Celebrating 50 Years of
Child Development Research

Celebrating 50 Years of Child Development Research

Past, Present, and Future Perspectives

edited by

Barbara Hanna Wasik, Ph.D.
William R. Kenan Distinguished Professor Emerita
Frank Porter Graham Child Development Institute
The University of North Carolina at Chapel Hill

and

Samuel L. Odom, Ph.D.
Frank Porter Graham Child Development Institute
The University of North Carolina at Chapel Hill

with invited contributors

Baltimore • London • Sydney

Paul H. Brookes Publishing Co.
Post Office Box 10624
Baltimore, Maryland 21285-0624
USA
www.brookespublishing.com

Typeset by BMWW, Windsor Mill, Maryland.
Manufactured in the United States of America by
Sheridan Books, Chelsea, Michigan.

Library of Congress Cataloging-in-Publication Data

Names: Wasik, Barbara Hanna, editor. | Odom, Samuel L., editor.
Title: Celebrating 50 years of child development research : past, present, and future perspectives /
    edited by Barbara Hanna Wasik and Samuel L. Odom; with invited contributors.
Other titles: Celebrating fifty years of child development research
Description: Baltimore : Paul H. Brookes Publishing Co., 2019. | Includes bibliographical references
    and index.
Identifiers: LCCN 2018046631 (print) | LCCN 2018061134 (ebook) | ISBN 9781681252773 (epub) |
    ISBN 9781681252780 (pdf) | ISBN 9781681252766 (paperback)
Subjects: LCSH: Child development—History. | Child development—Research. | BISAC:
    EDUCATION / Preschool & Kindergarten. | EDUCATION / Special Education / General. |
    PSYCHOLOGY / Developmental / Child.
Classification: LCC HQ767.9 (ebook) | LCC HQ767.9 .C3924 2019 (print) | DDC 305.231—dc23
LC record available at https://lccn.loc.gov/2018046631

British Library Cataloguing in Publication data are available from the British Library.

Contents

About the Editors

Barbara Hanna Wasik, Ph.D., Fellow, Frank Porter Graham Child Development Institute, and Professor Emerita, School of Education, University of North Carolina at Chapel Hill, Campus Box 8185, Chapel Hill, NC 27599-8185.

Barbara Hanna Wasik, Ph.D., William R. Kenan Distinguished Professor Emerita, University of North Carolina at Chapel Hill, is a clinical/school psychologist who has devoted her career to the study of children with social/emotional difficulties and language/literacy difficulties, as well as their families. A Ph.D. graduate of Florida State University in psychology, she completed a postdoctoral fellowship at Duke University. She then joined the faculty at the University of North Carolina (UNC), where she held a professorship in the School of Education as well as a research position with the Frank Porter Graham Child Development Institute (FPG). She taught master's and doctoral students in the School Psychology Program and held administrative positions in the UNC Graduate School, the School of Education, and FPG. She was one of the directors of Project CARE, a randomized study of child care and home visiting and served as an investigator on the longitudinal outcomes of both Project CARE and the Abecedarian Project. She was co-director for curriculum in the national study for low birth weight infants, the Infant Health and Development Program. Bringing together her interests in children and families, she is the developer of a comprehensive preschool and home intervention for preschool children and their families.

She served as President of the North Carolina Psychological Association, a member of the APA Council of Representatives, Chair of the APA Board of Educational Affairs, and Chair of the APA Committee on Early Childhood Education. She was one of the three co-chairs of the National Forum on Home Visiting and has served on numerous national boards. She was an invited participant to the White House Conference on Child Care and served as a member of the Committee on Early Childhood Pedagogy of the National Academy of Sciences that produced the study Eager to Learn—Educating Our Preschoolers. Her professional interests include the observational study of children, social and emotional behaviors, problem solving, parenting, language and literacy, and home visiting. The author of over 100 publications and five books, she continues her professional involvement as a fellow of the FPG Institute.

Samuel L. Odom, Ph.D., Senior Research Scientist, Frank Porter Graham Child Development Institute, and Research Professor, School of Education, University of North Carolina at Chapel Hill, Campus Box 8040, Chapel Hill, NC 27599-8040.

Samuel L. Odom, Ph.D., is the former Director of the Frank Porter Graham (FPG) Child Development Institute, where he remains as a Senior Research Scientist. Prior to his work at the University of North Carolina at Chapel Hill, Dr. Odom served in faculty positions at Indiana University and Peabody College/Vanderbilt University. Dr. Odom received a master's degree in special education in 1976 and an educational specialist degree in educational psychology from the University of Tennessee at Knoxville in 1979. He earned his doctorate in 1982 in education and human development from the University of Washington.

Throughout his career, Dr. Odom has held positions as a preschool teacher, student teaching supervisor, program coordinator, teacher educator, and researcher. Dr. Odom's research interests include interventions and teaching approaches that promote social competence of young children, effective intervention approaches for children with autism, and early childhood curricula that promote children's school success. He is the author or co-author of over 175 journal articles and book chapters and has edited 10 books on early childhood intervention and developmental disabilities. His current research is addressing treatment efficacy for children and youth with autism spectrum disorders in elementary and high school grades. Also, he is the co-director of the National Clearinghouse on Autism Evidence and Practice at FPG. Dr. Odom is an associate editor for *Exceptional Children* and is on the editorial board of the *Journal of Early Intervention, Topics in Early Childhood Special Education, Journal of Autism and Developmental Disabilities,* and *Early Childhood Research Quarterly.*

Dr. Odom received the Special Education Outstanding Research Award from the American Educational Research Association Special Education Special Interest Group in 1999, the Merle Karnes Contribution to the Field Award from the Division for Early Childhood of the Council for Exceptional Children in 2001, and the Outstanding Special Education Research Award from CEC in 2007. In 2013, he received the Arnold Lucius Gesell Prize awarded for career achievement in research on social inclusion and child development from the Theordor Hellbrugge Foundation in Munich, Germany. In 2016, he received an honorary doctoral degree from Stockholm University. He is currently a visiting professor at Stockholm University and San Diego State University.

About the Contributors

Oscar A. Barbarin, Ph.D., Chair and Professor of African American Studies & Professor of Psychology University of Maryland, 7236 Windsor Lane, Hyattsville, MD 20782

Oscar A. Barbarin earned a Ph.D. in clinical psychology from Rutgers University. His scholarly work has sought to illuminate how families, schools, and communities moderate the effects of adversity on the development of children, particularly boys of color. His scholarly work has been recognized for its Distinguished Contribution to Understanding International, Cultural and Contextual Diversity in Child Development by the Society for Research in Child Development. He serves on the executive committee of the International Union of Psychological Sciences.

W. Steven Barnett, Ph.D., Co-Director and Board of Governors Professor, National Institute for Early Education Research, Rutgers University, 73 Easton Ave, New Brunswick, NJ 08901

W. Steven Barnett is the founder and co-director of the National Institute for Early Education Research at Rutgers University. His research includes studies of the economics of early care and education, including costs and benefits, the long-term effects of preschool programs on children's learning and development, and the distribution of educational opportunities. Dr. Barnett earned his Ph.D. in economics at the University of Michigan. His best-known works include reviews of the research on long-term effects, benefit-cost analyses of the Perry Preschool and Abecedarian programs, and evaluations of large-scale public preschool programs.

Barbara Bowman, M.A., Professor of Child Development and Co-Founder of Erikson Institute Erikson Institute, 451 N. LaSalle Street, Chicago, IL 60654

Barbara Bowman is a pioneer in the field of early childhood education. Throughout her career, she has been an advocate for young children, applying knowledge about child development to her work integrating policy and practice. She is a founder and past president of Erikson Institute and has held local and national leadership positions in public education and professional organizations. She is currently on the faculty of Erikson Institute.

Donna M. Bryant, Ph.D., Senior Research Scientist, Frank Porter Graham Child Development Institute, University of North Carolina at Chapel Hill, 105 Smith Level Road, Campus Box 8180, Chapel Hill, NC 27199-8180

Dr. Bryant began her professional career at FPG in 1978. She has led dozens of research projects, including several Head Start consortia studies, North Carolina's Smart Start initiative, a five-state study of a professional development consultation model, home visiting interventions, and evaluations of the state Quality Rating and Improvement System systems. Current efforts include three studies within the Educare Learning Network of high-quality birth-to-5 schools.

Natasha J. Cabrera, Ph.D., Professor of Human Development and Quantitative Methodology, University of Maryland, 3942 Campus Drive, Suite 3304, College Park, MD 20742

Natasha J. Cabrera is Professor of Human Development at the University of Maryland. She conducts research on father involvement and children's social and cognitive development; adaptive and maladaptive factors related to parenting and cultural variations in ethnic minority families; and the mechanisms linking early experiences to children's school readiness. Dr. Cabrera has published on policy, methodology, theory, and the implications of fathering and mothering behaviors on child development in low-income minority families. She is the co-editor of the *Handbook of Father Involvement: Multidisciplinary Perspectives, 2nd Edition* and *Latina/o Child Psychology and Mental Health: Vol. 1 and 2*. Dr. Cabrera is an associate editor of *Child Development* and served on the National Academy of Sciences committee on parents of young children. She is co-principal investigator at the National Center for Research on Hispanic Families and Children.

Judith Carta, Ph.D., Senior Scientist in the Institute for Life Span Studies & Professor of Special Education, University of Kansas, 444 Minnesota Avenue, Suite 300, Kansas City, KS 66210

Dr. Carta is a senior scientist at the Institute for Life Span Studies and Professor of Special Education at the University of Kansas. She has directed research centers and projects focused on developing practices to promote children's early learning, particularly in vulnerable populations. She was the co-director of the Center for Response to Intervention in Early Childhood. She currently co-directs the Bridging the Word Gap Research Network—a collaborative of over 150 researchers, program implementers, civic leaders, and policy makers seeking to enhance children's language environments. She was formerly a teacher of young children with special needs, a member of the Federal Advisory Panel on Head Start Research and Evaluation, a commissioner on the Division of Early Childhood's Commission on Recommended Practices, and an editor of *Topics in Early Childhood Special Education*.

Mary Ruth B. Coleman, Ph.D., Senior Scientist, Emeritus, Frank Porter Graham Child Development Institute, University of North Carolina, Chapel Hill, 105 Smith Level Road, Chapel Hill, NC 27599-8180

Mary Ruth Coleman is Senior Scientist, Emeritus at the FPG Child Development Institute, University of North Carolina, Chapel Hill. She directs U-STARS~PLUS, a strength-based approach to supporting educationally vulnerable children from pre-K to fourth grade. Dr. Coleman is a past president of the Council for Exceptional Children and co-author of *Education Exceptional Children, 14th Edition* with James J. Gallagher.

Linda M. Espinosa, Ph.D., Professor of Early Childhood Education (Ret.) University of Missouri-Columbia, Columbia, MO 65211

Linda M. Espinosa has had experience as a preschool teacher, child care center director, elementary school principal, central office administrator, state program director, and corporate vice president of education. Her practical experience and research interests focus on the design and evaluation of optimal learning environments for young children who are at risk for school failure. Dr. Espinosa has worked extensively with low-income Hispanic/Latino children and families throughout the state of California. She completed her B.A. at the University of Washington, her Ed.M. at Harvard University, and her Ph.D. in Educational Psychology at the University of Chicago.

Nicole Gardner-Neblett, Ph.D., Advanced Research Scientist, Frank Porter Graham Child Development Institute, The University of North Carolina, Chapel Hill, 105 Smith Level Road, Campus Box 8180, Chapel Hill, NC 27599-8180

Nicole Gardner-Neblett is an advanced research scientist at the Frank Porter Graham Child Development Institute. Her research focuses on factors that promote children's language and literacy development, particularly among children from disadvantaged backgrounds. In particular, Dr. Gardner-Neblett's work examines the oral narrative (or storytelling) skills of African American children and the implications for literacy development and educational practice. Her work also examines professional development programs for early childhood educators to promote children's early language and communication development.

Ron Haskins, Ph.D., MAT, Senior Fellow and Co-Director, Center on Children and Families, Economic Studies, Brookings Institution, 1775 Massachusetts Avenue, NW, Washington, DC 20036

Ron Haskins is a senior fellow and holds the Cabot Family Chair in Economic Studies at the Brookings Institution, where he co-directs the Center on Children and Families. Dr. Haskins was appointed by Speaker of the House Paul Ryan to co-chair the Evidence-Based Policymaking Commission. He is the co-author of *Show Me the Evidence: Obama's Fight for Rigor and Evidence in Social Policy* (2015) and *Creating an Opportunity Society* (2009) and is the author of *Work over Welfare: The Inside Story of the 1996 Welfare Reform Law* (2006).

Governor James B. Hunt, Jr., J.D., Former Governor of North Carolina

Gov. Jim Hunt (1977–1985, 1993–2001) served four historic terms as governor of North Carolina. Under his leadership, North Carolina public schools improved test scores more than any other state in the 1990s, according to the Rand Corporation. Hunt focused on early childhood development and the improvement of quality of teaching. His Smart Start program received the prestigious Innovations in American Government Award from the Ford Foundation and the John F. Kennedy School of Government at Harvard University.

Marilou Hyson, Ph.D., Senior Consultant, Early Childhood Development and Education, The World Bank, UNICEF

Marilou Hyson is a national and international consultant in early childhood development and education. Marilou served as the associate executive director for professional development at the National Association for the Education of Young Children, was a former professor and chair of the University of Delaware's Department of Individual and Family Studies, and is a past editor-in-chief of *Early Childhood Research Quarterly*. She works on issues of early childhood professional development, early childhood teacher education, implementation of practices to support children's social-emotional development and approaches to learning, and quality improvement in low- and middle-income countries.

Iheoma U. Iruka, Ph.D., Chief Research Innovation Officer and Director of The Center for Early Education Research and Evaluation, HighScope Educational Research Foundation, 600 N. River Street, Ypsilanti, Michigan 49198

Iheoma U. Iruka's research addresses how early experiences impact poor and ethnic minority children's learning and development, and the role of the family and education environments and systems. She focuses on how evidence-informed policies, systems, and practices in early education can support the optimal development and experiences of low-income, ethnic minority, and immigrant children, through family engagement and support, quality rating and improvement systems, and early care and education systems and programs. She has been engaged in addressing how to ensure excellence for young diverse learners, especially Black children, through classroom observations, public policies, and publications geared toward early education practitioners and policy makers. She serves on numerous national boards and committees, including the National Academies of Sciences, Engineering, and Medicine.

Craig T. Ramey, Ph.D., Professor and Distinguished Research Scholar of Human Development, Virginia Tech Carilion Research Institute; Professor of Psychology, Neuroscience, and Human Development, Virginia Tech; and Professor of Pediatrics, Virginia Tech Carilion School of Medicine, Virginia Polytechnic Institute and State University, 2 Riverside Circle, Roanoke, VA 24016

Craig T. Ramey is the creator and founding director of the Abecedarian Project and its replicants, including Project CARE and the Infant Health and Development Program. His program of research centers on the role of early experience, especially education across the human life span, in the development of competence and robust health. His approach relies largely on experimental interventions in education, psychology, and pediatrics that provide rigorous tests of plausible developmental mechanisms of stability and change within dynamic, multilevel ecologies.

Patricia Snyder, Ph.D., Professor and David Lawrence Jr. Endowed Chair in Early Childhood Studies & Director, Anita Zucker Center for Excellence in Early Childhood Studies, University of Florida, College of Education, Norman Hall, 618 SW 12th Street, Suite 160, Gainesville, FL 32611

Patricia Snyder is a professor and the David Lawrence Jr. Endowed Chair in Early Childhood Studies at the University of Florida. She is the founding director of the Anita Zucker Center for Excellence in Early Childhood Studies. Dr. Snyder has worked for more than 40 years in the interdisciplinary field of early childhood studies. Her research interests focus on embedded instruction for early learning; social-emotional foundations of early learning; professional development, including practice-based coaching; and early childhood assessment and measurement.

Rud Turnbull, Ll.B., Ll.M., Distinguished Professor Emeritus, University of Kansas and Research Professor, University of North Carolina at Chapel Hill, University of North Carolina, Chapel Hill, 105 Smith Level Road, Chapel Hill, NC 27599

Rud Turnbull is a graduate of Johns Hopkins University (B.A., 1959), University of Maryland Law School (Ll.B., 1964), and Harvard Law School (Ll.M., 1969). With his wife Ann, he co-founded and was co-director of the Beach Center on Disability. He is also Distinguished Professor Emeritus, University of Kansas. He specializes in disability law and policy.

Pamela J. Winton, Ph.D., Senior Scientist and Research Professor, Frank Porter Graham Child Development Institute, University of North Carolina, Chapel Hill, 105 Smith Level Road, Campus Box 8185, Chapel Hill, NC 27599

Pamela J. Winton, a senior scientist at the Frank Porter Graham Child Development Institute, has been involved in research, outreach, technical assistance, professional development, and scholarly publishing related to early childhood for the last three decades. Winton has directed multiple national technical assistance centers, including the National Center on Professional Development on Inclusion, to help states create a cross-agency system of high-quality professional development for early childhood teachers; and CONNECT, bringing an evidence-based practice approach to professional development in early childhood. She has published numerous books, articles, chapters, and curricula on professional development, collaboration, systems change, family–professional partnerships, and inclusion. She has served on numerous advisory boards and review panels, and been recognized by local, state, and national awards.

Marlene Zepeda, Ph.D., Professor Emeritus of Child and Family Studies, California State University, Los Angeles, 5151 State University Drive, Los Angeles, CA 90032

Marlene Zepeda is Professor Emeritus in the Department of Child and Family Studies at California State University, Los Angeles. A former preschool and elementary school teacher, Dr. Zepeda's scholarship focuses on dual-language learning in Spanish-speaking preschool children and child development in Latino infants and toddlers. She also has authored a number of publications focused on workforce development, including a set of teacher competencies for dual language. Dr. Zepeda is a member of the Campaign for Quality Early Education, a California advocacy group that lobbies on behalf of dual-language learners, and currently is a member of the First Five Commission in Los Angeles.

Foreword

As I reflect on my 16 collective years as governor of North Carolina, I often think about the people and institutions that played key roles in assisting me with the important work of improving education, public schools, and early education so that our state's children and young adults could thrive. One of the key partners in all of this work was the Frank Porter Graham Child Development Institute (FPG) at the University of North Carolina (UNC) in Chapel Hill. This book captures some of the history and key moments in FPG's development and is a tribute to its rich history and worldwide reach.

Congratulations to all who have been involved in FPG's more than 50 years of successful and fruitful research on children's issues. Numerous young women and men have carried out some of the nation's most important research and public policy studies at FPG over this period. Each one of them focused on some aspect of child development that needed attention in our state and beyond. Furthermore, almost all of these researchers have carried the results of their research into practice in our communities. FPG has been a major force for the good of children for five decades—a remarkable achievement that is unmatched anywhere else in the nation.

FPG has been blessed from its beginning with inspirational leaders and directors with whom I have worked—men and women like Hal and Nancy Robinson, the first co-directors who were pioneers in leading an institute like FPG. The late Jim Gallagher, the longest-term director, was my close adviser and accomplice on many ventures in education, including the first competency testing program and the establishment of the School of Science and Mathematics. Other directors I depended on included Don Bailey, with whom I worked closely during my administrations, and Sam Odom, the first William Friday Professor of Child Development at UNC, who is one of the most productive researchers in autism in the nation. Important contributions to the field were made by other directors of FPG including Sharon Ramey whose work focused on interventions for at-risk children. Dick Clifford, another outstanding leader at FPG, helped us to create and manage the North Carolina Division of Child Development and guided the launch of Smart Start.

FPG has improved the lives and potential of children in North Carolina, particularly low-income children and their families. I believe that one of the major reasons North Carolina is seen as a leader in early childhood education is because of the quality of research that FPG conducts, as well as their ability to translate that research into recommendations for practice that assist policy makers. FPG researchers regularly advised the governor's office about best practices, programs, and policies based on current research. Having FPG in North Carolina meant that the most up-to-date research about the care and education of all children, including children with special needs, was readily available to my administration. Now, every state uses FPG's research and products, such as FPG's environmental rating scales, which became the basis for most states' quality rating systems.

Having FPG as a reliable resource was key to successfully launching and implementing Smart Start, the first initiative of its kind in the nation. Once it was launched, researchers studied all aspects of Smart Start, told us the kinds of things we should do, and advised us when we needed to revise and improve what we were doing or the way we were doing it. To improve the accountability of Smart Start in every county, FPG researchers, along with researchers from other universities, assisted in the development of Smart Start's performance standards. These standards are still being used, 25 years later.

Not only was North Carolina fortunate to learn from FPG's work; people from all over the world look to FPG for guidance and support. FPG's well-known Abecedarian Study, initiated by Craig T. Ramey and his colleagues in the early 1970s, has tracked children for more than 40 years. The study found significant educational and quality-of-life changes in children who experienced high-quality programs. This research is one of the most quoted nationwide studies on the long-term impacts of high-quality programs.

Although it is important to look back on the many accomplishments of this great institution, it is also important to look to the future. We need to continue working on issues that confront our children and their families, especially those living in poverty. Children need a healthy start and high-quality early care and education to build a foundation for their future success.

Our state has doubled in size since the 1960s when FPG first began its work. Furthermore, our children are now more diverse, and many are marginalized. We need to think about how we can help young families raise their children in the best ways to help assure their education and to help them become productive citizens. We need to continue to build strong public schools. Although we do not know what the future holds for our nation's children, I believe FPG will lead the nation in responding to the needs and circumstances of children and develop the research and training strategies that will be required to support the best quality of life possible.

Like our great state, like the great university of UNC (the oldest public university in the nation), and like the durable and persistent warrior Dr. Frank Porter Graham, I hope and trust that FPG will grow, thrive, and continue to be a major factor in strengthening the lives of our state's children and their families.

Governor James B. Hunt, Jr.
Governor of North Carolina, 1977–1985 and 1993–2001

Preface

This book is an outgrowth of the 50th anniversary celebration of the Frank Porter Graham (FPG) Child Development Institute of the University of North Carolina (UNC) at Chapel Hill in May 2016. In celebration of this significant anniversary, the planners included a major symposium designed to both summarize work over the past 50 years and to point out important future directions. To realize these goals, the planners put a unique framework into place to capture the significant accomplishments in child development and learning, specifically in the areas of early care and education, over the past 50 years. This framework included the following themes: 1) race, ethnicity, linguistic and cultural diversity; 2) early care and education, with an emphasis on children in poverty; and 3) interventions for children and youth with disabilities and their families.

This decision recognized the sizable overlap in some of the advances and issues in these three topic areas, while also recognizing that an analysis within each of these three areas would provide for more in-depth consideration. Each theme was explored through three lenses—research, professional development/ practice, and policy. This decision allowed for the presentation of the knowledge base in each area and in the preparation and role of practitioners, providing a foundation to view the social policies and legislation related to children and their families. A discussant for each theme then integrated the three foci and pointed to future directions.

Symposium presenters were carefully identified as highly respected professionals whose research and expertise have helped to shape the field of early childhood education. These same presenters are also the authors of the chapters in this volume. During the symposium, they presented on their respective topics and participated in a series of discussions about the presentations. Each presenter and the discussants prepared a chapter for this volume that reflected their presentations and symposium discussions. The keynote address by Jacqueline Jones identified critical issues discussed throughout the symposium.

A review of the chapters in this volume illuminates how frequently the content of the child's environment was considered in developing policy and practice decisions in the 1960s and 1970s. These decisions were often influenced by the early theories of Urie Bronfenbrenner, which focused on the ecological context of the child. Over time, Bronfenbrenner modified his earlier theory and focused directly on the child's interactions in his or her immediate environment as central to his theory. In the concluding chapter of this volume, we discuss Bronfenbrenner's final theory and how it can help drive new research, practice, and policy related to young children.

This volume and the 50th anniversary celebration of FPG would not have materialized without the outstanding leadership of Don Stedman, former Dean of the UNC School of Education and former Associate Director of FPG. Don brought a vision of this important milestone to the FPG administrators and staff, as well as to the FPG Executive Leadership Board. He was also instrumental in bringing together the 50th Anniversary Honorary Committee, who helped guide and support many of the celebration efforts. Other key individuals included Stephanie Ridley of FPG, who was the primary coordinator and facilitator; she helped to ensure that the planning and implementation for the symposium and other anniversary events occurred. Importantly, the 50th Anniversary Committee set the vision for the symposium and identified speakers and discussants. This group included Karen Blase, Donna M. Bryant, Peg Burchinal, Dick Clifford, Mary Ruth Blackwell Coleman, Lynn Kahn, Peter Ornstein, and Pamela J. Winton, as well as the two of us, Barbara Wasik and Sam Odom.

During the process of creating this volume, others at FPG made significant contributions. Dave Shaw, Stephanie Ridley, and Jennifer Robinette provided helpful editorial guidance. Donna M. Bryant provided a valuable historical perspective, Barbara Goldman located archival materials that made their way into presentations and chapters, and former FPG staff Gina Harrison provided expertise for visual displays at the symposium. Other FPG researchers took on the role of facilitators for the discussion sessions, helping to ensure that all participants had opportunities to engage in meaningful discussion with the presenters. Don Stedman, FPG Fellow, provided helpful reviews of parts of this volume.

Paul H. Brookes Publishing Company and FPG authors have enjoyed a deep collaboration over the years, with Brookes publishing the writings of more than 60 FPG authors. We are very pleased that Brookes partnered with us to publish this volume and we appreciate the strong support of the many staff at Paul H. Brookes who helped to shepherd this book through the steps involved in publishing a large edited volume. Brookes has indeed been very much a part of the history of FPG and this book is one more example.

To all we listed and the many others who contributed to make the symposium and this book possible, we say thank you. You have indeed stayed firm to our mission of advancing knowledge and enhancing lives.

*To all who have worked at the FPG Institute since its inception—
the directors, scientists, staff, fellows, teachers, and students—and to
all the children who attended the child care center and their families.
These individuals made the advances of FPG during its first 50 years
possible and laid the foundation for the next 50 years.*

I

Historical Overview
and Contemporary Issues

Throughout history, parents have undoubtedly thought about how they care for their children. Parents have nurtured their children, fed and clothed them, treated illnesses, protected children from the elements, and taught self-care and social skills. As society became more complex, so did the responsibilities of parents. By the time the United States was settled by Europeans in the 16th and 17th centuries, many child-rearing practices had extended to include religious education, early literacy skills, and self-support as adults.

As the education of children and adolescents became a more dominant feature of society, many philosophers and educators began to theorize about the best ways to rear children, both in the home and in child care settings. Governments also became involved in setting policies for educational settings. Over time, some of the early assumptions about children's development came to be questioned, especially questions about children's intellectual and developmental disabilities. Chapter 1 by Barbara Wasik and Donna Bryant elaborates on these occurrences as prologue for the 50 years of advances made from the 1960s to the present and addressed by the authors in this volume.

Wasik and Bryant also describe events beginning in the 1960s to anchor the 50-year time period reflected in this volume. The decade of the 1960s was a time of rapid social, cultural, and political progress, ushering in a number of dramatic events related to young children and their families. These events included laws against segregation in schools, concerns about children growing up in poverty, and the initiation of early care and education efforts, including Head Start. Within this milieu, the Frank Porter Graham Child Development Institute (FPG) at the University of North Carolina began as one of 12 research centers funded by the federal government to conduct research on children with intellectual and developmental disabilities. Influenced by individuals who believed that it was possible to change the trajectory of children reared in poverty through early educational experiences, FPG developed an early childhood program at the same time many other researchers were asking similar questions and initiating similar programs. The 1970s and 1980s saw considerable progress for children with disabilities through legislation that grant educational rights and methods developed to best help them gain knowledge and skills. Increased attention and sensitivity was directed toward minority children, children with health vulnerabilities, and pregnant women. States began to expand preschool programs. By the 1990s, immigration—especially of Spanish-speaking families—brought new issues related to language and culture to bear on early care and education for young children, recognizing that characteristics of these children and their families needed to be considered when developing educational programs. Early in the 21st century, issues of poverty, minority status, segregation, immigration, language, disabilities, and diversity remain priorities for research with young children and their families.

In Chapter 2, Iheoma Iruka expands on the focus of Chapter 1 by examining early childhood research in a globalized society. To organize this chapter, Iruka uses the four features of child development and learning identified by the National Academies of Science, Engineering, and Medicine: children's physical health and safety, cognitive competence, emotional and behavioral competence, and social competence. Children in the United States fall behind in these areas when compared to their peers in a number of other developed countries. Furthermore, within the United States, troubling racial disparities exist among groups of children. Demographic shifts related to population change, income, wealth, poverty, education attainment, family structure, and community change all contribute to young children's educational outcomes.

Iruka reviews various types of influences on children and their families, including immediate factors and more distance influences, such as federal policies and procedures. Specific federal efforts exist to support families, particularly pregnant women, expectant fathers, and parents and caregivers of children under the age of 5 years. Iruka identifies and reviews these efforts and policies, including the Maternal, Infant, and Early Childhood Home Visiting Program; Early Head Start and Child Care Partnership; preschool development grants; and Head Start. For each of these, Iruka identifies how these efforts support families, as well as the reasons why such support is essential for improving health, education, and living conditions.

Collectively, these two chapters provide the reader with a broad foundation about many circumstances affecting parents, children, and youth in our country from its earliest day to the present. This foundation helps the reader put into perspective the subsequent chapters in Sections II–IV, which address the themes of this volume, namely race, discrimination, linguistic, and cultural diversity; early care and education; and children with disabilities and their families.

1

Children and Families

Historical Trends in American Beliefs, Policies, and Practices

Barbara Hanna Wasik and Donna M. Bryant

The 1960s heralded a dramatic expansion of interest in the education and development of young children and their families—from the work of politicians, educators, and researchers to the implementation of significant research projects and the passage of unprecedented legislation regarding children and families. Within these social and cultural events, the authorization for 12 mental retardation centers (in the language of the time; now called Intellectual and Developmental Disabilities Research Centers) was signed into law by President John F. Kennedy in 1963. Designed to advance practice and policy through research, these centers unfolded in multiple ways influenced by the goals of researchers and practitioners at their local university or organization, as well as by national priorities. Several of these centers have been at the vanguard of advances in practice, policy, and professional development for the past 50 years, including the Frank Porter Graham Child Development Institute (FPG Institute) at The University of North Carolina. The celebration of the 50th anniversary of the FPG Institute became the impetus for this book, which was designed to provide an intensive review of the research, practice, and policy regarding children and their families over the past 50 years, as well as to present recommendations that challenge the field to be both thoughtful and bold in charting the next 50 years.

The FPG birth story began with the vision of several psychologists, educators, and pediatricians in Chapel Hill, North Carolina—all of whom were affiliated with the University of North Carolina. These visionaries were concerned with both the adverse consequences of poverty on the development of young children and the potential positive impact of early childhood care and education to improve their educational trajectory and life outcomes (Shaw, 2016). Notable among these leaders were Harold (Hal) and Nancy Robinson, who became the first directors of the FPG Institute at its initiation in 1966. Through a serendipitous meeting on an airplane between Hal Robinson and U.S. Senator Frank Porter Graham (a former president of the university), Robinson learned of Graham's deep commitment to education and subsequently proposed that the university's new child development institute be named for Graham. Fifty years later, the FPG community gathered with many invited speakers in an academic symposium to address the domains that have been central to FPG since its inception—namely poverty, disabilities, and diversity (race, ethnicity, language, and culture). Within each of these themes, three topics—research, professional practice, and policy—were addressed during the symposium and now in this volume.

OVERVIEW

Almost three decades ago, Shonkoff and Meisels (1990, p. 3) described the fundamental purpose of early childhood intervention as the need "to merge the knowledge and insights of scholars and practitioners with the creative talents of those who design and implement social policy initiatives, and to invest the products of such an alliance in the future of our children." Their cogent description remains highly pertinent to the central focus of this book—namely, to examine the knowledge base, practice issues, and policies in early childhood education. The authors in this volume examine these foci within the following content areas: 1) race, ethnicity, linguistic, cultural, and socioeconomic diversity; 2) early care and education primarily focused on children from low-income families; and 3) research and services for children with disabilities. The order of these topics recognizes different levels of influence, beginning with more macro-level influences in society (e.g., discrimination, segregation), followed by events in the child's more immediate environment (including home and child care), and ending with a focus on specific child characteristics (namely, children with disabilities). These three areas are not distinct areas of policy, research, and practice; rather, they have been intertwined throughout FPG's history, especially during periods when individuals with low socioeconomic status, individuals with disabilities, and individuals who were simply different from the majority culture were often grouped together by society. These areas form the basis of this book's organization across chapters and sections. Collectively, we hope they provide the reader with a thoughtful and provocative picture of the history of and advances in early childhood interventions.

In this first chapter, we examine the historical developments that have broadly influenced advances in early childhood education. Many recent developments had long roots in America and, even before that, in Europe, where beliefs about children's development arose from disparate philosophies. Our historical perspective begins in Colonial America by noting early ideas about children and families, then moves through the centuries to the present; along the way, we identify many salient beliefs, educational and economic events, cultural changes, and legislative accomplishments. This overview lays the foundation for consideration of the research, practice, and policy affecting children and families for the past 50 years, while also prompting consideration of issues that need to be considered in the future. Chapter 2 by Iheoma Iruka further addresses contemporary social, cultural, and educational phenomena.

THE EARLY YEARS: COLONIAL AMERICA, 1600–1750

From the time of the earliest American settlers, the family was recognized as having authority and responsibility for child rearing. Many child-rearing practices that originated in religious beliefs in England were carried forward to Colonial America, including the authority of the father over the household and the need to teach children obedience. Throughout the 1600s, numerous records show a very strong interest in ensuring that children did not grow up to be disorderly or rebellious. For example, beginning in 1642, Massachusetts Bay passed a series of acts intended to compel parents to "train up" their children properly and also authorized magistrates to take children from parents who neglected their duties (Bremner, 1970, p. 39). Town records show that men were instructed to go to the houses of families suspected of not teaching their children literacy and catechism to give warnings to the parents. Failure to follow through on the warnings could result in children being removed from these "unsuitable homes." Children were also "bound out" to other families when their own family could not provide for them, when their family neglected them, or when they became orphaned (Bremner, 1970).

In the early 17th century, families were also responsible for their children's education and were expected to provide them with instruction in reading and writing (Bremner, 1970). By 1647, Massachusetts moved beyond the expectation that families were the main source of education and required towns of 50 households to maintain a schoolmaster for elementary skills and larger towns (greater than 100 households) to maintain a grammar schoolmaster to teach boys Latin and Greek in order to prepare them for college (Bremner, 1970). Many of the dominant religious beliefs influencing child rearing also became part of the early schools when religious content was taught to children as a regular part of the curriculum.

Because of the compact nature of New England towns, they were subject to more regulations regarding education. In Middle Atlantic colonies, churches with limited private assistance helped to maintain some elementary schools. In Southern colonies, the only elementary schools were charity schools for poor children; secondary education was even sparser than in the North, confined to a few expensive private schools. Higher education also reflected major regional distinctions. Massachusetts was the first colony to establish a college. Land was secured for what became Harvard College in 1636, followed in 1701 by the founding of Yale College in Connecticut. Not until 1795 did any state-funded college enroll students. Our own University of North Carolina was the first public institution of higher learning to open its doors.

As the country matured and families became more settled, they could attend more to their children's education. Affluent families sometimes employed tutors for their children; some sent their children to Europe for further education. When more formal educational organizations were established, they were usually under the direction of religious denominations and often served to educate young men to become ministers (Bremner, 1970).

Throughout the 1600s and 1700s, many children had limited access to education because they were expected to help their family with household work or be part of the labor force. Children living on farms helped with farm work. Some were apprenticed to tradesmen to learn a skill for their future livelihood (Bremner, 1970). Others worked in mines and factories, often under dangerous circumstances. Families living on the edge of survival did not have the luxury of educating their children at home or sending them to school (Hansan, 2011).

Access to the types of education noted previously mainly applied to White children. When European settlers came to America, Native American tribes and nations occupied lands throughout the country, including the eastern seaboard. Native Americans had their own traditions and values; compared with families of European origin, they were more permissive in rearing their children. Spirituality and relationships were important concepts that influenced family life, and children were taught by their families to respect others and themselves (Horse, 1997). However, Native American children seldom had access to schooling. Black people were also part of America, albeit against their will, from the early 17th century when slaves first arrived from Africa. Their numbers increased dramatically in the 18th and 19th centuries. Although they had strong family values and traditions in their native countries, it was almost impossible to reestablish these values and traditions under their living conditions in America, where restrictive codes governed their lives. As Black individuals in the North gained freedom in the 1800s, opportunities opened for their education and employment; however, in the South, conditions remained harsh.

European Philosophical Underpinnings

Beliefs about rearing children in early America were not limited to religious tenets, physical necessity, or government policies; educators and philosophers also turned their attention to how children should be raised. Certain European philosophers were quite influential; among them was John Locke, an English philosopher who argued against the prevailing beliefs of his time that children have innate knowledge and predetermined behavior. Locke proposed that children acquire knowledge and skills over their lifetimes, that at birth the mind is a blank slate or *tabula rasa,* and that knowledge is gained through experience rather than innate ideas (Locke, 1689). His ideas significantly influenced 18th- and 19th-century thought on knowledge acquisition.

Building on the work of Locke, the Frenchman Jean-Jacques Rousseau emphasized the importance of children's environments in their development. He recommended a *laissez-faire* approach to childhood and education based on the child's own nature. Rousseau saw the need to preserve children from the influence of society so that their natural talents could develop. He described three stages of children's natural development that foreshadowed modern ones. Although Rousseau published several major books and treatises that continue to influence modern political and social thought, he considered his best work to be *Emile, or On Education* (1762; Bloom's 1979 translation).

Johann Heinrich Pestalozzi was a Swiss educator and social reformer writing in the 18th century who was especially concerned about the plight of children with low socioeconomic status. He believed that education should be based on the interests and needs of the child and proposed specific educational practices that became widely adopted (http://www.jhpestalozzi.org). Later, Friedrich Froebel, a German educator writing in the 19th century, strongly influenced educational practices by encouraging play and activity for young children as well as the use of objects for learning (http://www.froebelgifts.com/history.htm). He founded a preschool program in 1837 that he later called *kindergarten,* an innovative early childhood program that eventually spread to the United States. Until the United States developed its own cadre of educational philosophers, these four European thinkers had a strong influence on the advancement of education in America.

A DEVELOPING COUNTRY: 1750–1900

One of the most dominant beliefs influencing how children were reared in the United States in the 1800s and much of the 1900s for those of European backgrounds was the primacy of maternal care for young children and the potential negative impact of out-of-home care on children's behavior. These beliefs not only influenced practices from the earliest years of the United States, but they also have been inextricably related to public policy up to the present. However, policies vacillated at times by supporting poor mothers to keep their children at home (and thus out of almshouses or orphanages), as well as by supporting the role of working mothers through child care support. These policies also were influenced by government and religious leaders who questioned the ability of families living in poverty to effectively rear their own children, including the family's ability to promote moral development.

Educating Children With Low Socioeconomic Status

Concerns about educating disadvantaged children existed in America and England as early as the beginning of the 19th century. In England, this concern led to the "charity school" movement throughout the 1800s as a way to address "the decay of religion and the rise of ignorance among the poor" (Cahan, 1989, p. 8). Established primarily for children ages 5 through 7 years and typically supported through individual parishes, these schools taught children from poor families to read and write and facilitated their movement into a trade or other services. During the industrial revolution in the 19th century, significant changes in family life occurred throughout England and the United States as many families moved from rural areas to urban settings searching for better work opportunities. As parents, especially women, went to work in factories, they could not also be at home to care for their children—a situation that influenced the development of "infant schools" in both Europe and America in the 1820s. Rather misnamed, these schools actually served children up to approximately age 6 or 7 years.

Robert Owen, a reformist factory owner, established the first infant school in 1816 in Scotland, with the goal of shielding children from the effects of poverty. His school was designed to provide children with a pleasant school environment where they could think about practical problems and experience little punishment. Teachers encouraged children to help each other, dance, sing, and play outside (http://robert-owen-museum.org .uk/Robert_Owen_1771_1858/school). Influenced by Pestalozzi and Owen, infant schools expanded throughout Europe with practices characterized as child focused and informal, emphasizing a pervasive theme that has continued as a dominant belief into the 21st century—namely, that education can be a means of overcoming poverty and its potential long-term negative social consequences.

The development of infant schools in the United States was built on needs and beliefs similar to those in Europe—the need to provide child care for working parents, a concern that low-income families might be unable to appropriately socialize their children, and an interest in preparing children for elementary school. Both educators and social reformers saw these schools as a means to provide academic instruction, moral training, and child care—that is, more than just custodial child care. Unlike in Europe, infant schools fell out of favor in America because U.S. primary schools began to serve younger children; furthermore, it was still widely believed that children were best raised at home and were the responsibility of the mother. A third factor was promoted by Amariah Brigham (a doctor, writer, and administrator of an asylum for individuals with mental illnesses) who believed that overstimulating a child's mind would result in feeble-mindedness (Zigler & Styfco, 2010). Illustrating the fluctuating philosophies of education, the British infant school model experienced a revival of interest in the United States in the 1960s and 1970s, influencing Head Start and other preschool and elementary programs.

In the latter part of the 19th century, almshouses became an acceptable means of providing care for orphans, abandoned children, and children from low-income families. Since colonial time, almshouses had existed in the United States to house people who were sick, elderly, or destitute and individuals with disabilities. Almshouses had also become an alternative for children with intellectual or developmental disabilities whose families could not care for them, setting a precedent for out-of-home care for these children. These institutions were usually poorly funded and conditions were often abysmal. Reformers spoke out, the public took note, and yet another shift in social beliefs and interest in children was about to take place.

THE PROGRESSIVE ERA: 1900–1920

The Progressive Era began in the late 1800s as rapid industrialization, urbanization, and immigration led to greater economic and social problems. Progressive reformers began to work for change. When large numbers of immigrant families settled in urban areas in the Northeast and Midwest early in the 20th century, both day nurseries and settlement houses were established to provide services to immigrant and low-income families and their children. Day care for poor children expanded slowly beyond basic care to include social and educational goals. Educators began to believe that day nurseries could provide mothers with information on the health of their young children (Tank, cited in Cahan, 1989). This innovation in addressing the needs of both mothers *and* their children was not broad based but did anticipate later efforts at two-generation programs in modern times. The U.S. settlement houses were modeled on those in England, where more privileged individuals provided services for less fortunate families to help them improve their circumstances. The expansion of these houses in the Northeast and Midwest beginning in the late 1880s and continuing into the 20th century fit within the goals of the Progressive Era to address the needs of both low-income and immigrant families.

Cahan observed that these efforts were early examples of beliefs in the "plasticity and educability" of the young child (1989, pp. 8–9) and as compensatory programs for children living in poverty. Cahan also drew attention to the fact that these were two-tier systems: For more affluent families, the nursery school and kindergarten provided opportunities for child enrichment and social interactions, whereas "childminding" or day care were the options for lower-income parents and working women. This two-tier system was prevalent not only during the Progressive Era, but also throughout the remainder of the 20th century.

Whether their children could attend a custodial childcare program or an educational one was a non-issue for low-income White families and all Black families in the South, nor were these options relevant for Native American families. Most Black families at the turn of the century were living in the South, where resources in general were more limited and where the history of slavery still influenced society. As a result, Black families had considerably fewer educational opportunities than White families while also struggling with discrimination and racism. Native American families had lost most of their land over a period of two centuries through exchanges with the federal government and were living on isolated reservations in the West. It would be decades before early education opportunities came to these communities.

Home Visiting

Although placing children in almshouses lost favor in the early 20th century, home visiting enjoyed a resurgence of interest as the best way to provide services to children and families. Home visiting was not new; rather, it dated to Elizabethan England and was the dominant way to help individuals living in poverty in colonial America. Interest, however, waned in the 19th century as institutional care became more popular. Jane Addams and other social reformers in the early 20th century renewed interest in home visiting, coinciding with their beliefs that mothers could not manage employment outside the home along with caring for their children and household responsibilities. Subsequently, these beliefs became the prevailing position of efforts on behalf of families, influencing the development of settlement houses and home visiting to assist mothers in their own homes (Wasik & Bryant, 2001). Beginning in the late 19th century and continuing until the 1920s, home visiting was a prevalent means of reaching families and influenced the development of several professions, including social workers, visiting nurses, and visiting teachers.

Consistent with these social concerns of helping to keep children in their own homes rather than in institutions, in 1909 the U.S. government took a significant step toward organizing various efforts for children with the first White House Conference on the Care of Dependent Children. President Theodore Roosevelt initiated the conference and emphasized keeping children with their parents, prompted by the belief that "such aid being given as may be necessary to maintain suitable homes for the rearing of children" (Bremner, 1971, p. 364). This conference influenced the adoption of widows' pension laws in 1911, making public money available to help widowed mothers care for their children in their own homes; it also led to the establishment of the Children's Bureau. Begun under President Taft and becoming operational in 1913, the Children's Bureau was and is the only federal agency focused exclusively on children and families. Today, it continues as part of the Administration on Children, Youth and Families. Once again, however, these new efforts on behalf of White families were rarely extended to African American or Native American families.

Preschool Education and the Preparation of Preschool Teachers

As a number of Progressive Era philosophers, educators, and psychologists were emphasizing the role of education in society, universities began to attend to the education of young children. Indeed, Teachers College at Columbia University had already established itself as a leader in preschool education by the 1880s. Growing from simple roots to teach low-income immigrant women, it evolved into a preparation program for teachers of young children. Its early philosophy emphasized the importance of the learners' backgrounds and how to present materials in relevant, meaningful ways. By 1892, it had reorganized under the name Teachers College and developed a broad-based vision that included education, psychology, and health (Teachers College, n.d.) Among its leaders was John Dewey, who had a significant influence on both educational practices for young children and teacher education. He viewed schools as settings where children could realize their own potential, not simply as a place where children learned a set of predetermined knowledge and skills (Dewey, 1915).

Another early influence on formal preschool education was Maria Montessori, whose work was guided by Pestalozzi, Rousseau, and Froebel, and who in turn had a considerable effect on educational theory and practice in early childhood education in the early 1900s. Drawing on her work for children with intellectual disabilities and in medicine, she employed both the scientific method and observations of children to influence her educational theory. Based on this work, she proposed a structured environment, a very specific set of materials and instruction, and close observation of children (Montessori, 1912). Initially, her work was not met with widespread acceptance in the United States; however, by the middle of the 20th century, her methods began to receive considerable support. More than 4,000 certified Montessori schools operate in the United States today.

The establishment of preschool centers continued to expand during the early 20th century at many university settings and were used to help prepare teachers of young children. Relatedly, both educators and psychologists began to focus on young children's needs and pedagogical practices for teaching them. Bank Street was an early leader, beginning in 1916 as the Bureau of Educational Experiments, with the goal of studying children "to find out what kind of environment is best suited to their learning and growth, to create that environment, and to train adults to maintain it" (Bank Street, n.d.). Also in 1916, the Merrill-Palmer School was founded, which was another institution focused on young children. Beginning operation with an innovative multidisciplinary model to serve children in the Detroit area, the school reached professionals, parents, and other caregivers (Merrill-Palmer School, n.d.).

The Yale Child Study Center also was established during the early part of the century through the efforts of Arnold Gesell (http://childstudycenter.yale.edu/about/history.aspx). Influenced by G. Stanley Hall, one of the earliest psychologists to study children's development, Gesell was an innovator in conducting intensive studies of a small number of children—work that led to the highly influential Gesell Developmental Schedules; the developmental quotients from these scales were used to determine children's intelligence. His theory of maturation (Gesell, 1928), which proposed that children's development was guided from within, influenced both child rearing and primary education. Although he was originally interested in children with disabilities, Gesell later shifted to study typically developing infants and children.

During this time of expanding interest in children's education in the early 20th century, the United States was making advances related to compulsory education for young children. By 1920, attendance at school for at least part of the year was required for all students between the ages of 8 to 14 years. Although the requirement was not strongly enforced in much of the country, it was evidence of the country's maturing views on children's education. The establishment of the National Association for the Education of Young Children in 1926, with its goal of improving children's well-being through quality educational services, was another positive step for the education of young children.

Children With Disabilities

Interest and research on children's developmental disabilities also increased in the early part of the 20th century. *The Century of the Child*, a book by Ellen Key published in 1900, called for making children the central concern of society. Indeed, advances did follow in the 20th century, including "improvements on measurement, advances on developmental psychology, the advent of psychoanalysis, and the mental hygiene and child guidance movements" (Rey et al., 2015, p. 5). By the 1920s, these developments were influencing the views of children with developmental disabilities and the interventions created for them.

Another significant advance was made in 1922 when Elizabeth Ferrell, a teacher of children with disabilities, founded the Council for Exceptional Children. At the initial meeting, the Council identified three goals: 1) to emphasize the educational needs of the child (rather than the child's classification); 2) to establish standards for special education teachers; and 3) to bring together professionals interested in the education of "special children" (Kode, 2017). These goals foreshadowed work later in the century and remain part of the Council's mission today.

The New "Science" of Assessment in the 20th Century

At the turn of the 20th century, two instruments were developed to assess intellectual and mental abilities. These intelligence tests would come to have a significant effect on many aspects of policy, practice, and research with young children. The first was the Binet-Simon Scale, created in 1905 by Albert Binet and his co-worker, Theodore Simon, to address the French government's interest in identifying students who needed alternative educational experiences due to their lower intellectual skills. Lewis Terman at Stanford University standardized and renamed the Binet Scale in 1916; the resulting Stanford-Binet then became widely used as a measure of general intelligence for both adults and for children. Beginning in the 1960s, it also became a primary instrument for evaluating the outcomes of early intervention programs.

In the early 1900s, Henry Herbert Goddard, director of research at the Vineland Training School for Feeble-Minded Girls and Boys in New Jersey (Zenderland, 1998), translated Binet's intelligence test into English and used it with the Vineland School children as well as others in the public schools (http://www.apa.org/monitor/2009/01/assessment.aspx). Of considerable significance was his belief, building on his early research into heredity, that either isolation or sterilization of those with low intelligence was necessary for society. Although in later years Goddard reversed many of his early opinions and very publicly admitted his error, his work was unfortunately reprinted in German in the 1930s, significantly influencing the eugenics movement in Germany that led to tens of thousands of children being exterminated in the 1930s prior to World War II.

Other professionals concerned with children's development advanced the experimental study of children by creating research methods for the observational study of children's behavior. In particular, Mildred Parten introduced an observational study method to examine children's play (Parten, 1932). Current coding schemes are often quite similar to the methods Parten used to observe children's play behavior. Such efforts illustrated the strong professional interest in children's behavior and helped establish the experimental study of children as a serious scientific effort (Wasik, 1984).

MAJOR CHANGES: 1920–1960

During the first part of the 1920s, the relative prosperity of many Americans contrasted with the lives of a significant number of urban and rural low-income families. At the end of this decade, the stock market crash was followed by the Great Depression, which dramatically altered the economic situation of almost every American family. Millions of workers became unemployed and lost their financial savings, thrusting their families into poverty. Those who were already living in poverty suffered even more drastically; bread lines and soup kitchens were opened to provide for the poor and unemployed as the country fell deeper into the Depression. Under President Herbert Hoover, the U.S. government did not take a highly active role in addressing the national crises brought about by the Depression. However, when Franklin Roosevelt became president in 1933, the government moved quickly to stem the crisis with the banks and to initiate a host of programs to put people back to work and provide support to families (Goodwin, 1995).

Recognizing the need for mothers to work when possible, one of the programs provided funds for day care, although the support was often not sufficient for a family's needs. Providing government resources to working mothers was viewed more favorably during this time. However, once the country began to pull out of the Depression, these views shifted; they did not match the prevailing social and political beliefs about the role of women in society. Consequently, another significant social policy was enacted in 1935—namely, the federal assistance program called Aid to Dependent Children, which was changed later to Aid to Families with Dependent Children (AFDC). This funding was designed to make it possible for low-income mothers to remain at home to care for their children. AFDC was intended for White widows and families in which the husband could not work. Most Black mothers had always been in the labor force and were considered ineligible for this benefit (Carten, 2016).

Numerous changes were made in the AFDC regulations over the next 60 years as beliefs about the best way to support children in low-income families fluctuated, especially as negative opinions developed about providing assistance to unmarried mothers or families perceived to be taking advantage of the system. Changing beliefs about the financial needs of families, maternal work outside the home, and the positive versus detrimental effects of day care on young children continued to influence policies (see Chapter 9 for a more detailed discussion of these policies).

The Social Security Act of 1935, also signed into law by President Roosevelt, was a landmark action. We know it best as a pension program for adults over 65 years of age, but the Act was also the beginning of a long process to obtain financial support from the government for adults with disabilities, and later for children with disabilities. During the 1920s and 1930s, other shifts were occurring in social services. Services provided by clinics and hospitals came to be viewed more favorably than home services, while institutional care for children with disabilities increased. Once again, support for institutional care caused home visiting to recede as a major means of reaching families; it would not have another resurgence until the 1960s (Wasik & Bryant, 2001). By contrast, home visiting continued throughout Europe as a desirable means of providing family services. It received additional support from the writings of John Bowlby, who emphasized the importance of the relationship between maternal care and child health, resulting in a focus on keeping children in their own homes (Bowlby, 1952, 1969).

The War Years and the Recovery: 1940–1960

World War II, the dominant event of the 1940s, touched almost all facets of home and family life. The United States had not fully recovered from the Depression when it was pulled into international conflicts. President

Roosevelt committed national resources to help the war efforts in Europe while also beginning to prepare for the possibility of defending the country against an invasion (Goodwin, 1995). These efforts changed the national economy as tens of thousands of individuals were employed in war-related efforts. Both men and women responded to the call for service. As women, including those with children, moved into the workforce in record numbers during the war, filling positions previously held by men or in new war-related efforts, work by women came to be seen as patriotic and the government began providing day care support to families with lower incomes. Once the war was over, however, women were expected to return to the home; thus, financial support for mothers of young children in the workforce was dramatically reduced. However, because women had experienced more independence and acquired more workplace skills during the war, their own views about employment outside the home began to change. This shift in attitudes continued over the next half-century as women began to work outside the home in record numbers—a shift that altered the dynamics of family relationships and the responsibilities for child care. This trend of increasing numbers of women in the workforce has continued unabated into the 21st century, as documented in Chapters 2 and 9.

Other developments in the 1940s also significantly influenced political, social, and educational events, including segregation. Racial unrest was becoming an increasing concern, leading to a planned march on Washington in 1941 to protest the lack of opportunities for Black Americans resulting from the New Deal. This march, however, did not take place because President Roosevelt promised that opportunities would be made available, although few new opportunities materialized. Racial concerns also influenced Kenneth and Mamie Clark's doll studies on the perceptions of how White and Black children who attended either segregated or nonsegregated schools viewed dolls of different races (Clark & Clark, 1947). When asked about their preference for a White or Black doll, even the Black children showed a preference for White dolls—a striking finding used later (1954) in arguments before the U.S. Supreme Court in the case of *Brown v. Board of Education of Topeka* to support the detrimental effects of segregated schools.

Children With Intellectual or Developmental Disabilities

Historically, in the United States, little attention was given to children and adults with disabilities. Beginning in the 19th century, society began to differentiate between intellectual disability and developmental disability. By the mid-1800s, people working in the United States to reform the treatment of individuals with limited cognitive functioning became aware of Edouard Seguin's work in France and later in the United States, where he was implementing procedures to educate children who had severe disabilities (Seguin, 1856). Intellectual disability was beginning to be conceptualized along a continuum and viewed as a developmental phenomenon. As a result, reformers began to propose education for these children and worked to create schools where such education was possible. Part of the motivation for such schools was to remove these children from what was viewed as a detrimental home life. These beliefs about the family were consistent with Goddard's early studies (later refuted) that traced the intellectual performance of children over time. Reformers pushed states to create separate institutions for children, leading to increased efforts for the identification and classification of children with disabilities.

Along with the increased use of intelligence tests with children was the development of several mental ability tests to determine role assignments for recruits during World War I. Robert Yerkes, the president of the American Psychological Association, led a team that had tested almost 2 million soldiers by the end of the war. The results of this extensive testing revealed ethnic and racial differences among the men being evaluated. Although these results were criticized as being clearly related to acculturation (the test scores correlated highly with duration in the United States), the findings led to increased xenophobia and anti-immigrant feelings in the population (DuBois, 1970).

The adult testing results also led to an interest in studying differences among children from different races. Concerned with the absence of normative data for African American children, Kennedy, van de Riet, and Wilson (1963) conducted a detailed review of the research, finding that White children almost always outperformed Black children on measures of intelligence (e.g., Peterson, 1923). However, the reasons for the differences varied across studies, with some researchers attributing the differences to inferior home, school, and cultural environments (Garth, 1931; Peterson, 1923), whereas others thought race also played a role. (See Chapters 3, 4, 5, and 6 for more nuanced, strengths-based approaches to understanding minority children.)

Mid-century, several researchers contributed to the knowledge base of children with intellectual and developmental disabilities. In 1943, the psychiatrist Leo Kanner published his influential paper "Autistic Disturbances of Affective Contact," in which he described the symptoms of 11 children with a distinct syndrome characterized by deficits in normal social interactions (Kanner, 1943). One year later, Hans Asperger also referred to a group of children as autistic, noting similarities in behavior but reporting that the children he observed had scored high in intelligence and had large vocabularies (Asperger, 1944). His findings have gained considerable significance in the understanding of autism.

Other major advances were taking place for children with disabilities. In 1950, parents of children with disabilities established the Association for Retarded Citizens (ARC), working toward equal services for their children. Between 1950 and 1980, the efforts of parents and professionals led to many advances in deinstitutionalization and normalization efforts (Wehmeyer, 2013). Also during this time, several well-known parents of children with disabilities significantly influenced a shift in people's thinking. Pearl Buck's writings about her daughter with mental disabilities and Dale Evans Rogers' *Angel Unaware* about her daughter with Down syndrome helped to alter parents' acceptance of their children with disabilities. Also influential was Eunice Kennedy Shriver's story about her sister's intellectual disability in a 1962 article in the *Saturday Evening Post*.

As noted previously, questions were being asked about the immutability of intelligence in young children, including those with intellectual disabilities and those from poverty backgrounds. Dreger and Miller (1960) conducted a major review of testing outcomes and concluded that significant social and environmental variables had to be taken into account in interpreting test data because Black children did not have the social and cultural advantages of White children. About the same time, intelligence tests began to be seen as a valid instrument to determine the effects of environmental interventions on children's intellectual abilities. Several pioneering researchers began to ask if changes in the home or school environment could change the trajectory for these children, thus shifting the focus from the immutability of intelligence to the potential of increasing children's cognitive abilities through environmental changes.

Other researchers were concerned with mental retardation and became captivated by questions on the malleability of intellectual abilities. They began to ask if educational programs could make a difference in the development of children with disabilities—questions not unlike those being raised about children from minority backgrounds on the role of heredity and the environment on development. To explore this possibility, Kirk (1958) conducted a study that examined whether a preschool intervention for children with intellectual disabilities could change their developmental outcomes. In one of the earliest experimental studies on the positive benefits of preschool, Kirk compared children in preschool with those who remained at home, finding that those who attended preschool made major gains in IQ scores and social development (Kirk & Johnson, 1951). This work built on the efforts of earlier theorists about environmental factors as important determinants of children's development. For example, it was consistent with the findings of Skeels and Dye (1939) and Skeels (1966), who compared the effects of children in an orphanage with those who were removed from the orphanage and placed with families, finding that children who were placed with families outperformed those who remained in the orphanage. Although this research was criticized for its methodology, it was part of the early efforts to examine if intelligence could be modified by environmental factors.

POLITICAL, SOCIAL, AND CULTURAL ISSUES: The 1960s

Although the prevailing view at mid-century was that intelligence was immutable, events in the 1960s continued to call that belief into question. Other pioneering researchers were also asking if changes in the home or school environment could positively influence the projected outcome for these children. Susan Gray and Rupert Klaus at George Peabody College for Teachers developed an early childhood intervention program for children from low-income families. In a randomly assigned study of children to four treatment conditions, children in the treated groups scored higher on IQ tests after their first summer of participation (Gray & Klaus, 1970). Martin and Cynthia Deutsch at the Institute for Developmental Studies of New York University (Jordan, Grallo, Deutsch, & Deutsch, 1985) developed an early enrichment program designed to last 5 years for each child. Compared with children who did not attend the program, children in the treatment group made significant gains on a number of cognitive and language tests. The results of both studies captured the attention of several influential individuals, further stimulating interest in establishing a national early childhood program (Zigler & Styfco, 2010).

In the early 1960s, Bettye Caldwell and Julius Richmond developed a preschool program in Syracuse, New York, which broke new ground by going against the prevailing views on home care for young children and enrolling children as young as 6 months of age. Other innovative elements included a focus on health care and implementing a curriculum that included cognitive and socioemotional development as well as social services for the families. Their goal was to prevent the kinds of verbal and motivational deficiencies often observed when children from low-income families entered school (Caldwell & Richmond, 1968). All three of these programs were highly influential in the development of the new federal program that was to be called Head Start (Zigler & Styfco, 2010).

Two researcher theorists active in the 1950s and 1960s, B.F. Skinner and Jean Piaget, had an outsized influence on these new programs for children and on research in the field of child development. Skinner's research and writings were significant in bringing about a focus on a child's actual behavior and the role of immediate consequences in changing behavior (Skinner, 1953, 1968). His work and that of others influenced the development of applied behavior analysis as a clinical approach to understand and treat a large range of problematic child behaviors (Ullmann & Krasner, 1965; Baer, Wolf, & Risley, 1968). This work contrasted with the prevailing views in clinical psychology regarding disorders in children and adults that conceptualized maladaptive behavior as resulting from underlying causes, such as neurosis and psychosis (Skinner, 1953, 1968; Ullmann & Krasner, 1965). Jean Piaget was a Swiss psychologist who posited that all children went through universal stages of cognitive development and biological maturation. Although he did not specifically relate his theory to education, his theory has had enormous influence as, for example, his beliefs that children learn through discovery and by actively exploring rather than through social interactions (Piaget & Inhelder, 1969).

When John Kennedy assumed the presidency in 1961, the country was in a depression. Much of Kennedy's attention was focused on ways to improve the economy, but he could not ignore the growing civil unrest against racism. This unrest required attention to many of the struggles taking place in the country, especially in the South. Illustrative of this unrest was the March on Washington for Jobs and Freedom in the summer of 1963—a highly significant event that brought national attention to the concerns of African Americans. Spurred in part by the failure of Congress to pass the Civil Rights Act, the march attracted 250,000 people, Black and White, marching for more rights for Blacks. Remembered especially for the "I have a dream" speech by Martin Luther King, Jr., the march also facilitated the passage of the Civil Rights Act in 1964 and brought to national attention numerous other grievances of African Americans, including unemployment and segregated schools.

Kennedy was also cognizant of the debilitating consequences for children with intellectual and developmental disabilities—referred to at the time as "mentally retarded" and "mentally ill" children. Influenced by the realities of life for his sister with disabilities, in October 1963 President Kennedy signed two significant legislation acts. First was the Maternal and Child Health and Mental Retardation Planning Amendments of 1963 (PL 88-156), which specifically addressed mental retardation and mental illness. This action was the first large-scale public action recognizing the needs of children with disabilities. Kennedy (1963) noted, "We as a nation have long neglected the mentally ill and the mentally retarded. This neglect must end if our nation is to live up to its own standards of compassion and dignity." The following week, he signed a bill to fund construction of 12 mental retardation research centers to study the causes of intellectual disabilities, diagnostic treatment clinics, and community-based centers for the care of people with intellectual disabilities—the Mental Retardation Facilities and Community Health Centers Construction Act of 1963 (PL 88-164). The significance of these national acts cannot be overestimated. Among the very last legislative actions of President Kennedy, they fostered considerable professional interest in children with disabilities and prompted the initiation of significant research efforts focused on children with intellectual disabilities. Kennedy had previously signed into law another highly significant legislation for children that created the National Institute for Child Health and Development.

Although President Kennedy did not live to implement many of his plans to address social issues, his interest in the debilitating effects of children growing up in poverty was shared by President Johnson and became part of the impetus for the War on Poverty. President Johnson's initiatives resulted in the largest number of new federal programs since Franklin D. Roosevelt—many of which had a strong and positive bearing on the lives of low-income families. These included the Social Security Amendments of 1965 (Medicare and Medicaid; PL 89-97), the Food Stamp Act of 1964 (PL 88-525), the Housing and Urban Development Act of 1965 (PL 89-117), the Voting Rights Act of 1965 (PL 89-110), and federal support for the Elementary and Secondary Education Act of 1965 (PL 89-10), which provided significant funding for schools. Among its entitlement programs was Title I, which provided funding to schools and school districts with a high percentage of students from low-income families. Several of Johnson's Great Society efforts continued to expand under both Presidents Nixon and Ford. President Nixon, however, vetoed the Comprehensive Child Development Act of 1971, limiting federal support for child care and negatively influencing low-income families. By contrast, middle-income families were able to use child care costs to reduce their taxes.

One of the most enduring actions under President Johnson was the initiation of Head Start, which was a nationwide effort to provide educational and health resources for children living in poverty. Started as an 8-week summer program in 1965, Head Start provided a preschool setting for children or parenting education through home visiting to help alleviate the negative educational consequences of growing up in poverty. During this time, minority children were often described as "culturally deprived" or "disadvantaged," implying they were not receiving the early home experiences necessary to succeed in mainstream society (Reissman, 1962). Head Start was seen as a way to break the "cycle of poverty" by providing children from low-income families with a comprehensive preschool program that could address not only their educational needs but also their social, health, and nutritional needs and positively influence parents' child-rearing practices.

A number of events converged to provide the foundation for the creation of Head Start. President Kennedy's brother-in-law, Sargent Shriver, visited Gray and Klaus's early intervention projects at Peabody College and learned about the positive outcomes for children from attendance at a summer program combined with home visits to the parents during the school year (Zigler & Styfco, 2010). Shriver called on other professionals, including Edward Zigler and Urie Bronfenbrenner, to help design these Head Start programs (Zigler & Styfco, 2010), thus sparking considerable interest among psychologists and educators in Head Start (Zigler & Valentine, 1997) and in research examining the potential benefits of early childhood education.

FIFTY YEARS OF ADVANCES: 1966–2016

The social and political climates in the 1960s were ripe for researchers to ask how children's environments influenced their development and if educational experiences during the preschool years could change their developmental trajectory. Early empirical studies provided encouragement for the potential positive benefits of environmental changes on children's development. Many well-known researchers had been raising questions about whether retardation was primarily a hereditary phenomenon or if intellectual abilities could be modified through the environment. Others were examining the positive effects of early intervention on children growing up in poverty. Among the pioneers in the early intervention studies were the already mentioned work from the 1960s by Gray and Klaus, Deutsch and Deutsch, and Caldwell and Richmond, as well as the well-known study by David Weikart who initiated the High/Scope Perry Preschool Program in 1962 to examine the effects of a high-quality preschool program for children from low-income families with both center and home-based interventions (Schweinhart & Weikart, 1980). The teachers in the Perry Preschool Program made home visits every Friday; home visiting was increasingly being employed in early childhood as a way to enhance development for children growing up in poverty. Ira Gordon's Florida Parent Education Program made home visits with parents of preschool children and held backyard play groups (Gordon, Guinagh, & Jester, 1977). Data from these and other early studies were collected as part of the Cornell Consortium and report by Lazar and his colleagues (Lazar et al., 1982). Almost all these early researchers assessed the intellectual performance of children rather than measures of social behaviors or academic performance, thus underscoring the interest in intellectual malleability. Most programs enrolled children from families in poverty; however, because of the preponderance of minority families in many low-income communities, many of the research populations were predominantly minority.

In the 1970s, other researchers initiated well-designed studies on the effects of early childhood education. Influenced by research and theories in the 1960s about the malleability of children's intellectual performance, the Abecedarian Project of the FPG Institute was launched in 1972 by Craig Ramey and his colleagues, becoming one of the most significant longitudinal studies of early childhood intervention. This study and subsequent replications, described in Chapter 7, examined the effects of a quality child care program initiated in infancy on the intellectual outcomes of children from low-income families. Other early interventions studies proliferated—some spurred by the funding of Project Head Start. The Perry Preschool Study continued to follow the young children enrolled in the late 1960s. A renewed focus in the 1960s on home visiting as a strategy for reaching parents of young children influenced several programs in the 1970s and 1980s, which developed into model national programs (Wasik & Bryant, 2001).

When the Bureau for the Education of the Handicapped was established in 1967 as part of the U.S. Office of Education, James J. Gallagher served as its first chief and promoted legislation supporting children with disabilities. (Of note, Gallagher later served as the director of the FPG Institute from 1970 to 1987.) In 1975, Congress passed the Education for All Handicapped Children Act of 1975 (PL 94-142), later known as the Individuals with Disabilities Education Act of 1990 (PL 101-476), which guaranteed a free, appropriate, public education for all children with mental and physical disabilities. This highly significant and far-reaching act mandated that public schools evaluate disabled children and create an educational plan with input from parents. It also mandated that students be served in the

least restrictive environment and allowed maximum opportunity to interact with nonimpaired students. These federal policies, described in Chapter
13, spurred both research with children with disabilities as well as attention
to professional development (see Chapters 8 and 12).

Another influential event in understanding children's learning and
development was the pioneering publication by Hart and Risley (1995),
which dramatically illustrated differences in the home environments of
children in professional, working-class, and low-income families. These
data also illustrated the relation of the home environments with children's
language skills and later school performance. Interest in preschool education for children from low-income families also was increasing, especially at
the state level, with numerous pre-K programs initiated across the country.
The significant increase in the number of immigrant families with young
children, particularly Spanish-speaking families, prompted a major focus
on English-language learners, dual-language learners, and concerns with
how best to facilitate language development among non–English-speaking
children. In contrast to the "assimilation" views in the early part of the 20th
century, a growing number of educators were calling for new views on
educating children from non–English-speaking households (see Chapter 4).
Others raised concerns with theories that did not take into consideration
race, gender, and ethnicity. Of special note was the integrative conceptual
framework for understanding the development of minority children proposed by Garcia-Coll and her colleagues, who called out critical variables
often neglected in the study of minority children's development, including
racism, prejudice, discrimination, oppression, and segregation (Garcia-Coll
et al., 1996). Other advances made in research, policy, and practice served
as a lens for examining issues of race, ethnicity, language, and economic
diversity, as well as the needs of and services for children with disabilities
and children growing up in poverty. These issues are addressed in depth
by the authors in this volume. The final chapter uses the refined process-
person-context-time model of Bronfenbrenner (1979) to reflect on the lessons
we have learned over the last 50 years and to consider the unresolved challenges to be faced in the future.

SUMMARY

The United States has a long history of addressing the role of children in
society, from their education and upbringing in the home to when and
whether government should provide support to families with young children. Numerous philosophical, social, professional, and religious beliefs
and attitudes as well as research findings influenced many of the policies
and practices. As a result, disparate ways to address the educational, developmental, economic, and social needs of families and children have emerged
over time, leading at times to inequities in policies and services. In Sections
II, III, and IV of this volume, the authors address many of these phenomena.

Throughout much of the history of the United States, child and family services were provided primarily to White families. When changes were brought about related to desegregation in the 1950s and 1960s, the needs of minority children and their families became more salient, especially those of African American children and families. As immigration patterns changed in the 1980s and 1990s, bringing many non–English-speaking families with children, another set of events began to influence educational practices. These changes have influenced policy and practice throughout the past 50 years and are captured in the chapters presented in Section II on race, ethnicity, linguistic, and cultural diversity. This section begins with a consideration of the special needs of African American boys, followed by an examination of cultural and linguistic changes in the demographics of the country and how these have influenced the need for services. Then, a consideration of policies regarding children of color and minority children is presented, followed by a concluding chapter that reviews the current status of research and practice for these minority children and their families and makes recommendations for future directions.

The 1960s saw a significant increase in concerns with children growing up in poverty. It is not, however, always easy to separate services that came about related to race and ethnicity from those that developed out of social concerns for those living in poverty. Consequently, many of the initiatives that began in the 1960s and 1970s to address children from low-income families enrolled a majority of families from minority backgrounds. Nevertheless, concerns with children living in poverty, regardless of race or cultural status, has driven many of the initiatives designed to ameliorate the educational and social disadvantages of growing up in low-income families. In Section III, the authors present information on some of the most significant early childhood interventions that addressed children from low-income families. Also addressed in Section III are issues in the professional preparation of educators and other specialists who work with these children. A detailed presentation of federal policies and funding regarding early childhood programs over the past 50 years is presented. This section concludes with a detailed reflection on the research, practice, and policy advances of the past 50 years.

Section IV addresses the third theme of this volume—namely, children with disabilities and their families. Historically, children with disabilities were rarely provided services—a situation that did not change significantly in the United States until the 1960s, when the legislation initiated by President John Kennedy (discussed previously in this chapter) called for establishing research centers to address the needs of developmentally and intellectually disabled children. FPG (one of the originally funded research centers), along with other research centers, began to examine the needs of children with disabilities and their families. The outcomes of this ongoing work have contributed significantly to interventions for these individuals. The review of these advances is followed by a review of professional practice concerns, which is especially focused on preparation of the work force. Detailed information is then presented on the major policy advances of the past 50 years for services for children with disabilities. This section concludes with a review of the research, practice, and policy advances and makes recommendations for future directions.

The accomplishments reported over the past 50 years give us reason for celebration because much has been accomplished. However, the findings are tempered by observations of unresolved needs and challenges still faced when translating research findings into effective policy and practice (see especially Chapters 10 and 15). Nevertheless, when considered together, the findings from the past 50 years create an informative but complicated tapestry that can be used to help understand the advances across research, practice, and policy. The dilemmas, challenges, and progress identified by authors in this volume allow reflection on the past 50 years and provide an essential foundation for ensuring advances for the next 50 years.

REFERENCES

Asperger, H. (1944, June). Die "Autistischen Psychopathen" im Kindesalter [Autistic psychopaths in childhood]. *Archiv für Psychiatrie und Nervenkrankheiten, 117,* 76–136.

Baer, D. M., Wolf, M. M., & Risley, T. R. (1968). Some current dimensions of applied behavior analysis. *Journal of Applied Behavior Analysis, 1,* 91–97.

Bank Street. (n.d.). History. Retrieved from https://www.bankstreet.edu/discover-bankstreet/what-we-do/history

Blank, S. W., & Blum, B. B. (1997). A brief history of work expectations for welfare mothers. *The Future of Children, 7*(1), 28–38.

Bowlby, J. (1952). *Maternal care and mental health.* Geneva, Switzerland: World Health Organization.

Bowlby, J. (1969). *Attachment and loss* (Vol. 1). New York, NY: Basic Books.

Bremner, R. H. (1970). *Children and youth in America: A documentary history, Vol. 1: 1600–1865.* Cambridge, MA: Harvard University Press.

Bremner, R. H. (1971). *Children and youth in America: A documentary history, Vol. II: 1866–1932.* Cambridge, MA: Harvard University Press.

Bronfenbrenner, U. (1979). *The ecology of human development: Experiments by nature and design.* Cambridge, MA: Harvard University Press.

Cahan, E. D. (1989). *Past caring: A history of U.S. preschool care and education for the poor, 1820–1965.* New York, NY: National Center for Children in Poverty, Columbia University.

Caldwell, B. M., & Richmond, J. B. (1968). The Children's Center in Syracuse, New York. In L. L. Dittmann (Ed.), *Early child care: The new perspectives* (pp. 326–358). New York, NY: Atherton Press.

Carten, A. (2016). *How racism has shaped welfare policy in America.* Retrieved from https://the-conversation.com/how-racism-has-shaped-welfare-policy-in-america-since-1935-63574

Clark, K. B., & Clark, M. P. (1947). Racial identification and preference among Negro children. In E. L. Hartley (Ed.), *Readings in social psychology.* New York, NY: Holt, Rinehart, & Winston.

Dewey, J. (1915). *Schools of tomorrow.* New York, NY: Dutton.

Dreger, R. M., & Miller, K. S. (1960). Comparative psychological studies of Negroes and whites in the United States. *Psychological Bulletin, 57,* 361-402.

DuBois, P. H. (1970). *A history of psychological testing.* Boston, MA: Allyn & Bacon.

Education for All Handicapped Children Act of 1975, PL 94-142, 20 U.S.C. §§ 1400 *et seq.*

Elementary and Secondary Education Act of 1965, PL 89-10, 20 U.S.C. §§ 241.

Food Stamp Act of 1964, PL 88-525, 7 U.S.C. §§ 2011 *et seq.*

Garcia-Coll, C., Lamberty, G., Jenkins, R., McAdoo, H. P., Crnic, K., Wasik, B. H., et al. (1996). Toward an integrative theoretical model for the study of developmental competencies in minority children. *Child Development, 67,* 1891–1914.

Garth, T. A. (1931). *Race psychology: A study of racial mental differences.* New York, NY: McGraw-Hill.

Gesell, A. (1928). *Infancy and human growth.* New York, NY: Macmillan.

Goodwin, D. K. (1995). *No ordinary time.* New York, NY: Simon & Schuster.

Gordon, I. J., Guinagh, B. J., & Jester, R. E. (1977). The Florida Parent Education Infant and Toddler Program. In M. C. Day & R. K. Parker (Eds.), *The preschool in action: Exploring early childhood programs* (pp. 95–127). Boston, MA: Allyn & Bacon.

Gray, S. W., & Klaus, R. A. (1970). The Early Training Project: A seventh year report. *Child Development, 41,* 909–924.

Gray, S. W., & Ruttle, K. (1980). The Family-Oriented Home Visiting Program: A longitudinal study. *Genetic Psychology Monographs, 102,* 299–316.

Hansan, J. (2011). The American era of child labor. *Social Welfare History Project.* Retrieved from http://socialwelfare.library.vcu.edu/programs/child-welfarechild-labor/child-labor

Hansan, J. E. (2011). Settlement houses: An introduction. *Social Welfare History Project.* Retrieved from http://socialwelfare.library.vcu.edu/settlement-houses/settlement-houses

Hart, B., & Risley, T. (1995). *Meaningful differences in the everyday experience of American children.* Baltimore, MD: Paul H. Brookes Publishing Co.

Horse, J. R. (1997). Traditional American Indian family systems. *Families, Systems, & Health 15*(3), 243–250.

Housing and Urban Development Act of 1965, PL 89-117.

Individuals with Disabilities Education Act (IDEA) of 1990, PL 101-476, 20 U.S.C. §§ 1400 *et seq.*

Institute of Medicine. (2000). *From neurons to neighborhoods: The science of early childhood development.* Washington, DC: The National Academies Press.

Jordan, T. J., Grallo, R., Deutsch, M., & Deutsch, C. P. (1985). Long-term effects of early enrichment: A 20-year perspective on persistence and change. *American Journal of Community Psychology, 13,* 393–415.

Kanner, L. (1943). Autistic disturbances of affective contact. *Nervous Child, 2,* 217–250.

Kennedy, J. F. (1963). *Special message to the Congress on Mental Illness and Mental Retardation.* Retrieved from http://www.presidency.ucsb.edu/ws/?pid=9546

Kennedy, W. A., van de Riet, V., & Wilson, J. (1963). A normative sample of intelligence and achievement of Negro elementary school children in the southeastern United States. *Monographs of the Society for Research in Child Development, 28*(6), 1–112.

Kirk, S. A. (1958). *Early education of the mentally retarded: An experimental study.* Urbana, IL: University of Illinois Press.

Kirk, S., & Johnson, G. (1951). *Educating the retarded child.* Cambridge, MA: Riverside Press.

Kode, K. (2017). *Elizabeth Farrell and the history of special education* (2nd ed.). Arlington, VA: Council for Exceptional Children.

Lazar, I., Darlington, R., Murray, H., Royce, J., Snipper, A., & Ramey, C. T. (1982). The lasting effects of early education: A report from the consortium for longitudinal studies. *Monographs of the Society for Research in Child Development, 47*(2–3), 1–151.

Locke, J. (1689). *An essay concerning human understanding.* Retrieved from http://socialwelfare .library.vcu.edu/programs/child-care-the-american-history

Maternal and Child Health and Mental Retardation Planning Amendments of 1963, PL 88-156, 42 U.S.C. §§ 1305 *et seq.*

Mental Retardation Facilities and Community Mental Health Centers Construction Act of 1963, PL 88-164, 42 U.S.C. §§ 2670 *et seq.*

Merrill-Palmer School. (n.d.). *Our history.* Retrieved from http://mpsi.wayne.edu/about/history.php

Montessori, M. (1912). *The Montessori method* (A. E. George, Trans.). New York, NY: Frederick A. Stokes. Retrieved from http://digital.library.upenn.edu/women/montessori/method/method.html

Parten, M. (1932). Social participation among preschool children. *Journal of Abnormal and Social Psychology, 27*(3), 243–269.

Peterson, J. (1923). The comparative abilities of white and Negro children. *Comparative Psychology Monographs, 5,* 1–141.

Piaget, J., & Inhelder, B. (1969). *The psychology of the child.* New York, NY: Basic Books.

Pintner, R. (1931). *Intelligence testing: Methods and results.* New York, NY: Holt.

Reissman, F. (1962). *The culturally deprived child.* New York, NY: Harper.

Rey, J. M., Assumpção, F. B., Bernad, C. A., Çuhadaroğlu, F. C., Evans, B., Fung, D., et al. (2015). *History of child and adolescent psychiatry.* In J. M., Rey (Ed.), *IACAPAP e-textbook of child and adolescent mental health.* Geneva, Switzerland: International Association for Child and Adolescent Psychiatry and Allied Professions.

Rousseau, J. (1979). *Emile, or On education* (A. Bloom, Trans.). New York, NY: Basic Books.

Schweinhart, L. J., & Weikart, D. P. (1980). *Young children grow up: The effects of the Perry Preschool Program on youths through age 15.* Ypsilanti, MI: High/Scope Foundation.

Seguin, E. (1856). Origin of the treatment and training of idiots. *American Journal of Education.* Retrieved from http://www.disabilitymuseum.org/dhm/lib/detail.html?id=1437&page=all.

Shaw, D. (2016). *The promise of the premise: The first 50 years of the Frank Porter Graham Child Development Institute.* Chapel Hill, NC: The University of North Carolina, FPG Child Development Institute.

Shonkoff, J. P., & Meisels, S. J. (1990). Early childhood intervention: The evolution of a concept. In J. P. Shonkoff & S. J. Meisels (Eds.), *Handbook of early childhood intervention* (pp. 3–31). New York, NY: Cambridge University Press.

Skeels, H. (1966). Adult status of children with contrasting early life experiences. *Monographs of the Society for Research in Child Development, 31*(3), 1–65.

Skeels, H. M., & Dye, H. B. (1939). A study of the effects of differential stimulation on mentally retarded children. *Proceedings and Address of the American Association on Mental Deficiency, 4,* 114–136.

Skinner, B. F. (1953). *Science and human behavior.* New York, NY: Macmillan.

Skinner, B. F. (1968). *The technology of teaching.* New York, NY: Appleton-Century-Crofts.

Social Security Amendments of 1965, PL 89-97, 42 U.S.C. §§ 401 et seq.

Tank, R. M. (1980). *Young children, families, and society in America since the 1820s: The evolution of health, education, and child care programs for preschool children* (Doctoral dissertation). Department of History, University of Michigan, Ann Arbor. Retrieved from University Microfilms International (No. 8106233).

Teachers College. (n.d.). *About Teachers College.* Retrieved from http://www.tc.columbia.edu/abouttc/timeline

Ullmann, L. P., & Krasner, L. (1965). *Case studies in behavior modification.* New York, NY: Holt, Rinehart, & Winston.

Voting Rights Act of 1965, PL 89-110), 42 U.S.C. §§ 1973 et seq.

Wasik, B. H. (1984). Clinical applications of direct behavior observation: A look at the past and the future. In B. B. Lahey & A. E. Kazdin (Eds.), *Advances in clinical child psychology* (pp. 153–193). New York, NY: Plenum Press.

Wasik, B. H., & Bryant, D. (2001). *Home visiting: Procedures for helping families.* Thousand Oaks, CA: Sage Publications.

Wehmeyer, M. L. (Ed.) (2013). *The story of intellectual disability.* Baltimore, MD: Paul H. Brookes Publishing Co.

Yarrow, A. L. (2009). *History of U.S. children's policy, 1900–Present.* Washington, DC: First Focus.

Zenderland, L. (1998). *Measuring minds: Henry Herbert Goddard and the origins of American intelligence testing.* New York, NY: Cambridge University Press.

Zigler, E., & Styfco, S. J. (2010). *The hidden history of Head Start.* Oxford, UK: Oxford University Press.

Zigler, E., & Valentine, J. (Eds.). (1997). *Project Head Start: A legacy of the War on Poverty* (2nd ed.). Alexandria, VA: National Head Start Association.

2

Early Childhood Research in a Globalized Society

Accounting for Demographic Shifts and Changes

Iheoma U. Iruka

The importance of the early years (birth through age 8) has been documented in numerous reports and empirical studies. For these early years, four outcomes have been identified by the National Academies of Science, Engineering, and Medicine (2016) as being fundamental to children's well-being: physical health and safety, cognitive competence, emotional and behavioral competence, and social competence.

Physical health and safety—the first of the four fundamental outcomes—speaks to children starting life in a safe and secure environment where they are free from physical, emotional, social, and sexual maltreatment. It also includes caring for children in a way that supports their physical development, including access to nutritious food and health-promoting services and care, such as a medical home or primary doctor. Physical health and safety are also critical to meeting children's other competencies. The second critical outcome, cognitive competence, includes the capacities needed across the developmental life course to support children's school performance—and eventually their life success. These capacities include language, communication, reading, mathematics, knowledge of science and history, and skills that support learning, including persistence, flexibility, and attention. Emotional and behavior competence, the third critical outcome, encompasses the ability to cope with and manage unfamiliar and unwanted situations and stimuli, including obstacles and frustrations. These competencies include the ability to be resilient and hopeful, especially in the midst of stressors, as well as the ability to regulate one's emotions in developmentally appropriate ways. Finally, social competence includes children's abilities to cooperate with others; be responsible, empathetic, sympathetic, and assertive; and self-regulate one's emotions. Furthermore, noncognitive competencies are thought to support children's cognitive development and set them on track for positive school and life outcomes. Collectively, these four competencies are viewed as being critical to help children meet the long-term outcomes of being economically, emotionally, and socially stable and civically engaged. This chapter will address the social, cultural, educational, and political forces that have a bearing on these outcomes for young children.

One way of assessing how U.S. children are doing in these four areas is to compare them with their global counterparts regarding their later school performance. Most scholars generally agree that these four domains are critical for children's later school and life success. However, when examined within a global framework, one sees concerns about the ability of children in the United States to compete in a global market. The Programme for International Student Assessment (PISA)—an international assessment that measures 15-year-old students' reading, mathematics, and science literacy every 3 years (coordinated by the Organization for Economic Cooperation and Development, an intergovernmental organization of industrialized countries, and conducted in the United States by the National Center for Education Statistics)—found the United States to be lagging behind many countries. For example, the PISA 2015 assessed students' science, reading, and mathematics literacy in more than 70 countries and education systems (Kastberg, Chan, & Murray, 2016). Science was the focal subject of the 2015 data collection, including optional assessments of collaborative problem solving and financial literacy. U.S. 15-year-old students participated in both of these optional assessments. The average scores for the United States and Singapore were 488 and 552 points, respectively, with Singapore having the highest average score.

What is most staggering in the United States beyond these differences with other countries is the racial disparities in these scores: White Americans scored 519, Asian Americans scored 517, multiracial Americans scored 492, Hispanic Americans scored 465, and Black Americans scored 432—a spread of 87 points. These global and U.S. ethnic disparities have been documented in prior collections and for other subject areas (Winn et al., 2012). The National Assessment of Educational Progress, our nation's report card, also shows these racial gaps (Vanneman, Hamilton, Baldwin Anderson, & Rahman, 2009). In 1992, the fourth-grade reading scale score ranged from a high of 224 for White students to a low of 192 for Black students (a 32-point spread). A similar pattern was seen for eighth-grade reading scale scores, with a high of 267 for White students and a low of 237 for Black students (a 30-point spread). Although some improvements occurred in the past 20 years, the 2015 scores showed a similar gap. In 2015, the fourth-grade reading scale score ranged from a high of 239 for Asian/Pacific Islander students to a low of 205 for American Indian/Alaska Native students (a 34-point spread); the White–Black spread was 26 points. The range for eighth-grade reading scale scores in 2015 was from a high of 280 for Asian/Pacific Islander students to a low of 248 for Black students (a 32-point spread); the White–Black spread was 26 points. These consistent patterns of academic racial gaps are prevalent between White and Asian students in comparison with Black, Hispanic, and American Indian/Alaska Native students. Similar patterns are seen for mathematics scale scores.

Discrepancies are also evident when examined across socioeconomic status levels (SES). For example, the U.S. Department of Education's analyses of the Early Childhood Longitudinal Study–Kindergarten Cohort for 2010–2011 shows a considerable gap between children from low-, middle-, and high-SES households in the first few years of elementary school. The average science scale score for first-time kindergartners in the fall of 2010 differed by SES, and scores of children from high-SES households went from 33 points at kindergarten to 48 points by the second grade (a 15-point increase). During this same period, the science scale scores of children from low-SES households went from 24 to 39 points, which is also a 15-point increase; however, these children started lower and remained lower. Considering the changing demographic landscape of the United States, which has a growing population of low-income, ethnic minority, and linguistic minority individuals who experience multiple risk factors, these gaps are likely to continue over time.

THEORETICAL FRAMEWORK

One of the major education problems in the United States is the achievement gap, which may be a symptom of earlier opportunity gaps. For example, when low-income, ethnic, or language minority children do not experience high-quality early learning, then an achievement gap is likely to appear and persist over time. When these children do not have access to proper prenatal and medical care, gaps are also likely to develop. Both the bioecological model (Bronfenbrenner & Evans, 2000) and the Integrative Model for the Study of Developmental Competences in Minority Children (García Coll et al., 1996) provide a framework of factors that likely contribute to the persistent opportunity and achievement gaps among children from different backgrounds.

The bioecological model proposed by Urie Bronfenbrenner emphasizes the importance of various systems and settings close to children that affect children's development on a microlevel (e.g., families, schools, early education programs), as well as macrolevel contexts (e.g., policies, culture) that are also critical influences but are further from children's day-by-day development. Time is also a critical feature of the bioecological framework, which identifies the importance of examining the intersection of systems and time. A striking example of the importance of considering time is the change in immigration policies or patterns over time in the United States.

To further explicate issues that are more attuned to the needs of diverse children, the Integrative Model for the Study of Developmental Competences in Minority Children (García Coll et al., 1996) is used to inform this chapter. This integrative model underscores how the development of minority children is impacted by identifying several critical topics: 1) social position (e.g., race, gender, social class); 2) racism, discrimination, and oppression; 3) residential, economic, social, and psychological segregation; 4) school, neighborhood, and health care environments; 5) adaptive cultures (e.g., traditions, migration, economic history, acculturation); 6) physical, biological, and temperamental characteristics; and 7) family structure, roles, belief, racial socialization, and SES. Several of these topics inform sections of this chapter, such as examining the economic position of families over time and delving deeper into differences by race and ethnicity.

MICROSYSTEM CHANGES

When considering how to effectively address development, learning, well-being, and, more importantly, opportunity and achievement gaps, one must attend to the various demographic shifts in the micro- and macrosystems that affect children and have a bearing on research, programs, practices, and policies. This section focuses on microsystem changes—population change; income, wealth, and poverty; education attainment; family structure; and community change—which are likely influenced by microsystem factors, including tax structures, labor changes, and immigration policies. Although these factors are described separately, to some extent there is a need to recognize the intersectionality and relationships across these areas. For example, children of color are more likely to live in low-income and less educated, single-female-headed households with limited resources and opportunities in low-wealth communities with substandard housing—all factors that may exacerbate the achievement gap.

Population Change

Based on the 2010 U.S. Census, children make up almost 25% of the national population at 74.2 million (O'Hare, 2011). However, the child population grew by only 3% between 2000 and 2010, which is considerably lower than the rate of 14% between 1990 and 2000. The growth in the child population is attributable to growth in mixed-race children (46% increase), Hispanic children (39% increase), and Asian/Pacific Islander children (31% increase). During this decade, a noticeable decrease occurred in White children (10% decrease), American Indian/Alaska Native children (6% decrease), and Black children (2% decrease). This changing demographic has resulted in ethnic minorities making up more of the child population. Based on the U.S. Census Bureau 2014 National Projections, the minority population is projected to increase to 56% of the total population in 2060, compared with 38% in 2014.

The change in demographics is also seen in the native-born versus foreign-born population, the English-speaking vs. non–English-speaking population, and in different legal statuses. "Foreign born" refers to persons born outside of the United States, Puerto Rico, or other U.S. territories to parents who are not U.S. citizens. The terms "foreign born" and "immigrant" are sometimes used interchangeably in this chapter. There has been a sharp increase in the foreign-born U.S. population since 1970. In 2013, the foreign-born population reached a high of 13%, or more than 41 million people (Pew Research Center, 2015a). Furthermore, the demographics of foreign-born citizens have changed from being a majority of Europeans in the 1960s and 1970s to a majority of immigrants from Latin America, South or East Asia, and sub-Saharan Africa. This immigration trend may also be linked to language use. In 1980, 30% of immigrants reported speaking only English at home; this number decreased to 16% in 2013 (Pew Research Center, 2015a). Furthermore, this change also resulted in a shift in the number of immigrants who reported speaking English less than very well, from 43% in 1980 to 50% in 2013, reflecting the increasing number of immigrants who prefer to maintain primary use of their home language.

Unauthorized immigration into the United States is another documented phenomenon. In 1970, approximately 64% of immigrants were U.S. citizens; however, this percentage decreased to 47% in 2013. Estimates indicate that 26% of immigrants are unauthorized, meaning they are in the country illegally (Pew Research Center, 2015a). Although the number of unauthorized immigrants grew to 12.2 million between 1990 and 2007, this number has steadily decreased through 2017.

Using the 2013 Census Bureau's American Community Survey, the Center for Migration Studies reported the following statistics: 1) a total of 5,151,000 U.S.-born children were living with an undocumented parent in 2013; 2) approximately 300,000 children with undocumented parents were born in each of the past few years; and 3) approximately 3.6 million, or 70%, of the undocumented parents of U.S.-born children were from Mexico (Warren, 2013). The majority of children in these homes speak English well (95%), are enrolled in school (80% for those who are aged 3 years and older), and have health insurance (83%). However, they are more likely to live in poverty compared to all undocumented residents (39% vs. 28%).

The changes in the demographics of the United States (i.e., more majority-minority, non-English speakers, and immigrants from Latin America, Asia, and Africa) indicates a need to ensure that research captures the unique experiences of these populations. This increasing diversity may have implications for policies and practices, which may need to be refined and adjusted.

Income, Wealth, and Poverty

Countless studies have pointed to the links between income, wealth, school education, and life outcomes (Gershoff, Aber, Raver, & Lennon, 2007; Linver, Brooks-Gunn, & Kohen, 2002; Yeung, Linver, & Brooks-Gunn, 2002). These links are particularly concerning in light of the widening income and wealth gap. In their calculations from the U.S. Census Bureau's Current Population Survey and the Internal Revenue Service's Statistics of Income data compiled from a large sample of individual income tax returns, Stone, Trisi, Sherman, and Horton (2016) obtained three major findings. First, the income gap between higher-income and lower-income individuals grew substantially and then did not change much between the late 1940s and early 1970s. Second, by the 1970s, the income growth for middle- and lower-income households slowed considerably and the incomes for higher-income households grew sharply, with even more concentration of income at the very top. Third, "wealth—the value of a household's property and financial assets, minus the value of its debts—is much more highly concentrated than income. The best survey data show that the top 3% of the distribution hold over half of all wealth" (Stone et al., 2016, p. 1).

Income is used to determine one's poverty status. Individuals who live below the income threshold based on family size and composition are designated as living in poverty. This threshold is adjusted annually to reflect the consumer price index. For example, the threshold for a couple with two children was $24,339 in 2016 (compared to $8,351 in 1980, $13,301 in 1990, $17,463 in 2000, and $22,113 in 2010). Although income has generally remained steady for the average family, the poverty rate has seen a decrease; however, this rate varies among racial groups (Patten, 2016). Between 1980 and 2013, the poverty rate for Hispanic children increased from 29.1% to 32.7% (39% for foreign-born children and 32.3% for U.S.-born children). The poverty rate for Black children remained relatively level, although higher, during this same time period: from 37.7% in 1980 to 39.3% in 2013. The poverty rate increased almost 3% (from 10.4% to 13.6%) for White children, whereas it decreased for Asian children (from 15.0% to 13.2%) between 1980 and 2013.

On a positive note, there has been a steep decline in poverty since the 1960s, which can be attributed to the implementation of poverty-reducing measures, such as the Supplemental Nutrition Assistance Program (SNAP) and rental vouchers. The alternative to the official poverty measure, called the Supplemental Poverty Measure, accounts for a family's cash income as well as noncash benefits such as SNAP, housing assistance, Women with Infants and Children, school lunch, home energy assistance, and tax credits. This safety net cuts poverty nearly in half for children, from 26.8% to 16.1%. However, the rate for children in deep poverty—households that are below half of the poverty line (less than $12,170 annual income)—rose to 3% in 2005 from 2.1% in 1995 (Stone et al., 2016).

Educational Attainment

Parent education level was found to be an important predictor of children's early and later outcomes, with higher parental education attainment associated with better outcomes (Davis-Kean, 2005). Between the 1980s and 2013, there was a steady increase in U.S. adults with 2-year degrees or some college (from 17.8% to 29.1%) and baccalaureate degrees (from 16.2% to 29.6%)

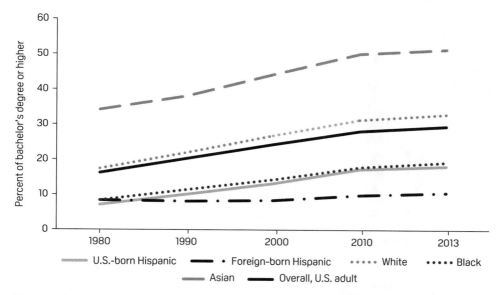

Figure 2.1.   Percent with a bachelor's degree or higher by race/ethnicity, 1980–2013. (*Source:* Pew Research Center tabulations of 1980, 1990, and 2000 census [5% Integrated Public Use Microdata Series] and 2010 and 2015a American Community Surveys [1% Integrated Public Use Microdata Series].)

(Patten, 2016). Although all ethnic/racial groups saw an increase in educational attainment, U.S.-born Hispanics and Black individuals saw a greater increase in 2-year degrees or some college. Asians earned the most bachelor's degrees and had a more pronounced increase compared to other racial and ethnic groups, from 34% in 1980 to 52% in 2013 (see Figure 2.1). In contrast, foreign-born Hispanics saw a minimal increase during the same time period, from 8% to 11%. Furthermore, Asian children were more likely to be in households with at least one parent with a bachelor's degree in comparison with Hispanic and Black children. This ethnic disparity in baccalaureate degrees has potential implications for a family's ability to provide an economically stable and enriching learning environment for children, subsequently impacting children's learning and well-being.

Family Structure

Family structure has been linked to children's overall well-being and behavior, with children in stable and two-parent families likely to function at a higher level than those in less stable and one-parent households (Brown, 2004; Iruka, 2009). Analyses by the Pew Research Center (2015b) found changes in children's living arrangements between 1960 and 2014. Specifically, more than 70% of children were living with two parents in a first marriage in 1960—a number which decreased to 46% in 2014. This change was accompanied by an increase in children living in single-parent families from 9% in 1960 to 26% in 2014, and 7% of children living with cohabiting parents in 2014.

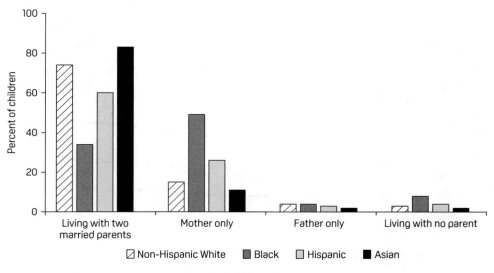

Figure 2.2.   Living arrangements of children by race and Hispanic origin, 2015. (*Source:* U.S. Census Bureau, 2015a.)

This change in family structure is particularly stark for racial and ethnic groups. In Figure 2.2, data on the living arrangements of children in
2015 show that more Asian (83%), non-Hispanic White (74%), and Hispanic
(60%) children are living with two married parents compared to Black children (34%), who are more likely to only live with their mothers than in two-
parent households. Forty-nine percent of Black children are living in a
single-female household compared with 26% of Hispanic children, 15% of
White children, and 11% of Asian children. Black children are also significantly more likely to live with no parent (instead often living with their
grandparents) than other children. One explanation for Black children residing with non-parents may be the imprisonment rate: 1 out of 3 Black males are
likely to be imprisoned in their lifetime, compared with 1 out of 9 for all males,
1 out of 6 for Latino males, and 1 out of 17 for White males. This racial
disproportionality is also evident for females: 1 out of 18 Black females are
likely to be imprisoned in their lifetime, compared with 1 out of 56 for all
females, 1 out of 45 for Latina females, and 1 out of 111 for White females.

Although, on average, more than 60% of Hispanic children are likely
to live with two married parents, this more favorable situation for Hispanic
children has been decreasing over time, especially for children in U.S.-born
households compared to foreign-born households (Patten, 2016). From 1970
to 2014, the percentage of Hispanic children living in single-parent homes
increased from 18% to 29% (Pew Research Center, 2016b). At this same time,
the marriage rate for Hispanics decreased from 76% to 54%. The trend of
children living in a single-female-headed household is particularly concerning because, compared to married couples with children, cohabiting/
unmarried couples with children tend to be younger, be less educated, have

a lower income, and have less secure employment (Child Trends Data Bank, 2015). Children who are living in single-parent, low-education, and low-income households are less likely to be school ready and successful (Evans, Li, & Whipple, 2013).

In addition to the change in marital status of families, an increase in same-sex families with biological and nonbiological children has occurred. Based on data from the 2014 U.S. Census Bureau American Community Survey, same-sex couples make up less than 1% of all married and unmarried couples. However, almost 17% of same-sex couples have biological and nonbiological children in their households, compared with almost 40% of married and unmarried couples. These households, compared with those of opposite-sex couples, are more educated (58.2% vs. 38.8%), younger (48.2 vs. 52.0 years), and have a higher median household income ($87,300 vs. $82,293).

Another changing aspect of children's everyday lives concerns dual-earning families and mothers in the labor force. From 1960 to 2010, the number of households with only fathers employed decreased by almost 40% to 31%. During this same period, households with dual earners increased from 25% to 60%, continuing a trend that began after World War II, which was also bolstered by a small increase in the number of households with only mothers working (4% increase). This increase in women in the labor force is even more staggering for mothers with children under 3 years old: from 34% in 1975 to 61% in 2014 (see Figure 2.3). These changes have significant implications for parenting and the experiences of children at home. Pew

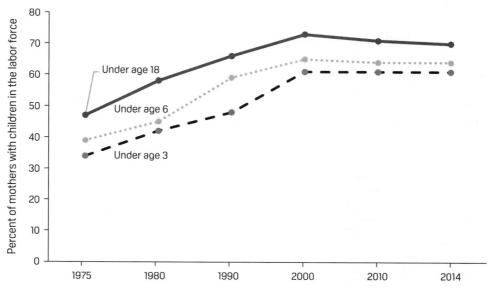

Figure 2.3. Percent of mothers in the labor force with children. Mothers working full time or part time are included as being in the labor force. (*Sources:* Pew Research Center 2015b; Bureau of Labor Statistics, 2009.)

Research Center (2015b) found that 39% of full-time working moms say they spend too little time with their children, compared with only 14% of moms who work part time or do not work outside the home at all.

The number of dual-earning households and mothers in the labor force has resulted in higher usage and need for out-of-home care placement. Burgess, Chien, Morrissey, and Swenson (2014) examined the use of early care and education (ECE) in the United States from 1995 to 2011. The authors found that little change occurred in the overall use of ECE between 1995 and 2005, but a shift occurred in more parents using community center-based child care rather than home-based care, especially for children under age 3; higher-income families were more likely to use community center-based child care at an earlier age than were low-income families. The authors reported that 4 out of 5 children with an employed mother were in some type of ECE arrangement, compared to only 1 out of 3 children with mothers who were not employed. They also found that the rates of public preschool enrollment increased between 1995 and 2011; highly-educated mothers were more likely to choose preschool, especially a private preschool, rather than a community-based child care program. The preschool enrollment gap between minorities and Whites in 2005 was no longer present in 2011. However, Hispanic children's enrollment, although it increased, still lagged behind their Black and White peers. The percent of children enrolled in public preschool was highest among Black children, followed by Hispanic children, and then White children; however, the percent of children enrolled in private preschool was highest among White children, followed by Black children, and then Hispanic children.

Cost is a critical component of parental decision making regarding selection of care. Since the 1960s, there has been a significant increase in the cost of child care. This increase is especially concerning for low-income households, who spend upward of 30% or more of their take-home pay for child care, compared with 10%–15% for upper-income households, depending on location (Giannarelli & Barimantov, 2000). A 2016 report from Child Care Aware of America (2016) found that approximately 60% of funding for child care comes directly from parents, in comparison with 23% of the cost for a public education coming directly from parents.

According to Schulte and Durana (2016, p. 5):

> The typical cost of full-time care in child care centers for all children ages 0–4 in the United States is $9,589 a year, higher than the average cost of in-state college tuition ($9,410). To cover the cost of full time in-center care for one child, a family earning at the median household income would need to spend one-fifth (18 percent) of its income. For an individual earning the minimum wage, full time in-center care is even less affordable: Child care costs two-thirds (64 percent) of their earnings.

Community Change

Beyond the changing landscape in children's family and home environments, there are also changes in communities. Communities have a direct impact on children's development and functioning (Clarke, Koziol, & Sheridan, 2017; Miller & Votruba-Drzal, 2013; Sheridan, Koziol, Clarke, Rispoli, & Coutts, 2014). One third of schools in the United States are rural, and 20% of the nation's children—close to 10 million students—are in rural settings (Johnson, Showalter, Klein, & Lester, 2014). According to the Economic Research Service, the total population in nonmetro counties (i.e., rural communities) stood at 46.2 million in July 2015. Therefore, 14% of U.S. residents are spread across 72% of the nation's land area. The population growth rates in nonmetro areas have been significantly lower than in metro areas since the mid-1990s, and the gap has widened. Compared to urban areas, rural residents are increasingly becoming educated; however, a gap still remains with urban residents, which varies across demographic groups. Furthermore, urban residents are employed at higher rates and earn more than their rural counterparts (U.S. Department of Agriculture, 2017). Specifically, in 2000, almost a quarter of rural residents 25 years and older did not have a high school diploma; however, this number dropped to 15% by 2015, which is similar to the urban rate of 13% (see Figure 2.4). Of concern is the gap in bachelor's degree attainment between urban and rural residents, which increased to 14% in 2015 from 11% in 2000. Numerous studies show the positive impact of parental education on a host of family and child outcomes, including economic stability and child health, well-being, and achievement.

Lynne Vernon-Feagans, a professor and researcher at FPG Child Development Institute at The University of North Carolina at Chapel Hill, has conducted seminal work on a multisite, multidisciplinary birth-cohort study of a representative sample of children born in three poor, rural Pennsylvania and North Carolina counties, called the Family Life Project (Vernon-

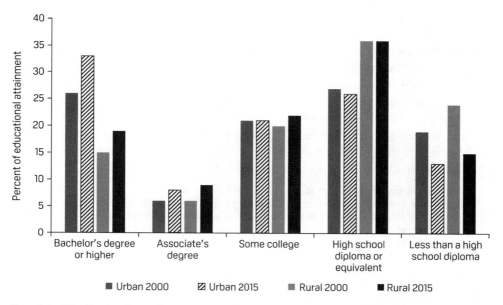

Figure 2.4. Educational attainment for adults ages 25 and older in rural and urban areas, 2000 and 2015. The 2015 metropolitan area definitions are from the Office of Management and Budget. (*Source:* U.S. Department of Agriculture, 2017.)

Feagans et al., 2013). This project provided deep knowledge about families in rural communities, such as poverty, biological markers of family stress, family health, family work, family interactions, and home and child care literacy activities, as well as child cognition, language, emotionality, and sociability. This work has provided extensive research linking parenting, home, child care, and neighborhood conditions to children's development in early childhood. It further provided insight about the heterogeneity of rural communities; the isolated nature of rural communities with barriers, such as geographic distance resulting in limited access to formal child care, living wage jobs, social services, and health, mental health, and recreational opportunities; and the positive aspects of rural communities having less exposure to violent crime, more access to extended family, stronger connections to religious institutions, a greater sense of community, and a strong emphasis on family and relationships.

MACROSYSTEM: EXAMINATION OF
CHILD-CENTERED INITIATIVES AND POLICIES

Many factors driving changes in the microsystem (i.e., family income, child care costs) include macrosystem contexts, such as federal and tax expenditures and policies. According to Edelstein, Hahn, Isaacs, Steele, and Steuerle (2016), adult spending in Social Security, Medicare, and Medicaid programs has increased over the past 50 years, from 2% of the gross domestic product in 1960 to 9% in 2015. In comparison, child-centered spending grew from 0.6% of the gross domestic product in 1960 to 2% in 2015. Spending for children shifted from programs and tax provisions serving all children toward means-tested programs serving low-income children. In 2015, federal expenditures on children totaled $471 billion, with 77% for outlays (spending from federal programs such as Medicaid and child nutrition programs, refundable tax credits) and 23% for tax expenditures (tax breaks to families with children provided through the dependent exemption). Medicaid is the largest source of spending for children, followed by three tax provisions: earned income tax credit, child tax credit, and the dependent exemption (see Figure 2.5). Well-known early childhood programs, such as Head Start, are not in the top 10 of federal spending for children. (See Chapter 9 for additional information on federal spending for children's programs.)

Edelstein et al. (2016, p. II) concluded the following:

> Total federal spending on children has been fairly flat over the past four years, in real dollars. However, spending in 2015 was slightly up from 2014, with increases in children's health and nutrition and other areas more than offsetting declines in children's education and income security. In the future, overall federal spending is projected to increase substantially, but virtually none of the additional funds will be directed toward children.

The federal expenditures and forecast have implications for meeting the needs of children to ensure that they experience high-quality environments in the first few years of life. A lack of available federal funding for children

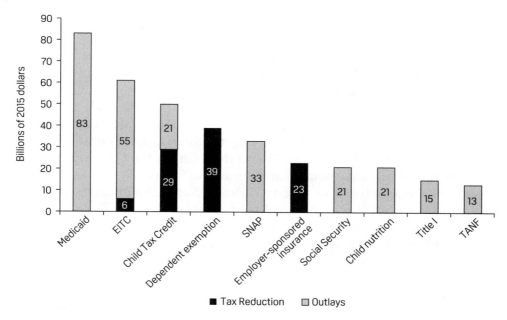

Figure 2.5. The 10 spending and tax programs with the highest expenditures on children, 2015. Child nutrition spending includes the National School Lunch Program, the School Breakfast Program, the Child and Adult Care Food Program, the Summer Food Service, and the Special Milk Program. (*Source:* Edelstein, Hahn, Isaacs, Steele, & Steuerle, 2016. Authors' estimates are based on the U.S. government budget for fiscal year 2017.)

means that the majority of the burden for funding will be placed on states. In the past few years, the federal government has provided the foundational funding to ensure that children who are most in need can access high-quality early childhood programming and services. For example, it supported more effective evidence-based home visiting interventions, partnerships between child care programs and Early Head Start, and strengthening and increasing the number of pre-K program and slots, as well as establishing more opportunities for states to strengthen, develop, and validate their quality rating and improvement systems or child care quality initiatives. The following sections describe some of these high-profile early childhood programs and initiatives, which are the basis for continuous quality improvement and strengthening of the ECE programs and systems.

Maternal, Infant, and Early Childhood Home Visiting Program

The Maternal, Infant, and Early Childhood Home Visiting Program (MIECHV) was established in 2010 by Congress to provide federal funds to states and tribal entities to support voluntary, evidence-based, home-visiting services. MIECHV reaches pregnant women, expectant fathers, and parents and caregivers of children under the age of 5. MIECHV is administered by the Health Resources and Services Administration in collaboration with the Administration for Children and Families. The program provides necessary resources and skills to raise children who are physically, socially, and emotionally healthy and ready to learn. The goals are to improve maternal and child health, prevent child abuse and neglect, encourage positive parenting, and promote child development and school readiness. The recent Home Visiting Evidence of Effectiveness funded by the U.S. Department of Health and Human Services provides evidence of the positive and long-term impacts of various home visiting programs (Avellar et al., 2016).

MIECHV received a $372.4 million appropriation, after accounting for sequestration, for fiscal year 2017. This funding supports grants to all 50 states, the District of Columbia, Puerto Rico, Guam, the U.S. Virgin Islands, the Northern Mariana Islands, and American Samoa, as well as awards to Native American tribes (or a consortium of Native American tribes), tribal organizations, and urban Native American organizations. By law, grantees must spend the majority of their grants to implement evidence-based home visiting models, with up to 25% of funding available to implement promising approaches that will undergo rigorous evaluation. This approach to funding evidence-based practices and supporting innovation ensures that families will receive services that will likely benefit them and their children, while also ensuring services can be improved. More information can be found at https://mchb.hrsa.gov/maternal-child-health-initiatives/home-visiting-overview.

Early Head Start–Child Care Partnership

The Early Head Start–Child Care Partnership (EHS-CCP) initiative brings the best of Early Head Start and child care through layering of funding to provide comprehensive and continuous services to low-income infants, toddlers, and their families. EHS-CCP enhances developmental services and supports for low-income infants and toddlers, and their families, by providing strong relationship-based experiences and preparing them for the transition into Head Start and preschool. Specifically, the early learning Head Start program performance standards are integrated into traditional child care and family child care settings that provide flexible and convenient full-day and full-year services and are strongly grounded in the cultural, linguistic, and social needs of the families and their local communities. The long-term outcomes of the EHS-CCP program as follows:

1. Sustained, mutually respectful, and collaborative EHS-CCP

2. A more highly educated and fully qualified workforce to provide high-quality infant/toddler care and education

3. An increased community supply of high-quality early learning environments and infant/toddler care and education

4. Well-aligned early childhood policies, regulations, resources, and quality improvement support at national, state, and local levels

5. Improved family and child well-being and progress toward school readiness

For more information about the EHS-CCP, see https://www.acf.hhs.gov/ecd/early-learning/ehs-cc-partnerships.

Preschool Development Grants

Funded in 2014, Preschool Development Grants (PDGs) provide support for states to build or enhance a preschool program infrastructure that would enable the delivery of high-quality preschool services to children, as well as expand high-quality preschool programs in targeted communities that would serve as models for expanding preschool to all 4-year-olds from low- and moderate-income families (see https://www2.ed.gov/programs/preschooldevelopmentgrants/index.html).

The goals of PDGs are to 1) create or expand high-quality preschool programs in high-need communities, 2) implement state-level infrastructure and quality improvements, 3) collaborate with selected programs and ensure strong partnerships between school districts and other early learning providers, 4) align preschool programs within a birth through third grade continuum of services, and 5) create sustainable programs by coordinating existing early learning funds. Based on the 2015 progress report, 18 states expanded access to high-quality programs for 4-year-olds from low- to moderate-income families in more than 230 high-need communities; more than 28,000 additional children benefited from high-quality preschool in their local communities because of these grants. Expanding access for children to experience high-quality early learning prior to formal schooling and providing a mechanism to improve and expand best practices will increase the likelihood that children, especially from disadvantaged communities, are prepared for school and lifelong learning.

Race to the Top–Early Learning Challenge

Established in 2011, the Race to the Top–Early Learning Challenge (RttT-ELC) supports states in building statewide systems that raise the quality of early learning and development programs and increase access to high-quality programs for children with high needs, so that all children enter kindergarten ready to succeed (see https://www2.ed.gov/programs/racetothetop-earlylearningchallenge/index.html). RttT-ELC is administered jointly by the U.S. Department of Education and the U.S. Department of Health and Human Services.

The program is organized around five key areas focused on an effective early learning and development system. The first is a focus on successful state systems built on broad-based stakeholder participation and effective governance structures. The second focuses on high-quality programs that are held accountable based on a common set of standards that align

Head Start, the Child Care and Development Fund (CCDF), the Individuals with Disabilities Education Act (PL 101-476), Title I of the Elementary and Secondary Education Act (PL 81–874), state-funded preschools, and similar programs to create a unified statewide system of early learning and development. The third area is focused on promoting early learning and development outcomes for children through the implementation of common statewide standards for young children, comprehensive assessments aligned to those standards across a range of domains, and clear guidelines for improving the quality of programs and services that promote health and engage families in the care and education of young children. The fourth area, focused on the early childhood education workforce, ensures that these professionals are supported through professional development, career advancement opportunities, differentiated compensation, and incentives to improve knowledge, skills, and abilities to promote the learning and development of young children. The fifth and final area addresses measurable outcomes and progress through the collection, organization, and understanding of evidence of young children's progress across a range of domains, as well as implementing comprehensive data systems and using data to improve instruction, practices, services, and policies.

Based on the 2015 RttT-ELC progress report, more early learning and development programs are being included in states' Tiered Quality Rating and Improvement Systems, more programs are at higher-quality levels, and more children with high needs are enrolled in high-quality programs. From a family and child perspective, this means that families, especially low-income families, across the United States have an increased likelihood of finding and accessing higher-quality programs, with the potential of leading to better child outcomes.

Beyond these grant initiatives, reauthorization of existing early learning and development policies have implications for the future of children's development and well-being.

Child Care and Development Block Grant

CCDF is the primary federal funding source devoted to helping low-income families whose members are working or participating in education and training pay for child care and improving the quality of care for all children (see https://www.acf.hhs.gov/occ/ccdf-reauthorization). It provides child care financial assistance for children, primarily under the age of 5 years. CCDF funds are also used to improve the quality of care. In 2014, CCDF was updated, reauthorized, and focused on strengthening child care to better support the success of both parents and children, while also providing a new emphasis on the importance of providing high-quality early education and care for young children.

This revised law accomplishes the following: 1) protects the health and safety of children in child care by establishing a baseline; 2) helps parents to make informed consumer choices and access information to support child development through knowledge about provider options and available services; 3) supports equal access to stable, high-quality child care for low-income children by lengthening eligibility periods; and 4) enhances the quality of child care by mandating set-asides and better support the workforce through mandated trainings and professional development. An effort is underway to evaluate the implementation and impact of this reauthorization for children and families (see https://www.acf.hhs.gov/opre/research/project/child-care-development-block-grant-ccdbg-implementation-research-and-evaluation-planning-grants).

Head Start

Head Start was most recently reauthorized by Congress in 2007 through the Improving Head Start for School Readiness Act of 2007 (PL 110-134). The law made sweeping changes to Head Start, such as introducing a competition system that programs are required to go through in order to receive another 5 years of funding, requirements for teacher education, and other significant changes to the proven Head Start Model. Preparations for the next Head Start reauthorization have been underway for a while—specifically, planning for what the next 50 years of Head Start should look like to pave the way for a strong future. Furthermore, in November 2016, the new Head Start Program Performance Standards went into effect. These standards reinforce Head Start as a research-based model of high quality that encourages continuous quality improvement over compliance, yet with the flexibility for innovation (U.S. Department of Health and Human Services, 2016).

Every Student Succeeds Act

The Every Student Succeeds Act (ESSA; PL 114-95) was signed into law in 2015 and reauthorized the 50-year-old Elementary and Secondary Education Act of 1965 (PL 89-10), the nation's national education law and long-standing commitment to equal opportunity for all students signed by President Lyndon Johnson in 1965. ESSA has the following six features:

1. Advances equity by upholding critical protections for America's disadvantaged and high-need students

2. Requires (for the first time) that all students be taught to high academic standards that will prepare them to succeed in college and careers

3. Ensures that vital information is provided to educators, families, students, and communities through annual statewide assessments that measure students' progress toward those high standards

4. Helps to support and grow local innovations, including evidence-based and place-based interventions developed by local leaders and educators

5. Sustains and expands investments in increasing access to high-quality preschool

6. Maintains accountability and action to affect positive change in the lowest-performing schools

Because this reauthorized law is currently being implemented, information is not yet available on its impact on schools and children's learning opportunities and achievement.

SUMMARY

The turn of the 21st century has resulted in many changes to children's microsystems that affect their daily lives. Demographic trends reveal increasing diversity among families, ranging from more ethnic minority families, families whose first language is not English, immigrants from non-European countries, single-parent-headed households, and same-sex and blended families. Although there has been an increase in education and fewer families in poverty, considerable disproportionality in wealth by race and ethnicity, as well as imprisonment, still exist. The increase in dual-earning families has also led to the need for greater use of out-of-home child care and the call for more affordable high-quality child care options (in addition to the growing evidence about the importance of quality ECE in the first few years of life). Although the U.S. population is relatively stable, the shift in the population from rural to urban and suburban settings also has implications for children's development and context. The importance of the ever-changing technology and social media potential also has implications on families' lives, and subsequently children's learning and development. With the diversity of changes in children's microsystems (i.e., home, school), more research is needed to better understand their effects on children's well-being.

To better understand the changes in children's microsystems, one must attend to the macrosystem changes that affect the lives of children and their families. For example, scholars have forecasted that federal expenditures for children will remain level for the foreseeable future, which can impact the availability of high-quality affordable early education programs for children. Furthermore, the large investment in supporting the expansion of and strengthening of early childhood education programs, systems, and initiatives would likely require continued funding from states and localities to remain viable, such as MIECHV, quality rating and improvement systems, and PDGs. These initiatives and programs have focused on children, especially children from low-income and disenfranchised homes and communities, from birth through the early years of formal schooling. These initiatives are seeking to address the opportunity gaps with the future goal of eliminating, if not preventing, the achievement gap. In particular, they have focused on families and children getting access to support and resources from birth (and sometimes prenatally) through school entrance. They have also tried to incentivize and mandate high-quality practices to support the ECE workforce, such as through recompetition and higher reimbursement rates when programs attain the highest quality. Furthermore, they have tried to ensure that current systems and programs, such as community-based child care programs, are supported and their value to families and children are recognized.

CONCLUSION

Children's learning, development, achievement, and general well-being are affecting by many things, including environments proximal to them (especially their family and ECE/school) and distal factors such as their community, parental workplace, and federal policies. Vast evidence exists about the demographic shift in the United States from a growing minority population, more non–English-speaking families, and a change in poverty rates. The demographic change with an increasing ethnic minority population along with the minimal rise in family income and wealth, especially for ethnic minority groups, has potential implications for the achievement gap and life success. For example, children who are not prepared for school are less likely to be successful and will likely drop out in high school, thus affecting their future earnings and contributions to society, including their families and communities.

To ensure that practice and policies are evidence-based, it is critical that attention be paid to the growing diversity and the unique needs of the U.S. populous. As the U.S. demographics shift from more rural and majority White to more urban and racially and economically diverse, research must examine the influence and impact of current policies and programs for this changing population. What may work for White families may not be as relevant or salient for Hispanic families; what may work in rural North Carolina may not be meaningful for the urban core in Michigan. Thus, although researchers and scientists seek to provide information that is generalizable, there is still a need to ensure that evidence is not presented as universal and monolithic, especially research focused on young children and programs serving young children. Research needs to better pinpoint what factors are critical to ensure that all children have the opportunity to learn and be successful, including identifying assets in children, families, and communities that support children's optimal development.

REFERENCES

Avellar, S., Paulsell, D., Sama-Miller, E., Grosso, P. D., Akers, L., & Kleinman, R. (2016). *Home visiting evidence of effectiveness review.* Washington, DC: U.S. Department of Health and Human Services, Administration for Children and Families, Office of Planning, Research and Evaluation.

Bronfenbrenner, U., & Evans, G. W. (2000). Developmental science in the 21st century: Emerging questions, theoretical models, research designs, and empirical findings. *Social Development, 9,* 115–125.

Brown, S. L. (2004). Family structure and child well-being: The significance of parental cohabitation. *Journal of Marriage and Family, 66*(2), 351–367.

Bureau of Labor Statistics. (2009). *Women in the labor force: A databook, Table 23. Married-couple families by number and relationship of earners, 1967–2007.* Washington, DC: Author. Retrieved from https://www.bls.gov/cps/wlftable23.htm

Burgess, K., Chien, N., Morrissey, T., & Swenson, K. (2014). *Trends in the use of early care and education, 1995–2011: Descriptive analysis of child care arrangement from national survey data.* Washington, DC: U.S. Department of Health and Human Services, Office of the Assistant Secretary for Planning and Evaluation.

Child Care Aware of America. (2016). *Parents and the high cost of child care.* Retrieved from https://usa.childcareaware.org/wp-content/uploads/2017/12/2017_CCA/High_Cost_Report_FINA.pdf

Child Trends Data Bank. (2015). *Family structure.* Bethesda, MD: Author. Retrieved from https://www.childtrends.org/indicators/births-to-unmarried-women

Clarke, B. L., Koziol, N. A., & Sheridan, S. M. (2017). The effects of rurality on parents' engagement in children's early literacy. In G. C. Nugent, G. M. Kunz, S. M. Sheridan, T. A. Glover, & L. L. Knoche (Eds.), *Rural education research in the United States: State of the science and emerging directions* (pp. 231–251). New York, NY: Springer.

Davis-Kean, P. E. (2005). The influence of parent education and family income on child achievement: The indirect role of parental expectations and the home environment. *Journal of Family Psychology, 19*(2), 294–304.

Edelstein, S., Hahn, H., Isaacs, J., Steele, E., & Steuerle, C. E. (2016). *Kids' Share 2016: Federal expenditures on children through 2015 and future projections.* Washington, DC: Urban Institute.

Evans, G. W., Li, D., & Whipple, S. S. (2013). Cumulative risk and child development. *Psychological Bulletin, 139*(6), 1342–1396.

Elementary and Secondary Education Act of 1965, PL 89-10, 20 U.S.C. §§ 241.

Every Student Succeeds Act of 2015, PL 114-95, 20 U.S.C. § 1001 *et seq.*

García Coll, C. T., Lamberty, G., Jenkins, R., McAdoo, H. P., Crnic, K., Wasik, B. H., et al. (1996). An integrative model for the study of developmental competencies in minority children. *Child Development, 67*(5), 1891–1914.

Gershoff, E. T., Aber, J. L., Raver, C. C., & Lennon, M. C. (2007). Income is not enough: Incorporating material hardship into models of income association with parenting and child development. *Child Development, 78*(1), 70–95.

Giannarelli, L., & Barimantov, J. (2000). *Child care expenses of America's families, Occasional paper number 40.* Washington, DC: Urban Institute.

Iruka, I. U. (2009). Ethnic variation in the association between family structure and practices on child outcomes at 36 months: Results from Early Head Start. *Early Education & Development, 20*(1), 148–173.

Johnson, J., Showalter, D., Klein, R., & Lester, C. (2014). *Why rural matters 2013–14: The condition of rural education in the 50 states.* Washington, DC: Rural School and Community Trust.

Kastberg, D., Chan, J. Y., & Murray, G. (2016). *Performance of U.S. 15-year-old students in science, reading, and mathematics literacy in an international context: First Look at PISA 2015* (NCES 2017-048). Washington, DC: U.S. Department of Education. National Center for Education Statistics.

Linver, M. R., Brooks-Gunn, J., & Kohen, D. E. (2002). Family processes as pathways from income to young children's development. *Developmental Psychology, 38*(5), 719–734.

Miller, P., & Votruba-Drzal, E. (2013). Early academic skills and childhood experiences across the urban-rural continuum. *Early Childhood Research Quarterly, 28*, 234–248.

National Academies of Science, Engineering, and Medicine. (2016). *Parenting matters: Supporting parents of children ages 0–8.* Washington, DC: The National Academies Press.

O'Hare, W. (2011). *The changing child population of the United States: Analysis of data from the 2010 Census.* Baltimore, MD: Annie E. Casey Foundation.

Patten, E. (2016). *The nation's Latino population is defined by its youth.* Washington, DC: Pew Research Center.

Pew Research Center. (2015a). *Modern immigration wave brings 59 million to U.S., driving population growth and change through 2065: Views of immigration's impact on U.S. society mixed.* Washington, DC: Author.

Pew Research Center. (2015b). *Parenting in America: Outlook, worries, aspirations are strongly linked to financial situation.* Washington, DC: Author.

Pew Research Center. (2016a). *On views of race and inequality, Blacks and Whites are worlds apart.* Washington, DC: Author.

Pew Research Center. (2016b). *Statistical portrait of Hispanics in the United States, 1980–2014.* Washington, DC: Author. Retrieved from http://www.pewhispanic.org/2017/09/18/facts-on-u-s-latinos

Schulte, B., & Durana, A. (2016). *The New America care report.* Washington, DC: New America.

Sheridan, S. M., Koziol, N. A., Clarke, B. L., Rispoli, K. M., & Coutts, M. J. (2014). The influence of rurality and parental affect on kindergarten children's social and behavioral functioning. *Early Education and Development, 25,* 1057–1082.

Stone, C., Trisi, D., Sherman, A., & Horton, E. (2016). *A guide to statistics on historical trends in income inequality.* Washington, DC: Center on Budget and Policy Priorities.

U.S. Census Bureau. (2015). *America's families and living arrangements: 2015.* Retrieved from https://www.census.gov/data/tables/2015/demo/families/cps-2015.html

U.S. Census Bureau. (2014). *National Population Projections Tables.* Retrieved from https://www.census.gov/data/tables/2014/demo/popproj/2014-summary-tables.html

U.S. Census Bureau (2014). *American Community Survey.* https://www.census.gov/acs/www/data/data-tables-and-tools/data-profiles/2014/

U. S. Department of Agriculture. (2017). *Rural education at a glance, 2017 edition.* Washington, DC: Author.

U.S. Department of Health and Human Services. (2016). *Head Start program performance standards, 45 CFR Chapter XIII.* Washington, DC: Author.

Vanneman, A., Hamilton, L., Baldwin Anderson, J., & Rahman, T. (2009). *Achievement gaps: How Black and White students in public schools perform in mathematics and reading on the National Assessment of Educational Progress* (NCES 2009-455). Washington, DC: National Center for Education Statistics, Institute of Education Sciences,

Vernon-Feagans, L., Cox, M., Blair, C., Burchinal, M., Burton, L., Crnic, K., et al. (2013). The Family Life Project: An epidemiological and developmental study of young children living in poor rural communities. *Monographs of the Society for Research in Child Development, 78*(5), Serial No. 310.

Warren, R. (2013). *US-born children of undocumented residents: Numbers and characteristics in 2013.* New York, NY: Center for Migration Studies.

Winn, D.-M., Iruka, I. U., Stevenson, H., McKinney, M., Harradine, C., & Buansi, A. (2012). *Providing opportunities despite the obstacles. Countering the adverse conditions that undermine the success of many African American boys.* Washington, DC: Grantmakers for Children, Youth, and Families Press.

Yeung, W. J., Linver, M. R., & Brooks-Gunn, J. (2002). How money matters for young children's development: Parental investment and family process. *Child Development, 73*(6), 1861–1879.

II

Theme A: Race, Ethnicity, Linguistic, Cultural, and Socioeconomic Diversity

The first theme of this volume begins with macro-level influences because of their pervasiveness and their potential detrimental effects on children and families. Many phenomena that are often beyond their control have a direct impact on children and families. These phenomena can be pervasive in a society, influencing possibilities for individual choice and actions from childhood through adulthood and beyond. Some phenomena, including racism and discrimination, have played an outsized role in almost all aspects of society in the United States. Closely associated with these phenomena are linguistic and cultural diversity because children and adults whose language and culture differ from mainstream culture are often at a disadvantage in terms of health, education, and living conditions.

This section opens with Chapter 3 by Oscar Barbarin, who observes that serving diverse populations is basic to the mission of early childhood programs, but the mission is confounded by issues of culture, ethnicity, and economic diversity. Barbarin brings diversity to the forefront by using the experiences of African American boys as a device to examine issues with all vulnerable groups, while providing the reader with compelling detail about the experiences of these children. Noting that racial diversity can no longer be conceptualized as a simple dichotomy of black and white, but rather one of "many shades and complexions," he also observes how the more recent increases in immigrant populations have shifted the focus on diversity to language, ethnicity, and national origin. Within these diverse groups, African American boys in particular experience multiple risk factors—some of which are not unique to them, although other risks appear unique. Barbarin elaborates on the risks of these young children by identifying impediments for achieving educational quality and concludes with recommendations for improving educational outcomes.

In Chapter 4, Linda Espinosa and Marlene Zepeda document the growing diversity in our preschool and school-age populations related to race, ethnicity, language, and levels of ability. Chapter 4 also discusses preparing the workforce to meet the needs of all children in our schools. Changing demographics, especially as related to dual-language learners, present numerous challenges to the educational workforce. Much as Barbarin identified gaps between African American boys and other groups, Espinosa and Zepeda note the poor performance of dual-language learners compared with their English-only peers and identify the unique contextual and societal circumstances that characterize the lives of dual-language learners. Observing the "deficit perspective" that sometimes dominates services for dual-language learners, the authors provide an alternative view of the positive competencies that arise from learning two languages. They then identify instructional strategies and enhancements linked to better achievement for these children and conclude with very specific recommendations for the preparation and training of personnel who work with this population.

Looking broadly at policies, programs, and practices that influence diverse children and their families, Barbara Bowman begins Chapter 5 with a description of diverse families. She then addresses the advantages and limitations of early childhood programs, noting that they can reduce some academic and social disadvantages for children living in poverty. Alternately, Bowman notes that preschool programs cannot in themselves reduce all educational disparity. Furthermore, she observes that the preschool experiences of young children vary considerably and that children's prior knowledge before entering school influences their later school performance. Noting that children of color are disproportionately underprivileged, she also observes the role of racism and segregation in young children's early experiences, as housing segregation and language segregation are pervasive in many communities. Although many early childhood programs are funded by the government, access to these programs and the quality of the programs differ. Bowman concludes by providing recommendations related to teacher education and training, curriculum and assessment, program coordination, and parent education that can lead to higher-quality programs.

To bring together the research, practice, and policy issues in this section, Natasha Cabrera, Nicole Gardner-Nisbett, and Iheoma U. Inruka suggest that the disparities in academic outcomes often seen for minority children at times overshadow this population's variability, as well as their strengths and resilience. Bringing in research from numerous sources, the authors discuss the achievement gap followed by a strengths-based approach for studying ethnic minority children. Their approach includes three domains: social competence, language, and ethnic identity. These authors then call for a major paradigm shift regarding the need for diversity throughout the research process, especially in the scientific workforce. They also call for conducting research that explicitly examines variables such as race, ethnicity, culture, language, and socioeconomic class with a more nuanced perspective that examines systematic factors contributing to child outcomes.

Collectively, the authors in this section confront pervasive issues with the education and social circumstances of minority children. They call for a major rethinking of the preparation of the workforce, understanding the role of families, examining classroom practices, and recognizing that early experiences differ considerably for children across economic, racial, and cultural backgrounds.

3

African American Boys in Early Childhood

Facing the Challenge of Diversity

Oscar A. Barbarin

Serving diverse populations is integral to the mission of early childhood programs, especially as the demographic diversity of this country has expanded. Although inadvertent and unintended, the populations in pioneering early childhood programs such as the Abecedarian Project, Perry Preschool, and the Child Development Centers in Chicago consisted mostly of low-income and African American children. Thus, from their inception, early childhood programs were confronted with a myriad of issues stemming from the cultural, ethnic, and economic diversity of the children they served. Facing up to the issues of ethnic, cultural, and linguistic diversity can be a source of anxiety and distress, especially for a predominantly White staff whose prior lives have been situated within a predominantly White community. As a result, issues of diversity have often been the elephant in the room that everyone looked past or avoided due to a lack of awareness of their importance or a lack of clarity about how to address them.

Early care and education are at a point where the issues cannot be sidestepped. Public support of pre-K programs has been justified as a pivotal strategy in the nation's efforts to foster children's development in general and to address the achievement gaps of low-income and ethnic minority children. Kindergarten readiness has become a primary goal and *raison d'etre* for public sponsored pre-K programs. In this context, the mandate of early childhood programs has shifted from a comprehensive focus on meeting the developmental and health needs of the child and supporting their parents to a narrower focus on academic outcomes. Accordingly, the success of public investment in pre-K programs is determined in large measure by the academic gains they accomplish for children from economically disadvantaged households and ethnically diverse communities. Consequently, the need to address the implications of ethnic, cultural, and linguistic differences between the children served and those serving them has become even more compelling today. In light of the nation's rapidly changing demographics, the early care and education (ECE) field has devoted significant efforts to reflecting on practices that might extend the effectiveness of pre-K programs for a broader array of ethnically, culturally, linguistically, and economically diverse groups of children.

To contribute to the reflection on diversity, this chapter uses the situation and experiences of African American boys (AABs) as a device—a literary conceit—to pinpoint problems that are widespread and potentially overlap with issues affecting children from other vulnerable groups, such as other ethnic minorities and those living in poverty. A central aspect of this chapter is the articulation of concerns about the academic and socioemotional status of AABs linked to risk processes of many other groups, including gender, poverty, and experiences. The chapter includes a model that draws attention to the social and biological risks faced by AABs. Finally, the chapter provides recommendations for three major steps that programs should take to improve outcomes for all children.

EVOLVING CONCEPTIONS OF RACE AND ECONOMIC DISADVANTAGE

The American experience of and the ways we talk about cultural diversity, ethnic/racial diversity, and economic disadvantage have evolved over time. Initially, diversity was conceptualized simply in Black–White racial terms contrasting African Americans and Americans of European descent. Diversity is no longer just a "black-and-white" issue but one of many shades and complexions. Increasing waves of immigrants, especially from non–English-speaking countries, have shifted the focus to diversity based on language, ethnicity, and national origin. Today, the challenges of serving diverse populations are expanding and becoming more complex as programs deal not only with young children whose first language is Spanish; for increasing waves of children from Asia, Africa, and the Middle East, not only language but also national identities, immigration status, and economic diversity need to be addressed. Even the terms used to describe some populations have changed: from Colored and Negro to Black and African American. A variety of terms have been used to signal economic deprivation, including ghetto, urban, inner city, culturally deprived, low income, disenfranchised, poor, and materially disadvantaged. As we have moved from imprecise subjective labels to depict economic status, different terms and measures have come into and fallen out of fashion or favor. Research and policy reports have relied on widely collected indicators, such as eligibility for free and reduced-price lunch, government poverty guidelines, or measures of food insecurity and material consumption. No matter the term for ethnicity and cultural or economic deprivation, their relationships to child development have remained remarkably robust. Socioeconomic status, ethnicity, and language/culture are often associated with stressors in the lives of young children. This chapter describes the relationship of diversity to adversity, specifically in the lives of AABs.

FOCUSING ON AFRICAN AMERICAN BOYS: A RATIONALE

Each year, approximately 300,000 AABs are born, with more than 67% born into households with incomes below the federal poverty guideline. As a consequence, most AABs are eligible for and many participate in public-sponsored early childhood programs, including child care block grants, Early Head Start, state-sponsored pre-K, and Title I programs designed to serve low-income families.

Largely as a consequence of growing up in impoverished households, AABs are exposed to multiple risks that undermine and militate against their positive development. Many AABs who are enrolled in early childhood programs come from homes that are materially disadvantaged, where children do not have sufficient resources and where food insecurity is common; housing may be unstable and work demands may be so great that parents have very little time to engage with children around learning and to connect with pre-K program staff. These economic disadvantages of children are among the more intractable difficulties for early childhood programs. They exemplify the most complex and difficult problems facing early childhood educators and therefore pose the most serious and stringent test for the effectiveness of early childhood programs. Specifically, they draw on the capacity of early childhood programs to socialize, inculcate executive function, and promote literacy, language numeracy, and other academic skills. Accordingly, they provide a useful model for representing and reflecting on the range of dilemmas associated with serving diverse populations in early childhood.

AABs are not unique in the challenges they present. However, they spark considerations of many important issues, such as how to promote school readiness in high-risk children, ensure uniform quality as programs go to scale with diverse populations, and bridge the cultural chasms between programs and families they serve. These issues are at the center of discussions about how to improve the effectiveness of early childhood programs for all children. A principal goal of ECE is to promote school readiness and reduce achievement and opportunity gaps, especially for children growing up in adversity and facing daily challenges associated with economic disadvantage. In considering ideas that should animate ECE's approach to serving AABs, we encounter issues related to how ECE can promote socioemotional learning, bridge the cultural divide with families, and address the role of implicit racism in program practices, especially as they affect behavior management and discipline. Discussion of AABs provides an opportunity to search for answers to several questions that have implications for the quality of ECE services offered to all children. Those questions are listed in the sidebar and are divided into three categories: socioeconomic skills, home–school relations, and stigma and implicit bias.

Questions Regarding the Quality of ECE Services

Socioemotional Skills

- How can ECE best nurture the development of academic skills and behavioral and emotional regulation among AABs?
- What steps can program staff take to understand and address the emotional burdens carried by children?
- To what extent do programs by their structure, practices, and responses give rise to or escalate behavioral problems in AABs?

Home–School Relations

- How do programs build a strong home–school partnership?
- What do staff need to know about a family's history and culture to bridge the differences between them on fundamental issues such as socialization goals and discipline?

Stigma and Implicit Bias

- To what extent do teachers' personal experiences and backgrounds shape how they see and respond to AABs?
- What steps can be taken to assure fair and even-handed approaches to discipline?
- How necessary are suspensions and expulsions to addressing problem behavior?
- What supports do teachers need to provide a safe environment for all children?
- How crucial are high-quality teacher–child relationships to children's success at school?

Answers to these questions go to the core of the thorny issues influencing the effectiveness of early childhood programs, particularly with AABs. Promoting the academic achievement and socioemotional learning of AABs are significant tests for early childhood programs. Practices developed to support the academic and socioemotional needs of AABs can have a wider utility and contribute to a program's effectiveness with many other groups of vulnerable children. Treatment of these issues will begin with a discussion of AABs' developmental status and the developmental needs they bring when they arrive at the doorsteps of early childhood programs.

DEVELOPMENTAL STATUS OF AFRICAN AMERICAN BOYS

Under developmental status, the first consideration is academic status, followed by a summary of what is known about the behavioral development of AABs.

Academic Achievement

The development of academic skills, particularly with respect to literacy and numeracy, has emerged as a major concern in the development of AABs and economically disadvantaged children in general. A plethora of data on the achievement of AABs underscores the scale of the issues. On learning outcomes from pre-K to 12th grade, AABs often lag behind their peers. For example, as seen in Figure 3.1, data from the 2013 National Assessment of Educational Progress show that AABs had the lowest rate of proficiency on the fourth-grade reading tests for all identified groups. The mean proficiency score attained by AABs was approximately 260, which was lower than that of Latino, White, Asian, and Native American children. Moreover, AABs scored lower than African American females. Poverty status accounts in part for the low proficiency rates, but it does not account entirely for ethnic differences that occur in both economic status groups.

Figure 3.2 shows the proportion of children in each group who attained proficiency disaggregated by household poverty levels. In general, children living in poverty were less likely to be proficient than higher-income children. Within both poverty and nonpoverty groups, African Americans had the lowest rates of proficiency. Only 10% of African Americans in low-income households were proficient. Approximately 25% of African Americans in nonpoverty households scored at the proficient level, suggesting an effect of household poverty on achievement. Ethnic differences are stark: The African Americans with relative economic advantage were no more likely to be proficient than economically disadvantaged White and Asian children. Even when poverty level is controlled, African American children were less likely to score at the proficient level than children of other ethnic groups. These data corroborate the concern about academic achievement

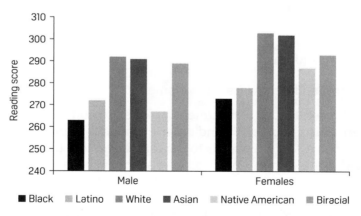

Figure 3.1. Reading scores on the 2013 National Assessment of Educational Progress fourth-grade reading test by gender and ethnicity. (*Source:* National Center for Education Statistics, 2013.)

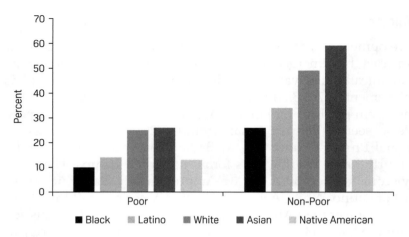

Figure 3.2. Percent of children who scored in the proficient range on the 2013 National Assessment of Educational Progress fourth-grade reading test by household poverty and ethnicity. (*Source:* National Center for Education Statistics, 2013.)

and the need for early childhood programs to lay a foundation on which future academic success can be built.

The findings from the Early Childhood Longitudinal Study–Kindergarten Cohort (ECLS-K; U.S. Department of Education, 2003) suggest that efforts need to be sustained beyond pre-K if they are to be successful. The ECLS-K data show that, although all children improve their reading and math skills, the rates of increase vary by race and gender and that racial disparities expand over the kindergarten year rather than diminish. These findings are consistent across assessments from multiple sources and leave little doubt about the magnitude of the problem. At the same time, there is confidence about the capacity and innate abilities of AABs to acquire the necessary and expected skills when provided with the necessary supports and learning experiences. However, effective pedagogical practices should be implemented by well-trained teachers with conviction about the cognitive capacity of AABs to learn.

Socioemotional and Behavioral Development

The acquisition of literacy and numeracy skills are undeniably important to the long-term success of AABs and other vulnerable populations. Teachers' experience with AABs often leads to the conclusion that the biggest impediment to AAB achievement and success at school is behavior, not the ability to learn. In other words, the achievement gap is due to gaps in behavioral adaptation and to the program's response to that behavior—not to intellectual ability. Thus, behavioral and emotional adaptations in the classroom represent a more serious concern and an overriding impediment to boys realizing their potential to excel in school.

From the perspective of early childhood programs, AABs can meet the academic standards; however, their long-term success in school may be abbreviated by slow progress in the development of self-regulation of behavior, attention, and emotions. Teacher evaluations of children enrolled in Head Start programs reflect these concerns. Using the attention, behavior, language, and emotions (ABLE) universal mental health screen (Barbarin, 2006), teachers indicated the severity of concerns they had about the children enrolled in Head Start programs in a large Midwestern city or in a rural county in the South. The data were gathered during mental health consultations in the fall of the pre-K year as part of a system of mental health care emphasizing prevention. In both urban and rural areas, approximately one in five boys was identified by the teacher as having some serious concern with respect to self-regulation of behavior. The prevalence of problems in boys was twice that reported for girls. Across all groups of children, the most common concern was related to oppositional behavior. Almost 16% of boys in the urban area and 11% of boys in the rural area were identified as having a serious problem related to oppositional behavior. The second most common problem was inattention and poor concentration, with 1 in 10 boys was designated as having a serious issue with inattention. Furthermore, serious concerns about opposition inattention, restlessness, and impulsivity often co-occurred.

Aggression and opposition are among the most common and serious childhood disorders, affecting 3%–10% of children in the United States (Lewinsohn, Hops, Roberts, Seeley, & Andrews, 1993). Teachers view fighting and aggression in early childhood as disturbing and especially disruptive to the classroom environment. Moreover, these behaviors are alarming because of their contributions to a chaotic environment that interferes with other children's learning; in addition, they have been linked to later academic difficulties and to problems such as substance abuse and criminal behavior. Often, teachers are hesitant to identify their young charges as having serious concerns with respect to self-regulation. In some cases, this hesitation is justified in that the observations of inattention or opposition are transient difficulties that children overcome as they adapt to the expectations of the classroom. However, these problems do not always resolve. In the absence of effective intervention, these problematic behaviors can become worse over time.

Concern about the long-term consequences of aggression and behavior problems in young children is especially salient and relevant for the development of AABs. What makes the development of AABs remarkable is that the trajectory they follow as a group with respect to conduct problems is somewhat atypical. Usually, conduct problems, oppositional behavior, and aggression decrease from a high at age 2 years to much lower levels by the time children are 4 years of age because of their improved capacity for self-regulation. This pattern of improved self-regulation is evident in all groups of children as they accommodate to the demands of family life and the regimen of early child care. The capacity for behavioral self-regulation grows as the prevalence of problem behaviors decrease and stabilize at age 4 or 5 years (Bub, McCartney, & Willett, 2007). At age 4 (usually the preschool year), the trajectories of AABs diverge from those of other groups. While the behavioral trajectories of other groups of children show stable or decreasing levels of aggression and conduct problems, the prevalence of these problems among AABs continues to rise. Studies using both cross-sectional (Barbarin & Soler, 1993) and longitudinal designs (Aber, Brown, & Jones, 2003; Bates, Brame, Dodge, & Vitaro, 2003; Olson et al., 2013) support this observation of increases in externalizing problems during this critical period from ages 4 to 10 years, or approximately pre-K through Grade 4. Thus, it appears that the routines, demands, and expectations of pre-K and formal schooling elicit higher levels of conduct problems among AABs, whereas other groups of children seem to accommodate more often to these demands and are therefore less frequently rated by teachers and parents as having difficulties with opposition, fighting, and attention dysregulation.

Data from a study of multiple school districts participating in a Kellogg-sponsored project (Barbarin, 2005) to promote the academic success of boys of color revealed a decline in peer relations due to fighting and poor conflict management across cohorts of boys in pre-K through second grade. These teacher-reported data comparing Latino boys and AABs between pre-K and second grade showed that, contrary to the expectations that self-regulation would increase and lead to more harmonious relations with peers, the quality of peer relations decreased for AABs. A similar pattern was observed in teachers' ratings of the emotion regulation of Latino boys and AABs, with AABs declining in emotion regulation while Latino boys showed a more typical pattern.

Although conduct problems are well recognized, emotional problems in AABs should not be discounted as a potential impediment to learning. Although they are often underreported, emotional problems also can affect classroom adaptation and academic achievement. The differences observed in self-regulation and peer relations likely result from a combination of endogenous factors, socialization experiences, and the social environment. The following section proposes ways to account for these differences in the behavioral and emotional development of AABs that have implications for early childhood educators.

TRIPLE RISKS: THE DEVELOPMENTAL CONTEXT OF AFRICAN AMERICAN BOYS

The atypical behavioral trajectories noted for AABs may be attributed to the unique context in which they are developing. This atypical context can be characterized by three distinctive but overlapping sets of risks that dominate the social and psychological landscape that comprise the social environment of AABs—namely, gender, poverty, and race. Figure 3.3 provides a schematic for the conceptual framework proposed here, with gender, poverty, and ethnicity identified as critical constituents of the developmental context of AABs. Specifically, AABs are situated at the nexus of vulnerabili-

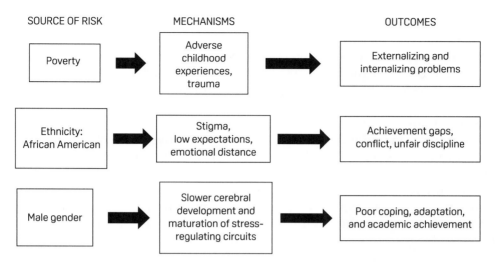

SOURCE OF RISK   MECHANISMS   OUTCOMES

Figure 3.3.   Triple risks in the developmental context of African American boys.

ties related to male gender, low economic status, and a disparaged ethnicity. The risks are influential and together are responsible for outcomes across multiple domains: academic, behavioral, and interpersonal. These risks are why AABs can be considered poster children for the challenges associated with ethnic, cultural, and economic diversity within early childhood education.

Poverty-Related Risks

A large proportion of AABs are born into economically disadvantaged households. Approximately 46% of AABs under the age of 6 years live in households that are poor (U.S. Census Bureau, 2014). This rate is about 3 times the rate for White children. When this level of poverty is translated into dollars, it means that 1 in 4 African American households lives on a meager annual income of less than $15,000 (U.S. Census Bureau, 2014). Poverty is associated with increased prevalence of exposure to adverse childhood experiences, which results in significant emotional distress and trauma.

Research on adverse childhood events centers around the prevalence and traumatic effects on children of experiences such as insults, humiliation, or physical threats; severe physical punishment (e.g., slapped, hit hard); sexual abuse; low affection and family support; food and social insecurity (e.g., child had to wear dirty clothes, child had no one to protect and care for him or her); disruptions of family life (e.g., parental separation, divorce); mother being hit, kicked, or threatened with weapon; living with a family member who has alcoholism, drug addiction, depression, mental illness, or suicidality; and arrest and incarceration of a household member. Such adverse events are ubiquitous in the lives of many AABs. When these events occur, they have a devastating effect on a child's socioemotional development. In addition to socioemotional impact, poverty-related adversity has been linked to aberrations in brain structures and functions, physical growth, cognitive and language development, and compromised neuroendocrine functioning (Shonkoff, Boyce, & McEwen, 2009). Thus, life in poverty is associated with a range of adverse experiences, including emotional trauma, material deprivation, poor nutrition and health, and exposure to violence.

The household is not the only locus contributing to the emotional distress of children living in poverty. The impact of poverty on children flows not only from parenting and what children are exposed to at home, but also to the accumulated disadvantages to which children are exposed at school and in their communities. These children live not only in low-income households but also in resource-deprived communities with high concentrations of other families living in poverty. Household poverty brings its own challenges, but living in communities with high concentrations of poverty is associated with an additional set of risks.

Poor communities are likely to be ethnically segregated and deprived of many of the resources that contribute to high quality of life. For example, economically disadvantaged children often attend failing schools with high concentrations of other children living in poverty. Communities with high concentrations of poverty are plagued by a host of social ills, including high unemployment, housing instability, homelessness, crime and violence, and crippling economic stagnation (Allard, 2008). There are fewer opportunities for adult mobility, as well as high rates of violent crime, limited access to quality health care, declining quality of housing stock, and residence in a "food desert" that lacks access to fresh and healthy foods, which all can weaken parents' capacity to cope and contribute to their demoralization. These conditions diminish parental well-being and the capacity of parents to provide the resources needed to invest in their children's development. Thus, the social and economic consequences for these children extend beyond family life to include disadvantages in community life. These effects trickle down to children and undermine their ability to adapt at school. Consequently, poverty-related risks can be understood as flowing from multiple sources. They arise not only from growing up in low-income families but also from residing in economically struggling communities and attending racially segregated schools. Therefore, it is unreasonable to expect that solutions to the challenges that AABs face in early childhood programs will be resolved without addressing the sources at these multiple levels.

Ethnicity-Related Risks

The disadvantages experienced by African American boys arise not only from inequality of access to material resources and opportunities, but also from the effects of explicit and implicit racial biases and microaggressions. Not even young children are spared from the toxic effects of negative racial stereotypes and biases. For young AABs, racial bias may take the form of scapegoating and disparagement at school and in the community (Nyborg & Curry, 2003). Scapegoating is the identification of an innocent victim to whom blame is attributed for misbehavior more broadly by the entire group. Disparagement refers to the tendency to belittle and to point out negative attributes. Under these conditions, weaknesses are amplified and strengths are minimized. Affirmation is rarely provided to disparaged populations. Instead, they are made to feel inadequate, unworthy, invisible, and unimportant. For young children, particularly boys, this situation can also take the form of disparate harsh punishment for behaviors that might be considered a minor infraction if committed by children of other racial/ethnic groups (Barbarin & Crawford, 2006).

The negative impacts of racial disparagement and stigma are especially evident in the domains of discipline at school and in the community. Suspension and expulsions of preschool children are not uncommon (Skiba, Peterson, & Williams, 1997). In 2002, 39% of the teachers in a Connecticut pre-K program reported expelling at least one child; a few expelled at least six children. Nationally, the data are not as bleak. One out of every 10 teachers in a national sample of state-supported pre-K programs reported expelling at least one child in the previous year; approximately 2% expelled more than one child. African American children are overrepresented among children suspended and expelled (Fenning & Rose, 2007). AABs are suspended from school at rates that exceed those of other ethnic groups. The disparate rates of suspension are greater for AABs than for African American girls in public education. For both African American boys and girls in grades pre-K to 12th grade, the percentage of children suspended from school increased between 1980 and 2006. The disparities are specially marked for AABs, whose suspensions rose from slightly above 15% to almost 25% of boys in 2006 (Wallace, Goodkind, Wallace, & Bachman, 2008). It is astounding and worrisome that almost 1 in 4 AABs in public school were suspended in the year 2006.

Rates of suspensions and expulsion are higher in programs serving high-need, impoverished, and ethnic-minority communities. For example, Black students are suspended and expelled at a rate that is 3 times higher than that of White students. Black students represent 16% of enrollment, but they account for 48% of preschoolers receiving more than one out-of-school suspension. By comparison, White students account for 43% of enrollment but only 26% of suspensions. Although boys account for 51% of preschool enrollment, they account for 72% of multiple out-of-school suspensions and 74% of expulsions (Office of Civil Rights, U.S. Department of Education, 2012). Although these findings might not be surprising, it is concerning that AABs in pre-K were suspended or expelled at rates that exceeded those for older boys in K–12 education.

It is tempting to express indignation when programs resort to suspensions and expulsions of children in preschool. The casual observer may find it difficult to imagine what behavior of a 3- or 4-year-old could be so egregious, dangerous, or disruptive that suspension and expulsion are the chosen remedy. Can a 3- or 4-year-old child be so disruptive and endangering of others that the only answer is to remove the child from the very programs intended to help them manage those very problems? This problem, however, is more complex than it appears on the surface. From the perspective of many program staff, suspensions are justified by the child's behavior or the lack of family support and follow-up at home. Suspensions may be used as a strategy to get the family's attention and involvement in promoting prosocial behavior in the child. Program staff may also concede that they resort to suspensions and expulsions because of their lack of training and ideas for managing the disruptions created by the child's behavior. Programs give many reasons for expelling children from their preschools. Most of these causes are linked to a child's behavior that the program finds disruptive but has been unable to correct. Children are suspended and expelled from early childhood programs most commonly for "prolonged tantrums, physical and verbal aggression, disruptive vocal and motor behavior, property destruction, self-injury, noncompliance, and withdrawal" (McCabe & Frede, 2007, p. 1). In a few cases, these problems may be serious and pose a risk to other children, but behaviors that endanger staff or peers are the exception rather than the rule.

The widespread use of expulsion has serious implications for the future development of young boys. It sets the affected boys on a course in which the seeds of future disconnection from school are sown. It provides a surprisingly early start to a process of alienation, which makes it increasingly likely that boys of color will drop out of school before earning a high school diploma and forestall any possibility that they will acquire the education they need for sustained future employment and engagement in civic life. Most importantly, the challenging behaviors that may lead to a child's suspension from pre-K are more easily susceptible to intervention that can be better addressed within the program classroom.

Given the prevalence of biases directed against AABs, it is not surprising that their parents expressed a high level of anxiety about the potential treatment of their sons at school. This high anxiety centers around safety, how the child might be viewed, whether the child will be disciplined fairly, and whether the child will be given positive or negative messages about who he is. In addition to concern about the treatment of their sons, parents may feel lack of trust because of a mismatch between socialization goals and cultural practices at home and at school. Bridging the gap between home and school in these matters is a critical and difficult task that programs are not free to ignore. Unless early childhood programs start from a position of understanding the difference between home and school, they will experience great difficulty in their efforts to help AABs adjust to the expectations and demands at school.

Suspensions and expulsions are ineffective means by which to address the needs of children who have difficulties adjusting to preschool settings. They should be rare to nonexistent. These tactics may also be an indicator of bias and stigma. Ubiquitous racial bias distorts the typical supportive relationships between AABs and their nonfamily caregivers (e.g., teachers) in a way that deprives AABs of the social and emotional resources they need to learn to cope with frustration, perceived threats, and demands for conformity to adult-initiated regimes.

Gender as a Risk Factor

Gender is the basis of biological vulnerability that affects the rate of physical growth and brain development. It is associated with differences in the rates of physical development and the development of brain circuits responsible for emotion regulation (Schore, 2017). Gender differences in the rate at which cerebral maturation proceeds can account for the some of the differences in language and behavior between boys and girls observed in early childhood programs. Specifically, the gender differences in the maturation of the left cerebral hemisphere responsible for language development contributes to slower language and acquisition of self-regulatory competencies in boys compared with girls. This delayed development affects boys' responses to stress, their emotion regulation, and their behavior. The delayed maturation of stress regulatory circuits in the brain renders boys vulnerable to environmental trauma and mundane stressors that arise in daily life. Boys are more often rated by teachers as exhibiting externalizing behavior than are girls (Deater-Deckard, Dodge, Bates, & Pettit, 1998; Juliano, Werner, & Cassidy, 2006; Keiley, Bates, Dodge, & Pettit, 2000). Boys engage in aggressive and rule-breaking behavior as a way of establishing a reputation, fitting in socially, and solidifying status within the peer group to a greater extent than girls. To wit, middle-school AABs associated aggression and rule breaking with high peer status and popularity more often than Whites and Latinos did (Xie, Dawes, Wurster, & Shi, 2013).

Male gender is also related to a tendency on the part of adults to overlook possible emotional difficulties experienced in boys. The failure to recognize emotional issues among boys may be due to the fact that boys are reluctant to manifest or signal their emotional distress to others out of fear of disapproval or retribution for violating established norms of masculinity. Findings across studies consistently show that boys display and report less fear and anxiety than girls; however, African American children, both boys and girls, have a greater prevalence of anxiety disorders than do White children (Beidel, Turner, & Träger, 1994; Neal & Turner, 1991). Foster, Kuperminc, and Price (2004) found that boys were less often diagnosed with anxiety disorders and reported fewer symptoms of posttraumatic stress than did girls. This situation may be the consequence of being taught that conveying pain and hurt are not socially permitted for boys. Boys are often socialized to believe that boys do not cry. If they violate the gender prohibition against expression of emotion, they are often sanctioned by teasing, name-calling, bullying, and other forms of social disapproval. This may also explain differences in how boys and girls cope with stress. Boys were more likely to employ physical means of regulating their emotions and girls more likely to express emotions and communicate about them in words (Carlson & Grant, 2008). Although it is generally true that boys tend to display fewer internalizing problems than girls, this finding does not hold true for AABs. Among AABs under the age of 9 years, rates of emotional difficulties, such as sad affect, were higher in boys than girls (Barbarin & Soler, 1994). Moreover, given the correlations between aggression, irritability, and depressive symptoms, emotional difficulties can also be expressed in terms of tantrums and emotional outbursts, which are ordinarily classified under the rubric of behavioral problems.

POVERTY AND BIOSOCIAL INFLUENCES ON THE BEHAVIORAL DEVELOPMENT OF AFRICAN AMERICAN BOYS

Implicit racial bias often leads to disparate discipline and undermines the ability of staff to serve as a resource for children who are struggling to adjust to preschool. These effects may be amplified when the child is economically disadvantaged. For this reason, the effects of poverty on AABs' adjustment to pre-K are important to consider. Poverty creates inauspicious conditions that exacerbate and amplify other sources of risk for child development. For example, in a latent growth curve analysis of aggression among boys from first to seventh grade, Schaeffer, Petras, Ialongo, Poduska, and Kellam (2003) identified four trajectories of aggression in an urban sample consisting of a majority of AABs. Although about a third of the boys were classified as nonaggressive, a majority (52%) exhibited moderate levels of aggression that were strongly related to early difficulties with concentration. Long-term adverse outcomes for boys with moderate levels of aggression were negligible. The boys with the highest probability of adverse outcomes had high and early-onset levels of aggression that persisted through seventh grade (9%) or had low but slowly increasing levels of aggression from first through seventh grades (7%). The boys at greatest risk of serious long-term difficulties were exposed to adverse childhood experiences and significant environmental risks associated with poverty.

Poverty has its own negative effects, but it can also be related to stigma and other adverse events that have biological consequences. Adversities linked to socioeconomic status and racial bias are interactive processes. Both are significant sources of distress in the lives of AABs (see Figure 3.4). Although the sequelae of poverty are a common topic in the professional literature, the more recent work linking poverty to brain development, neurohormonal functioning, and physical maturation is not frequently discussed and has not been well integrated into the early childhood discourse on the behavioral development of AABs. This work suggests that poverty-related adverse experiences and environmental conditions promote adaptations in neurohormonal functioning associated with externalizing problems.

SOCIAL/BIOLOGICAL RISKS   MEDIATORS   LIFE OUTCOMES

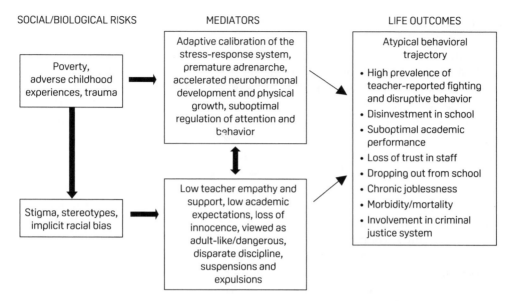

Figure 3.4. Model of the biosocial processes and atypical developmental outcomes of African American boys.

Research on biobehavioral and social processes that are associated with poverty can help to explain the accelerating trend of externalizing problems among AABs from ages 5 to 10 years. Specifically, biological and social mechanisms may account for atypical behavioral development, which undergirds many of the negative outcomes experienced by AABs (Romero, Richards, Harrison, Garbarino, & Mozley, 2015). The principal idea proposed in the Adaptive Calibration Model is that chronic adversity induces a recalibration of the stress response system. Specifically, this model proposes that chronic adversity may lead to early adaptations in cortisol response and to premature adrenarche (Del Giudice, Ellis, & Shirtcliff, 2011). An important idea is that this recalibration of the stress response based on early life events will have enduring effects on stress responsivity and behavior in adulthood. Although this effect of adversity on neuroendocrine functions related to aggression is more pronounced in boys than girls, the effect is moderated when boys receive strong parental support (Ellis & Essex, 2007).

Stigma and implicit bias also play an important role in accounting for the atypical trajectory behavioral trajectory of AABs. Stigma and implicit bias shape teachers' perspectives and expectations of AABs. The most deleterious effect of stigma is that it alters the teacher–child relationship, leading to emotional discomfort, conflict, and harsh discipline. Okonofua and Eberhardt (2015) linked racial disparities in discipline to racial stereotypes about African Americans. In their experimental research, they found that teachers exhibited more escalating negative responses directed to Black students over student misbehavior than they did for White students. Teachers were also more troubled by the behavior and responded with more severe punishment for repeated infractions for Black students than they did for White students.

Implicit bias can lead teachers to view AABs as being older, less innocent, and more dangerous than is justified. The result is that teachers blame these students for classroom disruptions, viewing them as less deserving of empathic responses in addressing the behavioral misconduct. Consequently, when behavior problems arise, teachers may be more likely to view them as requiring discipline than as opportunities for teaching or a mental health concern. Moreover, teachers may withdraw emotionally from the child and make themselves less accessible as a safe and secure base. This withdrawal deprives children of adult support and the possibility of co-regulation when children's own self-regulatory mechanisms are inadequate to handle the situation. As a result, AABs are suspended and expelled more frequently than other groups of children for the same infractions of rules. In time, the disparate and harsh discipline may leave a child feeling misunderstood, unblocked, and unfairly treated. These feelings can cause the child to withdraw and become less invested in the activities of the classroom and in learning. In turn, AABs lose trust in the teachers and are less likely to control an impulse to act out.

Through stigma, children are deprived of the very relational resources they need in order to learn to cope with disappointments, deal with conflict, and manage overwhelming emotional arousal. Lacking this support, AABs are left to their own devices, which are often inadequate and lead to disruptive, aggressive, or oppositional behavior. It is also true that difficult relationships with peers may be reflected in these behavioral trajectories. In some cases, peers may support deviations from routines and violations of rules. More than Whites and Latinos, AABs associated aggression and rule breaking with high peer status and popularity; however, this association decreased over the transition to high school (Xie, Dawes, Wurster, & Shi, 2013).

SUMMARY OF ISSUES EMBEDDED IN THE CONSIDERATION OF AFRICAN AMERICAN BOYS IN EARLY CHILDHOOD

Barbarin, China, and Wright (2014) identified nine impediments to achieving educational equality: harsh disparate school discipline, conflict and distance in teacher–student relationships, poor instructional quality, an anti-academic peer culture, attending schools with high concentrations of children with significant academic needs, the absence of male mentorship, poor home–school partnership, trauma, exposure to violence, and cultural stereotypes that African American males are dangerous and incompetent. Some of the identified impediments are the direct consequences of poverty and racism in education, as discussed previously. These social processes may not be unique to AABs and may affect other groups of children growing up in poverty. Although early childhood programs alone cannot overcome these impediments, there are clear recommendations that can contribute to reducing their effects. Three major recommendations are articlulated in this section.

Recommendation 1: Implement a System of Preventive Mental Health Service Delivery Consisting of Universal Behavioral Health Screening Followed by Classroom-Embedded Consultation

Adopting a proactive, multitiered approach can result in a health-promoting environment that is beneficial to all children. Central to such a system is a universal behavioral health screening to detect emergent problems/concerns. The screen should be used to gather concerns and insights from both program staff and parents. Assessments should be followed by interventions, which include universal classroom programming to prevent potential problem behavior, child-focused interventions for children with persistent problematic behavior, and direct therapeutic services for some children and families. The system may follow a Response to Intervention (RTI) model in which interventions involving positive behavior supports are titrated to the extent and nature of the problem. The elements of this RTI preventive approach include multiple steps, which include following up the screening with consultative support and training in the classroom for teachers. Another step is offering professional development on universal tier 1 socioemotional learning programs. A small number of children with the most severe difficulties and delays in self-regulation may need direct services. Family support programs and behavioral health classroom consultation for pre-K teachers are also promising approaches. For example, the Family Check-up (Dishion & Stormchak, 2007), which provides time-limited focused assistance with periodic follow-up, has been well received by distressed families.

Recommendation 2: Animate Home–School Partnerships by Increasing Staff's Cultural Competence

Cultural diversity is a reality in the United States. To be successful, programs must be able to serve segments of society that are different from the majority White teaching staff. The term *cultural competence* has been used to describe an amorphous status of attitudes, behaviors, and relationships whereby in-groups learn or develop facility in interacting smoothly with out-groups. Cultural competence is based on attitudes, perspectives, and knowledge. It requires taking the view that differences are not to be minimized or discounted but should be understood and sometimes celebrated. From this perspective, cultural differences are not impediments that need to be overcome but assets that need to be cultivated.

Although the reasons for celebrating and embracing diversity are many, serving diverse populations in early childhood programs is complex and easier said than done. First and foremost, it requires the motivation to move beyond cultural myopia and learn about lives other than one's own with a sense of curiosity, adventure, and most of all humility. Culturally diverse families may have very different worldviews and values about behavior. Consequently, an effort to learn about these differences in a nonjudgmental way is an essential step toward serving children well.

The knowledge needed to develop cultural competence can vary. Although it can be as broad and encompassing as knowledge of the history, religious celebrations, and heroes of a particular group, sometimes it is much narrower and focused on learning about the mundane lives of families. This latter approach is probably more realistic for staff to achieve. It will involve learning about multiple aspects of family life, including family organization, its members, and their roles, including gender-based roles; beliefs about childhood; socialization practices and goals for children; and what the family celebrates. This information can be gleaned most efficiently by taking advantage of naturally occurring situations and events planned specifically for families, such as open-ended conversations with family members in their homes or at family events at school.

The California Department of Education Child Development Division (2011a, 2011b) has developed an exemplary set of materials that elaborate on strategies proposed by a range of professionals for improving the cultural responsiveness of programs. The framework developed for the State of California early childhood providers is a useful guide for early childhood staff to address the issue of cultural competence. The process of developing cultural competence begins with self-awareness of one's own culture and recognition of how that culture influences personal beliefs, values, and behavior. It requires relinquishing any vestiges of cultural superiority and moving to a position of respecting and honoring differences. This involves activities to bridge home and programs such as home visiting, bringing in community elders to engage with children, providing books with diverse home languages that parents can use at home, and embracing the ways diverse cultures celebrate and mark important life transitions.

Recommendation 3: Address the Effects of Implicit Bias by Nurturing More Empathic Teacher–Child Relationships and Banning Child Suspensions/Expulsions From Pre-K

Concerns about bias and diversity are not new. Anti-bias curricula have been developed for and used in early childhood programs for some time (Derman-Sparks, 1989). However, these efforts were intended primarily to expose children to ideas and experiences that would help children grow up free of bias and stereotypes. The National Association for the Education of Young Children has promulgated standards with broader targets that include staff and programming (Derman-Sparks, LeeKeenan, & Nimmo, 2015). Studies of the effects of inadvertent and unconscious biases have raised awareness of possible implicit biases in staff and the need to support practices to overcome their effects on children, especially in the domain of discipline. For example, Okonofua, Paunesku, and Walton (2016) described an innovative intervention to mitigate the effects of implicit bias and reduce the prevalence of disparate harsh discipline, such as suspensions and expulsions. This intervention focused on improving the quality of relationships between teachers and students as a way to reduce the deleterious effects of biased discipline. The authors theorized that increased empathy lowers stress between teachers and students and builds children's trust and respect for teachers, both of which are related to students' proclivity to follow rules and adhere to the expectations of classroom decorum and behavior. The invention consisted of two online modules that reminded teachers of the importance of high-quality teacher–student relationships for student learning, self-control, and adhering to classroom regimes. In addition, teachers were asked to think about how this empathic approach helps teachers to maintain control of the classroom. As a consequence of this relatively brief intervention, teachers were less likely to resort to punitive discipline than the teachers in the control group. Moreover, the intervention was successful in reducing school suspensions by 50% over the academic year.

A second strategy for reducing disparate discipline targets program policy. It involves prohibitions against the use of suspensions and expulsions to address student infractions of rules. Suspensions and expulsions are ineffective and often create more harm by removing children from the very setting in which they can best acquire self-regulation. In addition to the disruption of the child's education, suspensions and expulsions may result in loss of time at work and income for parents. The use of child exclusion strategies can build parental resentment toward the program and staff and introduce conflict and discord into the home–school relationship. To date, 18 states and the District of Columbia have passed legislation that bans the use of suspensions and expulsions from preschool. However, bans do not go far enough and thus have unintended effects. Some staff may feel trapped because the one tool they had to deal with serious problem behavior has been taken away. In response, they may develop alternatives that are equally problematic for children's' well-being. Along with banning exclusionary practices, support for teachers to deal with challenging behaviors is important. Recommendation 1 for a universal behavioral health system is an example of a supportive response to help program staff.

In summary, the implementation of these three recommendations could make a considerable difference in helping schools to serve AABs more effectively and to reduce the achievement gap. Employing a comprehensive system of mental health service delivery can help identify and remediate behavioral and emotional problems in their early stages, when they may still be malleable. In-classroom consultation could provide teachers with the support they need when they are at a loss on how to respond to difficulties in the classroom. Moving away from the use of expulsions and suspensions will keep AABs in the classroom, where they can be best helped. Finally, families can be an important resource in addressing difficulties children may have adapting to the school environment. Forming a positive working partnership with families is one of the most effective things teachers can do. Strong alliances with families rest on regular two-way communication between the program and the family. Very positive relationships can result from showing genuine interest in families, their culture, and what they want for their children.

REFERENCES

Aber, J. L., Brown, J. L., & Jones, S. M. (2003). Developmental trajectories toward violence in middle childhood: Course, demographic differences, and response to school-based intervention. *Developmental Psychology, 39,* 324–348.

Allard, S. (2008). Place, race, and access to the safety net. In A. C. Lin & D. Harris (Eds.), *The colors of poverty* (pp. 232–260). New York, NY: Russell Sage Foundation.

Barbarin, O. (2005). Promoting Academic Success of Boys of Color: Family, School, and Community Intervention Research Project. Chapel Hill, NC: Frank Porter Graham Child Development Institute.

Barbarin, O. (2006). *Using ABLE to assess mental head needs in early childhood.* Paper presented at the Head Start Research Conference, Washington, DC.

Barbarin, O. A., Chinn, L., & Wright, Y. (2014). Creating developmentally auspicious school environments for boys of color. In L. Liben and R. Bigler (Eds.), *Advances in child development and behavior: The role of gender in educational contexts and outcomes* (pp. 75–106). Philadelphia, PA: Elsevier.

Barbarin, O., & Crawford, G. (2006). Acknowledging and reducing stigmatization of African American boys. *Young Children, 61*(6), 79–86.

Barbarin, O., & Soler, R. (1993). Behavioral, emotional and academic adjustment in a national probability sample of African American children: Effects of age, gender and family structure. *Journal of Black Psychology, 19*(4), 423–446.

Bates, J. E., Brame, B., Dodge, K. A., & Vitaro, F. (2003). Developmental trajectories of childhood disruptive behaviors and adolescent delinquency: A six-site, cross-national study. *Developmental Psychology, 39,* 222–245.

Beidel, D. C., Turner, M. W., & Trager, K. N. (1994). Test anxiety and childhood anxiety disorders in African American and White school children. *Journal of Anxiety Disorders, 8*(2), 169–179.

Bub, K. L., McCartney, K., & Willett, J. B. (2007). Behavior problem trajectories and first-grade cognitive ability and achievement skills: A latent growth curve analysis. *Journal of Educational Psychology, 99,* 653–670.

Carlson, G., & Grant, K. E. (2008). The roles of stress and coping in explaining gender differences in risk for psychopathology among African American urban adolescents. *The Journal of Early Adolescence, 28*(3), 375–404.

California Department of Education Child Development Division. (2011a). Family engagement framework. Retrieved from http://www.cde.ca.gov/ls/pf/pf/documents/famengage frameenglish.pdf

California Department of Education Child Development Division. (2011b). The early childhood educator competencies. Retrieved from http://www.cde.ca.gov/sp/cd/re/documents/ececompetencies2011.pdf

Deater-Deckard, K., Dodge, K., Bates, J., & Pettit, G. (1998). Multiple risk factors in the development of externalizing behavior problems: Group and individual differences. *Development and Psychopathology, 10,* 469–493.

Del Giudice, M., Ellis, B. J., & Shirtcliff, E. A. (2011). The Adaptive Calibration Model of stress responsivity. *Neuroscience and Biobehavioral Reviews, 35*(7), 1562–1592.

Derman-Sparks, L. (1989). *Anti-bias curriculum: Tools for empowering young children.* Washington, DC: National Association for the Education of Young Children.

Derman-Sparks, L., LeeKeenan, D., & Nimmo, J. (2015). *Leading anti-bias early childhood programs: A guide for change.* New York: Teachers College Press.

Dishion, T. J., & Stormshak, E. A. (2007). *Intervening in children's lives: An ecological, family-centered approach to mental health care.* Washington, DC: American Psychological Association.

Ellis, B. J., & Essex, M. J. (2007). Family environments, adrenarche, and sexual maturation: A longitudinal test of a life history model. *Child Development, 78,* 1799–1817.

Fenning, P., & Rose, J. (2007). Overrepresentation of African American students in exclusionary discipline: The role of school policy. *Urban Education, 42,* 536–559.

Foster, J. D., Kuperminc, G. P., & Price, A. W. (2004). Gender differences in posttraumatic stress and related symptoms among inner-city minority youth exposed to community violence. *Journal of Youth and Adolescence, 33*(1), 59–69.

Juliano, M., Werner, R. S., & Cassidy, K. W. (2006). Early correlates of preschool aggressive behavior according to type of aggression and measurement. *Journal of Applied Developmental Psychology, 27*(5), 395–410.

Keiley, M., Bates, J., Dodge, K., & Pettit, G. (2000). A cross-domain growth analysis: Externalizing and internalizing behaviors during 8 years of childhood. *Journal of Abnormal Child Psychology, 28,* 161–179.

Lewinsohn, P. M., Hops, H., Roberts, R., & Seeley, J. (1993). Adolescent psychopathology: I. Prevalence and incidence of depression and other *DSM-III-R* disorders in high school students. *Journal of Abnormal Psychology, 102,* 110–120.

McCabe, L. A., & Frede, E. C. (2007). *Challenging behavior and the role of pre-school education* (National Institute of Early Education Research Pre-School Policy Brief #16). Retrieved from http://nieer.org/wp-content/uploads/2016/08/16.pdf

National Center for Education Statistics. (2013). *National Assessment of Educational Progress 2013.* Washington, DC: U.S. Department of Education. Retrieved from https://nces.ed.gov/nationsreportcard/naepdata/dataset.aspx

Neal, A., & Turner, S. M. (1991). Anxiety disorders in African Americans. *Psychological Bulletin, 109,* 400–410.

Nyborg, V. M., & Curry, J. F. (2003). The impact of perceived racism: Psychological symptoms among African American boys. *Journal of Clinical Child and Adolescent Psychology, 32*(2), 258–266.

Office of Civil Rights, U.S. Department of Education. (2012). *Civil rights data collection data snapshot: School discipline.* Retrieved from https://ocrdata.ed.gov/downloads/crdc-school-discipline-snapshot.pdf

Okonofua, J. A., Paunesku, D., & Walton, G. M. (2016). A brief intervention to encourage empathic discipline halves suspension rates among adolescents. *Proceedings of the National Academy of Sciences, 113,* 5221–5226.

Okonofua, J. A., & Eberhardt, J. L. (2015). Two strikes: Race and the disciplining of young students. *Psychological Science, 26*(5): 617–624.

Olson, S. L., Sameroff, A. J., Lansford, J. E., Sexton, H., Davis-Kean, P., Bates, J. E., . . . (2013). Deconstructing the externalizing spectrum: Growth patterns of overt aggression, covert aggression, oppositional behavior, impulsivity/inattention, and emotion dysregulation between school entry and early adolescence. *Development and Psychopathology, 25,* 817–842.

Romero, E., Richards, M. H., Harrison, P. R., Garbarino, J., & Mozley, M. (2015). The role of neighborhood in the development of aggression in urban African American youth: A multilevel analysis. *American Journal of Community Psychology, 56,* 156–169.

Schaeffer, C. M., Petras, H., Ialongo, N., Poduska, J., & Kellam, S. (2003). Modeling growth in boys' aggressive behavior across elementary school: Links to later criminal involvement, conduct disorder, and antisocial personality disorder. *Developmental Psychology, 39,* 1020–1035.

Schore, A. N. (2017). All our sons: The developmental neurobiology and neuroendocrinology of boys at risk. *Infant Mental Health Journal, 38*(1), 15–52.

Shonkoff, J. P., Boyce, W. T., & McEwen, B. S. (2009). Neuroscience, molecular biology, and the childhood roots of health disparities: Building a new framework for health promotion and disease prevention. *Journal of the American Medical Association, 301*(21), 2252–2259.

Skiba, R. J., Peterson, R., & Williams, T. (1997). Office referrals and suspension: Disciplinary intervention and middle schools. *Education & Treatment of Children, 20,* 295–315.

U.S. Census Bureau. (2014). *Current population survey: Annual social and economic supplements.* Washington, DC: Author.

U.S. Department of Education. (2003). *Early childhood longitudinal study, kindergarten class 1998–99.* Washington, DC: National Center for Education Statistics.

Wallace, J. M., Goodkind, S., Wallace, C. M., & Bachman, J. G. (2008). Racial, ethnic, and gender differences in school discipline among U.S. high school students: 1991–2005. *The Negro Educational Review, 59*(1–2), 47–62.

Xie, H., Dawes, M., Wurster, T. J., & Shi, B. (2013). Aggression, academic behaviors, and popularity perceptions among boys of color during the transition to middle school. *American Journal of Orthopsychiatry, 83,* 265–277.

4

Linguistic and Cultural Diversity

Knowledge Utilization in Early Care and Education

Linda M. Espinosa and Marlene Zepeda

> Children in [early care and education] settings are substantially more diverse in terms of race, ethnicity, language, and special needs, all of which call for new knowledge and skills among their teachers. And as scientific understanding of the profound influence of children's early years on brain development, behavior, and learning has grown exponentially, it has become a high-stakes concern to assure that our nation's [early care and education] settings provide high-quality, enriching experiences for young children. (Whitebook, Phillips, & Howes, 2014, p. 1)

Since the Bilingual Education Act of 1968 (PL 90–247), the educational needs of children who speak a language other than English in the home have received increasing attention for many reasons: The proportion of these children has increased from approximately 11% of all students in 1980 to almost 25% in 2017 (National Academies of Sciences, Engineering, and Medicine [NASEM], 2017); the number of different languages present in classrooms has increased to more than 140 (Office of Head Start, 2017); enduring educational disparities continue to exist between native and nonnative English speakers; and the teaching profession has a limited pool of qualified bilingual professionals. As child and family diversity continues to grow in the United States, the challenge of providing high-quality early care and education (ECE) consistently across all groups continues to confront ECE practitioners. Children from diverse backgrounds are typically those from immigrant families whose first language is not English, those who are from racial minority groups, or those who are not growing up in a mainstream cultural context (i.e., White and middle-class; see Chapters 3 and 5), many of whom are living in poverty. For one particular group of diverse children, dual-language learners (DLLs; children who are aged 0–5 years and speak a language other than English in the home), a number of challenges exist that contribute to decreased educational attainment and have implications for ECE knowledge utilization (Castro, García, & Markos, 2013). (Note that the

term *English-language learners* is used to refer to children who are not proficient in English and are enrolled in the K–12 education system.)

The growth of DLLs in the child population has meant that many ECE
settings, such as Head Start and state pre-K programs, now serve high numbers of families and children who primarily speak languages other than
English. Current demographics reflect the increasing linguistic diversity
of our children and families. The Office of Head Start reported that more
than 30% of preschool children in their programs are considered to be DLLs
(Office of Head Start, 2017); in the state of California, 60% of children aged
birth to 5 years are so identified (First Five California, 2017).

The substantial and persistent achievement gap between DLLs and
native English speakers is of concern to educators and policy makers across
the United States. In many studies, DLLs show language gaps during
infancy (although language is almost always assessed only in English in
these studies) and have had fewer opportunities to learn English (Fuller,
Bein, Kim, & Rabe-Hesketh, 2015). DLLs perform significantly below their
English-only peers at kindergarten entry, have much lower reading and
math scores at third grade, and are likely to be classified as long-term English learners in the upper grades, which provides little access to the general
curriculum when they may have higher probabilities of dropping out of
school (NAESM, 2017; Olsen, 2010).

To effectively address the achievement gap for DLLs, the professional
learning experiences and pedagogical practices of the personnel who work
with these children must be improved. For children in the early years,
teacher effectiveness has been identified as one of the most important variables for DLL student learning and achievement (Garcia & Garcia, 2012).
During the ECE years, practitioners come from a variety of disciplines and
often play different roles than in the K–12 educational system. A report from
the Institute of Medicine and National Research Council (2015, p. 27) identified "professionals with regular (daily or near-daily), direct responsibilities
for the care and education of young children" as educators and expanded
the use of the term to associated roles such as home visitors, early intervention specialists, and mental health consultants, who may have less frequent
direct interaction. The report referenced "care and education practitioners"
(CEPs) throughout. Therefore, this chapter uses the acronym CEPs to refer
to all personnel who have direct responsibilities for the care and education
of young children.

CONCEPTUAL FRAMEWORK FOR UNDERSTANDING THE
DEVELOPMENT AND LEARNING OF DUAL-LANGUAGE LEARNERS

Historically, most research examining the growth, progress, and achievement of DLLs has focused on differences between DLLs and non-DLLs,
judging DLLs' performance on norms designed for English-only populations without considerations for the unique linguistic and developmental

trajectories of children growing up with more than one language (Center for Early Care and Education Research—Dual Language Learners, 2011). This approach has often led to a "deficit perspective" that views these children as less capable than their monolingual English peers because of their lack of English proficiency. This view, however, is contrary to current research, which has found that learning more than one language during the ECE years can be accomplished by all young children and carries significant linguistic and cognitive advantages (NASEM, 2017). To understand how to best prepare CEPs to meet the needs of DLLs, one must first understand what typical development and school readiness looks like for these children, what factors contribute to their growth and learning, and what teaching practices and classroom conditions best support their achievement. To improve the knowledge utilization of CEPs, we propose a shift in our conceptual framework for understanding and improving ECE teacher knowledge utilization— essentially broadening and redefining what is critical knowledge for CEPs and how to apply it to diverse populations, such as DLLs.

The first priority regarding critical knowledge for CEPs is to recognize that the development of DLLs differs in significant aspects from that of children who are English-only speakers due to the unique context and societal circumstances of their upbringing. For example, DLLs are often the children of immigrants, some of whom may be new to the United States and unfamiliar with social and cultural norms as well as school expectations. Some of these families may be experiencing trauma associated with migrating to the United States, a phenomenon that can have negative consequences for their children's development. In addition, by definition, the families of DLLs speak a language other than English in the home—a characteristic that can lead to family isolation and, in some cases, can be a source of shame for the children (Halgunseth, Jia, & Barbarin, 2013).

Culture-specific parenting goals, values, and practices vary across different ethnic groups, which also contribute to disparities in the early social, language, and literacy learning opportunities of DLLs. For instance, culturally specified parenting concepts such as *familismo, respeto*, and being *bien educado* among Latino families (e.g., Halgunseth et al., 2013) and concepts such as *guan* and *chiao shun* among Chinese families (e.g., Chao, 1994) emphasize the importance of harmonious relationships with others, respect for adult authority, prioritizing the needs of the family, and conducting oneself in a manner that reflects well on the family. These particular values that children are exposed to early in life may lead to patterns of behavior in the ECE setting that are inconsistent with program goals. Furthermore, these patterns of behavior can result in judgments of DLLs' capacities that are misleading.

Language and literacy practices at home are another area that reflects the unique experiences of DLLs and their families. In many ways, such practices are likely influenced by parents' and other family members' proficiency in the first language and in English, as well as by family members' beliefs about how exposure to English and continued use of the home language affects their children's development, learning, and potential for success as adults (Billings, 2009). Such beliefs about bilingualism may also reflect broader family processes related to acculturation, racial and ethnic socialization, and language socialization. Families may view their children's development of the home language as critical for maintaining ties to the family's cultural heritage and the connection with family members in their countries of origin. Alternatively, newly arrived immigrant families may prize the rapid acquisition of English over maintenance of their heritage language and encourage their children to speak only English. Adult family members may also consider their own experiences and competencies in their first language and their second language, which may influence their goals for their children. Thus, beliefs and goals about cultural and language maintenance can play a key role in how much exposure and opportunity children have to use their two languages.

Racial and ethnic identity may also impact the development of DLLs, especially their language development. When DLLs enter an ECE program, they are likely to be taught by teachers who are monolingual speakers of English (Migration Policy Institute, 2015) and English is typically the primary language of instruction in their classroom, giving children the message that English is the desired language of communication (Espinosa, 2015). This message, in turn, may affect their developing abilities and attitudes about continuing to use their home language (DeHouwer, 2007). Although the role of racial and ethnic identities has received minimal attention in research on DLLs, research on older language learners has shown that English-language learners from ethnic groups who are culturally similar to the mainstream cultural group have better academic achievement outcomes in school than English-language learners from culturally dissimilar backgrounds (Ellis, 2008).

Finally, the amount and quality of DLLs' exposure to and usage of their two languages are also important features of their early development that affect later school success. Multiple studies have shown that preschoolers' and school-age children's exposure to the home language supports their development of that language (Hammer et al., 2012). Use of the child's first language in the home or in the school setting does not appear to affect the rate or level of English acquisition; however, an emphasis on English in the ECE setting does appear to negatively impact DLLs' development in the home language. This is likely due to the higher value given to English proficiency in the broader social context. Given the research findings about the impact of exposure to their two languages by their parents and teachers, attention needs to be devoted to the amount and quality of exposure DLLs experience in each language.

This attention is especially important given the current scientific consensus that children who become fully proficient in both their home language and English are likely to reap benefits in cognitive, social, academic, and professional outcomes as well as be protected from brain decline at older ages (NASEM, 2017). These findings suggest that all CEPs should understand the benefits of early bilingualism and view the development of DLLs through the lens of potential advantages of having more than one language and not as being deficient because of limited English skills. The framework for understanding and promoting advanced levels of academic achievement for DLLs needs to broaden to include the assets inherent in emerging bilingualism.

DLLs have a wide range of early learning environments, amount and quality of language exposure, family resources, and level of educational support, all features that influence development and achievement; thus, they should not be considered as a homogeneous group or only in comparison to their English-only peers. Broadly, this situation means that CEPs need in-depth knowledge of the circumstances, values, and culture of DLL children and their families to better understand how to foster their learning and achievement. Specifically, it means these personnel must expand their thinking beyond simple comparisons between DLLs and English-only children, not use norms or expectations for achievement based on English only, and develop methods to collect important information about DLLs' background (e.g., the age of acquisition of each language, the extent and nature of exposure to each language, key family characteristics) as well as family histories. They also must be knowledgeable about the process, benefits, and methods of early bilingualism to promote the future school success of DLLs.

Current Perspectives on Professional Development in Early Care and Education

As described in Chapter 8, ECE knowledge utilization is driven by both the knowledge base of the profession and the multiple ways it is applied or utilized to influence classroom practices. Persistent challenges have existed with defining the knowledge base essential and unique to working with DLLs as well as the instructional competencies and best practices that ECE personnel need to be able to improve educational outcomes for these children.

Fortunately, recent scientific evidence has shed light on four key points: 1) the typical developmental trajectories of DLLs, 2) the factors that contribute to their rate and levels of second language acquisition, 3) the consequences of exposure to more than one language during the early childhood years, and 4) the specific CEP competencies and teaching practices that foster school success for DLLs (NASEM, 2017). This section presents a discussion of what CEPs need to know and be able to implement to meet the needs of linguistically diverse children. By clearly defining the content of the essential knowledge base for CEPs, defining the specific competencies and best practices for ECE service providers, and integrating this knowledge and practical competencies into ECE preservice and in-service professional development, CEPs can strengthen the educational opportunities for DLLs and improve their chances for success.

What Do Care and Education Practitioners Need to Know About the Development of Dual-Language Learners?   As the knowledge base concerning the language development of DLLs continues to expand, it is increasingly used as a foundation to support and inform ECE practice. Currently, the field is informed by a number of lines of empirical inquiry. First, research on early brain development has shown that infants can learn two languages simultaneously and that the early years are the optimal period to become bilingual (Ramirez & Kuhl, 2017). Brain science suggests that the bilingual brain is more active than the monolingual brain due to the need to process two languages (Bialystok, 2017) and is associated with greater control of task-relevant attention and the ability to switch tasks more efficiently (Conboy, 2013). These cognitive skills are associated with enhanced executive function in DLLs. Second, research has shown that although DLLs follow a similar general language trajectory as monolingual children, their development will demonstrate unique characteristics as a function of learning two languages. These characteristics include language mixing, smaller vocabularies in each language (Bedore, Pena, Garcia, & Cortez, 2005), and differences in the emergence of certain linguistic benchmarks.

A recent report from NASEM (2017) provides a research synthesis on the development of English-language learners and DLLs from birth to age 21 years. This consensus study connected research to educational practices and policies that are consequential for DLLs' development and school success. Three major interrelated conclusions inform the CEP knowledge base and underpin the recommended instructional strategies in this chapter. The first conclusion is that high levels of proficiency in both the home language and English are critical for children's future academic success; the second is the finding that a child has greater chances for future school success the earlier that he or she is exposed to a second language; and the third conclusion is that home language loss may place the child at risk for unhealthy family relationships, including estrangement from their cultural heritage.

There is evidence that DLLs show greater growth in learning English compared with monolingual English-speaking children when they participate in high-quality early childhood programs (Gormley, 2008); furthermore, better outcomes are achieved when more time is spent in high-quality early childhood programs (i.e., 2 years vs. 1 year; Yazejian, Bryant, Freel, & Burchinal, 2015). In addition, when programs systematically support the child's home language, children show greater growth in both their home language and English (Farver, Lonigan, & Eppe, 2009). Because English constitutes the primary language that DLLs hear outside of their home and is often the preferred language in social contexts, a strong possibility exists that DLLs will lose their desire and ability to understand and speak their home language, especially after they are exposed to English; this may have negative consequences for their psychosocial development (NASEM, 2017). Because maintenance of a home language is associated with a healthy sense of identity as well as future school success (Bialystok, 2017) and the ability to communicate with family members who only speak the home language, home language preservation should be considered a priority for all ECE programs.

Culturally Responsive Early Care and Education

Because the majority of DLLs come from cultures that are distinct from mainstream U.S. culture, the role of culture in language development needs to be understood. Basically, language and culture are deeply intertwined. It is through language that the values and beliefs of a culture are transmitted from one generation to another. Parents use language to operationalize culture through their parenting practices that stress behavioral expectations for their children. The interconnection of language and culture obliges CEPs to be knowledgeable not only of the processes and consequences of first and second language development, but also the role that culture plays in a child's life. Thus, in serving DLLs, CEPs should understand what is included in culturally and linguistically responsive practices.

There are many definitions of culturally responsive teaching. One definition that is often referenced is from Gay (2010), who described it as possessing cultural knowledge of diverse children, including understanding their prior experiences, their frames of reference, and their approaches to learning in order to accommodate instruction. This perspective echoes the recommendations of the NASEM report (2017) to include the presence of staff that represent the children and families served, to select curricula that is culturally relevant, and to conduct outreach to families to form strong mutually respectful partnerships.

The concept of linguistically responsive teaching overlaps with culturally responsive teaching, but it specifically targets teaching strategies that have been shown to promote optimal language learning in DLLs. Lucas, Villegas, and Freedson-Gonzalez (2008) described three areas where educators need to develop their skills and strategies. Although developed for the K–12 educator, the outlined skills and strategies can be adapted to learning settings for young children. These skills and strategies include the following: 1) knowledge of the language and educational backgrounds of children, 2) understanding the program's expectations for first and second language development, and 3) the instructional skills needed to scaffold learning to engage DLLs in the learning environment.

Assessment of Young Dual-Language Learners

Knowledge of linguistically appropriate assessment practices is particularly crucial for DLLs. The valid and comprehensive assessment of young DLLs' development and achievement is essential and often challenging for CEPs

(Espinosa & Garcia, 2012). Individualized instruction enhances young children's learning opportunities and promotes the important developmental and achievement outcomes necessary for school success. Individualized instruction, however, requires comprehensive, ongoing assessments that are fair, valid, and linguistically, culturally, and developmentally appropriate. Such assessments show educators how children are progressing and what adaptations need to be made for individual children.

For DLLs, the language in which an assessment is given may have serious implications for how capable they are judged to be by CEPs and for the educational services they receive. Because DLLs acquire their knowledge of the world around them in and through two languages, their knowledge and skills will be distributed across both of their languages. Therefore, to have an accurate picture of what young DLLs know and do not know, it is necessary to assess them in each of their languages. A DLL child may know some words and concepts in one language and other words in the second language. Depending on the child's experiences and learning opportunities, he or she may not perform as well as monolingual speakers of each language in all domains. This pattern is a typical and, most often, temporary phase of emergent bilingualism (Paradis, Genesee, & Crago, 2011). A child who demonstrates difficulties in both languages, however, should be referred for further evaluation to determine whether he or she needs additional services.

An appropriate approach to the assessment of DLLs should consist of both formal and informal methods to determine a child's trajectory in both their first and second languages (Espinosa & Magruder, 2015). Initial assessment should include a formal family interview or questionnaire about the languages spoken in the home and by which family members. Other formal child assessments, such as a measure of language proficiency like the preLAS (Duncan & De Avila, 1985), can be administered to individual children to more specifically inform CEPs about a child's receptive and expressive language abilities. In addition to formal assessment, ongoing informal observational assessment that is both structured or unstructured provides CEPs with a means to monitor a child's progress and plan appropriate learning activities. Knowledge of a DLL's language exposure and language proficiency will help CEPs to understand how much a child may or may not know in their first and second language and plan targeted educational interactions.

Family Engagement

Another area that is of salience for DLLs is family engagement. Because families are the primary informants of a child's development and because many early educators do not share the same racial and/or cultural heritage of the children they serve, it is important for CEPs to initiate and maintain a dialogue with parents and other family members about the child's early learning experiences; the family's expectations, values, and language preferences; and areas where they can collaborate, such as classroom volunteers. Educators who acknowledge that families possess "funds of knowledge" reflective of their own culturally derived skills and competencies (Moll, Amanti, Neff, & Gonzalez, 1992) and who utilize that knowledge in their practice can help reduce incongruity for the young child. Opening the lines of communication between CEPs and families will benefit both through mutual understanding of their goals and objectives for the child's development.

In summary, personnel serving young DLLs need a strong knowledge base in a number of areas specific to this population of children. These areas include knowledge about first and second language development, an understanding of relationship between language and culture as reflected in culturally and linguistically responsive teaching strategies, knowledge about appropriate assessment, and the important role of the family in shaping language learning.

CARE AND EDUCATION PRACTITIONER COMPETENCIES AND BEST PRACTICES FOR DUAL-LANGUAGE LEARNERS

In addition to having knowledge about factors that influence the development of young DLLs, CEPs need to implement strategies and practices that promote positive child outcomes for DLLs consistently across ECE settings. One of the core challenges in addressing the educational needs of DLLs is to recognize they are learning content or conceptual knowledge at the same time that they are also learning the language in which that content or concept is expressed. Thus, instructional approaches that focus on monolingual English speakers need adaptations and additional enhancements (Castro, Espinosa, & Páez, 2011) to build on what the child already knows in their first language while also adding English.

This section briefly describes crucial instructional strategies for developing optimal early learning environments for young DLLs. It should be noted that particular educational approaches will differ based on a program's specific language model and its goals and objectives for first and second language development, as well as on children's ages (e.g., infants and toddlers versus preschool-age children). Regardless of the goals and objectives for language development, it is critical that teachers possess a positive disposition toward DLLs that recognizes their potential and creates a positive learning climate that capitalizes on their unique strengths and language needs (Castro et al., 2011). The following instructional strategies and enhancements have been shown to be effective in promoting important academic outcomes for DLLs.

Instructional Supports

Although effective pedagogical practice is beneficial for all children, DLLs will require additional instructional supports, including the use of the child's home language to promote the best educational outcomes. The report from NASEM (2017) outlined a number of instructional strategies and enhancements that have been linked to improved achievement of DLLs in early education settings.

Use of the Home Language   Because the use of the home language while the child acquires English is associated with higher rates of English proficiency (Méndez, Crais, Castro, & Kainz, 2015), CEPs who intentionally use the home language across content areas will assist DLLs in the development of their conceptual knowledge. In addition, if DLLs are given opportunities to develop listening, speaking, writing, and reading skills in both their languages, over time they will demonstrate higher levels of academic achievement in elementary school (Valentino & Reardon, 2015). There are several language models that an ECE program can adopt, ranging from full two-way immersion programs to primarily English-language instruction with systematic support for the home language. It is beyond the scope of this chapter to discuss in detail all possible language models for ECE settings, but the underlying principle is that DLLs need explicit bridges from what they know in their first language to conceptual content in the second language (English) to increase DLLs' comprehension of important subject matter. Ideally, the same instructional content is offered in the home language to promote early balanced bilingualism; at the very least, specific classroom strategies (described in the following sections) should be employed to address the child's need for a strong first language as the foundation for acquiring English.

Explicit Vocabulary Instruction   Providing DLLs with the definitions of specific vocabulary words in both their home language and English and exposing them to print in a variety of contexts (e.g., storybook reading, daily schedules, labels on objects) will assist in comprehension and oral language skills. Repetition of vocabulary across different activities will assist in expanding their understanding of word meaning.

Intentional Oral Language Development   Because strong oral language skills are associated with such future literacy capabilities as narrative and discourse production and reading comprehension (Shanahan & Lonigan, 2010), young children need ample opportunities in listening and speaking. For DLLs, the need to practice listening and speaking is greater because they must process verbal information using two different sound systems and grammatical patterns. According to NASEM (2017), oral language development includes a focus on phonological awareness, vocabulary development, listening comprehension skills, speaking and narrative skills, and is enhanced by frequent interactions with speakers who are proficient in the second language and adults who provide corrective feedback during verbal interactions. For example, if a child responds with a one-word response in the home language to a question posed in English, the teacher acknowledges the response as an attempt to communicate and provides the answer in English.

Explicit Bridging Between the Home Language and English   The provision of pictures, visuals cues that convey meaning, and physical gestures linked to particular meanings will help children comprehend and retain academic content. Although these approaches are good practice for all young children, they are especially needed for children who do not understand English and cannot be expected to rely solely on oral language input.

Opportunities to Participate in Small Groups   DLLs, just like all young children, need individual attention. However, because DLLs are learning a new language, they benefit from additional practice time to reinforce both comprehension and production of language. During small-group time, more hands-on and interactive activities that allow DLLs to converse with their others will assist in promoting comprehension and language production.

Opportunities to Interact With Peers   Research has demonstrated the important role that peers play in language development for DLLs (Sawyer et al., 2018). It is during informal peer interaction that DLLs have more opportunities to practice their budding language skills without feeling adult pressure. Structuring early learning environments that promote informal peer interaction provides additional learning time.

Incorporate Elements of the Children's Home Cultures   Evidence suggests that creating a supportive environment reflective of a child's language and culture will help to engage the child and support a positive learning climate. Displaying pictures and artifacts representing children's home languages and cultures provides a welcoming and familiar atmosphere.

OPPORTUNITIES AND CHALLENGES IN THE PREPARATION AND TRAINING OF CARE AND EDUCATION PRACTITIONERS

Although there is an increasing focus on the developmental needs of young DLLs that includes a strengths-based approach, including support for the home language and culture, professional preparation of early educators remains a challenge. Recent evidence points to the conclusion that CEPs are not well prepared through their preservice education or their in-service professional development opportunities to meet the needs of DLLs. The literature described in this chapter provides guidance on what CEPs should know and what specific competencies they should possess in order to effectively promote the development and learning of DLLs. Currently, the ECE field is disadvantaged in providing high-quality professional preparation and training to CEPs by the following factors: 1) the lack of or limited experience of higher education faculty with respect to issues of diversity, including appropriate practice for DLLs (Freedson, Figueras-Daniel, Frede, Jung,

& Sideris, 2011); 2) the low numbers of qualified CEPs who are bilingual and bicultural (NASEM, 2017); 3) the need for professional development trainers with expertise about DLL development and instructional practice; 4) the low priority given to the topic of DLLs within early childhood professional development; and 5) the scarcity of assessment measures that are culturally and linguistically appropriate.

Higher Education Faculty

The issue of who comprises the teacher educator workforce and how qualified they are to prepare prospective CEPs to understand and address the pedagogical needs of DLLs is a long-standing concern of experts in the field (Freedson, 2010). There is a pressing need to develop a cadre of teacher educators that have the knowledge, skills, and dispositions to not only work effectively with nontraditional adult learners (who are often from underrepresented linguistic and cultural groups) but also have knowledge and experience with young DLLs.

In their analysis of 226 colleges and universities offering bachelor's degrees in early childhood education, Ray, Bowman, and Robbins (2006) found that programs indicate an interest in the needs of children of color and second-language learners, but very few hours of coursework are actually offered (8.37 total semester hours across the 11 diversity categories studied). These authors concluded that early childhood teacher preparation programs may say that they promote the importance of meeting the needs of children of color and second-language learners; however, in reality, they deliver little content or practical experiences to prospective teachers of DLLs. Recommendations stemming from this study are that teacher preparation programs should require that all prospective ECE teachers receive education and training in how bilingualism develops, provide fieldwork experiences with child populations that include children from minority and linguistically diverse backgrounds, and develop metrics to assess how well teachers implement best practices with children of color and second-language learners.

In her review of how institutions of higher education can increase their capacity to educate teachers working with dual-language learners, Freedson (2010) noted the urgency to diversify the faculty. The National Prekindergarten Center's survey of early childhood teacher preparation in 2- and 4-year institutions of higher education found that 8 of 10 faculty were non-Hispanic White (Maxwell, Lim, & Early, 2006). One possible consequence of the lack of diversity in higher education faculty is a failure to meet the needs of prospective or current teachers seeking degrees who themselves are members of ethnic and language minorities. It should be no surprise that a positive correlation has been found between the presence of diverse faculty in a teacher preparation program and coursework related to cultural diversity or second-language development (Lim, Maxwell, Able-Boone, & Zimmer, 2009).

The Bilingual and Bicultural Workforce

As the child population has become more diverse, there is a growing concern in the field about the lack of diversity found in the educator workforce. For the birth-to-5 workforce, the Department of Labor projected a 14% increased need for child care educators and a 17% increase in preschool teachers from 2012 to 2022 (Whitebook et al., 2014). In a comprehensive study of the condition of diversity in the nation's education workforce (Albert Shanker Institute, 2015), it was found that minority teachers are more motivated to work with minority children in high-poverty communities and tend to demonstrate higher expectations for their students. This analysis goes on to say that minority children benefit from having positive role models reflective of their own backgrounds, which, in turn, helps to reduce stereotypes. For the birth-to-5 workforce, profiles of the ethnic and racial characteristics, including immigrant status, suggest that educators of color tend to inhabit the lower rungs of the field's occupational ladder with paid and unpaid home-based educators at the bottom. In general, there is an urgency to strengthen the infrastructure supporting the educator pipeline. However, with the nationwide increase of DLLs, there needs to be a targeted focus on workforce development to serve this group of children.

Early Childhood Professional Development
Providers' Competence to Address the Needs of DLLs

There is a growing movement in the field to identify and describe the competencies of early childhood professionals who deliver professional development (see Chapter 8). This concern has been translated into a number of efforts by individual states. For example, New York has developed an early learning trainer credential and Georgia has outlined expected competencies for professional development providers. Generally, these competencies focus on aspects of professionalism, facilitation skills, the design of training and assessment, and evaluation of training. However, the content of professional development relies on the professional standards adopted by a particular state or licensing entity (National Association for the Education of Young Children [NAEYC], 2016). Thus, unless a state's early learning standards or a licensing entity's requirements explicitly describe standards for serving young DLLs, it may be less likely that professional development about second-language learning is addressed. The extent to which individual states focus on the needs of DLLs varies widely, as reported by Espinosa and Calderon (2015). In their analysis of a subset of states (21 states plus Washington, DC), they found that many states describe some early learning expectations for DLLs and provide some guidance, but only one state had a full comprehensive set of standards that addressed the unique needs of DLLs.

Because the field is shifting away from limited one-time workshop presentations to approaches that focus on pedagogical practice through positive modeling of adult–child interaction with opportunities for observation, feedback, and reflection (Zaslow, Tout, Halle, Whittaker, & Lavelle, 2010), we are seeing new approaches to professional development that include classroom coaching, mentoring, and communities of practices. Often, the topics of coaching and mentoring are based on the results of observation tools used to measure quality in the early learning setting. Yet, the majority of these measures were developed for settings where only English is spoken and are general snapshots of environmental quality and teacher interaction that do not target DLLs specifically; thus, they may overlook or miss the needs of DLLs. Frequently, the scores from classroom quality measures that were not developed with DLLs in mind are used to identify the topics for professional development. Because few of these measures capture the amount of support and instructional enhancements that are important for DLLs, these topics are rarely covered in general ECE professional development.

DLL-focused quality rating tools, such as the Early Language and Literacy Classroom Observation for DLLs (Castro, 2005) and the Classroom Assessment of Support for Emergent Bilingual Acquisition (Freedson et al., 2011) focus specifically on pedagogical practices relevant to DLLs. However, few ECE programs consistently administer these DLL-specific measures of classroom quality unless they are conducting focused studies or evaluating dual-language programs.

Although research on the efficacy of coaching in improving instructional practices holds promise, its use with teachers serving DLLs needs further study. There are myriad questions that arise regarding the qualifications of coaches who work in dual-language classrooms that need to be explored as we continue to implement this form of professional development. Specifically, what are the qualifications of coaches who assist teachers in understanding DLLs? What types of experiences should coaches have working in environments populated by DLLs? What are coaches' attitudes and beliefs regarding bilingualism, and are those compatible with the teachers they assist? When coaching is done online, what do the coaches know about the neighborhoods in which teachers work?

PROMISING SIGNS OF SYSTEM CHANGES THAT RECOGNIZE CULTURAL AND LINGUISITIC DIVERISTY

The importance of a child's language and culture is now integrated into a number of policy documents promoting the importance of understanding the development of diverse children and identifying appropriate teaching practices. Through their Quality Benchmarks for Cultural Competence initiative, NAEYC (2010) developed a self-assessment tool to review the presence of culturally competent practices. The Office of Head Start (2009) updated their multicultural principles, originally published in 1991, to stress the role of culture within the teaching-learning context and the importance of supporting a child's primary language while they learn English. More recently, Zero to Three developed a set of cross-sector competencies for professionals working with children from birth to age 5 years. Among the eight major domains, one was dedicated to cultural and linguistic responsiveness (Zero to Three, 2017).

Other important signs focused specifically on DLLs include the position statement of the NAEYC (1995) on best practices for children whose home language is not English and the most recent performance standards from the Office of Head Start (2017), which recommend specific approaches for caring and educating DLLs. In January 2017, the U.S. government reissued guidance outlining high-quality and appropriate supports in programs in programs serving DLLs (U.S. Department of Health and Human Services & U.S. Department of Education, 2017). This guidance underscores the importance of respecting diversity and the importance of communities in reflecting cultural context, as well as provides support for safeguarding the home language and children's cultural identities as they learn English.

CONCLUSIONS

As described in this chapter, improved knowledge and pedagogical practices for CEPs serving DLLs is a matter of urgency for a large and growing proportion of our children and families. There is no dispute that the implementation and delivery of effective education and social services to young DLL children rests in the hands of the practitioners who educate and care for them. Furthermore, there is no dispute that DLLs are disadvantaged when they do not receive the educational enhancements essential to their learning and development. Connecting these two propositions leads to the obvious conclusion that there is a critical need to improve the capacity of the CEP workforce to achieve positive outcomes for DLLs. As our knowledge base continues to expand about DLLs, we must be vigilant in linking what we know about their development and the practices critical to their success to the competencies of CEP. How well we are able to ensure that CEPs are qualified to meet the needs of DLLs has real-life consequences for many young children and their families.

We have proposed that all CEPs should have a perspective toward the education of DLLs that recognizes their strengths and potentials for cognitive, linguistic, and social advantages, not one that views DLLs' development as "deficient" because of their limited English skills or one that is based on their expectations for monolingual English-only children. We have reviewed literature that shows the importance of partnering with parents to better understand the child—and the child's early learning opportunities—as well as family values, cultures, and norms. An expanded knowledge base for CEPs that includes knowledge of the process and consequences of early bilingualism, appropriate assessment methods and instruments, and specific teaching competencies has been presented. The challenges to including this expanded perspective and DLL-specific knowledge into the complex system of ECE preservice and professional development, although significant, must be addressed through diversification of higher education faculty and a focus on ECE workforce development, which integrates the knowledge and competencies outlined in this chapter.

REFERENCES

Albert Shanker Institute. (2015). *The state of teacher diversity in American education*. Washington, DC: Author. Retrieved from https://assets.documentcloud.org/documents/2426481/the-state-of-teacher-diversity.pdf

Bedore, L. M., Pena, L. D., Garcia, M., & Cortez, C. (2005). Conceptual versus monolingual scoring: When does it make a difference? *Language, Speech and Hearing Services in Schools, 36*, 188–200.

Bialystok, E. (2017). The bilingual adaptation: How minds accommodate experience. *Psychological Bulletin, 143*(3), 233–262.

Bilingual Education Act of 1968, PL 90–247, 81 Stat. 816.

Castro, D. C. (2005). *Early language and literacy classroom observation: Dual language learners* (ELLCO-DLL).

Castro, D. C., Espinosa, L., & Páez, M. (2011). Defining and measuring quality early childhood practices that promote dual language learners' development and learning. In M. Zaslow, I. Martinez-Beck, K. Tout, T. Halle, & H. P. Ginsburg (Eds.), *Quality measurement in early childhood settings* (pp. 257–280). Baltimore, MD: Paul H. Brookes Publishing Co.

Castro, D. C., García, E. E., & Markos, A. M. (2013). *Dual language learners: Research informing policy*. Chapel Hill, NC: Frank Porter Graham Child Development Institute.

Center for Early Care and Education Research—Dual Language Learners. (2011). *Research brief #5: Early care and education quality measures: A critical review of the research related to dual language learners*. Chapel Hill, NC: Frank Porter Graham Child Development Institute.

Chao, R. K. (1994). Beyond parental control and authoritarian parenting style: Understanding Chinese parenting through the cultural notion of training. *Child Development, 65*(4), 1111–1119.

Conboy, B. (2013). *Neuroscience research: How experience with one or multiple languages affects the developing brain*. In Governor's State Advisory Council on Early Learning and Care Sacramento (Ed.), *California's best practices for young dual language learners research overview papers* (pp. 1–50). Sacramento, CA: California Department of Education.

De Houwer, A. (2007). Parental language input patterns and children's bilingual use. *Applied Psycholinguistics, 28*(3), 411–424.

Ellis, R. (2008). Investigating grammatical difficulty in second language learning: Implications for second language acquisition research and language testing. *International Journal of Applied Psycholinguistics, 18*(1), 4–22.

Espinosa, L. (2010). Assessment of young English language learners. In E. E. Garcia & E. C. Frede (Eds.), *Young English language learners: Current research and emerging directions for practice and policy* (pp. 119–142). New York, NY: Teachers College Press.

Espinosa, L. (2013). *Early education for dual language learners: Promoting school readiness and early school success*. Washington, DC: Migration Policy Institute.

Espinosa, L., & Calderon, M. (2015). *State early learning and development standards, policies and related practices: How responsive are they to the needs of young dual language learners?* Report for BUILD Initiative. Retrieved from http://www.buildinitiative.org/Portals/0/Uploads/Documents/State%20Early%20Learning%20and%20Development%20Standards,%20Policies%20and%20Related%20Practices%20.pdf

Farver, J. M., Lonigan, C. J., & Eppe, S. (2009). Effective early literacy skill development for young Spanish-speaking English language learners: An experimental study of two methods. *Child Development, 80*, 703–719.

First Five California. (2017). *What constitutes high quality early learning experiences for California's young Dual Language Learners: Working Paper*. Retrieved from http://www.ccfc.ca.gov/partners/gsync/pdf/Dual%20Language%20Learner/Dual%20Language%20Learner%20Pilot%20Working%20Paper.pdf

Freedson, M. (2010). Educating preschool teachers to support English language learners. In E. E. Garcia & E. C. Frede (Eds.), *Young English language learners: Current research and emerging directions for policy and practice* (pp. 165–183). New York, NY: Teachers College Press.

Freedson, M., Figueras-Daniel, A., Frede, E., Jung, K., & Sideris, J. (2011). The Classroom Assessment of Supports for Emergent Bilingual Acquisition (CASEBA): Psychometric Properties and Initial Findings from New Jersey's Abbott Preschool Program. In C. Howes & R. Pianta (Eds.), *Investigating the classroom experiences of young dual language learners*. Baltimore, MD: Paul H. Brookes Publishing Co.

Fuller, B., Bein, E., Kim, Y., & Rabe-Hesketh, S. (2015). Differing cognitive trajectories of Mexican American toddlers: The role of class, nativity, and maternal practices. *Hispanic Journal of Behavioral Sciences, 37*(2): 139–169.

Garcia, E. H., & Garcia, E. E. (2012). *Understanding the language development and early education of Hispanic children*. New York, NY: Teachers College Press.

Gay, G. (2010). *Culturally responsive teaching: Theory, research, and practice* (2nd ed.). New York, NY: Teachers College Press.

Gormley, Jr., W. T. (2008). The effects of Oklahoma's pre-K program on Hispanic children. *Social Science Quarterly, 89*(4), 916–936.

Halgunseth, L., Jia, G., & Barbarin, O. (2013). *Family engagement in early childhood programs: Serving families of young dual language learners*. Sacramento, CA: Governor's State Advisory Council on Early Learning and Care.

Institute of Medicine and National Research Council. (2015). *Transforming the workforce for children birth through age 8: A unifying foundation*. Washington, DC: National Academies Press.

Lim, C., Maxwell, K., Able-Boone, H., & Zimmer, C. (2009). Cultural and linguistic diversity in early childhood teacher preparation. *Early Childhood Research Quarterly, 24*(1), 64–76.

Lucas, T., Villegas, A. M., & Freedson-Gonzalez, M. (2008). Linguistically responsive teacher education: Preparing classroom teachers to teach English language learners. *Journal of Teacher Education, 29*(4), 361–373.

Maxwell, K. L., Lim, C.-I., & Early, D. M. (2006). *Early childhood teacher preparation programs in the United States: National report*. Chapel Hill, NC: Frank Porter Graham Child Development Institute.

Méndez, L. I., Crais, E., Castro, D., & Kainz, K. A. (2015). Culturally and linguistically responsive vocabulary approach for young Latino dual language learners. *Journal of Speech, Language and Hearing Research, 58*(1): 93–106.

Migration Policy Institute. (2015). *The impact of discrimination on the early schooling experiences of children from immigrant families*. Washington, DC: Author.

Moll, L. C., Amanti, C., Neff, D., & Gonzales, N. (1992). Funds of knowledge for teaching: Using a qualitative approach to connect homes and classrooms. *Theory Into Practice, 31*(2), 132–141.

National Academies of Sciences, Engineering, and Medicine. (2017). *Promoting the educational success of children and youth learning English: Promising futures*. Washington, DC: National Academies Press.

National Association for the Education of Young Children. (1995). *Position statement. Responding to linguistic and cultural diversity: Recommendations for effective early childhood education*. Retrieved from https://www.naeyc.org/sites/default/files/globally-shared/downloads/PDFs/resources/position-statements/PSDIV98.PDF

National Association for the Education of Young Children. (2009). *Where we stand on responding to linguistic and cultural diversity*. Retrieved from https://www.naeyc.org/sites/default/files/globally-shared/downloads/PDFs/resources/position-statements/diversity.pdf

National Association for the Education of Young Children. (2010). *Pathways to cultural competence guide*. Washington, DC: Author.

National Association for the Education of Young Children & National Association of Early Childhood Specialists in State Departments of Education. (2002). *Early learning standards: Creating the conditions for success* (Joint position statement). Retrieved from https://www.naeyc.org/sites/default/files/globally-shared/downloads/PDFs/resources/position-statements/position_statement.pdf

Office of Head Start. (2008). *Revisiting and updating the multicultural principles for Head Start programs serving children ages birth to five*. Retrieved from https://eclkc.ohs.acf.hhs.gov/sites/default/files/pdf/principles-01-10-revisiting-multicultural-principles-hs-english_0.pdf

Office of Head Start. (2015). *Head Start early learning outcomes framework: Birth to five*. Retrieved from https://eclkc.ohs.acf.hhs.gov/school-readiness/article/head-start-early-learning-outcomes-framework

Office of Head Start. (2017). *Home language support.* Retrieved from https://eclkc.ohs.acf.hhs
.gov/culture-language/article/home-language-support

Olsen, L. (2010). *Reparable harm: Fulfilling the unkept promise of educational opportunity for California's long term English learners.* Long Beach, CA: Californians Together.

Paradis, J., Genesee, F., & Crago, M. (2011). *Dual language development & disorders: A handbook on bilingualism & second language learning* (2nd ed.). Baltimore, MD: Paul H. Brookes Publishing Co.

Ramirez, N. F., & Kuhl, P. (2017). The science of bilingualism. *Young Children, 72,* 38–44.

Ray, A., Bowman, B., & Robbins, J. (2006). *Preparing early childhood teachers to successfully educate all children: The contributions of four-year undergraduate teacher preparation programs.* Chicago, IL: Erikson Institute.

Sandhofer, C., & Uchikoshi, Y. (2013). *Cognitive consequences of dual language learning: Cognitive function, language and literacy, science and mathematics and socioemotional development.* Retrieved from https://www.cde.ca.gov/sp/cd/ce/documents/dllresearchpapers.pdf

Sawyer, B., Atkins-Burnett, S., Sandilos, L., Hammer, C.S., Lopez, L., & Blair, C. (2018). Variations in classroom environments of preschool children who are low income and linguistically diverse. *Early Education and Development, 29*(3), 398–416.

U.S. Department of Health and Human Services & U.S. Department of Education (2017). *Policy statement on supporting children who are dual language learners in early childhood programs.* Retrieved from https://www.acf.hhs.gov/sites/default/files/ecd/dll_policy_statement_final.pdf

Valentino, R. A., & Reardon, S. F. (2015). Effectiveness of four instructional programs designed to service English learners: Variation by ethnicity and initial English proficiency. *Educational Evaluation and Policy Analysis, 37*(4), 612–637.

Whitebook, M., Phillips, D., & Howes, C. (2014). *Worthy work, STILL unlivable wages: The early childhood workforce 25 years after the National Child Care Staffing Study.* Retrieved from http://cscce.berkeley.edu/files/2014/ReportFINAL.pdf

Yazejian, N., Bryant, D., Freel, K., & Burchinal, M. (2015). High-quality early education: Age of entry and time in care differences in student outcomes for English-only and dual language learners. *Early Childhood Research Quarterly, 32,* 23–39.

Zero to Three. (2017). *Cross-sector core competencies for the prenatal to age five field.* Retrieved from https://www.zerotothree.org/resources/2059-cross-sector-core-competencies-for-the-prenatal-to-age-five-field#downloads

5

Programs, Practices, and Policies Affecting Diverse Children and Families

Barbara Bowman

Fifty years of research has shown that early childhood programs can reduce some of the academic and social disadvantages of poverty and racism (see Chapters 3 and 7). Evaluations of model programs have shown the potential effectiveness of early educational interventions to improve children's educational and social outcomes (Duncan et al., 2007). However, just because early childhood programs can be effective does not mean that effectiveness is guaranteed (Phillips et al., 2017). Although many studies show benefits from early childhood programs, conflicting research indicates less successful outcomes as well (Farran & Lipsey, 2015; Phillips et al., 2017). This inconsistency reinforces the importance of this volume's look at programs, policies, and practices to bring into focus the characteristics of those programs that are most likely to be effective.

Who are the diverse children and families to which this chapter calls special attention? For the purpose of this chapter, I use the term *minorities* because these individuals historically lacked numbers and power in the United States. However, the demographics are rapidly changing; low-income and black and brown people are a growing proportion of the American population. They are African Americans, Native Americans, Latinos, and immigrants of color, and their families are stressed by both poverty and racism, placing their children at risk for healthy development and academic achievement (American Psychological Association, Presidential Task Force on Educational Disparities, 2012). Compared to the general population, diverse families are more likely to experience employment, housing, education, and health inequities, thus combining biological and social/economic hazards (Cuddy, Venator, & Reeves, 2015). The everyday stresses on these families are enormous, challenging their child rearing and compromising their children's development and learning. The most pernicious assumption, however, is that their misfortunes are all their own fault and that their behavior reflects ignorance or perversity rather than the strength of the forces that challenge them.

School failure is a serious and long-term disadvantage for these children. Because education is an increasingly important aspect of American life, failure not only limits career and work opportunities, but also health and family functioning. Because education plays a critical role in both individual and community advancement, there is an economic and social cost to not addressing school achievement. Early childhood programs are of special interest because of their potential to alleviate some of the educational disadvantages for children.

Interest in preschool as a strategic intervention reflects two major bodies of research. One is work on the flexible nature of intelligence (Hunt, 1961). Understanding the important role of experience in children's development has made early intervention a realistic option (Bruner, 1960; Piaget, 1955). This perspective was solidified as neural scientists showed the malleability of the brain and its vulnerability to experience (Shonkoff & Phillips, 2000). Instead of accepting differences as genetic or "waiting until the child is ready," educators could change achievement through how they structured children's early experiences.

A second research theme provoking interest in early education was the evidence of long-term benefits of preschool. Although an early evaluation of Head Start (Besharov, Germanis, Higney, & Call, 2011) showed few achievements lasting beyond the program year, later studies of High Scope, Chicago Child Parent Centers, and Abecedarian showed meaningful long-term effects (see Chapter 7). These programs showed that the trajectory of low-income children's lives could be altered by their preschool experiences.

This chapter focuses on how government-sponsored programs and policies have adapted this research to the educational needs of low-income, minority children. It discusses how programs that target these children measure up to the challenges they face, with a focus on Head Start, the Child Care and Development Block Grant (CCDBG), state-funded preschool, and special education and what they are doing to reduce educational disadvantages. These programs are as diverse as the children who attend them. They are lodged in a variety of organizations: nongovernmental and philanthropic organizations; national, state, and city governments and public schools; and religious organizations and businesses—resulting in little standardization. Nevertheless, the pattern of program challenges and responses is worthy of attention.

DEVELOPMENT AND LEARNING

Differences in the educational achievement of low-income, minority children begin early. Acquisition of school skills and knowledge depend on experiences that occur long before formal schooling. At conception, experience starts shaping children's genetic potential and lays an increasingly complex foundation for learning. To understand the interplay between development, learning, and school achievement, it is useful to make a distinction between two overlapping dimensions of development: biogenetic and social-cultural learning. The human genetic blueprint supports biogenetic learning, which includes social attachment, acquiring language, recognizing patterns, representing ideas with symbols, and much more. This kind of learning is achievable at some level in all typically developing children. The other dimension of learning, social-cultural, reflects how different communities display and support the expression of biogenetic characteristics. It includes everything from blowing kisses and knowing how to celebrate birthdays to the names for different numbers and literacy conventions. Both types of learning are essential. Readers, for example, must learn to talk, focus their eyes, use symbols, and recognize patterns. However, they also need to learn specific information and skills, such as the vocabulary and sentence structures of a particular language and the names, shapes, and sounds of letters or characters in that language.

Most low-income and racially diverse children achieve the biogenetic developmental benchmarks at approximately the same age as other children. They attach to others; they walk, make categories, learn language, and play, as do other children. However, what they learn may look quite different from what schools expect. For example, children do not just acquire language; they acquire a particular language or dialect. This may not be the language of school. They may not know the vocabulary, sentence structure, and pronunciation of the school language or use language in expected ways. Despite having reached the appropriate benchmark of language acquisition, they are disadvantaged in school because they lack the necessary social knowledge.

The two dimensions of learning go hand in hand. When children fail to read, for example, one must ask whether the problem is with their genetic or biological development. Can the child see? Does he or she have language? Does the child understand symbols? Does he or she recognize patterns? Or, does the child lack specific information? Is his or her vocabulary sufficiently varied? Has the child been taught the names of letters and their sounds? Has he or she heard stories or poems? Does the child understand the difference between the oral and literary uses of language?

CULTURAL DIFFERENCES AND SCHOOL ACHIEVEMENT

The greater the differences between a child's home environment and the expectations of schools, the more difficult it is for him or her to achieve. Children who are not from middle-class, White communities are disadvantaged in school. For example, low-income children hear fewer words growing up than do more economically advantaged children; therefore, they have smaller vocabularies than middle-class children (Hart & Risley, 1995). Similarly, African American children's language may use different grammatical rules than standard English, but we have no reason to believe that this dialect is inherently better or worse than standard English. Nevertheless, children who speak Black English tend to have smaller vocabularies and have a steeper learning curve in school than do children who have larger vocabularies and who speak the standard form of English. Furthermore, the disadvantage increases as the discrepancy between what a child knows and what the child needs to know grows. Children with small vocabularies are likely to have difficulty mastering more complex reading text; children who speak a different dialect are likely to have trouble writing in standard English—not because they have a biogenetic disability or delay, but because of limited social knowledge. However, because development depends on both types of learning, what starts out as a social/cultural difference may soon become the basis for school failure.

Often, low-income, minority children are lacking the task-specific social/cultural learning needed for school, which includes not only language and literacy but also attitudes, beliefs, social skills, and behaviors. For instance, Shade (1982) reported that young African American children were apt to make analogical responses when they were asked to tell a story—responses that connected things by their personal relationships (e.g., "I like my dog"). Conversely, White children's responses to the same request were likely to be referential or have a strong objective structure (e.g., "My pet is a dog"), which was the type of response preferred by teachers. It should not be assumed that even ubiquitous events and behaviors have similar meaning for all children. Without question, children can become bicultural and families can adapt to changes in their personal and cultural lives, but recognition of differences in cultural practices and the strengths of families from different cultural communities needs to be the starting point.

STRESS

Stress is natural for children and often functions to enhance the development of skills and knowledge. However, a number of studies have shown a correlation between excessive stress caused by abuse and neglect in childhood and adult health and social problems. Exposure to extremes of disease, violence, neglect, and inconsistent and unreliable care in early childhood can be so stressful that they compromise a child's developmental potential. Such stress, unless buffered by human and/or pharmacologic resources, can become toxic, restrict intellectual development, and cause mental and physical health problems. Parental warmth and protection are buffers for stress.

Although children in all social classes can experience high levels of stress, poverty places extra limits on the resourcefulness of families and communities to buffer the stress. Thus, low-income, minority children are often exposed to greater stress and fewer resources than are children from economically advantaged families. Unfortunately, the treatment of children subjected to highly stressful environments is both difficult and expensive and, along with children with special needs, requires special resources and sensitivities, which are often unavailable.

Given this understanding of toxic stress, how do our policies measure up? Not too well. Interventions to ameliorate stress are generally aware of the risks facing children and families; however, few have the necessary resources to intervene effectively. There is a serious shortfall between resources (culturally sensitive and trained staff, funds for referrals, and emergency services) and some families' numerous and often serious problems. Well-meaning early childhood educators cannot be expected to deal with threats to development that include violence, drug usage, hunger, poor housing, inadequate health care, and adult mental and physical disabilities. Current efforts, primarily in the form of home visiting and preschool programs, rarely have the intensity and breadth that families needing intervention require.

Fortunately, in the United States, most low-income and minority parents do a sufficient job of buffering children from the most serious effects of poverty, racism, and toxic stress. However, many government policies and programs are built on a platform of deprivation and disability that fail to appreciate the developmental competence of children and families. Too often, they assume that there is something wrong, inferior, or even pathological about why children do not have school-related skills and knowledge. In reality, what is lacking is the opportunity to learn what is required for school and an environment that encourages that learning. However simple that may seem, success in school is complex; it is enmeshed in a plethora of individual, family, community, and family issues that range from racial identity to classroom behavior.

Also serious is the tendency to treat the problems of low-income and minority families as solely personal, rather than systemic. In doing so, we transfer responsibility from the health and welfare systems and institutions that contribute to family stresses to the individuals who succumb to them. Without alleviating the poverty and racism that contribute to family problems, programs are unlikely to be outstandingly successful in treating them and are likely to have a continuous supply of candidates for intervention.

THE ACHIEVEMENT GAP

The gap in formal knowledge between groups is well documented. By fourth grade, 82% of African Americans, 79% of Hispanics, and 78% of Native Americans scored below proficient, as compared with 47% of Asians and 54% of non-Hispanic Whites (Annie E. Casey Foundation, 2016). In 2011, Asian students had the highest reading and math scores, followed by Whites, Latinos, African Americans, and Native Americans (U.S. Department of Education, 2015). These differences can have serious consequences. The education achievement gap between African American, Latino, and

Native American children and White children results in lower earnings, poor health, and higher rates of incarceration for individuals and "imposes the economic equivalent of a permanent recession on the nation" (Auguste, Hancock, & Laboissiere, 2009, Exhibit 2).

While the achievement gap does have tragic consequences for some children, the meaning of the "gap" is less clear. All ethnic groups scored lower than Asian children on tests of formal knowledge; nevertheless, the gap between White children and Asian children is not generally considered to be a handicap for White children. Further, despite the academic superiority of Asian children, they generally do not garner the same economic and social advantages as White children. These findings suggest that the "gap" is not merely a difference in formal knowledge between groups; rather, it is interpreted as a mark of inferiority for some but not others.

POVERTY

The correlation between poverty and school achievement is well established. Reading and math knowledge is lowest for kindergartners in households with incomes below the federal poverty level (U.S. Department of Education, 2015). There are a number of theories to explain the education gap between children from low-income families and others as researchers focus on deficits in culture and resources to explain the poverty–education connection. These explanations include the following: 1) the culture of low-income families is different and does not support academic achievement; 2) low-income families are more dysfunctional and do not provide adequate physical care and social guidance for their children; 3) the unequal distribution of resources, such as wages and health care, exacerbates family stress and negatively affects school performance; 4) the informal curriculum that middle-class parents provide, such as a more extensive vocabulary, enriches their children's experience; 5) the strengths of low-income, minority children and families are ignored or considered valueless. Underlying all of these explanations is the failure to recognize and appreciate the strengths of low-income, minority children and families.

How have government-sponsored early childhood programs responded to the nexus between poverty and school achievement? Government-funded preschool interventions have an uneven record. Head Start, as a signature program of the War on Poverty, made addressing poverty one of its primary goals. Head Start was unique in giving equal attention to the economic development of adults and to children's development. It sought to empower low-income communities and, at the same time, bring health and education resources to children and families. The children's program was as focused on health and nutrition as it was on education; it also often served as an employment program for parents and community members. Furthermore, it promoted adult education, with classes in everything from voter education, consumer education, General Educational Development, and writing a resume for a job application. Head Start, by focusing on poverty, highlighted its intersect in the lives of adult and children.

Soon, however, Head Start moved away from economic development to concentrate on the development and education of individual children. Parent involvement revolved around supportive parenting and paid less attention to the economic well-being of families. It is open to question whether the two-generation, economic-focused policy would have worked better than one based primarily on children's achievement.

The separation of Head Start from anti-poverty efforts did lead to gradual improvements in the administration of programs and, eventually, to efforts to improve their educational quality. Head Start began working systematically to provide guidance on literacy, evaluation, and teacher education and training. However, one might argue that by putting the stress on individuals instead of economic issues, intervention policies and programs pathologized children and families and did little to ameliorate poverty. Too often, low-income children and families are viewed as having deficits that need to be fixed as opposed to being victims of unequal systems that created the problem. Consequently, Head Start has served generations of children from the same family.

By the 1990s, the underachievement of low-income children was (as it still is) viewed by many as a national crisis, with effects that include high rates of crime and incarceration, unemployment and underemployment, premature parenting, and other social ills. Early childhood programs have increasingly been accepted as a viable strategy to help derail these outcomes. The research on early learning has led to the belief that early childhood programs work like an inoculation, warding off poverty's effects and changing the educational trajectory of poor children. This belief has sponsored an increase in government funding, but until recently little attention was paid to the qualities that might make programs more effective. Today, Head Start is leading the effort to make academic education and intentional curricula important components of early childhood programs for low-income children. It has not addressed the systemic problems caused by family poverty, thus ensuring the continuing risk of low-income children for school failure.

RACISM

Although poverty undermines formal education no matter what color or culture the child, the contextual differences that children in various communities face ameliorate or intensify its effects on children and their families. Poverty is unevenly distributed across the population and children of color are disproportionately living in poverty. In all, 70% of Black children live in poverty (Children's Defense Fund, 2017). In general, they are exposed to the deepest poverty over the longest periods of time and live in the most depressed neighborhoods with the fewest material and social resources. Multigenerational and homogenous poverty reinforced by racism casts a shadow on educational achievement and helps explain why low-income minorities also have the worst developmental and learning outcomes.

Black families are the poorest group in the United States, they are subject to the most persistent prejudices, and their children are the lowest achieving in school. Racism plays a major role in academic underachievement. Sustained racism is the pervasive belief that people of color are inferior to others (Jensen, 1969). Although government policies and programs may explicitly deny this position, few question this belief is widespread. Prejudice and discrimination underlie segregated housing, limited employment opportunities, poor education and health care, and underresourced community services. Racial bias is found in classrooms and affects teacher attention and approval, school quality, and discipline (Gershenson & Dee, 2017). For example, young children of color are disproportionately excluded from preschool and childcare programs and suspended from school programs for the same behavior as White children (Gilliam, 2014; Khalifa & Briscoe, 2015).

SEGREGATION

Despite the 1954 *Brown v. Board of Education of Topeka* decision making racially segregated schools illegal, most African American and Latino children attend such schools. Today, segregated schools are increasingly widespread due to the confluence of housing and school policies and practices. In 1991, 34% of schools reported more than 90% minority students. By 2011, that number had risen to 39%; the number of African Americans attending essentially mixed schools decreased from 35% in 1991 to 28% in 2011 (Rothstein, 2014). Social service organizations that sponsor Head Start and child care programs draw children from the low-income communities where they are located; because of residential segregation, they mirror the community. Consequently, young children who attend pre-K programs will generally attend segregated ones and will continue in schools where achievement is the lowest.

As housing patterns increasingly reflect race and economic status, early childhood programs for low-income, minority children are increasingly "ghettoized." Head Start, the largest program for low-income children, makes it administratively and economically difficult to integrate nonpoverty students into their programs. Although some of the restrictions in Head Start reflect the political need to reserve funds for only very-low-income individuals, their effect is the perpetuation of race segregation.

LANGUAGE SEGREGATION

Many preschools also segregate English-language learners (ELLs). For example, Head Start, in encouraging home language support, often groups children with the lowest English skills, thus decreasing the opportunity for them to interact with English-speaking teachers and peers. Such programs fail to take advantage of the special ability of young children to learn language and thus deprive children of early bilingual competence. This practice creates a barrier to the acquisition of school skills and knowledge for many children, particularly in school districts without high-quality K–3 bilingual programs. For example, only 14 states have written plans for working with preschool English learners; a lack of adequate monitoring and supervision makes these programs less effective than they could be (National Institute for Early Education Research, 2017). Truly bilingual programs serving both English speakers and English learners would go a long way toward evening the playing field for ELLs and providing linguistic advantages for English-speaking children, but they are in short supply.

Research shows that children who attend racially and economically segregated preschool programs are educationally disadvantaged. Reid, Kagan, Hilton, and Potter (2015) argued that quality and equity are inextricably linked, that programs segregated by race/ethnicity and income are rarely of equal quality, and that efforts to make early childhood investments sustainable must take these facts into account.

Publicly funded early childhood programs are under no legal obligation to promote racial and social class mixing. However, concentrating children whose communities are subject to the oppression of racism and the deprivations of poverty is hardly the solution to solving the achievement gap (Rothstein, 2014; Duncan et al., 2007). Without explicit direction and enhancements toward desegregation, the current drift is toward more rather than less segregation, making the search for equity even more difficult and unlikely.

GOVERNMENT-FUNDED PROGRAMS

Government-funded programs currently serving children between birth and kindergarten include state pre-K, child care, Head Start, Early Head Start, and special education. Each of these is described in the following sections.

State Pre-K

States have increased their funding for pre-K programs substantially over the past 15 years. With a short hiatus during the 2008 economic rollback, states have increasingly used state money to fund early childhood programs. State involvement in funding for pre-K has taken a number of different forms. Some states have added to the Head Start budget, which permits Head Start to serve more income-eligible children. Others have funded community-based programs to extend or improve their programs and/or have funded programs in elementary school. States have also extended programs to include children from working and middle-class families, when parents want these services for their children. Today, 43 states plus the District of Columbia and Guam provide some type of pre-K program at a cost of about $7.4 billion, an 8% increase from 2014–2015. Some states are enrolling up to 80% of eligible children, but others are enrolling only a small number. Furthermore, although state funding of pre-K is increasing in California and Texas, seven states provide no funding at all for pre-K. A few states provide preschool for all; however, in none of these states are 100% of children enrolled (National Institute for Early Education Research, 2017).

Child Care

The Child Care and Development Block Grant is the primary source of federal/state funding for child care subsidies for low-income working families. The funds are used to pay for state licensed and regulated care for children whose low-income parents are working or in school. Child care does not include a required education component, although the legislation has included unfunded quality enhancements for this purpose (Walker & Matthews, 2017). Less than 16% of eligible children receive child care subsidies through CCDBG—a percentage that steadily declined from 2010 to 2018 (Matthews, Schulman, Vogtman, Johnson-Staub, & Blank, 2016; Walker & Matthews, 2017). In 2018, this trend was reversed, but the benefits and limitations for low-income participants has yet to be assessed. Participation in CCDBG is far from equitable, with 21% of eligible Black children and only 8% of eligible Hispanic or Latino children receiving services (Matthews et al., 2016). However, of note, with intentionality and effort, Chicago has raised the participation rate of Latinos substantially (López, Grindal, Zanoni, & George, 2017). Nevertheless, many low-income and minority families have not found easy access to high-quality child care through CCDBG, with inadequate funding, large family co-payments, quick shutout policies, and family work patterns being major barriers to enrollment.

Head Start

Head Start is the flagship of government programs addressing educational disparities, yet in 2016 it enrolled fewer than half of eligible children (Matthews et al., 2016). Its funding reflects considerable state differences, with some states receiving a larger share of the Head Start budget than others. Federal funding levels and state policy also determine significant state-level differences in access to Head Start and CCDBG child care. Furthermore, participation in Head Start varies by race and ethnicity.

Early Head Start

By 3 years of age, many children have already begun to fall behind their age mates in school-related skills and knowledge. To address these concerns, Early Head Start, like Head Start, was designed as a comprehensive program by making referrals for health, nutrition, psychosocial services, and, most importantly, by providing educational services to children and families. Its agenda is accomplished through home visits and group meetings designed to educate parents about children's development. However, regardless of the potential benefits, fewer than 5% of eligible infants and toddlers are enrolled in Early Head Start (Matthews et al., 2016).

Special Education

Children with untreated disabilities are candidates for school failure, yet more children are in need of services than are currently being served in special education. Even before birth, low-income and minority children are disadvantaged. Many get off to a poor start because their mothers do not receive adequate prenatal care, they are born prematurely, or they have low birth weights. During the first 3 years, there are limited opportunities for them to participate in early intervention through Early Head Start, early intervention services, home-visiting, or other such programs. The lack of therapeutic services is also a problem for 3- to 5-year-old pre-K children in child care and others who lack transportation to a public school.

Questions frequently arise as to what extent diagnoses and treatments in special education reflect social class and ethnic bias as minority children are underidentified in some categories (learning disabilities) and overidentified in others (behavior). Given the threats to low-income and minority children, it is not surprising that there is a greater need for intervention with this population; nevertheless, as noted, bias is evident throughout the education and care systems. Children of color are excluded and suspended from early childhood programs at a higher rate for the same behavior as White children (Gilliam, 2014). Moreover, even when the system is working appropriately, parents' work schedules often cause refusal of both home and center services.

ACCESS TO SERVICES

Access to early childhood services are especially problematic for low-income, minority children (Magnuson & Waldfogel, 2005). The need is great: More than half of low-income children are not considered ready for kindergarten. Yet, funding levels still preclude attendance for all who need it. Fewer than half of eligible preschoolers attend Head Start and only 15% receive CCDBG funding (U.S. Department of Education, National Center for Education Statistics, 2017). Although Black children are more likely than White children to be enrolled in some form of center-based preschool, they attend ones of lower-quality than their White peers (Magnuson & Waldfogel, 2005).

Even when free programs are available, many low-income parents do not take advantage of the opportunity to enroll their children. Undoubtedly, some eligible families fail to take advantage of the opportunity because of the complexities in their lives. Preschool is often not a priority for families struggling with joblessness, illness and disabilities, homelessness, and the myriad of emergencies that characterize their lives. Additionally, enrollment is not easy. Head Start documentation of eligibility is a deterrent for many families, as is the copay required for CCDBG enrollment. The result is that learning opportunities depend as much (or more) on chance than on how great the need (National Institute for Early Education Research, 2017). Children who gain the most from preschool are the least likely to attend and obtain its advantages (U.S. Department of Education, 2015).

Low-income and minority children's access to high-quality education is hampered by funding inadequacies. Congress has not provided full funding for any of the programs designed to address inequalities in development and learning, and most states have not provided substantial alternative coverage. Certainly, we need to fund enough high-quality educational programs for children at risk for school failure. Equally important, however, we need to fix aspects of the system that are stacked against particular groups of children. (For a fuller discussion of children with disabilities and their families, see Section IV of this volume.)

QUALITY OF SERVICES

Research studies have shown that early education programs can be effective, but they have been less helpful in identifying the program ingredients that lead to the best outcomes. A number of structural factors (e.g., group size, teacher–child ratios, teacher training) and process variables (e.g., teacher–child relationships, child activity and engagement, teacher focus) have been identified in program effectiveness. In addition, a wide range of models has shown some educational promise (Bowman, Donovan, & Burns, 2000). However, as yet, few programs have been able to reproduce the same outcomes as the early models (Perry Preschool, Chicago Child–Parent Centers, Abecedarian Project), and many have shown considerably less effectiveness.

Child care has been particularly lacking in serious efforts to improve educational quality. Because low-income and minority children are likely to need smaller classes and more expert teachers to close the achievement gap, cost is a serious consideration. Preschoolers require a large number of adults to care for a small number of children. Because states regulate child care, the ratio of adults to children is not standardized; however, a popular model for infants requires 1 adult for every 4 infants and 1 adult for every ten 4- to 5-year-old children. Even when paying staff minimum wage, the cost of child care is out of reach for most low-income parents. In Illinois, a full-time caregiver's hourly minimum wage is $8.25 and the cost to the parent for an infant in child care is more than $12,000 (Progress Illinois, 2015). Yet, the child care worker's wage of just over $17,000 is too low to support a family and would clearly preclude them from using child care themselves. Even for the average worker who is earning $51,500 (U.S. Bureau of Labor Statistics, 2017), spending more than 20% of income on child care is not sustainable. Staffing exerts downward pressure on reimbursement for well-educated teachers and accounts for the difference in how much teachers earn in community agencies compared to public school teachers. However, benefits for children are inevitably related to workforce wages. Experimentation with different arrangements, such as adding a strong Head Start educational program to child care, might stretch funding and still achieve goals; however, such experimentation would necessitate leadership. So far, government programs have shown little interest in supporting the drive to try out new models.

TEACHER EDUCATION AND TRAINING

Teachers are key to effective early childhood education. Two areas have been identified as needing improvement. The first is preservice education. Advocates contend that substantial education and training are necessary to teach preschool children. They contend that more and specific preservice education is necessary for at least one teacher with a group of children and recommend a bachelor's degree in early education as the standard. Criticisms of this recommendation note that the research does not show clear advantages for teachers who have a 4-year college education (bachelor's level) as opposed to other types of post–high school training (Early et al., 2007). Arguments also reference the disproportionate effect that such requirements would have on many minority members of the workforce, who are less likely to reach this standard. To the extent that program effectiveness is compromised by not having "teachers who look like the children," funds to support continuing education for teachers from minority groups are essential, but not widely available.

The reasoning behind the recommendation to increase the education of teachers is that the skills and knowledge necessary to teach young children are just as extensive and complex as those needed to teach older children. The research does show that better-educated teachers display more of the characteristics that programs want to promote (e.g., more varied language, less autocratic interactions) than do less-educated teachers (Bowman et al., 2000). In addition, given the high correlation between a mother's education and her child's achievement, there is little reason to believe that more education does not have a similar value for teachers. Head Start has given credence to the argument favoring more education for teachers by requiring gradually that 50% of teachers have a bachelor's degree with an emphasis in early childhood. In most states, child care continues to have minimal educational requirements for teachers. In both Head Start and child care, current salary structures operate as an impediment to having more educated teachers. Without a change in workforce compensation, improvement of quality through the education of professionals is not likely. (See the analysis of teacher education programs in Chapter 8 for a further analysis of teacher education and professional development.)

The second recommendation for improving teacher quality is to better prepare teachers for work with diverse populations. Little attention has been given in early childhood programs to preparing teachers for diversity. Teacher knowledge is essential when there is a disconnect between a child's prior experiences and the knowledge and skills needed for school. Working with diverse families from low-income and nonmainstream communities requires more than a recipe book of activities. If they are to introduce bicultural thinking and behavior, teachers need knowledge of child development, respect for cultural differences, and the ability to apply flexibly different pedagogies. (See Chapter 10 for how teachers can take a more active role in research studies.)

CURRICULUM AND ASSESSMENT

Another controversial recommendation for addressing the achievement gap is to help children focus more intentionally on literacy and math concepts (Fuller, Bein, Bridges, Kim, & Rabe-Hesketh, 2017). The rationale for focusing on school-type skills, such as alphabetic and number knowledge, is that prior knowledge facilitates later learning; children who enter kindergarten with a beginning knowledge of literacy and mathematics are more successful in school. Duncan et al. (2007) conducted a meta-analysis of the research on school readiness; they found the "strongest predictors" of later achievement to be knowledge of math and attention skills on entering kindergarten. Another reason to promote academic skills in preschool is that many low-income children do not get the background knowledge and skills for school learning at home. Low-income parents are often overwhelmed with survival concerns, do not understand the importance of beginning these skills early, or do not have the skills themselves.

Critics have seen a conflict between the traditional free-play emphasis in early childhood curriculum and a more focused academic content. Play and activities based on young children's interests are seen as compromised by more "school"-type learning (e.g., the alphabet) and instruction (e.g., listening to directions). Some early childhood teachers believe formal curriculum and instructional strategies are nondevelopmental. They believe that children should learn primarily through indirect guidance and play. It is interesting that most of the criticism of academic content comes from middle-class teachers and parents whose children already know and use these skills regularly. Before even entering kindergarten, the average cognitive score of children in the highest SES group are 60% above the scores of the lowest SES group (Jones, 2017). Just because economically advantaged children tend to learn these skills informally, in small bits over several years spent with educated parents, does not mean that is the only way to acquire them.

Not surprisingly, the most successful intervention programs have well-thought-out curricula delivered by teachers who had the time and skills to plan implementation, could figure out how to make learning interesting and engaging, and knew when children were learning. No one curricula or teaching style is effective with all children (Bowman et al., 2000). Diversity in content and methods and a balance between teacher-directed and child-initiated activities has the most research support (Bowman et al., 2000).

To promote children's learning, assessment is essential. To know what needs to be taught and how, teachers need to know what they want children to learn and their current level of development and skills. With this information, teachers can develop lesson plans with clear objectives, which can be assessed throughout the year. This is a different pedagogy than one based on waiting for the teachable moment. Instead, it focuses on stimulating the child's interest in learning and teaching to it. Effective teachers for low-income, minority children need to not only recognize individual differences, but also understand the culture of children whose backgrounds are less synchronous with school demands. Unfortunately, there is little evidence that most teachers of low-income, minority children in any government program are able to meet this challenge. Low wages, vague standards, little planning time, and inadequate assessment combine to stress teachers and make the children's preparation for kindergarten uncertain.

Standardized tests are used to demonstrate a gap in academic achievement between groups of children. However, there is little agreement about how they should be used in planning curricula and assessing learning. They are rightly criticized for use with young children of color because they fail to accurately assess them (Kohn, 2000). However, failure to acknowledge that children are not learning in school is a serious problem. When children's performance is not tracked, poor programs and teachers go undetected. Furthermore, when assessment is delayed, it is often too late to develop an effective intervention and failure is inevitable. Standardized tests can provide useful information when used in combination with other assessment tools.

Currently, only Head Start requires standard assessment procedures for both teaching and learning. These include a classroom observation of the teacher (using a standardized form) and teachers conducting quarterly assessments of children, again using a standardized form. Child care programs generally have no requirements for assessment of teaching or learning, and public school practice varies from district to district.

Without question, new assessment instruments and strategies need to be developed. In the meantime, school personnel must be responsible for using multiple measures of teaching and learning. Most important, however, is the participation of parents and community members in assessment, which is currently only required by Head Start. This participation means that teachers, administrators, parents, and the community all need to understand the purpose of assessment (to be sure that children are learning and, if not, why) and how different measures can inform their evaluations.

COORDINATION BETWEEN PROGRAMS

One of the significant contributors to the achievement gap is the lack of alignment between preschool and kindergarten programs. It is common to hear early childhood teachers complain that children who did so well in pre-K are not doing as well in kindergarten. Some of the reason is the difference in expectations between the two systems. A chasm often exists between what children learn in preschool and what is expected in kindergarten. Traditions, competing belief systems, professional training, administrative controls, and requirements are all apt to be quite different between community settings and public schools, which adds to the disadvantage of low-income, minority children. Head Start has taken several steps in the direction of alignment in principle if not in practice; however, this action is not the case for child care, where little (if any) preparation of children for kindergarten is required. Without explicit alignment of curricula between pre-K and kindergarten, low-income, minority children will continue to arrive at kindergarten without the necessary precursor skills and knowledge.

Kindergartens in schools serving low-income families enroll preschool children whose prior experience is markedly different from children who attended a high-quality program. Only a few of those children will have attended a high-quality early childhood program. Instead of kindergarten and primary teachers moving forward with children having a common knowledge base, they often spend years catching up those children whose background is more limited.

This gap reinforces the need for better coordination between preschool programs and public schools. The achievement gap is serious enough without adding to it with different standards for pre-K and K–12. Currently, each state has its own early learning standards, which are not related to those in K–12. This disconnect between what is expected in pre-K and later schooling is very serious for children whose cultures are different from that of the school.

PARENT EDUCATION

Parent education to support children's development and learning is a frequent component of early childhood programs. Significant changes in child outcomes from such programs have often been modest at best (Halpern, 1999). Home-visiting programs in the United States show uneven evidence of effectiveness across program goals and few consistent findings for any program. More recently, parent programs, especially home visiting serving infants and toddlers, have shown outcomes that are more positive with diverse groups of parents. For example, the Nurse–Family Partnership Program serving pregnant women and infants (age 12–34 months) had high or moderate outcomes on maternal health, child health, child development and school readiness, reductions in child maltreatment, juvenile delinquency, family violence, and crime, as well as positive results in parenting practices and family economic self-sufficiency. However, a report from the U.S. Department of Health and Human Services (Sama-Miller et al., 2017) found that "model effectiveness is limited." Many models do not have high- or moderate-quality studies of their effectiveness or evidence of effectiveness of models with different types of families, particularly immigrant families with diverse cultural backgrounds (Sama-Miller et al., 2016). Although different parent program models have been successful, particularly health-related ones, both in the United States and abroad, programs have been most effective when carried out by professionals with clear objectives for a specific group of parents (Holzer, Higgins, Bromfield, & Higgins, 2006).

Inevitably, there is a cultural disconnect between parent programs promoting middle-class values and behavior and the low-income and minority parents they want to influence. For example, Holochwost et al. (2016) noted that parent behaviors supporting executive function in young African American children are different from those that are effective with White children. African American children reportedly respond less negatively to demeaning discipline from parents and report feeling more loved than White children do (Perry, Leerkes, Dunbar, & Cavanaugh, 2017). Minority parents are warned against spanking, although this disciplining technique does not seem to have the same effect on African American and Latino children as compared to White children (Slade & Wissow, 2004). Recently, in response to research on vocabulary differences, some programs advised parents to change how they talk to their children, as if language is not embedded in a complex system of identity and social relationships that are not easily changed. When cultural differences are defined as deficits, even if the goal is to bring families more into the cultural mainstream, changes are unlikely to have long-term effects.

Programs that fail to appreciate the special hazards of living in poor, segregated communities are also less likely to be successful. For example, parents are encouraged to shop sales from inexpensive chain stores when they live in the mercantile desert of inner cities or rural communities. The stress of living in poverty colors almost every aspect of child rearing and must be recognized in program expectations and support. Programs that understand the realities of families and accept the validity of home practices can offer children the opportunity to learn new things while respecting what they already know.

CONCLUSIONS

Although the research clearly shows early childhood programs can significantly reduce some of the academic and social disadvantages of poverty and race, it has certainly not shown that these programs can eradicate them. Even the most effective programs have not fully compensated for systemic deprivations. Indeed, it is unlikely that early childhood programs alone, no matter how many or how good, can fully compensate young children for the stresses of living in poverty, particularly for children of color. Unless poverty, racism, and their attendant systemic problems are addressed directly, developmental and educational disparities are likely to persist. By continuing to focus attention on individuals (children and families), programs do little to change the paradigm in which low-income children attend poor schools, among other inequalities, and get a poor education, which keeps them poorly educated, living in poverty, and with greater vulnerability to inequalities. It is a vicious circle.

Similarly, there is no evidence that preschool programs alone can fully compensate for poor K–12 schools. The effect on students enrolled in schools that systematically provide unequal educational opportunities (segregated schools, deteriorated facilities, inadequate materials, weak curricula, and inexperienced and/or prejudiced teachers) cannot be averted by high-quality preschool programs. The advantages of a preschool education cannot persist in the face of an inadequate K–12 education; nevertheless, early childhood programs at their best can make some difference in the lives of children and families by enhancing both short-term and long-term social and academic outcomes.

Over the past 50 years, the complexity of intervening in the lives of low-income, minority families has become crystal clear as simplistic answers and silver bullets have failed to achieve the desired results. How to increase the pace of change for low-income, minority children is a critical question and will require institutional as well as educational change. The following recommendations regarding policy, programs, and program innovations are designed to speed up the process.

Policy Recommendations

1. *Address the issues of race and class.* Systemic racism and classism make the goal of school equity more of a stretch and more of a priority. Racial inequality is costly and discourages achievement.

2. *Coordinate public services.* Early childhood programs need to form alliances with other community services (public housing, public health, libraries, and parks) to coordinate support for families. Programs need to form partnerships with adult training, employment, and recreational programs to extend funds and impact.

3. *Increase access to early childhood programs.* Enroll all children likely to be at risk for school difficulties into a high-quality early childhood program. Extend the child care block grant so that it supports workers with non-traditional hours and encourages job advancement. Potential new federal support for child care is salutary, but alone is not sufficient unless accompanied by quality and family support improvements.

4. *Support the early childhood workforce.* Increase resources allocated for the education of teachers (tuition benefits as well as increased wages) so that they have the skills and knowledge to do the job and make the programs effective.

5. *Address overlap in programs.* Examine the overlap and differing requirements between early childhood programs and other mandated programs: Head Start and The Patient Protection and Affordable Care Act

of 2010 (PL 111-148), Head Start and the Individuals with Disabilities Education Act of 1990 (PL 101-476) for special education, and Common Core and Early Learning Standards.

Program Recommendations

1. *Improve curricula.* Diverse children living in diverse environments will not get ready for school with the same curriculum. The dichotomy that some early educators make between social-emotional development and learning school skills is an artificial one. Both can and should happen at once.

2. *Require professional development.* Programs and practices based on mis-understandings of cultures and the stress of families living in poverty are not effective.

3. *Evaluate learning and program effectiveness.* Assess what is working and change what is not. Examine both teacher instructional quality and child outcomes.

4. *Align pre-K and K–3.* Create aligned standards for pre-K and K–3. Coordinate the preschool delivery system administered by small nonprofit agencies with public schools to facilitate funding, administration, workforce preparation, and ideology.

5. *Develop new parent involvement models.* The Parent-Teacher Association and Head Start models, which brought parents into the center or school to learn about and support children's education, are not as feasible today because most parents of young children work or go to school. One model of parent involvement will not work for all parents.

Innovation Recommendations

1. *Experiment.* Try out new models. Explore new staffing models, curricula, and alignment standards and evaluate them.

2. *Ask new economic questions.* What is the right mix of programs to invest in? Should we provide high-quality infant care to everyone or pay a parent to stay home the first year when child care is so expensive? What are the costs and benefits between funding preschool and birth-to-3 programs?

In conclusion, if we look at the early childhood policies and programs with our lens on diverse children and families, there is much to be done. Policies must focus on the systems that reinforce poverty and racism and continue to put children at risk. Programs must promote quality, as well as ensure that what they do actually changes outcomes for children. Moreover, practitioners must recognize the uniqueness and guard the strengths of the different communities whose children they want to change. On the positive side, most Americans understand that early childhood is a crucial period for human development *and* that providing high-quality education for all children is an important national economic and social investment.

REFERENCES

Annie E. Casey Foundation. (2016). *2016 Kids Count data book: State trends in child well-being.* Baltimore, MD: Annie E. Casey Foundation. Retrieved from http://www.aecf.org/m/resourcedoc/aecf-the2016kidscountdatabook-2016.pdf

Auguste, B. G., Hancock, B., & Laboissiere, M. (2009, June). *The economic cost of the U.S. education gap.* Retrieved from http://www.mckinsey.com/industries/social-sector/our-insights/the-economic-cost-of-the-us-education-gap

Besharov, D. J., Germanis, P., Higney, C. A., & Call, D. M. (2011). Westinghouse Learning Center/Ohio University report on Head Start. In *Assessing the evaluations of early childhood education programs* (pp. 21-1 to 27-15). College Park, MD: Welfare Reform Academy, School of Public Policy, University of Maryland. Retrieved from http://www.welfareacademy.org/pubs/early_education/pdfs/Besharov_ECE%20 assessments_Westinghouse_Head_Start.pdf

Bowman, B. T., Donovan, M. S., & Burns, M. S. (2000). *Eager to learn: Educating our preschoolers.* Washington, DC: National Academies Press.

Bruner, J. S. (1960). *The process of education.* Cambridge, MA: Harvard University Press.

Children's Defense Fund. (2017, September 12). *Children remain the poorest age group despite poverty drop; we must move forward, not backwards.* Retrieved from http://www.childrens-defense.org/newsroom/cdf-in-the-news/press-releases/2017/ChildrenRemainthePoorest AgeGroupDespitePovertyDrop.html

Cuddy, E., Venator, J., & Reeves, R. V. (2015, May 7). *In a land of dollars: Deep poverty and its consequences.* Retrieved from https://www.brookings.edu/research/in-a-land-of-dollars-deep-poverty-and-its-consequences/

Duncan, G. J., Dowsett, C. J., Claessens, A., Magnuson, K., Huston, A. C., Klebanov, P., et al. (2007). School readiness and later achievement. *Developmental Psychology, 43*(6), 1428–1446.

Early, D., Maxwell, K., Burchinal, M., Alva, S., Bender, R., Bryant, D., et al. (2007). Teachers' education, classroom quality, and young children's academic skills: Results from seven studies of preschool programs. *Child Development, 78*(2), 558–580.

Farran, D. C., & Lipsey, M. W. (2015, October 8). *The Tennessee pre-K study.* Retrieved from https://www.brookings.edu/blog/up-front/2015/10/08/the-tennessee-pre-k-study/

Franke, H. A. (2014). Toxic stress: Effects, prevention and treatment. *Children, 1*(3), 390–402.

Fuller, B., Bein, E., Bridges, M., Kim, Y., & Rabe-Hesketh, S. (2017). Do academic preschools yield stronger benefits? Cognitive emphasis, dosage, and early learning. *Journal of Applied Developmental Psychology, 52*(Supplement C), 1–11.

Gershenson, S., & Dee, T. S. (2017, March 20). *The insidiousness of unconscious bias in schools.* Retrieved from https://www.brookings.edu/blog/brown-center-chalkboard/2017/03/20/the-insidiousness-of-unconscious-bias-in-schools/

Gilliam, W. S. (2014, December 13). *What could make less sense than expelling a preschooler?* Retrieved from https://psychologybenefits.org/2014/12/13/preschool-expulsions/

Halpern, R. (1999). *Fragile families, fragile solutions: A history of supportive services for families in poverty.* New York, NY: Columbia University Press.

Hart, B., & Risley, T. R. (1995). *Meaningful differences in the everyday experience of young American children.* Baltimore, MD: Paul H. Brookes Publishing Co.

Holochwost, S. J., Gariépy, J.-L., Propper, C. B., Gardner-Neblett, N., Volpe, V., Neblett, E., et al. (2016). Sociodemographic risk, parenting, and executive functions in early childhood: The role of ethnicity. *Early Childhood Research Quarterly, 36*(Supplement C), 537–549.

Holzer, P., Higgins, J. R., Bromfield, L., & Higgins, D. (2006). The effectiveness of parent education and home visiting child maltreatment prevention programs. *Child Abuse Prevention Issues, 24,* 1–23.

Hunt, J. M. (1961). *Intelligence and experience.* New York, NY: Ronald Press Co.

Individuals with Disabilities Education Act (IDEA) of 1990, PL 101-476, 20 U.S.C. §§ 1400 *et seq.*

Jensen, A. (1969). How much can we boost IQ and scholastic achievement? *Harvard Educational Review, 39*(1), 1–123.

Jones, J. (2017, September 20). *One-third of Native American and African American children are (still) in poverty.* Retrieved from http://www.epi.org/publication/one-third-of-native-american-and-african-american-children-are-still-in-poverty/

Khalifa, M. A., & Briscoe, F. (2015). A counternarrative autoethnography exploring school districts' role in reproducing racism: Willful blindness to racial inequities. *Teachers College Record, 117*(8), 1–34.

Kohn, A. (2000, September 27). *Standardized testing and its victims.* Retrieved from http://www.edweek.org/ew/articles/2000/09/27/04kohn.h20.html

López, M., Grindal, T., Zanoni, W., & George, R. (2017). *Hispanic children's participation in early care and education: A look at utilization patterns of Chicago's publicly funded programs.* Retrieved from http://www.hispanicresearchcenter.org/wp-content/uploads/2017/04/2017-20HispCtr ChicagoECE.pdf

Magnuson, K. A., & Waldfogel, J. (2005). Early childhood care and education: Effects on ethnic and racial gaps in school readiness. *The Future of Children, 15*(1), 169–196.

Matthews, H., Schulman, K., Vogtman, J., Johnson-Staub, C., & Blank, H. (2016). *Implementing the child care and development block grant reauthorization: A guide for states.* Retrieved from https://www.clasp.org/sites/default/files/publications/2017/08/CCDBG-Reauth-Guide-Updated.pdf

National Institute for Early Education Research. (2017, May 24). *New research reveals growing inequality among states in access to high-quality public preschool.* Retrieved from http://nieer .org/wp-content/uploads/2017/05/YB2016_National.pdf

Patient Protection and Affordable Care Act of 2010, PL 111-148, 124 Stat. 119-1025, 42 U.S.C. §§ 18001 *et seq.*

Perry, N. B., Leerkes, E. M., Dunbar, A. S., & Cavanaugh, A. M. (2017). Gender and ethnic differences in young adults' emotional reactions to parental punitive and minimizing emotion socialization practices. *Emerging Adulthood, 5*(2), 83–92.

Phillips, D. A., Lipsey, M. W., Dodge, K. A., Haskins, R., Bassok, D., Burchinal, M. R., et al. (2017). *Puzzling it out: The current state of scientific knowledge on pre-kindergarten effects: A consensus statement.* Retrieved from https://www.brookings.edu/wp-content/uploads/2017/04/ consensus-statement_final.pdf

Piaget, J. (1955). *The language and thought of the child.* New York, NY: Meridian Books.

Progress Illinois. (2015, October 19). *The high cost of childcare on Illinois working families.* Retrieved from http://www.progressillinois.com/quick-hits/content/2015/10/15/high-cost-child-care-illinois

Reid, J. L., Kagan, S. L, Hilton, M., & Potter, H. (2015). *A better start: Why classroom diversity matters in early education.* Retrieved from http://www.prrac.org/pdf/A_Better_Start.pdf

Rothstein, R. (2014). Why our schools are segregated. *Educational Leadership, 70*(8), 50.

Sama-Miller, E., Akers, L. Mraz-Esposito, A., Zukiewicz, M., Avellar, S., Paulsell, D., et al. (2017). *Home visiting evidence of effectiveness review: Executive Summary.* Washington, DC: U.S. Department of Health and Human Services. Retrieved from https://homvee.acf.hhs .gov/homvee_executive_summary_august_2017_final_508_compliant.pdf

Shade, B. (1982). Afro-American cognitive style: A variable in school. *Review of Educational Research, 52*, 219–244.

Shonkoff, J. P., & Phillips, D. A. (Eds.). (2000). *From neurons to neighborhoods: The science of early childhood development.* Washington, DC: National Academies Press.

Slade, E. P., & Wissow, L. S. (2004). Spanking in early childhood and later behavior problems: A prospective study of infants and young toddlers. *Pediatrics, 113*(5), 1321–1330.

U.S. Bureau of Labor Statistics. (2017, March 31). *May 2016 OES state occupational employment and wage estimates, Illinois.* Retrieved from https://www.bls.gov/oes/current/oes_il.htm

U.S. Department of Education. (2015). *A matter of equity: Preschool in America.* Retrieved from https://www2.ed.gov/documents/early-learning/matter-equity-preschool-america.pdf

U.S. Department of Education, National Center for Education Statistics. (2017). *The condition of education 2017.* Retrieved from https://nces.ed.gov/pubs2017/2017144.pdf

Walker, C., & Matthews, H. (2017, January). *CCDBG participation drops to historic low.* Retrieved from http://www.clasp.org/resources-and-publications/publication-1/CCDBG-Participation-2015.pdf

6

Reflections on Racial, Ethnic, Linguistic, Cultural, and Socioeconomic Diversity

Natasha J. Cabrera, Nicole Gardner-Neblett, and Iheoma U. Iruka

The U.S. Census estimates that the proportion of minority children is projected to increase from about one half in 2016 to more than two thirds by 2060 (Vespa, Armstrong, & Medina, 2018), including a large proportion of children born to immigrant parents (Hernandez & Napierala, 2012). This demographic shift directs our collective attention to disparities in academic outcomes, the preparation of the workforce to serve a diversity of children and their families, and the federal policies that directly and indirectly influence ethnic and racial minority children's development. Scholars view the achievement gap between Black and Latino students and White and Asian American students as one of the most intractable educational puzzles in the United States (Ladson-Billings, 2006). In this chapter, the terms *Black* and *African American* are used interchangeably to refer to Black American children of African descent.

Despite the attention and investments (e.g., early childhood education) that may have had some effect on class differences, little progress has been made in reducing academic racial disparities (see Chapter 3; Chetty, Hendren, Jones, & Porter, 2018). In fact, we could argue that the research and programmatic focus on racial academic disparities has had the unintended consequence of obscuring the variability in ethnic minority children, including the strengths, perseverance, and resilience of ethnic minority populations. Moreover, comparatively little effort has focused on ensuring that the early childhood labor force is ready and trained to teach an ethnically and racially diverse population of children (see Chapter 4), as well as focusing on policies and programs that can support their development.

In this chapter, we address these issues by integrating and reflecting on the information from Chapters 3–5, which addressed racial, cultural, and linguistic diversity. More specifically, we present a brief synopsis of the achievement gap, offer a strengths-based approach to studying minority children, describe efforts to prepare the workforce, describe a paradigm shift for conducting research with ethnic minority children identify a strengths-based approach to educating the educators, and end with conclusions and future directions.

THE ACHIEVEMENT GAP

The causes of the achievement gap between racial and ethnic minority children and their White peers are complex, numerous, and confounded by socioeconomic disparities and opportunity gaps. Nearly two thirds of black and Latino children are likely to live in low-income households compared to a third of White children (Jiang, Granja, & Koball, 2017). The National Center for Education Statistics found that compared to their White peers, Black children on average were more likely to be from single female-headed households, live in poverty, have less educated mothers, attend high-poverty schools, have less educated teachers, and be less school ready, as well as less likely to graduate high school and attend college (Aud, Fox, & KewalRamini, 2010). Additionally, Black children and families who are also low-income are likely to live in racially segregated communities, which may limit their access to quality resources, such as high-quality early education programs and health care services, while also exposing them to more violence. These structural characteristics pose a risk for children's learning and development, which partly explains the achievement gap.

In comparison, Latino children are projected to make up nearly one third of the child population by 2050 and are more likely to live in poverty than other groups. For instance, 62% of Latino children live in low-income households and the percentage of children living in married-couple families has declined from 72% to 65% since the 1970s. Latino children are also likely to reside in homes with mothers without a high school education. The family resources available to Latino children have been linked to a mixed-set of outcomes for children. Although some improvements have been documented over the past few years (e.g., gains in educational attainment, health insurance coverage), Latino children still lag behind in cognitive skills (see Chapter 3), graduate at lower rates, and perform lower on national reading and math assessments than do their White counterparts. However, Latino children seem to outperform their White and Black peers in the area of social skills and outperform their Black peers in the academic skills of reading and math (Padilla, Cabrera, & West, 2017).

The main line of scholarship addressing the White–Black achievement gap is based on the view that it reflects mostly socioeconomic (SES) disparities, particularly income and education. However, this view ignores that racial disparities in achievement are also related to racism and discrimination (see Chapter 5). Chetty et al. (2018) used longitudinal income data from 1989 to 2014 to show that SES and family structure explain very little of the income gap between Blacks and Whites; in addition, they found that the gap is worse for boys. Controlling for parental income, Black boys have lower incomes in adulthood than White boys. Furthermore, the authors found that intergenerational persistence of disparities varies across racial groups, such that Latino Americans have higher rates of intergenerational income mobility compared to Black Americans. Moreover, Black children also seem to perform worse when compared to other ethnic minority groups. For example, Padilla, Cabrara, and West (2017) reported that low-income Black children scored lower on measures of academic (reading and math) and social skills than did low-income Latino children and low-income White children.

These findings suggest that efforts to understand academic disparities must include research that helps us to understand how intergenerational and institutional racism and discrimination, not just SES, have resulted in the achievement gap. Studies on disparities in early childhood often do not acknowledge that the experiences of children vary because of their race and are more likely to control for these potential effects than to investigate how ethnic minority children have differential access to resources and experiences in the early years (Black et al., 2017). An analysis by the U.S. Government Accountability Office (2018) found that, across type of disciplinary action, level of school poverty, and type of school, Black boys and students with disabilities were disproportionately disciplined (e.g., suspensions and expulsions) in K–12 public schools, particularly in pre-K. These statistics are particularly alarming because Black students accounted for 16% of all public school students but represented approximately 39% of students suspended from schools.

A STRENGTHS-BASED APPROACH FOR STUDYING ETHNIC MINORITY CHILDREN

The social positions of racial- and ethnic-minority dual-language learners (DLLs) and English-language learners (ELLs) and poverty are often viewed from a deficit lens that does not recognize within-group variability, view learning a second language as an asset, or recognize the strength and resilience among ethnic minority families.

To capture the ecology of ethnic minority children's experiences, García Coll et al. (1996) developed an integrative model for the study of developmental competencies in minority children, which highlights competencies beyond language and social-emotional development, including bicultural and bilingual competences and coping mechanisms for racism. The model posits that child development is influenced by a set of proximal and distal factors and processes, including the following: 1) social position, including race, social class, ethnicity, and gender; 2) race-based factors, such as racism, prejudice, discrimination, and oppression; 3) residential, economic, social, and psychological segregation; 4) schools, neighborhoods, and health care facilities; 5) adaptive cultural factors, such as tradition and cultural legacies, economic and political factors, and migration and acculturation; 6) child characteristics, such as age, temperament, health status, biological factors, and physical characteristics; and 7) family structure and roles, values, beliefs, goals, and racial socialization.

In addition to these processes and competencies, home language and dialect should be included. A National Academies of Sciences, Engineering, and Medicine consensus report (2017) indicated that DLLs and ELLs who have limited English proficiency face systemic barriers to academic achievement and success in school (see Chapter 4). The lack of support for the native language either at home or in school is another source of inequality because many of these children are likely to live in poverty with parents who have low levels of education, in low-wealth communities, and in neighborhoods with underresourced schools.

The deficit-focus view on the development of ethnic minority children is part of the reason why the research community has overlooked or understudied the developmental assets among minority children (Bialystock, Majumder, & Martin, 2003). Moreover, the research community itself lacks diversity. Thus, research is conducted without the voices, experiences, and knowledge of ethnic minority researchers, practitioners, and community members who are steeped in those cultures. Clearly, we are at a crossroads where we need to change the type of research that is done on ethnic minority children, who conducts such research, and how the workforce is prepared to work effectively with ethnic minority children. Although some progress has been made (Cabrera & Leyendecker, 2017), further research needs to document the unique and protective and promotive factors, parenting practices, and strategies that promote excellence in ethnic minority children, even in the face of social, familial, and institutional obstacles. Efforts to prepare the early childhood workforce should take into account the diversity of the children and families and acknowledge the challenges and assets of these families.

A strength-based approach to the study of ethnic minority children highlights specific skills (e.g., learning a second language, oral narrative skills) and shows the variability in child outcomes. This approach is useful for addressing opportunity and achievement gaps as well as identifying the promotive and protective factors that result in such variability (Werner, 1995). Findings from recent studies show that, overall, minority children show strengths in at least three domains of development: social competence, language, and ethnic identity. These three domains are addressed in the following sections. Following these three domains, family processes that support development are presented.

Social Competence   Many low-income ethnic minority children exhibit relatively high levels of self-regulation and social skills that can help them succeed in school (Galindo & Fuller, 2010; Li-Grining, 2012). Similarly, studies show that Mexican American youth have been found to engage in high levels of prosocial behaviors and exhibit more cooperative behavior than European American youth (Knight & Carlo, 2012).

Studies of low-income African American children also document social competencies in various contexts. African American preschoolers have been found to exhibit adaptive social and social-cognitive skills during play, psychosocial adaptation, and social and cognitive competence (Brody, Murry, Kim, & Brown, 2002). In a more recent study, African American preschoolers were found to engage in positive peer play interactions at home and in school, which support early learning and development (Bulotsky-Shearer et al., 2012).

Linguistic Strengths   Although low-income African American preschoolers are often found to exhibit delays in expressive vocabulary (Champion, Hyter, McCabe, & Bland-Stewart, 2003), their oral narrative (or storytelling) skills, which are rooted in a rich culture of African ancestry and tradition, may be a unique area of strength. Strong narrative skills may partly explain why early language skills are important for later reading, particularly for boys (Gardner-Neblett & Iruka, 2015; Gardner-Neblett, Pungello, & Iruka, 2012). However, narrative skills do not always translate into academic gains for Black children, which may suggest that either these skills are not assessed and supported in school settings or that teachers are unaware of how to leverage the elaborative narrative style to capitalize on these strengths and improve children's language skills.

Similarly, linguistic strengths have been reported for ethnic minority children who are growing up in bilingual environments (Engel de Abreu, Cruz-Santos, Tourinho, Martin, & Bialystok, 2012). Exposure to high-quality multiple languages, especially before the age of 5 years, is robustly related to better language outcomes and stronger metacognitive higher-order skills (McCabe et al., 2013). The cognitive benefits of being bilingual include enhanced executive and inhibitory control (Bialystok, Fergus, & Craik, 2010). Yet, despite these noted strengths, studies also report poorer language outcomes for DLLs and ELLs. This discrepancy may reflect several factors: 1) many DLLs/ELLs are exposed to lower-quality language at home and attend low-quality programs and schools, which may trump the potential cognitive advantage of learning two languages; 2) many studies that have not used conceptual coding may have underestimated DLLs' language skills; and 3) being bilingual may have costs, at least initially, such as having smaller vocabularies and weaker access to lexical items in each language (Bialystok, Luk, Peets, & Yang, 2010). It is possible, however, that the costs are overemphasized while the benefits are deemphasized (see Chapter 4).

Ethnic Identity   The formation of a strong ethnic identity and positive attitudes toward civic engagement are potentially promotive factors of positive youth outcomes (competence, confidence, character, connection, and caring). Security and pride in one's own racial and ethnic identity promote more positive peer and family relationships and self-esteem among racial and ethnic minorities (Neblett, Rivas-Drake, & Umaña-Taylor, 2012). Positive youth outcomes are often directly supported through traditional racial socialization messages at home (e.g., preparation for bias, self-worth, and egalitarianism; Evans et al., 2012), as well as through meaningful shared activities with others that promote positive other-oriented prosocial behavior, decrease risky behaviors, and foster citizenship (e.g., voting and campaigning; Flanagan & Levine, 2010). Having a strong sense of collective efficacy, based on group identity, is related to reduced problem behavior and substance use (Smith, Osgood, Caldwell, Hynes, & Perkins, 2013).

Family Processes That Support Development

Research on how families contribute to the positive development of children and youth has exploded recently (e.g., McLoyd, 2006). Two aspects of family life in particular have been linked to children's positive adaptation: family orientation and cultural/racial socialization.

Family Orientation   Family orientation, or *familism,* is a multidimensional construct emphasizing family support, solidarity, and obligations within the family (Updegraff, McHale, Whiteman, Thayer, & Delgado, 2005). Not surprisingly, the family plays a strong role in how children grow and develop, representing children's primary source for love, affection, support, monitoring, caregiving, and teaching children culturally and community-relevant values, beliefs, and expectations that can guide their social interactions with others in the community.

A strong sense of family orientation has been related to ethnic minority children's positive development; these children exhibit fewer behavior problems, have more friends, and are socially competent (Kiang, Supple, Stein, & Gonzalez, 2012). Mexican American children who have a strong sense of *familism* are less likely to become involved with deviant peers (Roosa et al., 2011) and to engage in antisocial behavior over time (Morcillo et al., 2011). A review of the literature revealed that *familism* may have a protective role in the socialization of Latino preschool-aged children's self-regulation (Li-Grining, 2012), such that a strong sense of family cohesion and loyalty may create a more positive and less conflicting home environment (e.g., reduced interparental conflict), which is associated with better child adjustment (Taylor, Larsen-Rife, Conger, & Widaman, 2012). Similarly, recent studies with Native American and Alaska Native youth show that traditional family values and worldviews can protect youth from risky behaviors (Kenyon & Hanson, 2012).

Cultural and Racial Socialization   Parental racial and cultural socialization (i.e., teaching children about the norms, values, and expectations of their particular cultural group) are prevalent and adaptive among ethnic minority families (Evans et al., 2012: Neblett et al., 2012). In addition to promoting cultural and personal pride, racial and ethnic socialization includes teaching children to be aware of and cope with racism and bias, which results in higher self-esteem, a greater sense of belonging, and a more positive outlook, protecting children against the negative effects of discrimination and prejudice (Evans et al., 2012; Hughes, Witherspoon, Rivas-Drake, & West-Bay, 2009).

For younger children, Caughy, O'Campo, Randolph, and Nickerson (2002) found that African American preschoolers performed better on cognitive tests and exhibited fewer emotional and behavioral problems when they resided in home environments reflecting elements of African American culture. Similarly, Native American and Alaska Native youth who reported higher levels of identification with their culture and participation in cultural activities were more likely to be classified as resilient (Kenyon & Hanson, 2012). One of the mechanisms by which cultural socialization is related to adaptation is through its impact on racial-ethnic identity (Schweigman, Soto, Wright, & Unger, 2011), which is also predictive of positive psychosocial adjustment (Umaña-Taylor, Gonzales-Backen, & Guimond, 2009).

In contrast, the sparse research on the cultural socialization of Asian American children shows that they confront stereotypes about being a "model minority" because of their higher rates of academic success (Qin, Way, & Mukhejee, 2008). Asian youth are also more likely to be perceived as perpetual foreigners who fail to assimilate properly to American culture (Kim, Wang, Deng, Alvarez, & Li, 2011). These stereotypes ignore the marked variability in this group and overlook issues that can undermine positive development (Zhou et al., 2012). For example, although having a strong Western orientation or a lower anchoring in Chinese culture may be related to fewer delinquent behaviors (Deng, Kim, Vaughn, & Li, 2010), it can also be related to cross-generational tensions, which may contribute to psychosocial maladaptation (Phinney, Ong, & Madden, 2000). To confront racial discrimination, Asian American parents might help children learn about American cultural values and norms in a way that capitalizes on Asian American cultural strengths (Zhou et al., 2012).

PARADIGM SHIFT: THE NEXT GENERATION OF STUDIES ON RACIAL AND ETHNIC MINORITY CHILDREN

Considering the gaps in achievement and opportunities for minority and low-income children in the United States and the high stakes of these gaps for the country's economic viability, future research has a key role to play in increasing the current knowledge base about the development of children from diverse backgrounds to inform policy and practice on how best to support children and families. In this section, we highlight the need for the inclusion of diversity throughout the research process, the methodological issues that need to be considered for high-quality inclusive research, and the need for research that explicitly examines race/ethnicity, culture, language, and socioeconomic class.

Inclusion of Diversity Throughout the Research Process

Greater inclusivity is needed throughout all stages of the research process. Historical accounts, such as *Even the Rat Was White* (Guthrie, 1976), have documented the ways in which racial/ethnic minorities have been excluded from behavioral and social science research under the assumption that Whites were considered the default category that represented all humans and minority populations were undeserving of scientific attention, unless it was to support the idea of deviance in non-White populations (Cundiff, 2012). This exclusion has continued, with more recent accounts documenting underrepresentation in the scientific workforce (e.g., researchers, editors) and participant pools (e.g., Cundiff, 2012; Hur, Andalib, Maurer, Hawley, & Ghaffarzadegan, 2017; Kameny et al., 2014) and perpetuating a sense of invisibility in the field of developmental psychology (Syed, Santos, Yoo, & Juang, 2018). When racial and ethnic minorities are included in research, the research tends to be mostly about adversity and failure rather than about strength and resilience (McLoyd, 2006).

Representation in the Scientific Workforce   A lack of racial and ethnic diversity has been documented within the scientific workforce. In 2013, Asians comprised 7% of the behavioral and social science workforce, Blacks comprised 5%, and Hispanic/Latinos comprised 4% compared to Whites at 82% (Hur et al., 2017). These disparities also translate into disparities in the makeup of decision makers and leaders within the research enterprise. Although racial and ethnic minorities comprise 34% of the U.S. population, they make up 11% of editors of peer-reviewed journals and 16% of senior authors (Cundiff, 2012). Disparities are also seen in access to research funding, with Black researchers less likely to receive federal grants compared with White researchers (Ginther et al., 2011).

A segment of the behavioral and social science workforce is responsible for studying a range of topics related to racial and ethnic minority children and families, building the knowledge base used to inform decisions affecting minority children and families. As such, the workforce has a critical role to play in the research topics explored, the types of research questions asked, the measures designed to address these research questions, the interpretations used to explain the resulting data, and the perspectives used to draw conclusions, which have implications for policies and practices. In addition to generating the research, the workforce is responsible for deciding which research is deemed worthy of being published (e.g., peer reviewers and editors). Thus, when White researchers dominate the scientific workforce, the resulting knowledge is shaped and constrained by the perspective of the dominant group, while the perspectives of racial and ethnic minorities are more likely to be ignored or devalued. Furthermore, the lived experiences and perspectives that racial and ethnic minority researchers bring to conducting research based on their social positioning can drive the selection of pertinent research topics and contribute to the generation of more informed knowledge of racial and ethnic minority children and families. To improve the racial/ethnic diversity of the workforce, systemic change is needed to overcome the institutional barriers and biases that minority researchers face in the behavioral and social sciences (Kameny et al., 2014).

Representation in Participant Pools   In addition to an underrepresentation of racial and ethnic researchers, there is also an underrepresentation of racial and ethnic minority populations as participants in research studies. For example, an analysis of research studies published in mainstream peer-reviewed journals in psychology found that Native American, Black American, and Latino groups were underrepresented as research participants compared to their composition in the U.S. population (Cundiff, 2012), contributing to a dearth of research on the normative development of minority children.

Methodological Considerations

A challenge to understanding positive adaptation of ethnic minority children is the limited toolkit (Knight, Roosa, & Umana-Taylor, 2009). To improve the resources available to researchers, the field needs better research designs that recognize the unique resources upon which ethnic minorities draw. Furthermore, the links among theory, research questions, and study design that are relevant to the experiences and resources of ethnic minorities must be clearly articulated. For example, scholars have emphasized the importance of culturally informed theory in guiding quantitative research conducted with ethnic minority children (Garcia Coll et al., 1996; Knight et al., 2009; Rogoff, 2011; Weisner, 2002).

    Analytical approaches and methods should also be questioned. Gillborn, Warmington, and Demack argue (2018, p. 175) argued that "quantitative data are socially constructed in exactly the same way as other forms of research material (including interviews and ethnographic observations). Numbers' authoritative façade often hides a series of assumptions and practices which mean, more often than not, that statistics will embody the dominant assumptions that shape inequity in society." Although we agree on the need to study the association between cultural environments and children's development using critical race theory lens, these links may not be linear, or the measures used to gather the environment may not be culturally salient (Iruka, LaForett, & Odom, 2012). For analytical purposes, researchers often represent these associations as if they were losing some of the complexity of these associations (Weisner, 2012).

Similarly, research with minority children is more likely to use either quantitative or qualitative methodology. However, scholars have argued that using multiple methods that integrate qualitative and quantitative approaches to research are essential to more accurately represent the diverse, cultural learning environments of all children (Hughes et al., 2009; Weisner, 2012). This multifaceted approach can yield rich information on the dynamic processes that lead to positive developmental outcomes among diverse groups. That is, researchers should employ experimental designs or large community samples that include intensive qualitative and ethnographic methods and are nested and fully integrated within them (e.g., Huston et al., 2005).

What Is the Right Comparison Group?   A persistent issue in research with ethnic minority children and youth is determining the appropriate control or comparison group (Syed, 2012). The deficit view to studying ethnic minority children takes a static between-groups/comparative approach that focuses on average between-group differences. Including a White comparison group is problematic because of SES disparities among groups, which contributes to negative stereotypes about minority children (McLoyd, 1991). This view has been ardently debated in the literature (e.g., McLoyd, 2006; Wong & Rowley, 2001). Of course, the opposite argument is not necessarily true or expected. Studies of White youth do not require an ethnic minority "control" group, for instance.

The decision about whether or not to include a White sample may depend on the particular research question, which has implications for how we theorize about the role of race and ethnicity in development (Syed, 2012). If the goal is to examine differences on some aspect of development between one or more racial and ethnic minority groups and Whites, then a White sample equivalent to the minority group(s) in SES and other contextual factors should be included. If the research question is to describe the experiences of a particular group or to examine individual differences within an ethnic group—and makes no claims to uniqueness or difference between groups—then including a White comparison sample is not necessary (Syed, 2012).

Furthermore, when examining data for ethnic or racial differences, it is essential to develop theoretical and empirical methods for ensuring that a between-groups comparative design that includes a White sample is not conceptualized or interpreted within a deficit framework (Syed, 2012). Syed suggested analytically replacing static social group markers (e.g., ethnicity) with dynamic psychological constructs (e.g., ethnic identity) that may have a stronger potential to explain group differences. Such analyses, Syed contended, can help to clarify whether existing theories have universal applicability or whether a theory needs to be revised or discarded altogether.

Finally, it is worth noting that the bulk of research on minority and disadvantaged families has not used rigorous sampling and recruitment strategies, which can also limit generalization to the larger population and confound interpretation (Knight et al., 2009).

Disentangling the Effects of Race and Ethnicity From the Effects of Socioeconomic Status on Children's Development What we currently know about minority children's skills and developmental trajectories is, in general, based on research that tends to confound racial and ethnic minority status with SES. Research often focuses on highly select samples of ethnic and racial minority children from high-risk and disadvantaged environments. Studies that have tried to disentangle the effects of SES from ethnicity show that differences between groups are mostly accounted for by differences in SES (Hill, 2006). However, many analyses show that disparities remain even after controlling for SES and family structure (Aratani, Wight, & Cooper, 2011; Chetty et al., 2018; Padilla et al., 2017). A study found that race and ethnicity were initially associated with subtle differences in children's mother–child interactions, which in turn predicted children's later outcomes (Bradley, Corwyn, McAdoo, & Garcia Coll, 2001). A closer look at data revealed that SES differences exerted stronger effects on children's outcomes than race and ethnicity. A review showed that maternal sensitivity is lower among low-income minority families due to poverty-related stress (Mesman, van IJzendoorn, & Bakermans-Kranenburg, 2012). Another analysis showed that the greatest source of inequality is SES rather than race (Duncan & Murnane, 2011). Yet, the issue of SES versus race/ethnicity is not settled. A new intergenerational study showed that race matters and that SES and family characteristics account for little of the variance in incomes for White and Black men (Chetty et al., 2018). Collectively, these findings suggest that immeasurable changes due to intergenerational discrimination and racism and concentrated disadvantage might play out differently for certain outcomes.

Research that disentangles race and SES can shed light onto the processes that are similar or different across groups. For example, research suggests that the family stress model holds for African Americans, Whites, and English-speaking Latinos (Iruka et al., 2012). That is, across ethnic groups, poverty means experiencing material hardship and living in dangerous neighborhoods, which can result in parental depression, irritability, and harsh parenting; this, in turn, may lead to child adversity. Similarly, an investment model that explains how parents' education and income matter for children's developmental outcomes was shown to hold across ethnic and racial groups (Mistry, Biesanz, Chien, Howes, & Benner, 2008)—but not always, because there may be other cultural-based family investments that are not measured (Iruka et al., 2012). Moreover, within-ethnic group differences may also reflect variations among participants in the level of parental education or other factors, which might explain why some studies have found that middle-class minority families are more similar to middle-class majority families than to low-income minority families. Preliminary findings from a study comparing middle-class and low-middle-class Chinese immigrant parents found that middle-class Chinese parents were more likely to be engaged in literacy activities with their children than were low-income Chinese parents, and that low-income Chinese children performed worse than middle-class Chinese children in reading and math (Yamamoto & Li, 2012).

Need for Research That Explicitly Examines Race and Ethnicity

Over time, research on ethnic minority children based on strengths-based models (e.g., a positive youth development model) has increased through national publications and convenings (as discussed in Cabrera, Beeghly, & Eisenberg, 2012). Despite these efforts, research is still needed that focuses on how race and ethnicity operate to produce the disparities that are evident in children's outcomes. This research needs to take a more nuanced perspective that goes beyond comparative designs or biological determinism to examining the systemic factors that contribute to disparities in child outcomes.

Scholars have noted that research takes place in an ideological setting that minimizes race and ethnicity as important factors and that are rarely examined to determine the processes involved in driving outcomes (Syed et al., 2018). This minimization of race and ethnicity serves to reflect and reproduce a color blindness that limits research from uncovering the underlying constructs or processes that drive outcomes. Furthermore, the minimization contributes to a weakened knowledge base, where gaps in our knowledge about the normative development of racial and ethnic minority children in many domains abound. Thus, there is a need for research that uncovers the mediators between race/ethnicity and child outcomes, examines the context in which racial/ethnic minority children develop, and provides a window into the normative development of minority children. Such research can provide society with a more complete understanding of the role of race and ethnicity in children's development.

A STRENGTHS-BASED APPROACH TO EDUCATING THE EDUCATORS IN EARLY CARE

The current workforce in early childhood is largely unprepared to meet the needs of ethnic minority children, particularly children who are learning two languages (see Chapter 4). This lack of preparation has implications for the extent to which the workforce can provide the high quality of care and education that young children need for optimal developmental outcomes and school readiness.

Preparation of the workforce needs to start with providing professional development, both preservice and in-service, that increases knowledge about racial and ethnic minority children and their families. This knowledge includes understanding of the role that culture plays in children's development, instructional practices that are culturally and linguistically responsive, and appropriate assessment of children's development and achievement (see Chapter 4). Professional development experiences should focus on how best to apply knowledge to classroom practices. Experiences that provide opportunities for active participation, self-reflection, and application of knowledge to solve everyday challenges can increase competence and create conditions that are optimal for learning (e.g., Castro et al., 2017; Trivette, Dunst, Hamby, & O'Herin, 2009; Trotter, 2006). Effective professional development experiences, however, tailored to meet the needs of racially, ethnically, and linguistically diverse children, remain a challenge for the early childhood field (e.g., Chapter 4; Zepeda, Castro, & Cronin, 2011).

Professional Development Programs

As discussed in Chapter 5, one of the current issues surrounding teacher education focuses on whether early childhood teachers should be required to have a bachelor's degree to increase their effectiveness in reducing the achievement gap. The issue we raise in this section is more related to the content of the education. In the same way that questions have been raised about the way we do research among low-income families, questions also need to be raised about revisions in the preparation of the workforce. We need to examine how teachers are trained to ensure that they learn about the strengths of low-income and ethnic and linguistic minority children and not just about the adversity these families experience. Furthermore, there is a need to incorporate insights from strengths-based research into programs designed for parents.

In a National Academies of Sciences, Engineering, and Medicine (2016) report on supporting parents, the Committee on Supporting Parents of Children Ages 0–8 focused part of their recommendations on the workforce. This committee recommended that the U.S. Department of Health and Human Services and the U.S. Department of Education should convene a group of experts in teaching and research as well as representatives of relevant practice organizations and research associations to review and improve professional development for providers who work with families of young children across sectors (e.g., education, child welfare, health). They urged that professional development should be evaluated to determine whether its core elements include best practices in engagement of and joint decision making with parents. They also argued for the need to create a toolbox of evidence-informed engagement and joint decision-making models, programs, and practices for implementation in early education settings. These recommendations and accompanying outputs are especially important for educators who work with children and families from low-income and ethnic and linguistic minority backgrounds. The following themes are based on the research outlined previously and may be helpful as we think about how to prepare the educators to be effective teachers.

1. *Not every low-income child is at risk and not every ethnic minority child is living in poverty.* The heterogeneity and variability in low-income and ethnic minority children, in terms of both their early experiences and outcomes, should be highly emphasized in the training teachers receive. Part of the problem is that research findings about the challenges and difficulties are taken as universals when in fact they are based on select samples or do not represent the entire population. For example, children living in low-income families are more likely to have a high cumulative risk factor when they live in chronic poverty, have been exposed to it during the early years, or have parents with serious mental health issues. Children who grow up in low-income families may not develop serious difficulties if the parents are working, are making ends meet, and have social support. Furthermore, it is important to recognize the economic, social, and cultural variability in this group, which may begin to challenge implicit biases about all children in poverty.

2. *Many low-income children have social and cognitive competencies that may not be recognized by teachers and that may be adaptive in other contexts.* There is an untested assumption that children who are living in poverty cannot have any competencies. For example, although we refer to children who are learning another language as dual-language learners, in the classroom these children are often referred to as students who "do not speak English" rather than who "speak Spanish and are becoming bilingual." This tendency to highlight what children do not have rather than what they have supports the negative view that low-income, ethnic minority children are deficient. This narrative does not integrate the findings that show that bilingual children are more adept at inhibitory control than monolingual children. Teachers who know and understand the cognitive advantage of bilingual children would have different beliefs and expectations about the learning success of bilingual children compared to teachers without this knowledge base. Similarly, children who have strong ethnic identity and better outcomes have been found to engage in practices called "cultural straddling" or "code switching." These are strategies used by minority students to negotiate and embrace being part of a majority culture while also holding onto their native cultural styles (Carter, 2005; Morton, 2014). Thus, teachers should be skillful in helping children maintain their cultural identity and cultural traditions in the midst of the expectations of the dominant cultural traditions and norms. In the same vein as DLLs and ELLs, this knowledge and use of the knowledge could help support positive teacher–child relationships and culturally responsive pedagogy.

3. *Low-income families and ethnic minority families have a strong family orientation.* The family unit is the source of support and strength for many ethnic minority families. This means that families, which include fathers, siblings, aunts, uncles, and grandparents, should be viewed as the central unit to partner and collaborate with to support children's healthy development and positive learning.

CONCLUSIONS: RESEARCH, PRACTICE, AND POLICY

Overall, research on ethnic minority child development increasingly reflects the recognition that a clearer understanding of cultural resources and constraints, as well as children's unique ecological contexts (Weisner, 2002), are critical to the study of positive development in these groups (Cabrera et al., 2012; Neblett et al., 2012). The bulk of the research to date, however, has been conducted with Latino American and African American children. There is an urgent need to understand the cultural aspects of family dynamics among Asian American and Native American/Alaska Native children and their families (Kenyon & Hanson, 2012). Ethnic minority groups are heterogeneous across contexts (e.g., rural), immigration patterns, historical trauma, and class. The time has come to broaden our view of poverty from a view that is almost exclusively focused on economic resources—income and education—to one that examines the way systemic and intergenerational racism has ensured that generations of ethnic minority families do not move out of poverty.

Progress has been made in examining issues of race, ethnicity, and diversity in social science from a strengths-based perspective, as evidenced by special journal issues and professional conferences addressing these issues (see Cabrera et al., 2012). However, these efforts are not enough. The studies on middle-class ethnic minority families are still too few to make a difference. Moreover, we must make structural changes to the pipeline to increase the number of ethnic minority scholars conducting and reviewing research and ensuring equitable access to external funding and resources. Including ethnic minority researchers into the academy will lead to more systemic investigations of issues of racism, for example, because it affects them personally. To date, there are no national longitudinal studies with high-quality data on racism and discrimination. This situation is not acceptable. Furthermore, attention needs to be given to the types of questions being asked, methods and analytical approaches, and interpretation because they have implications for practices and policies with generational impact.

In summary, to address the opportunity and achievement gaps in earnest, four research guidelines can significantly move the field forward: 1) ensure that all aspects of race and ethnicity are explicitly considered and addressed; 2) conduct analyses separately by race and ethnic group rather than control for or ignore racial differences; 3) challenge norms and paradigms that do not consider issues of race, ethnicity, and privilege; and 4) conduct research that has meaningful implications and impact for the well-being of children, families, and communities, especially those who have historically been marginalized.

Following these research guidelines has implications for the strategies used by the early care and education workforce, who care for and teach young children. It is critical to understand how race and ethnicity, along with income and education, have implications for children's development and learning and how teachers can support children's individual needs. The 2015 Institute of Medicine and National Research Council report, entitled *Transforming the Workforce for Children Birth through Age 8: A Unifying Foundation,* put forth a list of recommendations for improving the workforce, including the need for an early education workforce to be highly educated and competent to meet the needs of diverse learners. The committee stressed the importance of early education teachers being able to build on the resources of diverse children who have "funds of knowledge" (culturally developed and historically accumulated bodies of knowledge and skills) that can be used to develop children's understandings. To better connect classroom instruction to children, educators must familiarize themselves with children's backgrounds, traditions, and customs. Early education professional (and leaders) should develop an authentic two-way dialogue with families to share decision making and also learn about home and community contexts that may influence children's learning. For example, teachers who understand the adversity children experience are likely to personalize their instructions and interactions with children. Similarly, teachers who view ethnic minority children as having a rich culture and supportive and caring families are likely to have high expectations of students and create a learning environment that leverages children's learning.

Bowman, in Chapter 4, and Espinoza and Zepeda in Chapter 5, strongly argued that we must educate the educators if they are to meet the needs of a growing population of ethnic and language minority students, especially those who face many adversities from poverty, racism, and concentrated disadvantage. To achieve this goal, we need the following: 1) more experienced and educated early education professionals with expertise on issues of diversity and best practices for DLLs/ELLs and minority children; 2) qualified early education professionals who are bilingual and bicultural; 3) early education coaches and trainers who are bilingual and bicultural with expertise in diversity and strategies for DLLs and minority children; and (4) child-, teacher-, and classroom-level tools that are culturally and linguistically relevant to support ethnic and language minority children's development to ensure equitable learning opportunities and strengths-based assessments to support their learning and development. In essence, it is critical that the professional preparation of teachers in early care and education provides effective and appropriate ways for teaching children from different ethnic and racial backgrounds, if all children are to benefit from their educational experiences.

Although policy making often considers the need of all children (and families and communities), certain policies, such as the Supplemental Nutrition Assistance Program and the Children's Health Insurance Program (which support children's nutrition and health, respectively), were developed to support children with the most need. On the early education side, Head Start is a program primarily for children who are living in poverty, similar to the approach taken by many states with pre-K programs that serve mostly high-need children. Research provides evidence of the universal versus localized (e.g., based on income or geography) policies that are needed. If policy assumes that all children need the same thing, then we will continue to have inequities in the system. That is, if many children of color are likely to live in concentrated disadvantage primarily due to lack of opportunities and discrimination, then policies could potentially be instituted to address these systematic inequities. However, if science is scant on understanding the causes and effects of the opportunity and achievement gaps, especially for low-income ethnic and linguistic minority children and their families, then policies cannot be devised and examined. Furthermore, if a deficit and bias lens are used to understand these issues, then it is likely that these same lenses will be used for policies, which may minimize the impact of such policies.

As was articulated almost 30 years ago (McLoyd, 1990), it is a national imperative to address the knowledge gap in the research with ethnic and linguistic minority children and their families and communities. We must engage in research that examines universal and cultural specific processes and contexts. We must apply the critical race lens to ask the following:

1. To what extent have all race and ethnic groups been explicitly involved and their perspectives considered?

2. Have analyses been conducted separately by race and ethnic group for the data used as the basis for policies?

3. Are there biases and norms based on issues of race, ethnicity, and privilege that should be acknowledged?

4. Will a specific policy have meaningful implications and impact for the well-being of all children, families, and communities, especially those who have historically been marginalized?

5. Are the outcomes equally distributed or equitably distributed?

Addressing these questions should move us closer to addressing inequities while ensuring that all children, their families, and their communities continue to thrive.

REFERENCES

Aratani, Y., Wight, V. R., & Cooper, J. L. (2011). *Racial gaps in early childhood: Socio-emotional health, developmental and education outcomes among African-American boys.* New York, NY: Columbia University, Teachers' College, National Center for Children in Poverty.

Aud, S., Fox, M. A., & KewalRamani, A. (2010). *Status and trends in the education of racial and ethnic groups (NCES 2010-015).* Washington, DC: U.S. Department of Education National Center for Education Statistics. Retrieved from https://files.eric.ed.gov/fulltext/ED510909.pdf

Bialystok, E., Fergus, I., & Craik, M. (2010). Cognitive and linguistic processing in the bilingual mind. *Current Directions in Psychological Science, 19*(1), 19–23.

Bialystok, E., Luk, G., Peets, K. F., & Yang, S. (2010). Receptive vocabulary differences in monolingual and bilingual children. *Bilingualism: Language and Cognition, 13*(4), 525–531.

Bialystok, E., Majumder, S., & Martin, M. M. (2003). Developing phonological awareness: Is there a bilingual advantage? *Applied Psycholinguistics, 24*(1), 27–44.

Black, M. M., Walker, S. P., Fernald, L. C. H., Andersen, C. T., DiGirolamo, A. M., Lu, C., et al. (2017). Early childhood development coming of age: Science through the life course. *The Lancet, 389*(10064), 77–90.

Bradley, R. H., Corwyn, R. F., McAdoo, H. P., & García Coll, C. (2001). The home environments of children in the United States Part I: Variations by age, ethnicity, and poverty status. *Child Development, 72*(6), 1844–1867.

Brody, G. H., Murry, V. M., Kim, S., & Brown, A. C. (2002). Longitudinal pathways to competence and psychological adjustment among African American children living in rural single-parent households. *Child Development, 73*(5), 1505–1516.

Bulotsky-Shearer, R. J., Manz, P. H., Mendez, J. L., McWayne, C. M., Sekino, Y., & Fantuzzo, J. W. (2012). Peer play interactions and readiness to learn: A protective influence for African American preschool children from low-income households. *Child Development Perspectives, 6*(3), 225–231.

Cabrera, N. J., Beeghly, M., & Eisenberg, N. (2012). Positive development of minority children: Introduction to the special issue. *Child Development Perspectives, 6*(3), 207–209.

Cabrera, N. J., & Leyendecker, B. (Eds.). (2017). *Handbook on positive development of minority children*. Cham, Switzerland: Springer International Publishing.

Carter, P. (2005). *Keepin' it real: School success beyond black and white*. Oxford, UK: Oxford University Press.

Castro, D. C., Gillanders, C., Franco, X., Bryant, D. M., Zepeda, M., Willoughby, M. T., et al. (2017). Early education of dual language learners: An efficacy study of the Nuestros Niños School Readiness professional development program. *Early Childhood Research Quarterly, 40*(3), 188–203.

Caughy, M. O., O'Campo, P. J., Randolph, S. M., & Nickerson, K. (2002). The influence of racial socialization practices on the cognitive and behavioral competence of African American preschoolers. *Child Development, 73*(5), 1611–1625.

Champion, T. B., Hyter, Y. D., McCabe, A., & Bland-Stewart, L. M. (2003). "A matter of vocabulary": Performances of low-income African American head start children on the Peabody Picture Vocabulary Test—III. *Communication Disorders Quarterly, 24*(3), 121–127.

Chetty, R., Hendren, N., Jones, M. R., & Porter, S. R. (2018). *Race and economic opportunity in the United States: An intergenerational perspective*. Stanford, CA: Stanford University. Retrieved from http://www.nber.org/papers/w24441

Cundiff, J. L. (2012). Is mainstream psychological research "womanless" and "raceless"? An updated analysis. *Sex Roles, 67*(3-4), 158–173.

Deng, S., Kim, S. Y., Vaughan, P. W., & Li, J. (2010). Cultural orientation as a moderator of the relationship between Chinese American adolescents' discrimination experiences and delinquent behaviors. *Journal of Youth and Adolescence, 39*(9), 1027–1040.

Duncan, G. J., & Murnane, R. J. (Eds.). (2011). *Whither opportunity? Rising inequality, schools, and children's life chances*. New York, NY: Russell Sage Foundation.

Engel de Abreu, P. M. J., Cruz-Santos, A., Tourinho, C. J., Martin, R., & Bialystok, E. (2012). Bilingualism enriches the poor: Enhanced cognitive control in low-income minority children. *Psychological Science, 23*(11), 1364–1371.

Evans, A. B., Banerjee, M., Meyer, R., Aldana, A., Foust, M., & Rowley, S. (2012). Racial socialization as a mechanism for positive development among African American youth. *Child Development Perspectives, 6*(3), 251–257.

Flanagan, C., & Levine, P. (2010). Civic engagement and the transition to adulthood. *The Future of Children, 20*(1), 159–179.

Galindo, C., & Fuller, B. (2010). The social competence of Latino kindergartners and growth in mathematical understanding. *Developmental Psychology, 46*(3), 579–592.

García Coll, C., Lamberty, G., Jenkins, R., McAdoo, H. P., Crnic, K., Wasik, B. H., et al. (1996). An integrative model for the study of developmental competencies in minority children. *Child Development, 67*(5), 1891–1914.

Gardner-Neblett, N., & Iruka, I. U. (2015). Oral narrative skills: Explaining the language-emergent literacy link by race/ethnicity and SES. *Developmental Psychology, 51*(7), 889-904.

Gardner-Neblett, N., Pungello, E. P., & Iruka, I. U. (2012). Oral narrative skills: Implications for the reading development of African American children. *Child Development Perspectives, 6*(3), 218–224.

Gillborn, D., Warmington, P., & Demack, S. (2018). QuantCrit: Education, policy, 'Big Data' and principles for a critical race theory of statistics. *Race Ethnicity and Education, 21*(2), 158–179.

Ginther, D. K., Schaffer, W. T., Schnell, J., Masimore, B., Liu, F., Haak, L. L., et al. (2011). Race, ethnicity, and NIH research awards. *Science, 333*(6045), 1015–1019.

Guthrie, R. V. (1976). *Even the rat was white: A historical view of psychology*. New York, NY: Harper and Row.

Hernandez, D. J., & Napierala, J. S. (2012). *Children in immigrant families: Essential to America's future*. New York, NY: Foundation for Child Development. Retrieved from https://www .fcd-us.org/assets/2016/04/FINAL-Children-in-Immigrant-Families-2_1.pdf

Hill, N. E. (2006). Disentangling ethnicity, socioeconomic status and parenting: Interactions, influences and meaning. *Vulnerable Children and Youth Studies, 1*(1), 114–124.

Hughes, D., Witherspoon, D., Rivas-Drake, D., & West-Bay, N. (2009). Examining the mediating role of ethnic identity and self-esteem. *Cultural Diversity and Ethnic Minority Psychology, 15*(2), 112–124.

Hur, H., Andalib, M. A., Maurer, J. A., Hawley, J. D., & Ghaffarzadegan, N. (2017). Recent trends in the U.S. behavioral and social sciences research (BSSR) workforce. *PLoS ONE, 12*(2), 3–18.

Huston, A., Duncan, G., McLoyd, V., Crosby, D., Ripke, M., Weisner, T., et al. (2005). Impacts on children of a policy to promote employment and reduce poverty for low-income parents: New hope after 5 years. *Developmental Psychology, 41*(6), 902–918.

Iruka, I. U., LaForett, D. R., & Odom, E. C. (2012). Examining the validity of the family investment and stress models and relationship to children's school readiness across five cultural groups. *Journal of Family Psychology, 26*(3), 359–370.

Jiang, Y., Granja, M. R., & Koball, H. (2017). *Basic facts about low-income children: Children under 18 years, 2015*. New York, NY: National Center for Children in Poverty. Retrieved from http://www.nccp.org/publications/pdf/text_1170.pdf

Kameny, R. R., DeRoiser, M. E., Taylor, L. C., McMillen, J. S., Knowles, M. M., & Pifer, K. (2014). Barriers to career success for minority researchers in the behavioral sciences. *Journal of Career Development, 41*(1), 43–61.

Kenyon, D. B., & Hanson, J. D. (2012). Incorporating traditional culture into positive youth development programs with American Indian/Alaska Native youth. *Child Development Perspectives, 6*(3), 272–279.

Kiang, L., Supple, A. J., Stein, G. L., & Gonzalez, L. M. (2012). Gendered academic adjustment among Asian American adolescents in an emerging immigrant community. *Journal of Youth and Adolescence, 41*(3), 283–294.

Kim, S. Y., Wang, Y., Deng, S., Alvarez, R., & Li, J. (2011). Accent, perpetual foreigner stereotype, and perceived discrimination as indirect links between English proficiency and depressive symptoms in Chinese American adolescents. *Developmental Psychology, 47*(1), 289–301.

Knight, G. P., & Carlo, G. (2012). Prosocial development among Mexican American youth. *Child Development Perspectives, 6*(3), 258–263.

Knight, G. P., Roosa, M. W., & Umaña-Taylor, A. (2009). *Studying ethnic minority and economically disadvantaged populations: Methodological challenges and best practices*. Washington, DC: APA Books.

Ladson-Billings, G. (2006). From the achievement gap to the education debt: Understanding achievement in U.S. schools. *Educational Researcher, 35*(7), 3–12.

Li-Grining, C. P. (2012). The role of cultural factors in the development of Latino preschoolers' self-regulation. *Child Development Perspectives, 6*(3), 210–217.

McCabe, A., Tamis-LeMonda, C. T., Bornstein, M. H., Cates, C. B., Golinkoff, R., Guerra, A.W., et al. (2013). Multilingual children: Beyond myths and toward best practices. *Social Policy Report, 27*(4), 1–37.

McLoyd, V. C. (1990). Minority children: Introduction to the special issue. *Child Development, 61*(2), 263–266.

McLoyd, V. C. (1991). What is the study of African American children the study of? The conduct, publication, and changing nature of research on African American children. In R. L. Jones (Ed.), *Black Psychology* (pp. 419–440). Berkeley, CA: Cobb & Henry.

McLoyd, V. C. (2006). The legacy of Child Development's 1990 Special Issue on Minority Children: An editorial retrospective. *Child Development, 77*(5), 1142–1148.

Mesman, J., van IJzendoorn, M. H., & Bakermans-Kranenburg, M. J. (2012). Unequal in opportunity, equal in process: Parental sensitivity promotes positive child development in ethnic minority families. *Child Development Perspectives, 6*(3), 239–250.

Mistry, R. S., Biesanz, J. C., Chien, N., Howes, C., & Benner, A. D. (2008). Socioeconomic status, parental investments, and the cognitive and behavioral outcomes of low-income children from immigrant and native households. *Early Childhood Research Quarterly, 23*(2), 193–212.

Morcillo, C., Duarte, C. S., Shen, S., Blanco, C., Canino, G., & Bird, H. R. (2011). Parental familism and antisocial behaviors: Development, gender, and potential mechanisms. *Child and Adolescent Psychiatry, 50*(5), 471–479.

Morton, M. J. (2014). Cultural code-switching: Straddling the achievement gap. *Journal of Political Philosophy, 22*(3), 259–281.

National Academies of Sciences, Engineering, and Medicine. (2016). *Parenting matters: Supporting parents of children ages 0–8.* Washington, DC: National Academies Press.

National Academies of Sciences, Engineering, and Medicine. (2017). *Promoting the educational success of children and youth learning English: Promising futures.* Washington, DC: National Academies Press.

Neblett, E. W., Rivas-Drake, D., & Umaña-Taylor, A. J. (2012). The promise of racial and ethnic protective factors in promoting ethnic minority youth development. *Child Development Perspectives, 6*(3), 295–303.

Padilla, C. M., Cabrera, N., & West, J. (2017). *The development and home environment of low-income Hispanic children: Kindergarten to third grade.* Bethesda, MD: National Research Center on Hispanic Children and Families. Retrieved from http://www.hispanicresearch center.org/wp-content/uploads/2017/09/Developmental-Profiles.pdf

Phinney, J. S., Ong, A., & Madden, T. (2000). Cultural values and intergenerational value discrepancies in immigrant and non-immigrant families. *Child Development, 71*(2), 528–539.

Qin, D. B., Way, N., & Mukherjee, P. (2008). The other side of the model minority story: The familial and peer challenges faced by Chinese American adolescents. *Youth & Society, 39*(4), 480–506.

Rogoff, B. (2011). *Developing destinies: A Mayan midwife and town.* Cary, NC: Oxford University Press.

Roosa, M. W., Zeiders, K. H., Knight, G. P., Gonzales, N. A., Tein, J. -Y., Saenz, D., et al. (2011). A test of the social development model during the transition to junior high with Mexican American adolescents. *Developmental Psychology, 47*(2), 527–537.

Schweigman, K., Soto, C., Wright, S., & Unger, J. (2011). The relevance of cultural activities in ethnic identity among California Native American youth. *Journal of Psychoactive Drugs, 43*(4), 343–348.

Smith, E. P., Osgood, D. W., Caldwell, L., Hynes, K., & Perkins, D. F. (2013). Measuring collective efficacy among children in community-based afterschool programs: Exploring pathways toward prevention and positive youth development. *American Journal of Community Psychology, 52*(1–2), 27–40.

Syed, M. (2012, February). *Interdisciplinary and theoretical approaches.* Paper presented at the Positive Development of Minority Children meeting of the Society for Research in Child Development, Tampa, FL.

Syed, M., Santos, C., Yoo, H. C., & Juang, L. P. (2018). Invisibility of racial/ethnic minorities in developmental science: Implications for research and institutional practices. *American Psychologist, 73*(6), 812–826.

Taylor, Z. E., Larsen-Rife, D., Conger, R. D., & Widaman, K. F. (2012). Familism, interparental conflict, and parenting in Mexican-origin families: A cultural-contextual framework. *Journal of Marriage and Family, 74*(2), 312–327.

Trivette, C. M., Dunst, C. J., Hamby, D. W., & O'Herin, C. E. (2009). Characteristics and consequences of adult learning methods and strategies. *Winterberry Research Syntheses, 2*(2), 1–33.

Trotter, Y. D. (2006). Adult learning theories: Impacting professional development programs. *Delta Kappa Gamma Bulletin, 72*(2), 8–13.

Umaña-Taylor, A. J., Gonzales-Backen, M. A., & Guimond, A. B. (2009). Latino adolescents' ethnic identity: Is there a developmental progression and does growth in ethnic identity predict growth in self-esteem? *Child Development, 80*(2), 391–405.

United States Government Accountability Office. (2018). *K–12 education: Discipline disparities for Black students, boys, and students with disabilities.* Washington, DC: Author. Retrieved from https://www.gao.gov/assets/700/690828.pdf

Updegraff, K. A., McHale, S. M., Whiteman, S. D., Thayer, S. M., & Delgado, M. Y. (2005). Adolescent sibling relationships in Mexican American families: Exploring the role of familism. *Journal of Family Psychology, 19*(4), 512–522.

Vespa, J., Armstrong, D. M., & Medina, L. (2018). *Demographic turning points for the United States: Population projections for 2020 to 2060.* Current Population Reports, P25-1144. Washington, DC: U.S. Census Bureau. Retrieved from https://www.census.gov/content/dam/Census/library/publications/2018/demo/P25_1144.pdf

Weisner, T. S. (2002). Ecocultural understanding of children's developmental pathways. *Human Development, 45*(4), 275–281.

Weisner, T. S. (2012, February). *Interdisciplinary and theoretical approaches.* Paper presented at the Positive Development of Minority Children meeting of the Society for Research in Child Development, Tampa, FL.

Werner, E. E. (1995). Resilience in development. *Current Directions in Psychological Science, 4*(3), 81–84.

Wong, C. A., & Rowley, S. J. (2001). The schooling of ethnic minority children: Commentary. *Educational Psychologist, 36*(1), 57–66.

Yamamoto, Y., & Li, J. (2012). What makes a high-quality preschool? Similarities and differences between Chinese immigrant and European American parents' views. *Early Childhood Research Quarterly, 27*(2), 306–315.

Zepeda, M., Castro, D. C., & Cronin, S. (2011). Preparing early childhood teachers to work with young dual language learners. *Child Development Perspectives, 5*(1), 10–14.

Zhou, Q., Tao, A., Chen, S. H., Main, A., Lee, E., Ly, J., et al. (2012). Asset and protective factors for Asian American children's mental health adjustment. *Child Development Perspectives, 6*(3), 312–319.

III

Theme B: Early Care and Education

Research studies on early care and education caught the attention of many researchers and educators in the 1960s, setting the stage for 50 years of advances in early interventions. The initial work on early care and education reflects interest in the malleability of intelligence, as well as the potential for environmental changes to enhance the developmental and educational outcomes for children reared in poverty. Researchers designed early "compensatory" programs that would help prepare these young children for school. Based on outcomes from several early research studies, beliefs about the malleability of intelligence, and national concerns about children growing up in poverty, several significant events took place, including the initiation of Head Start and increased attention to environmental influences on children's intellectual and developmental outcomes.

Building on the momentum in the 1960s, the Frank Porter Graham Institute initiated a child development program to examine the benefits for children who were growing up in poverty. In 1972, this early effort became the foundation for the Abecedarian Project, initiated by Craig Ramey and his colleagues. In Chapter 7, Ramey places in theoretical and historical context the Abecedarian Project—a study that was to become one of the most referenced early childhood intervention programs in the United States. Using the term *Abecedarian Approach*, he describes this term as encompassing concepts and procedures used in a series of experimental studies, including the Abecedarian Project, Project CARE, and the Infant Health and Developmental Program. A central feature of the Abecedarian Approach was a set of "learning games" that provided many opportunities for adult–child dyadic interactions. Positive educational, social, and economic outcomes are presented. The author concludes by addressing the relevance of the Abecedarian Approach to today's U.S. population and circumstances.

Tackling one of the vexing issues in early care and education—namely, how do we best prepare personnel to work with young children—Marilou Hyson identifies major issues in professional development and practices in

Chapter 8. Of critical importance is her observation that, despite a strong empirically established knowledge base about child development and learning, knowledge utilization practices often do not reflect this evidence base; practitioners often fail to use available insights from research and professional expertise. This theme of an existing and compelling knowledge base, with a disconnection between knowledge and practice, guides her chapter. She provides examples of low uptake of such knowledge and, even when uptake is evident, low sustainability of knowledge-informed practices. Although the professional field has recommended a skills-focused approach to teacher preparation, including such recommendations in accreditations standards, Hyson observes that this approach is infrequently implemented. To address the disconnection between knowledge and practice, both within and beyond higher education, she proposes that the field employ key concepts from implementation science to guide the field.

Policies related to children and their families also had considerable impact beginning in the 1960s, with significant legislation funding research centers, Head Start, and numerous social programs for children and adults. Ron Haskins, an expert on policy for more than four decades, takes the reader through a concise review of the political landscape influencing early childhood education from the 1960s to the present in Chapter 9. He identifies the change in public perceptions and policy since the 1960s toward sponsoring early childhood programs, based in part on empirical support and theory and, second, on the vast numbers of families that need child care as a result of working mothers. Making the distinction between early childhood programs designed to provide primarily child care for working parents and ones designed to enhance child development, he reviews the growth of these programs, especially Head Start, the State Pre-K Movement, the Child Care and Development Block Grant, and the Temporary Assistance for Needy Families. These major programs are supplemented by 50 additional programs eligible to support different forms of child care. Haskins contrasts this federal support with funding at the state level, noting the reliance of states on federal grants, but concluding that future funding may be more likely to come from state than from federal sources. He also identifies a significant cultural shift toward recognizing the importance of high-quality early childhood environments for children from low-income families.

These three themes of early care and education are brought together by Steve Barnett in the detailed synthesis in Chapter 10, which is used as a foundation to make recommendations for future work. Building on his expertise in evaluating the outcomes of early intervention studies, Barnett reviews the outcomes of both smaller classic studies as well as large-scale public programs, noting the frequent finding that large-scale programs have smaller impacts. He identifies several significant cultural factors in attempting to compare current large-scale studies with those conducted several decades ago. In particular, he observes that health and educational benefits are stronger for low-income families than they were 30 to 40 years ago. Furthermore, the characteristics of children enrolled in preschool programs have changed significantly, with more dual-language learners, more children with developmental disabilities, and more children who are being reared in single-parent households—all factors that likely contribute to smaller impacts. Barnett calls for major shifts in practice if significant change is to come about. In particular, he calls on the field to shift from the paradigm of seeing research as continuous improvement to one of team-work among researchers, policy makers, and practitioners, who must work together to accomplish meaningful outcomes.

The authors in this section have challenged the reader to go well beyond current thinking about issues in early care and education to recon-ceptualizing how researchers, practitioners, and policy makers help bring about significant and lasting changes in the outcomes for young children and their families. Their calls for change have the potential to significantly alter the early care and education of low-income and minority children and potentially raise the base for all early education and care experiences.

7

The Abecedarian Approach to Full Development in Early Childhood

Craig T. Ramey

Some questions about human existence are so basic as to require scientific address, if possible. The question of human malleability is one such question. Can the course of human development be altered by intentional and directed acts? If so, through what systematic means and by how much? To what ends should systematic efforts be focused?

The question of human malleability has a long and controversial history in the United States. It began with racial and social class assumptions that predate the founding of the republic and that became cornerstones of public polices concerning education, housing, health care, employment, and marriage. Scientists have contributed to the controversies, with some individuals taking strongly predetermined and genetic views, such as Galton (1883), Jensen (1969), and Herrnstein and Murray (1994). Conversely, others have favored an experiential and/or environmental viewpoint (e.g., Bijou & Baer, 1961; Hunt, 1961), particularly with respect to cognitive performance.

What became clear to me was that this basic controversy needed an experimental approach (see Lazar et al., 1982). This controversy could not be adequately addressed via correlational analyses of naturalistic observations. The most basic question became whether individuals from highly vulnerable populations would benefit significantly if given access to more adequate resources. Chief among these resources were high-quality early care and education, as well as health care, nutrition, and family-oriented social services. These are factors that we attempted to control experimentally in the work I describe in this chapter. This work followed on the vision of the early founders of the Frank Porter Graham (FPG) Institute, Hal and Nancy Robinson, who believed in the potential of early care and education to change the trajectory of children from vulnerable populations.

This chapter deals with some of the experimental work that my colleagues and I began at FPG almost five decades ago. I realize there are practice, policy, and ethical implications to these basic questions; however, this chapter is primarily about the research that we have been privileged to carry out on human malleability.

THE ABECEDARIAN APPROACH TO EARLY CHILDHOOD

This chapter provides an overview of the Abecedarian Approach developed and used in the Abecedarian Project (e.g., Ramey et al., 1976) and its replications, Project Carolina Approach to Responsive Education (CARE; e.g., Ramey, Bryant, Sparling, & Wasik, 1985; Wasik, Ramey, Bryant, & Sparling, 1990) and the Infant Health and Development Program (IHDP; e.g., Infant Health and Development Program, 1990; Ramey et al., 1992). The word "approach" is used to indicate the main Abecedarian concepts and procedures that have been used as tools in a series of experimental studies. The procedures are what behavioral scientists often call the "experimental treatment." In that sense, the Abecedarian Approach (summarized in the sidebar) is a set of standards, curriculum resources, and practices that were used in the interventions conducted for the Abecedarian Project, Project CARE, and the IHDP.

Major Features of the Abecedarian Approach

- An education program that began in early infancy
- A structured curriculum grounded in developmental theory and research findings (Sparling & Lewis, 1979, 1984, 2008)
- A highly trained and actively monitored teaching staff committed to implementing the curriculum and documenting each child's progress with biweekly summaries
- Provision of high-quality health and safety practices, including active health/safety monitoring of all children within an environment that emphasized nutritious food, lots of exercise and play, and health promotion (good hygiene, appropriate rest)
- Low adult-to-child ratios (1:3 until babies were walking, 1:4 for toddlers and age 2 years; 1:6 for ages 3 and 4 years)
- Ongoing professional development from the child development center director and other learning specialists, with weekly meetings and frequent monitoring and in-classroom supports for teachers; active instruction and supervision for all teachers to implement the curriculum daily and to document each child's engagement in specific games that were part of the educational program
- Individualization of pace in the curriculum and attention to special needs of the child and family, including provision of social work services in a timely manner with follow-up supports
- Provision of transportation to children as needed from their homes to center and back
- Full-day, full-week, year-round program (center open from 7:30 a.m. to 5:30 p.m., operating 5 days a week, 50 weeks per year) with major emphasis on full attendance by all children

- Parent engagement component, including group meetings and special topic sessions, as well as teacher meetings with parents about their own children's progress
- Stable and stimulating adult–child interactions, with a central commitment to ensuring that each child engaged daily in many rich and varied language and learning activities

The research that drove the creation of the Abecedarian Project came out of basic behavioral research, which clearly established that even young infants were capable of learning, remembering, and generalizing from environments that were responsive to their behaviors (see Ramey & Finkelstein, 1978; Watson & Ramey, 1972). The three main experiments to be described sought to determine whether the provision of a theory-guided set of active learning experiences could produce significant benefits in language and learning for children from highly impoverished, multirisk families (who were known from an epidemiological perspective to be at risk for poor school achievement and subsequent life difficulties) and for children with known biological risks for poor cognitive development (i.e., low birth weight and prematurity). The control group children who did not attend the child development centers received support for health care, free and unlimited nutritional supports, and active social work services to the families, as well as timely referrals when any developmental problems were detected or suspected. Because the control groups received these multiple supports, the research findings provide a strong basis for concluding that it was the educational features of the Abecedarian Approach that produced the documented positive differences between the children in the experimental groups versus the control groups.

THE THREE ABECEDARIAN LONGITUDINAL RESEARCH STUDIES

The Abecedarian Approach was employed in three independent longitudinal Abecedarian studies—two single site and one multisite randomized controlled trials. The protocol was applied in these studies with some variations, as Table 7.1 summarizes.

The overall Abecedarian program and the specific educational practices and curricula were designed to be highly engaging, fun, and active—with learning occurring throughout the day in various activities (including daily caregiving, transitions, physical play and exploration, as well as more structured learning activities). Activities included many adult–child individualized interactions, as well as small-group activities as babies became older.

The systematic educational curriculum was based on the identification of multiple types of learning processes in infants, toddlers, and young children. Furthermore, it was paced to be appropriate for a child's developmental stage and to continuously provide challenges that were individualized for each child (Sparling & Lewis, 1979, 2008). The Abecedarian Approach strongly acknowledged the centrality of communication to the development of intelligence (see McGinness & Ramey, 1981). Thus, the planned "learn-

Table 7.1. Three longitudinal applications of the Abecedarian Approach

	The Abecedarian Project (1971–2017)	Project CARE (1977–2017)	Infant Health and Development Program (1983–1992)
Criteria for inclusion in the sample	Multicomponent socioeconomic risk (high risk score > 11)	Multicomponent socioeconomic risk (high risk score > 11)	Low birth weight (< 2,500 g) and premature (< 37 weeks' gestational age)
Duration of the child development center program	Age: 6 weeks to 5 years	Age: 6 weeks to 5 years	Corrected age: 12 months to 3 years
Amount of child development center program offered	Full day,[a] 5 days per week, 50 weeks per year	Full day, 5 days per week, 50 weeks per year	Full day, 5 days per week, 50 weeks per year
Visits in homes	As needed, for social support[b]	Weekly educational visits (*LearningGames*®, 1979, 1984)	Weekly educational visits (*LearningGames*®, 1979, 1984 and *Partners for Learning*, 1984, 1995)
Health care	Onsite with nurses and physicians	Onsite with nurses and physicians	By family's own provider
Transportation to center	Provided by program	Provided by program	Provided by program
Parent education group sessions	Several per year	Several per year	Every other month
Educational program	Abecedarian Approach	Abecedarian Approach	Abecedarian Approach

[a]Most children received approximately 8 hours per day.

[b]For the Abecedarian Project, 50% of the child development center children and 50% of the preschool control also received a home-school liaison follow-up program with a summer educational program for the first 3 years of public school. This included both home and school visits.

ing games" activities included many ways to use signs, symbols, sounds, words, sentences, stories, and interactive conversations—starting early in the first year of life. Even conversational reading and play began in infancy with specially written picture/word books. Adults used varied, complex, and informative language throughout the day; the use of Standard English in the child development center was emphasized. (Note that none of the children or families in Abecedarian Project or Project CARE were bilingual.)

The Commitment to High Quality in the Abecedarian Approach

In the Abecedarian Approach, four areas were considered especially critical to help children to grow and thrive. These areas recently have been described in detail as the Four-Diamond Model of High-Quality Early Care and Education (C. T. Ramey & Ramey, 2017; S. L. Ramey & Ramey, 2005); S. L. Ramey, Ramey, & Sonnier-Netto, 2008, 2012.

- *Health and safety practices:* Behaviors that seek to prevent accidents and promote physical and mental health and safety, consistently implemented at all times

- *Adult–child interactions:* Frequent, warm, and responsive to the individual child

- *Language and learning activities:* Adapted for the child's age and developmental level to maintain high interest and motivation; frequent, enjoyable, and promoting new and more advanced levels of child competence and independence

- *Caregiver–family relationships:* Respectful, supportive, and informative; frequent communication between adults in the program and parents and other family members

In the Four-Diamond Model, there are many other environmental influences (e.g., staffing ratios, the physical environment) displayed as potentially supportive, but these are considered indirect rather than direct influences on the child.

THE ABECEDARIAN STUDY SAMPLES

The Abecedarian Approach was applied in three separate longitudinal investigations while I was at FPG from 1971 to 1990. The following are some details on the study samples in these research projects:

- *The Abecedarian Project:* The sample consisted of 111 low-income, high-risk families in Orange County, North Carolina, whose children were born between 1972 and 1977. Of the families in the Abecedarian Project, 98% were African American and 76% were single mothers. The mothers had an average educational level of 10th grade.

- *Project CARE:* The sample consisted of 65 low-income, high-risk families in Orange County, North Carolina, whose children were born between 1978 and 1980. Of the CARE families, 91% were African American and 81% were single mothers. The mothers had an average educational level of 11th grade.

- *The Infant Health and Development Program:* The sample across eight sites comprised a total of 985 premature and low birth weight infants from eight cities. The families were from all socioeconomic classes and were 38% White/non-Hispanic, 53% African American, and 11% Hispanic.

These three are the longest-term and most extensively published Abecedarian Approach studies, but there have been shorter-term research studies that employed all or parts of the Abecedarian Approach. In the listing of investigations in Table 7.2, the eight sites of the IHDP study are broken out to show the independently randomized IHDP site samples; each was approximately the size of the original Abecedarian Project or larger. In total, this list identifies 10 samples that have been studied in randomized controlled trials that tested the efficacy of the Abecedarian Approach.

Table 7.2.   Randomized Abecedarian Approach studies

Randomized samples	Location	n	Duration of program	Type of program	Oldest age of follow-up
Abecedarian 1 (The Abecedarian Project)	Chapel Hill, NC	111 children	Birth to age 5 years	Center + social work + home visits + health care	40 years
Abecedarian 2 (Project CARE)	Chapel Hill, NC	64 children	Birth to age 5 years	Center + social work + educational home visits + health care	21 years
Infant Health and Development Program (IHDP)					
Abecedarian 3	Boston, MA	138 children	Birth to age 3 years	Center + educational home visits	18 years
Abecedarian 4	New Haven, CT	112 children	Birth to age 3 years	Center + educational home visits	18 years
Abecedarian 5	Bronx, NY	138 children	Birth to age 3 years	Center + educational home visits	18 years
Abecedarian 6	Philadelphia, PA	101 children	Birth to age 3 years	Center + educational home visits	18 years
Abecedarian 7	Miami, FL	100 children	Birth to age 3 years	Center + educational home visits	18 years
Abecedarian 8	Little Rock, AK	128 children	Birth to age 3 years	Center + educational home visits	18 years
Abecedarian 9	Dallas, TX	137 children	Birth to age 3 years	Center + educational home visits	18 years
Abecedarian 10	Seattle, WA	131 children	Birth to age 3 years	Center + educational home visits	18 years

Admission Criteria for the Longitudinal Studies

Before launching the Abecedarian Project, we created a High-Risk Index (Ramey & Smith, 1977) to establish eligibility for admission of children into the research sample. We used epidemiological data concerning the demographic factors linked to developmental delay and poor school achievement. We assigned weights to these variables based upon the best available evidence about their predictive importance.

In the Abecedarian Project and in Project CARE, the criteria for inclusion was a High-Risk Index score greater than a pre-established value and being healthy at birth. We randomly assigned children to either the experimental or the control group via a computer program.

In the eight-site Infant Health and Development Project, the only criteria for inclusion were low birth weight and prematurity (< 37 weeks' gestational age). Children were randomly assigned to one of two strata: birth weight between 2,500 and 2,000 g and birth weight less than 2,000 g.

Highlights of the Longitudinal Studies

The children in the Abecedarian Project were randomly assigned to two groups: an experimental treatment group (57 children) and a control group (54 children). All 111 children in the study were healthy, full-term infants with a normal birth weight, but they lived in families that were extremely challenged. Their family characteristics included the following:

- Very low incomes (well below 50% of the federal poverty line, adjusted for family size)

- Very low levels of education (approximately 10 years) among mothers

- Low intellectual test scores for mothers (the average intelligence quotient [IQ] score was near 85)

- Single parenthood (in approximately 75% of the families)

- Unemployed mothers (almost all at time of study recruitment)

The study was designed to test the effects of a high-quality, supportive educational program, the Abecedarian Approach, over the first 5 years of life. We sought to answer the following question: Can the cumulative developmental toll experienced by high-risk children be prevented or reduced significantly by providing systematic, high-quality early childhood education from birth through kindergarten entry?

Table 7.3 summarizes the services received by the treatment and control groups. Both groups received the following:

- Adequate nutrition (i.e., free, unlimited supply of iron-fortified formula); none of the mothers chose to breast-feed

- Supportive social services for the family with referrals as needed (e.g., for housing, job training, mental health and substance abuse problems) over the first 5 years of life

- Free or reduced-cost medical care (consistent with the highest levels of professionally recommended pediatric care) for the children's first 5 years of life

With this design, the control group was not untreated. Rather, the basic nutrition, health, and social service needs of the families and children were addressed systematically during the children's first 5 years of life.

The key factor distinguishing the treatment group was being enrolled in our child development center, starting as early as 6 weeks of age, and lasting until the children entered public kindergarten. The Abecedarian program was provided full day, 5 days per week, 50 weeks per year.

Table 7.3.   The Abecedarian Project: Comparison of treatment and control groups

The Abecedarian treatment group	Control group
Adequate nutrition	Adequate nutrition
Supportive social services	Supportive social services
Free primary health care	Low-cost or free primary health care
Transportation	Transportation
Preschool treatment: intensive (full day, 5 days/week, 50 weeks/year, 5 years)	

Health Studies Embedded in the Abecedarian Project

Because all of the families were living in poverty, it was difficult for them to access high-quality health care; therefore, we provided on-site child health care. In the process of providing this free health care, the medical team of the FPG Child Development Center were able to study important issues regarding health and illness in group child care settings. At the time, infant and toddler group care outside the family's home was new and highly controversial. Reasonably, there was serious concern about the spread of infectious diseases and other health and safety risks, including the potential disruption of mother–infant attachment relationships.

Studies of the Abecedarian children produced many journal articles and book chapters that added new knowledge to the field of young children's health. For example, contributions to knowledge were made on lung growth and functioning (Collier et al., 1978; Williams, Fulton, Tsai, Pimmel, & Collier, 1979; Williams, Pimmel, Fulton, Tsai, & Collier, 1979), otitis media (Etzel, Pattishall, Haley, Fletcher, & Henderson, 1992; Henderson et al., 1982), the role of mycoplasma and viral infections (Fernald, Collier, & Clyde, 1975; Henderson, Collier, Clyde, & Denny, 1979), and other infectious diseases (Carson, Collier, & Hu, 1985).

Overall, the careful monitoring of the daily health of the Abecedarian children provided first-ever evidence that an early childhood program did not result in poor health outcomes if the program consistently followed good hygiene practices, spaced beds apart, and provided prompt care for illnesses and injuries. Data from the Abecedarian Project and Project CARE contributed to later guidelines established by the American Academy of Pediatrics regarding infant and toddler group care.

Preschool Intellectual Results

In the Abecedarian Project, we measured many aspects of the children's growth and development at frequent intervals in their first 5 years. The assessments included cognitive, linguistic, and social-emotional outcomes for children and potential educational and employment benefits for mothers.

Qualified psychologists who had no involvement in the children's treatment group administered and scored individual developmental and cognitive assessments for all children in both groups between 3 and 54 months of age. The key findings, which are presented in Figure 7.1, were as follows:

- For the first 12 months, the treatment and control groups performed similarly and essentially at the national average.

- After 12 months, the control group's mean scores declined precipitously. At 24 months of age, the control children were performing at the low end of the normal range (at an average developmental quotient of 85 on the Bayley Scales of Infant Development).

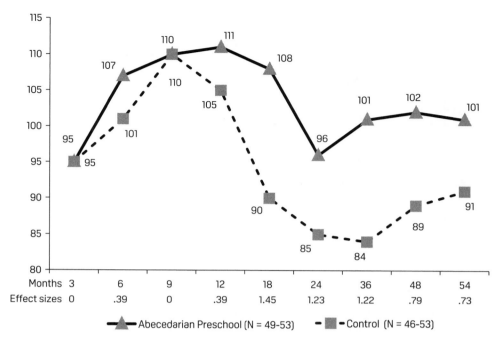

Figure 7.1.   Intellectual scores for early intervention and control participants in the Abecedarian Project.

- For the remaining preschool years, the treatment group scored an average of 10–15 points higher than did the control group, on three different types of developmental assessments (Ramey, Campbell, & Ramey 1999).

   In the education field, an effect size of 0.25 standard deviation or more is widely accepted as a sufficient basis for changing practice and policy. In the Abecedarian Project, the effect sizes ranged from 0.73 to 1.45 for children from the ages of 18 months to 4.5 years.

   A clinical perspective offers another view. Figure 7.2 shows the percentage of children in each group who scored in the normal range of intelligence (i.e., earning IQ scores of 85 or higher on tests that have a national average of 100 and a standard deviation of 15 or 16 depending on the test) at ages 6 months to 4 years. The findings were as follows (Martin, Ramey, & Ramey, 1990):

- For the control group, 93% were in the normal range at age 6 months, but this dropped to 45% by age 4 years. This is clearly consistent with the hypothesis of a cumulative toll due to lack of cognitive, language, and social-emotional learning opportunities.

- For the early educational treatment group, 95%–100% scored in the normal range at all ages tested. This pattern of consistent and large differences between the groups supports the hypothesis that high-quality early education can prevent cognitive delays or below normal intelligence in children from very-low-resource families.

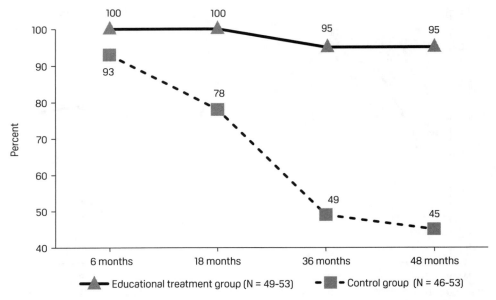

Figure 7.2. Percent of children in normal IQ range (>84) by age, control, and treatment groups in the Abecedarian Project. (*Source:* Martin, Ramey, & Ramey, 1990.)

Benefits for Mothers

The Abecedarian preschool intervention had other benefits as well, which included advantages for the children's mothers. For example, during the preschool years, the teenage mothers of children in the treatment group were significantly more likely to continue their own education. The teenage mothers continued their own educational advancement throughout their children's school years. By the time their children were 15 years old, 80% of these mothers had some post-high school education, compared with only 30% of the teenage mothers of children in the control group (Ramey et al., 2000).

The project staff encouraged the mothers of children in both groups to seek additional education through the social services component, but we did not provide any formal educational program or pay tuition and other costs. Figure 7.3 shows the percentage of teenage mothers in both groups who obtained additional education after enrolling in the study.

Replications: Project CARE and the Infant Health and Development Program

The hallmark of science is replicability of procedures and findings. The Abecedarian Project was replicated in two additional longitudinal studies conducted at nine different sites:

- Project CARE (Ramey et al., 1985; Wasik et al., 1990), which was initiated in 1978 in North Carolina

- The Infant Health and Development Program (1990), which was initiated in 1985 and conducted at eight sites (Little Rock, Arkansas; New Haven,

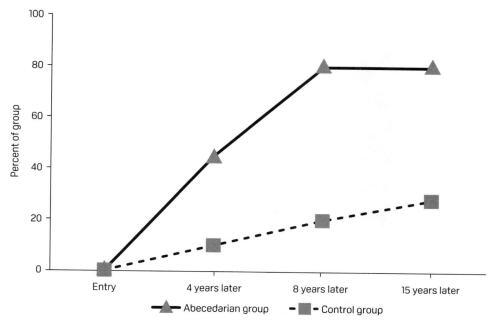

Figure 7.3. Percent of teenage mothers who obtained post–high school education after their infants entered the Abecedarian Project. (*Source:* Ramey et al., 2000.)

Connecticut; Miami, Florida; Boston, Massachusetts; New York, New York; Philadelphia, Pennsylvania; Dallas, Texas; and Seattle, Washington)

Children in the early education group of Project CARE served as a true replication for the Abecedarian Project, receiving 5 years of the same educational program at the same site (FPG Child Development Center); the IHDP replication was limited to only the first 3 years of life and included some accommodations for the children's low birth weight and premature conditions. At all nine replication sites, significant effects of the early Abecedarian Approach occurred with benefits in tested intelligence, language, and social-emotional development at 3 years of age.

TARGETED EARLY CHILDHOOD PROGRAMS

A pressing policy issue has to do with whether all young children need early educational enrichment. For example, do all premature and low birth weight infants need a special early educational intervention program?

The findings from the IHDP, which focused on 985 low birth weight, premature infants are informative. The findings support the well-established effects of maternal education on children's intellectual and cognitive performance in the control group condition.

Among the control group of 608 children, those whose mothers had not graduated from high school performed at the very lowest level (i.e., had the lowest IQs), followed next by those whose mothers graduated from high school, attended college, and graduated from a 4-year college. This stepwise

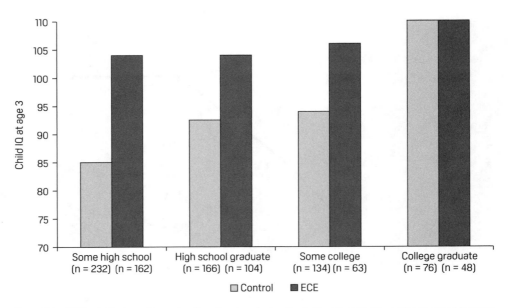

Figure 7.4. Children's IQ at age 3 as a function of maternal education in the Infant Health and Development Program (From Ramey, Sparling, & Ramey, 2012; adapted by permission.) (*Key:* ECE, early care and education.)

and cumulative difference reflects the well-recognized influence of parental education on children's IQ scores. The children who scored the lowest had an average IQ at age 3 years of approximately 85, which was one standard deviation below average (100).

In the treatment group of 377 children, the pattern was very different. Essentially, the Abecedarian preschool program "leveled the playing field" for these children and enabled them to perform at levels slightly higher (IQs of 104–107) than the national average (Ramey & Ramey, 1998).

For children whose mothers were college graduates, the early education program neither increased nor decreased their intelligence test scores at age 3 (see Figure 7.4). We hypothesize that the parents of these low birth weight, premature infants were able to provide opportunities for learning that were comparable in quality, quantity, and content to that in the IHDP child development centers (i.e., the Abecedarian Approach). Children in the IHDP control group often received a combination of community-based, home-based, and specialist care and treatment that these college-degreed families were able to seek out and afford. These children performed well above the national average—even if they were born prematurely and with a low birth weight and regardless of whether they received the Abecedarian treatment or other natural stimulation and programs that their parents arranged for them.

This finding confirms similar results from a number of other studies. That is, not all children need additional education or enrichment in the form of a planned preschool program to perform in the average range of cognition and intelligence. Rather, the children whose families have the least amount of resources, as estimated by parents' educational and intellectual skills, are those who are most likely to need and benefit from systematic provision of enriched learning opportunities in child development educational programs.

Educational Process Data

How Levels of Participation Influence Child Outcomes In the IHDP, linking the process of early educational intervention to outcome provided important insights. The extensive data collected on implementation of the IHDP pointed to a variety of process factors that are predictive of a child's developmental progress in an early childhood intervention. The factors include, for example, the level of children's participation, the amount of curriculum activities, the rate of delivery of curriculum activities, and the degree of active experience for parents and children.

A major outcome demonstrated in the IHDP was a 9-point overall difference in IQ between the control and treatment groups at age 3. To explore a possible relationship between this 9-point difference in IQ and the level of children's participation in the intervention, we devised a participation index. This index was the sum number of contacts between each family and the intervention program, as measured by the number of days a child attended the child development center, the number of home visits completed, and the number of group meetings parents attended. The differences in the percent of children at borderline (≤ 85) or lower IQ at age 3 years across the three levels of participation were 19.6% in the low-participation group, 11.9% in the medium-participation group, and 6.9% in the high-participation group. The control group had 35.5% with IQs ≤ 85 (Ramey et al., 1992).

Amount of Curriculum Activities Another consideration is how much of the instructional curriculum each child receives when attending the center. Table 7.4 shows the mean IQ of children in the treatment group at age 36 months matched to birth weight and level of curriculum activities (low, medium, high) received in the child development center and at home. The data show a positive correlation between mean IQ and level of curriculum activities for both low-birth-weight groups. The higher the number of activities, the higher was the child's IQ. Furthermore, among the children who received a low level of activities, those who had a smaller birth weight

Table 7.4. Mean IQ at age 36 months for 3 levels of curriculum activity received by children of two varying birth weight ranges in the Infant Health and Development Program

Birth weight	Level of participation		
	Low	Medium	High
$\leq 2,000$ g	82	95	97
2,001–2,500 g	92	98	100

Source: Sparling et al., 1991.

(< 2,000 g) had a 10-point lower IQ than did those who had a higher birth weight (2,001–2,005 g) (Sparling et al., 1991).

Rate of Curriculum Delivery and Active Experience   In an independent analysis of the year-by-year levels of participation of individual children and families, Blair, Ramey, and Hardin (1995) discovered a clear association between participation levels and cognitive progress at ages 2 and 3 years. For each year from ages 1–3 years, the days attended by the child in the IHDP Abecedarian Approach Center, the number of home visits, and the number of parent meetings attended predicted cognitive advances or benefits, whereas the child's background characteristics, such as maternal education and birth weight, did not. That is, these high-risk children's early educational experiences exerted an effect that served to eliminate the usual negative toll of low parent education, family income, and other indicators of very low levels of home stimulation. This outcome (Blair et al., 1995) represented the strongest evidence to date about a dosage effect of the Abecedarian Approach: the greater the level of exposure to high quality learning opportunities, the more the child gained in terms of IQ points each year.

SCHOOL-AGE RESULTS FROM THE ABECEDARIAN PROJECT

The long-term outcomes from the Abecedarian Project are equally informative. The children in the preschool treatment group continued to receive benefits from their participation in the early childhood program—lasting throughout their school years and into their adulthood. During the school years, and in comparison with the control group, the children who participated in the Abecedarian preschool intervention had the following:

- Significantly higher achievement scores in reading and math (according to independently administered Woodcock-Johnson Tests) at ages 8, 12, and 15 years, and even later at 21 years (Campbell, Pungello, Miller-Johnson, Burchinal, & Ramey, 2001)

- A lower rate of grade retention (i.e., failing at least one grade) that was almost half the rate for the control group (30% of the Abecedarian education group vs. 56% of the control group children)

- A lower rate of placement in special education by age 15 (only 12% of the treatment group vs. 48% of the control group that received no preschool or school-age intervention services), with the placement for children in the control group often occurring after repeated academic failures, social-adjustment problems, or conduct disorders (Ramey & Ramey, 1999)

The standardized tests for reading and math were individually administered by highly qualified assessors who did not know about the children's preschool treatment or their performance on earlier tests. Although the sustained benefits for reading and math are encouraging, they did not raise the children to the high levels of performance typical of children in their college-town community, where many parents had advanced graduate degrees. However, children's "real-world" school performance is of paramount interest and the fact that the educational treatment group had a much lower rate of grade retention argues well for the Abecedarian Approach for highly disadvantaged children.

The reduced need for special education also is an important educational and social outcome with both fiscal implications for governments and personal consequences for children and families. The cost of special education programs is approximately 2.5 times the cost of regular education. Children in special education are entitled to free public education until age 22 (approximately 4 additional years compared to students in regular education). The U.S. average for placement in special education programs is approximately 11%. For many children, the personal stigma associated with attending a special education program is considerable. This stigmatization is particularly difficult for children whose need for special education derives from their families' low-income or minority status rather than from medically diagnosed developmental disabilities.

EARLY ADULTHOOD RESULTS

In the Abecedarian Project, we had the rare opportunity to be able to follow more than 95% of the children living into adulthood. At age 21, the children who participated in the preschool intervention still showed signs of benefit from their participation compared to the control group. These long-term data show the following (Campbell, Ramey, Pungello, Sparling, & Miller-Johnson, 2002):

- Of the treatment group, 67% were engaged in a skilled job (i.e., Hollingshead category 4 or higher) or were enrolled in higher education, in contrast with only 41% of the control group.

- The young adults from the treatment group were three times more likely to have attended, or to be attending, a 4-year college than were those from the control group (35.7% vs. 13.7%).

- The percentage of teen parents (defined as having a first child at or before age 19) was significantly reduced in the treatment group compared with the control group (25% vs. 45%). Young adults who had received the Abecedarian early education treatment reported fewer symptoms of depression at age 21 years. Thus, the negative effects of lower-quality home environments on young adult depressive symptoms were almost entirely offset by the Abecedarian Approach.

- Data from both Project CARE and the Abecedarian Project indicate that young adults who had experienced the early childhood treatment showed evidence of adopting healthier lifestyles. For participants who received the center-based treatment, the odds of reporting a healthy lifestyle in young adulthood were 3.9 times greater compared with participants from the control groups.

- The use of illegal substances (e.g., marijuana within the past 30 days) was significantly lower for the treatment group compared to the control group (18% vs. 39%, respectively).

The results from age 30 years showed that those who received the Abecedarian early education, compared with controls, were almost 4 times as likely to graduate college (23% vs. 6%), more likely to be employed full-time (75% vs. 53%), less likely to have used extensive welfare supports (3.9% vs. 20.4%), and more likely to report being in excellent health (69% vs. 59%) (Campbell et al., 2012). Other beneficial outcomes at age 30 years with effect sizes > 0.25 included higher earned income, higher job prestige, and higher age at birth of first child. Above all, those who received high-quality early Abecedarian education were more likely than controls to have entered the middle class rather than remain in the lower class, as evidenced by educational levels, employment, and income.

SUMMARY OF THE ABECEDARIAN PROJECT RESULTS

The key findings from the Abecedarian Project are encouraging and are consistent within themselves and with the findings from other studies. The benefits—from 18 months through 21 years—for the children who participated in this early educational intervention can be summarized as follows:

- Higher IQ, reading, and math scores at 8, 12, 15, and 21 years of age (Campbell et al., 2012)

- Children's improved understanding of their role in the educational process, as reflected in their improved "academic locus-of-control" scores, whereby the children equated their effort and learning with their grades and achievement (rather than attributing them to factors such as teacher bias, chance, or luck; Walden & Ramey, 1983)

- Increased social competence (Ramey & Haskins, 1981)

- Additional years of educational accomplishment (Ramey et al., 2000; Campbell et al., 2002)

- Greater likelihood of full-time, higher-status employment and higher income (Campbell et al., 2012)

- Significantly lower rates of grade repetition, placement in special education, early teen pregnancy, smoking, and drug use (Ramey et al., 2000)

To achieve these long-lasting results, the Abecedarian intervention studies relied on broad and multifaceted intervention strategies, as noted in the sidebar at the beginning of the chapter. Broad, inclusive early intervention strategies appear to be essential for enhancing the basic cognitive and social skills of children at high risk. Children's ongoing and optimal long-term achievement in school is one of the basic pathways to every country's social equity and economic growth. The principal way to support this pathway is by providing children with a strong social-cognitive foundation—the hallmark of high-quality early childhood programs.

Mother–Child Attachment

Because the Abecedarian Approach began with children attending the Child Development Center beginning in early infancy, we were concerned that early group educational day care might have a negative effect on mother–child relationships and particularly attachment. In short, we were concerned that cognitive and language gains, if there were any, might be at the expense of the child's social relations with the family. This concern was a particularly delicate topic because attachment theory, stressing the importance of the mother–child bond during infancy (Bowlby, 1969), was approaching great saliency in the early 1970s when the Abecedarian Project was being launched. Thus, the Abecedarian Approach was highly controversial because we were beginning early childhood education at a much earlier age (as young as 6 weeks) than any other known research program at the time. Furthermore, we were operating a full-day program (7:30 a.m. to 5:30 p.m.) for 5 days per week and 50 weeks per year. We chose to directly address this issue through systematic and frequent examination of mother–child interaction patterns both in the home and in laboratory situations, including the so-called frequently used Ainsworth Strange Situation Protocol.

We are pleased to note that in a series of publications we found no evidence of negative effects on mother–child interaction patterns or attachment, even though there is clear evidence in both the treated and control groups that mother–child interaction patterns were, in fact, related to children's cognitive development (e.g., Burchinal, Bryant, Lee, & Ramey, 1992; Burchinal, Lee, & Ramey, 1989; Farran & Ramey, 1977; Farran & Ramey, 1980; Ramey & Farran, 1981; Ramey, Farran, & Campbell, 1979; Ramey, Yeates, & Short, 1984).

Differential Risk and Response to Treatment

The recruitment strategy for the selection of participants in all three randomized controlled trials adhered to a basic idea. That idea was to prespecify the inclusion cutoff points (e.g., a risk score of > 11 in the Abecedarian Project and Project CARE and birth weight of < 2,500 g and a gestational age of < 37 weeks in IHDP) and to assume that significant variation on important other parameters would likely occur. Given that random assignment should result in initial equivalence of treatment and control groups, this strategy allowed for a potentially useful data analytic approach to better understand different levels of risk as expressed in assessments of control group participants and how similar individuals or families responded to the delivery of the educational treatment.

An example of this research strategy comes from the study by Breitmayer and Ramey (1986) concerning biological nonoptimality and quality of the postnatal environment as codeterminants of intellectual development. In that publication, we demonstrated that even nonoptimal perinatal status (1-minute Apgar score of ≤ 8) had a negative relationship with cognitive scores at 4.5 years of age in the Abecedarian control group; however, comparable test scores of children with optimal or nonoptimal Apgar scores did not differ within the group that received the Abecedarian Approach educational treatment but were significantly higher than the control group.

These differential risk and response to treatment results are similar in form and outcomes to the mild fetal malnutrition reported by Zeskind and Ramey (1978, 1981). The general pattern has forced me to consider whether clinical cut points that have been established with general population samples need to be conditioned by an appreciation of the social context in which a child is likely to be reared. Low-resource environments may need to be taken into account when assigning risk status. In many ways, these general findings parallel the results from IHDP in which the Abecedarian Approach leveled the relationship between parental educational level and the child's cognitive performance at 3 years of age.

Cost-Benefit Analyses

Cost-benefit analyses have become an expected feature in public policy concerning child and family programs, particularly for economically disadvantaged families. This work was pioneered by Steven Barnett (1996) using data from the Perry Preschool Project. Barnett and Masse (2007) also conducted a preliminary cost-benefit analysis of the Abecedarian program through age 21 years.

From the age-21 results, Barnett and Masse estimated the benefit-cost ratio was approximately 3:1 for every dollar invested. More recently, Heckman, Garcia, Leaf, and Prados (in press) have amalgamated data from the Abecedarian Project and Project CARE into middle adulthood. Their current estimates are a benefit-cost ratio of 7.3:1 with an annualized rate of return of 13.7%. The main point that I draw from these perspectives is that there is no adequate substitute for longitudinal data from experimental designs that incorporate a life span approach and that simultaneously include information about educational attainment, employment, and health. In short, the economic perspective needs to be contextualized by the interdependence of outcomes that are affected by lifestyle and opportunities for advancement.

Multifactorial Influences on Intellectual Development

By the early 1980s, it was becoming clear that simple models of human development were inadequate to describe and account for intellectual development. Clearly, multiple and interacting forces that changed over time were a more likely dynamic model. After a period of intense discussion and reconceptualization, David MacPhee, Keith Yeates, and I presented our version of General Systems Theory applied to differential intellectual development in vulnerable populations (Ramey, MacPhee, & Yeates, 1982). We illustrated this perspective with data from multiple domains of influence using Abecedarian Project data.

After consolidating our new perspective, we were able to pursue these ideas more fully in a series of empirical articles (Martin et al., 1990; Ramey, Yeates, & Short, 1984; Yeates, MacPhee, Campbell, & Ramey, 1983). In this series of papers, we documented how the correlations between maternal IQ, the developmental quality of the home environment, and the influence of participation in the educational intervention changed in a systematic way over the first 5 years, such that maternal IQ became less powerful while the explanatory power of the intervention increased and the home environment remained an important contributor. These findings have caused me to question the applicability of single-point estimates of heritability, such as maternal IQ. We later captured these insights into an extended chapter on developmental genetics (Moser, Ramey, & Leonard, 1990) where we identified appropriate developmental research designs.

IS THE ABECEDARIAN APPROACH RELEVANT TO TODAY'S U.S. POPULATION AND CIRCUMSTANCES?

The Abecedarian CARE and IHDP projects were launched in the 1970s and 1980s and completed the active preschool interventions between 1981 and 1990. Between then and now, there have been significant changes in the U.S. population and the economy. For example, the population has become more diverse due to migration, particularly from Mexico and Latin America, with attendant changes in languages spoken at home and in public. These changes have been particularly dramatic in small and mid-size towns throughout the United States, especially in the South.

The national economy has gone through major boom and bust phases, with attendant impacts on job opportunities, employment patterns, and requisite skill expectancies, particularly at the entry level of the job market. Welfare has been reformed with time limits on eligibility and an explicit focus on completing high school (or obtaining General Educational Development certification) and obtaining employment. A crackdown on crime with a special focus on drug-related issues has led to a swelling prison population with an overrepresentation of Black males.

Finally, racial discrimination has continued to be a major characteristic of U.S. society, with predicable patterns in educational attainment, income distribution, housing patterns, and death rates. Given these and other trends too numerous to detail in this chapter, it is germane to ask whether the Abecedarian Approach is relevant to contemporary life in the United States. I think the answer is a clear *yes* for two major reasons.

First, we know better today than ever before, from a scientific perspective, that learning and development occurs early and is powerfully cumulative and consequential. Without a systematic and comprehensive approach that begins early in development, I know of no good reason to expect the quality of life for the intergenerationally disadvantaged to improve substantially.

Second, if I had it to do over again, I would place greater emphasis and resources on assisting the educational and occupational achievement of parents. Close ties with community colleges and local businesses could be very beneficial in accelerating the transition to middle-class status and improving their children's development.

REFERENCES

Barnett, W. S. (1996). *Lives in the balance: Benefit–cost analysis of the Perry Preschool Program through age 27. Monographs of the High/Scope Educational Research Foundation.* Ypsilanti, MI: High/Scope Press.

Barnett, W. S., & Masse, L. N. (2007). Comparative benefit–cost analysis of the Abecedarian program and its policy implications. *Economics of Education Review, 26,* 113–125.

Bijou, S. W., & Baer, D. M. (1961). *Child development: A systematic and empirical theory.* New York, NY: Appleton-Century-Crofts.

Blair, C., Ramey, C. T., & Hardin, M. (1995). Early intervention for low birth weight premature infants: Participation and intellectual development. *American Journal on Mental Retardation, 99,* 542–554.

Bowlby, J. (1969). *Attachment and loss, Vol. 1: Attachment.* New York, NY: Basic Books.

Breitmayer, B. J., & Ramey, C. T. (1986). Biological nonoptimality and quality of postnatal environment as codeterminants of intellectual development. *Child Development, 57,* 1151–1165. PMID 3769604

Burchinal, M. R., Bryant, D. M., Lee, M. W., & Ramey, C. T. (1992). Early day care, infant-mother attachment, and maternal responsiveness in the infant's first year. *Early Childhood Research Quarterly, 7,* 383–396.

Burchinal, M., Lee, M., & Ramey, C. T. (1989). Type of day-care and preschool intellectual development in disadvantaged children. *Child Development, 60,* 128–137.

Campbell, F. A., Pungello, E. P., Burchinal, M., Kainz, K., Pan, Y., Wasik, B. H., et al. (2012). Adult outcomes as a function of an early childhood educational program: An Abecedarian Project follow-up. *Developmental Psychology, 48*(4), 1033–1043.

Campbell, F. A., Pungello, E. P., Miller-Johnson, S., Burchinal, M., & Ramey, C. T. (2001). The development of cognitive and academic abilities: Growth curves from an early childhood educational experiment. *Developmental Psychology, 37,* 231–242.

Campbell, F. A., Ramey, C. T., Pungello, E., Sparling, J., & Miller-Johnson, S. (2002). Early childhood education: Young adult outcomes from the Abecedarian Project. *Applied Developmental Science, 6,* 42–57.

Carson, J. L., Collier, A. M., & Hu, S. S. (1985). Acquired ciliary defects in nasal respiratory epithelium of children with acute viral upper respiratory infections. *New England Journal of Medicine, 312,* 463–468.

Collier, A. M., Pimmel, R. L., Hasselblad, V., Clyde, W. A., Knelson, J. H., & Brooks, J. G. (1978). Spirometric changes in normal children with upper respiratory tract infections. *American Review of Respiratory Diseases, 117,* 47–53.

Etzel, R., Pattishall, E., Haley, N., Fletcher, R., & Henderson, F. W. (1992). Passive smoking and middle ear effusion in preschool children. *Pediatrics, 90,* 228–232.

Farran, D. C., & Ramey, C. T. (1977). Infant day care and attachment behaviors towards mothers and teachers. *Child Development, 51,* 1112–1116.

Farran, D. C., & Ramey, C. T. (1980). Social class differences in dyadic involvement during infancy. *Child Development, 51,* 254–257.

Fernald, G. W., Collier, A. M., & Clyde, W. A. (1975). Respiratory infections due to *mycoplasma pneumoniae* in infants and children. *Pediatrics, 55,* 327–335.

Galton, F. (1883). *Inquiries into human faculty and its development.* New York, NY: Macmillan.

Heckman, J. J., Garcia, J. L., Leaf, D. E., & Prados, M. J. (in press). Quantifying the life-cycle benefits of a prototypical early childhood program. *Journal of Political Economy.*

Henderson, F. W., Collier, A. M., Clyde, W. A., & Denny, F. W. (1979). Respiratory-syncytial-virus infections, reinfections and immunity: A prospective longitudinal study in young children. *New England Journal of Medicine, 300,* 530–534.

Henderson, F. W., Collier, A. M., Sanyal, M. A., Watkins, J. M., Fairclough, L. L., Clyde, W. A., et al. (1982). A longitudinal study of respiratory viruses and bacteria in the etiology of acute otitis media with effusion. *New England Journal of Medicine, 306,* 1377–1383.

Herrnstein, R. J., & Murray, C. A. (1994). *The bell curve: Intelligence and class structure in American life.* New York, NY: Free Press.

Hunt, J. M. (1961). *Intelligence and experience.* Oxford, UK: Ronald.

The Infant Health and Development Program. (1990). Enhancing the outcomes of low-birth-weight, premature infants: A multisite randomized trial. *Journal of the American Medical Association, 263*(22), 3035–3042.

Jensen, A. (1969). How much can we boost IQ and scholastic achievement? *Harvard Educational Review, 39,* 1–123.

Judkins, D., St. Pierre, R., Gutmann, B., Goodson, B., von Glatz, A., Hamilton, J., et al. (2008). *A study of classroom literacy interventions and outcomes in Even Start* (NCEE 2008-4028). Washington, DC: National Center for Education Evaluation and Regional Assistance, Institute of Education Sciences, U.S. Department of Education.

Lazar, I., Darlington, R., Murray, H., Royce, J., Snipper, A., & Ramey, C. T. (1982). Lasting effects of early education: A report from the consortium for longitudinal studies. *Monographs of the Society for Research in Child Development, 47*(2/3), 1–151.

Martin, S. L., Ramey, C. T., & Ramey, S. (1990). The prevention of intellectual impairment in children of impoverished families: Findings of a randomized trial of educational daycare. *American Journal of Public Health, 80,* 844–847.

McCormick, M. C., Brooks-Gunn, J., Buka, S. L., Goldman, J., Yu, J., Salganik, M., et al. (2006). Early intervention in low birth weight premature infants: Results at 18 years of age for the Infant Health and Development Program. *Pediatrics, 117,* 771–780.

McGinness, G., & Ramey, C. T. (1981). Developing sociolinguistic competence in children. *Canadian Journal of Early Childhood Education, 1,* 22–43.

Moser, H. W., Ramey, C. T., & Leonard, C. O. (1990). Mental retardation. In A. E. H. Emery & D. L. Rimoin (Eds.), *The principles and practices of medical genetics* (Vol. II) (pp. 495–511). New York, NY: Churchill Livingstone.

Ramey, C. T., Bryant, D. M., Sparling, J. J., & Wasik, B. H. (1985). Project CARE: A comparison of two early intervention strategies to prevent retarded development. *Topics in Early Childhood Special Education, 5*(2), 12–25.

Ramey, C. T., Bryant, D. M., Wasik, B. H., Sparling, J. J., Fendt, K. H., & LaVange, L. M. (1992). The Infant Health and Development Program for low birthweight, premature infants: Program elements, family participation, and child intelligence. *Pediatrics, 3,* 454–465.

Ramey, C. T., Campbell, F. A., Burchinal, M., Skinner, M. L., Gardner, D. M., & Ramey, S. L. (2000). Persistent effects of early intervention on high-risk children and their mothers. *Applied Developmental Science, 4,* 2–14.

Ramey, C. T., Campbell, F. A., & Ramey, S. L. (1999). Early intervention: Successful pathways to improving intellectual development. *Developmental Neuropsychology, 16,* 385–392.

Ramey, C. T., Collier, A. M., Sparling, J. J., Loda, R. A., Campbell, F. A., Ingram, D.L., et al. (1976). The Carolina Abecedarian Project: A longitudinal and multidisciplinary approach to the prevention of developmental retardation. In T. D. Tjossem (Ed.), *Intervention strategies for high risk infants and young children* (pp. 629–665). Baltimore, MD: University Park Press.

Ramey, C. T., & Farran, D. C. (1981). The functional concern of mothers for their infants. *Infant Mental Health Journal, 2,* 48–55.

Ramey, C. T., Farran, D. C., & Campbell, F. A. (1979). Predicting IQ from mother-infant interactions. *Child Development, 50,* 804–814.

Ramey, C. T., & Finkelstein, N. W. (1978). Contingent stimulation and infant competence. *Journal of Pediatric Psychology, 3,* 89–96.

Ramey, C. T., & Haskins, R. (1981). The causes and treatment of school failure: Insights from the Carolina Abecedarian Project. In M. Begab, H. Garber, & H. C. Haywood (Eds.), *Causes and prevention of retarded development in psychosocially disadvantaged children* (pp. 89–112). Baltimore, MD: University Park Press.

Ramey, C. T., MacPhee, D., & Yeates, K. O. (1982). Preventing developmental retardation: A general systems model. In J. M. Joffee & L. A. Bond (Eds.), *Facilitating infant and early childhood development* (pp. 343–401). Hanover, NH: University Press of New England.

Ramey, C. T., & Ramey, S. L. (1998). Prevention of intellectual disabilities: Early interventions to improve cognitive development. *Preventive Medicine, 27,* 224–232.

Ramey, C. T., & Ramey, S. L. (2017). Reframing policy and practice deliberations: Twelve hallmarks of strategies to attain and sustain early childhood gains. In A. J. Reynolds, J. A. Temple, A. J. Rolnick, & Human Capital Research Collaborative (Eds.), *Sustaining early childhood learning gains: Program, school, and family influences.* Cambridge, UK: Cambridge University Press.

Ramey, C. T., & Smith, B. J. (1977). Assessing the intellectual consequences of early intervention with high-risk infants. *American Journal of Mental Deficiency, 8,* 318–324.

Ramey, C. T., Sparling, J. J., & Ramey, S. L. (2012). *Abecedarian: The ideas, the approach, and the findings.* Los Altos, CA: Sociometrics Corporation.

Ramey, C. T., Yeates, K. O., & Short, E. J. (1984). The plasticity of intellectual development: Insights from preventive intervention. *Child Development, 55,* 1913–1925.

Ramey, S. L., & Ramey, C. T. (1999). Early experience and early intervention for children "at risk" for developmental delay and mental retardation. *Mental Retardation and Developmental Disabilities Research Reviews, 5,* 1–10.

Ramey, S. L., & Ramey, C. T. (2005). How to create and sustain a high-quality workforce in child care, early intervention, and school readiness programs. In M. Zaslow & I. Martinez-Beck (Eds.), *Critical issues in early childhood professional development* (pp. 355–368). Baltimore, MD: Paul H. Brookes Publishing Co.

Ramey, S. L., Ramey, C. T. & Sonnier-Netto, L. (2008, 2012). *The Four Diamonds Checklist.* Unpublished manuscript.

Sparling, J., & Lewis, I. (1979). *LearningGames® for the first three years: A guide to parent/child play.* New York, NY: Walker and Company.

Sparling, J., & Lewis, I. (1984). *LearningGames® for threes and fours: A guide to adult/child play.* New York, NY: Walker and Company.

Sparling, J., & Lewis, I. (2008). *The Creative Curriculum® LearningGames®* (5 volumes). Washington, DC: Teaching Strategies.

Sparling, J., Lewis, I., & Ramey, C. T. (1984, 1995). *Partners for learning: Birth to 36 months.* Lewisville, NC: Kaplan Press.

Sparling, J., Lewis, I., Ramey, C. T., Wasik, B. H., Bryant, D. M., & LaVange, L. M. (1991). Partners, a curriculum to help premature, low-birth-weight infants get off to a good start. *Topics in Early Childhood Special Education, 11,* 36–55.

Walden, T., & Ramey, C. T. (1983). Locus of control and academic achievement: Results from a preschool intervention program. *Journal of Educational Psychology, 75,* 347–358.

Wasik, B. H., Ramey, C. T., Bryant, D. M., & Sparling, J. J. (1990). A longitudinal study of two early intervention strategies: Project CARE. *Child Development, 61*(6), 1682–1696.

Watson, J. S., & Ramey, C. T. (1972). Reactions to response-contingent stimulation in early infancy. *Merrill-Palmer Quarterly, 18,* 219–227.

Williams, S. P., Fulton, J. M., Tsai, M. J., Pimmel, R. L., & Collier, A. M. (1979). Respiratory impedance and derived parameters in young children by forced random noise. *Journal of Applied Physiology, 47,* 169–174.

Williams, S. P., Pimmel, R. L., Fulton, J. M., Tsai, M. J., & Collier, A. M. (1979). Fractionating respiratory resistance in young children. *Journal of Applied Physiology, 47,* 551–555.

Yeates, K. O., MacPhee, D., Campbell, F. A., & Ramey, C. T. (1983). Maternal IQ and home environment as determinants of early childhood intellectual competence: Developmental analysis. *Developmental Psychology, 19,* 731–739.

Zeskind, P. S., & Ramey, C. T. (1978). Fetal malnutrition: An experimental study of its consequences on infant development in two caregiving environments. *Child Development, 49,* 1155–1162.

Zeskind, P., & Ramey, C. T. (1981). Preventing intellectual and interactional sequelae of fetal malnutrition: A longitudinal, transactional, and synergistic approach to development. *Child Development, 52,* 213–218.

8

A Long and Winding Road

Using Knowledge to Inform
and Improve Early Care and Education

Marilou Hyson

The goal of grounding early childhood practices upon a firm knowledge base has a long history (e.g., Lascarides & Hinitz, 2011); yet, as in The Beatles' 1970 song, achieving this goal has been a "long and winding road," and the field is still far from its destination.

This chapter examines the ways in which knowledge has typically been used in the early care and education (ECE) field, as well as how this knowledge could be used more consistently and effectively. Within this chapter, "knowledge" will include a broad array of concepts, principles, information, and evidence. Such knowledge has informed multiple decisions about early childhood practices, and the Frank Porter Graham (FPG) Child Development Institute's accomplishments in this regard are remarkable. While acknowledging these achievements, this chapter highlights the many ways in which the research-to-practice road has not been smooth and has, at times, been impossible to discern.

This chapter begins by acknowledging that the ECE field has had a complex and sometimes turbulent relationship with knowledge, pointing out that the multidisciplinary nature of our field has historically created challenges in gaining consensus about the most important theoretical and research-based sources of knowledge about critical ECE issues. The next section of the chapter moves from a focus on *knowledge* to a focus on *knowledge utilization*—that is, the uses of knowledge in the ECE field. Beginning at a broad level, I examine and compare the various ways knowledge utilization has been defined and the various terms that have been used to describe the connections between knowledge (concepts, information, evidence derived from research) and early childhood practices (specific professional competencies or skills). With these conceptual and definitional questions in mind, I make the case that knowledge, as defined here, has had a relatively weak and inconsistent impact on early childhood practices. Examples will illustrate a pattern of frequently low uptake of such knowledge and, even when uptake is evident, low sustainability of knowledge-informed practices.

Next, these issues are illustrated through an in-depth discussion of one specific area of the broader early childhood field—the preservice preparation of early childhood personnel, also known as early childhood teacher education (ECTE). Although research and professional recommendations underscore the value of a practice- or skills-focused approach, this approach has seldom been well implemented either in higher-education course work or in well-planned and well-integrated field experiences. Improving connections between the knowledge base and professional practice, within and beyond higher education, is likely to be advanced by systematic attention to the growing field of implementation science. To that end, the last section of this chapter provides an overview of some key concepts and central questions from that field and shows how their application can lead to better use of evidence to inform better practices. The chapter's key messages are then summarized, with their broader implications highlighted for the improvement of early care and education.

SOURCES OF KNOWLEDGE IN THE CONTEXT OF DISCIPLINARY AND IDEOLOGICAL DIVERSITY

Over time, the early childhood field has drawn from multiple sources of knowledge, with little consensus about the value and validity of these sources and with frequent gaps between knowledge and its application in early childhood practice.

Nature and Breadth of the Early Childhood Knowledge Base

Compared with other fields of education, ECE has drawn from notably diverse disciplines and sources of knowledge. Even the terms that have been used to describe the field reflect differing knowledge emphases (e.g., child development and early education, early childhood development, early care and education, child care and early education, early learning). Despite this diversity, the historical roots of the ECE field, at least in the United States, have been closely tied to the discipline of child study or child development (e.g., Lascarides & Hinitz, 2011; Morrison, 2012), with priority given to Erikson, Piaget, Vygotsky, and other developmental theorists.

Over the past 20 years, however, these ties have become looser than they were, with increasing critiques of the scope and nature of the field's primary sources of knowledge. For example, in 1996, *Early Childhood Research Quarterly* published a special section of articles written by early childhood leaders who called into question assumptions about the field's child development foundations as the primary basis for preparing teachers (e.g., Katz,

1996; Lubeck, 1996; Stott & Bowman, 1996). The title of one of the articles captures the special section's broader theme: "Child development knowledge: A slippery base for practice" (Stott & Bowman, 1996). The authors of articles in this special section emphasized the risks of overreliance on developmental-constructivist theory and research—focused primarily but not exclusively on Piaget and Vygotsky—as "the" foundation for the early childhood field. The articles reflected concern about the cultural narrowness of many applications of child development knowledge and also described the underrepresentation of other relevant disciplines and theoretical perspectives within the field, such as postmodern, feminist, and sociocultural theories. Similar concerns had a major influence on the National Association for the Education of Young Children (NAEYC)'s series of revisions of its developmentally appropriate practice position statements, which went beyond the original NAEYC position (Bredekamp, 1986) in providing increasingly detailed discussions of linguistic, cultural, and contextual considerations; greater attention to practices for young children with disabilities; and more focus on academic content disciplines (Bredekamp & Copple, 1997; Copple & Bredekamp, 2009).

The Knowledge Base as Reflected in Early Care and Education Research Handbooks

The field's expanding and diverse knowledge base is reflected in the content of the many handbooks of early childhood research. In 1993, Spodek published the first edition of the well-known *Handbook of Research on the Education of Young Children*. Beginning with a group of chapters on the major domains of child development, the following sections included curriculum addressing a number of content areas, as well as play and multicultural education, policy, and research strategies. The *Handbook* went through two more editions (Spodek & Saracho, 2005; Saracho & Spodek, 2012); over time, the structure remained the same but significantly more attention was given to issues such as dual-language learners, the sociocultural context of language development, and the effects of childhood poverty.

Four other handbooks published between 2006 and 2016 further illustrate the diverse ways in which the field has identified and prioritized areas of knowledge. *The Blackwell Handbook of Early Childhood* (McCartney & Phillips, 2006) includes sections describing overarching conceptual frameworks (e.g., risk and resilience) and developmental domains, followed by a set of chapters on "The social ecology of early development" and a final section on "Policy issues." The *Handbook of Early Childhood Education* (Pianta, 2012) begins with eight chapters on "Early Education Opportunities in the United States," including discussions of accountability, federal and state investments, cultural and language issues, and poverty. This section is followed by others on curriculum and instruction; developmental processes, early education, and families; and systems of effective early intervention supports for diverse children and practitioners. The *Sage Handbook of Early Childhood Research* (Farrell, Kagan, & Tisdall, 2016) begins with an introductory chapter on "Early childhood research: An expanding field," and includes chapters with themes such as "theorizing identities in early childhood" and "participation, rights, and participatory methods." Another volume, the *Handbook of Early Childhood Development Research and Its Impact on Global Policy* (Britto, Engle, & Super, 2013) has an explicitly international emphasis, with review chapters addressing economic perspectives, risk and protective influences on development in low-income countries, nutrition-based approaches, and social protection and welfare systems. Collectively, these publications reflect a continuing emphasis on the developmental foundations of the field while also documenting the diverse contexts of, and influences upon, early development and learning as seen from the perspective of multiple disciplines.

Controversies Over What Knowledge Is Most Valuable

Despite the recent broadening and diversifying of the ECE knowledge base, a thorny question persists: Of all this knowledge, what should be prioritized as the basis for professional practices? Early childhood theorists and researchers continue to disagree on the answer to this question (e.g., Bloch, Swadener, & Canella, 2014; National Institute of Child Health and Human Development & National Council for the Accreditation of Teacher Education, 2006; Pianta, Hitz, & West, 2010; Yoshikawa et al., 2013), with some scholars emphasizing new insights from fields such as neuroscience and others looking to knowledge derived from postmodern, feminist, and sociocultural investigations. Differing priorities are also reflected in debates over research methods, with some urging the use of randomized controlled trials of early childhood interventions and others prioritizing case studies, ethnographic approaches, and other qualitative methods. Although mixed methods may frequently be recommended, some degree of polarization continues in the field (Mackenzie & Knipe, 2006).

A Compelling Knowledge Base, Disconnects Between Knowledge and Practice, and the Importance of Knowledge Utilization

Despite a body of persuasive knowledge about child development and learning, practices often do not reflect this evidence base, failing to use available insights from research and professional expertise.

Compelling Evidence with Potential for Practice: Four Examples   This overview of competing claims about the early childhood knowledge base and its value should not obscure the fact that the field does have robust evidence in many areas. Four examples are highlighted here. In each, a solid foundation of knowledge has clear implications for practice.

1. *Teacher–child relationships and interactions.* Persuasive evidence from multiple contexts (e.g., Brock & Curby, 2014; Hamre et al., 2013) has shown the positive developmental effects of close relationships and supportive interactions between teachers and children from infancy through elementary school. The effects have been shown to persist and to be associated not only with social-emotional development but also with positive approaches to learning and academic competence.

2. *Early intervention and inclusion.* Likewise, the evidence is compelling on the value of early intervention for infants and toddlers with disabilities, as well as on the benefits of natural, inclusive environments through the early childhood years. Developmental trajectories are altered by these kinds of interventions when they are well-designed and well-implemented (e.g., Lawrence, Smith, & Banerjee, 2016; National Early Childhood Technical Assistance Center, 2011).

3. *Environments to support language and literacy development.* Even a quick review shows the extent of current knowledge about what is needed to promote language and literacy development, especially for children living in poverty and children who are dual-language learners (e.g., Castro, Espinosa, & Paez, 2011; Neuman & Dickinson, 2010). This evidence illustrates the kinds of interactions, intentional teaching strategies, and individual and contextual responsiveness that predict good outcomes.

4. *Coaching as part of early childhood professional development.* Although research is still uncovering the key elements of effective coaching models, recent syntheses point to the potential of on-site coaching to improve practices in a sustainable way (Aikens & Akers, 2011; Artman-Meeker, Fettig, Barton, Penney, & Zeng, 2015). Contributors to coaching's effectiveness include the close relationships that develop during coaching, the identification of specific targets for improving classroom skills, and the use of a structured cycle of goal-setting, observation, feedback, and action planning (National Center on Quality Teaching and Learning, 2014).

Persistent Disconnects Between the Knowledge Base and Practices   The kind of evidence just described has great potential to improve early childhood programs and practices. Some of that potential has been realized, but most has not. There is continuing concern that the implications of the ECE field's knowledge base have not consistently informed decisions about early childhood programs and practices. Discouraging examples abound. Children, especially African American boys, are punitively disciplined, suspended, and expelled from preschool, depriving them of the nurturing, stimulating environments essential for early learning (Gilliam, 2005, 2016). (See Chapter 3 for additional information on African American boys.) State child care policies seldom support positive infant-toddler development, which relies on continuity of care and low staff-to-child ratios (Ackerman, 2008; Norris, Horm, & McMullen, 2015; Schmit & Matthews, 2013). Despite evidence of the value of very early intervention for children at risk of developmental delays and disabilities, only a handful of states extend Part C eligibility criteria to "at-risk" groups (Early Childhood Technical Assistance Center, 2015). Teachers are ill prepared to implement the inclusive practices known to influence the developmental trajectories of children with disabilities (Chang, Early, & Winton, 2005; Horm, Hyson, & Winton, 2013). Furthermore, the research about effective curricula and environments for young dual-language learners is unevenly reflected in states' standards and policies (Castro, Páez, Dickinson, & Frede, 2011). (See Chapter 4 for additional information on dual-language learners.)

Some of these disconnects between knowledge and practice arise because evidence-based interventions are never taken up by early childhood programs and personnel. In other situations, there may be initial uptake with efforts to apply knowledge to program design and day-to-day practices, but the efforts are not sustained over time. These issues are the focus of the broad field of *knowledge utilization*—if, how, and at what level of effectiveness knowledge comes to be used.

Knowledge Utilization: What Does It Mean and Why Does It Matter?   Whatever one's beliefs about what knowledge is most valuable, there is still a pressing need to define the ways in which the most important and relevant knowledge—whatever its scope, source, and priority—becomes connected with the realities of the ECE field (Odom, 2009). In an article in the journal *Implementation Science*, Nilsen (2015) noted that many terms are used to describe the process of using knowledge: "The terms knowledge translation, knowledge exchange, knowledge transfer, knowledge integration and research utilization are used to describe overlapping and interrelated research on putting various forms of knowledge, including research, to use" (p. 2). Related terms (Straus, Tetroe, & Graham, 2013) include translational research, knowledge utilization, knowledge diffusion, knowledge uptake, and implementation research (Metz, Naoom, Halley, & Bartley, 2015). The language used to describe this process is a matter of importance: Some terms appear to reflect a relatively one-directional process (e.g., knowledge transfer, diffusion), some terms implicitly acknowledge the need for a more dynamic approach (e.g., knowledge translation), whereas others seem to focus specifically on how knowledge becomes employed within policy-and-practice contexts (e.g., knowledge utilization, implementation science).

THE POTENTIAL AND CHALLENGES OF KNOWLEDGE UTILIZATION IN EARLY CHILDHOOD TEACHER EDUCATION

So far, I have described the knowledge-to-practice challenges as they apply to the early childhood field as a whole. A better understanding may come from looking more deeply into one sector of that field—preservice professional development, also known as early childhood teacher education or ECTE. Some general background information on ECTE is followed by a discussion of the effects of a growing knowledge base about the value of practice- or skills-focused professional development on current ECTE programs.

Higher Education and the Early Childhood Field: Some Background

Recent examinations of early childhood workforce issues consistently identify higher education as a key route to preparing competent professionals in a reimagined field of practice (Goffin, 2015). Higher education is the priority in several key recommendations from the groundbreaking 2015 workforce report from the Institute of Medicine (IOM) and National Research Council (NRC). Additionally, ECTE has been the specific focus of other influential national reports (e.g., Bornfreund, 2011; Washington, 2008), an integral component of NAEYC's new "Power to the Profession" collaborative initiative (NAEYC, 2018), and a key element in the current vision and grant-making strategies of the Foundation for Child Development (2016).

Size and Scope of Programs in the Early Childhood Teacher Education System
According to the national database of the NAEYC (2017a), there are currently 1,300 early childhood-related associate degree programs and 1,064 bachelor's degree programs in the United States. For current and potential students (many of whom are early childhood teachers), both access and degree completion pose challenges. Obstacles include limited funds, class scheduling that is incompatible with work hours and family responsibilities, and lack of mechanisms to transfer credits and receive credit for prior learning (Whitebook, Gomby, Bellm, Sakai, & Kipnis, 2009). Despite these obstacles, tens of thousands of students graduate annually, entering the ranks of degreed teachers. Thus, the number of ECTE programs and graduates offers a significant opportunity to develop the competence of large numbers of early childhood practitioners; in turn, these graduates can potentially affect the developmental and educational potential of hundreds of thousands of young children.

Trends in Degree Requirements
Requirements that early childhood teachers hold college or university degrees, primarily bachelor's degrees, have increased in recent years. Specific requirements vary by setting and auspices. However, of 60 state-funded pre-K programs located in 43 states and the District of Columbia, 34 require lead teachers to have a bachelor's degree (National Institute of Early Education Research, 2018), and Head Start now requires that at least half of a program's lead teachers possess a bachelor's degree.

College Degrees' Benefits for Early Childhood Educators
Despite this emphasis on higher education as a route to a more competent workforce, the evidence for the positive impact of degrees on teaching skills or child outcomes has been mixed. A comprehensive review of research on effective professional development (Zaslow, Tout, Halle, Whittaker, & Lavelle, 2010,

pp. 11–12) concluded that the secondary analyses of large-scale studies by a consortium of researchers (Early et al., 2007) "provided little indication that degree, highest education level among those with an early childhood major, or having an early childhood major among those with a bachelor's degree were related either to observed classroom quality or to children's gain scores on measures of academic achievement." Recent research reviews offer somewhat more positive interpretations of the evidence (IOM/NRC, 2015). However, efforts to find straightforward, robust links between the possession of a degree and better teaching skills—let alone better child outcomes—have not been a success.

This finding in no way suggests that we should abandon the study of ECTE as a path to improvements in the broader early childhood field. Researchers and other experts are turning to a more nuanced, complex set of questions about the potential impact of ECTE (e.g., Foundation for Child Development, 2016; Hyson, Horm, & Winton, 2012; IOM/NRC, 2015; Ryan & Gibson, 2015; Whitebook et al., 2012; Whitebook & Austin, 2015). This new direction for ECTE research focuses on variations in the quality and pedagogical approach of ECTE programs, asking, for example, what kinds of higher education pedagogies or program approaches 1) may have the greatest benefit for graduates' teaching practices and 2) may be most effective in promoting children's positive development and early learning as a result of graduates' improved practices.

Skills-Focused Professional Development: Definition and Evidence of Effectiveness

Consistent with these questions, there is a substantial knowledge base about a specific professional development approach that has potential to raise the quality and impact of ECTE. In this chapter, I refer to this approach as "skills-focused professional development."

Definition   In a conceptual framework (Zaslow, Tout, Halle, & Starr, 2010) and in their comprehensive research review of effective early childhood professional development (Zaslow, Tout, Halle, Whittaker et al., 2010), Zaslow and colleagues contrasted two approaches to improving educators' competence: knowledge-focused and practice-focused. In this formulation, knowledge-focused professional development—what this chapter terms an *information-focused approach*—emphasizes participants' understanding of concepts, theories, and research on key early childhood issues. This information might include an understanding of child development theories, comparisons of and research on curricula, and principles of developmentally appropriate practices. In contrast, practice-focused professional development—what this chapter calls a *skills-focused approach*—directly highlights and provides feedback on teachers' (or future teachers') interactions with children and their use of specific evidence-based skills. Skills-focused approaches to professional development tend to be individualized and interactive, with an emphasis on giving professional educators, or future educators, opportunities to observe, model, reflect, discuss, and receive feedback.

Skills-Focused Approaches: Recommendations and Evidence from In-Service Professional Development   The IOM/NRC (2015, p. 361) review of research on the early childhood workforce states that an "emphasis on applying theory to practice, including field- and practice-based professional learning experiences" is one of the features of professional development initiatives that has been shown to predict positive outcomes for teacher competence. Although many of the studies examine in-service training, the results appear relevant for preservice ECTE programs as well. For example, Sheridan, Edwards, Marvin, and Knoche (2009) described the characteristics of in-service training shown to be effective in improving classroom competence. They reported that effective in-service training helps participants practice critical skills and gives participants feedback either during the group training sessions or as part of on-site workplace coaching.

Skills-Focused Approaches as Part of Preservice Teacher Education: Recommendations and Evidence   Is a skills-focused approach relevant only for in-service professional development? The IOM/NRC (2015) report explicitly addressed this question, emphasizing that such an approach is equally relevant for community-based professional development (in-service) and for higher education (preservice preparation). Certainly, the IOM/NRC report and others (e.g., National Council for the Accreditation of Teacher Education [NCATE], 2010; Zaslow, Tout, Halle, Whittaker, et al., 2010) acknowledge that skills-focused and information-focused approaches must be woven throughout effective teacher preparation programs. Programs are responsible for ensuring that their graduates 1) demonstrate mastery of content knowledge, theory, and research; and 2) demonstrate the ability to apply that information in skillful interactions and other classroom practices.

There is converging evidence that a strong skills focus—not just mastery of information—is essential for effective teacher preparation, including preparation of early childhood educators (NCATE, 2010; Sheridan et al., 2009; Zaslow, Tout, Halle, Whittaker, et al., 2010). Background papers for NCATE's major report on clinical preparation indicate that a strong skills-focused approach is associated with higher retention of new teachers and beginning teachers' greater sense of efficacy.

Although controlled studies are still limited, in its report *Preparing Teachers: Building Evidence for Sound Policy*, the National Research Council (2010) described this skills-focused approach (which they called "clinical preparation" or "field experiences") as one of the components of teacher education that has the greatest likelihood of improving child outcomes. One of the few studies to document this association (Boyd, Grossman, Lankford, Loeb, & Wyckoff, 2009) was conducted with more than 700 first- and second-year teachers of fourth- to eighth-grade children; teachers had graduated from one of 18 New York City preservice programs. Multiple sources of data showed that these programs varied considerably in their emphasis on skills-focused preparation, as reflected in the number and timing of field experiences, how well-designed and well-supervised the field experiences were, and whether there was a final project that served as a teacher preparation "capstone." These skills-focused features were significant predictors of better reading and math achievement by the children who were taught by graduates of the more skills-focused programs. (However, the study was not able to observe the graduates' classroom practices.) To date, similar research has not been conducted in ECTE programs, but such research has clear relevance.

FROM RESEARCH TO REALITY: EARLY CHILDHOOD TEACHER EDUCATION PROGRAMS' LIMITED EMPHASIS ON SKILL DEVELOPMENT

The preceding discussion showed that a skills-focused approach to teacher preparation is strongly recommended by professional associations and is supported by evidence from the in-service early childhood professional development literature (e.g., Zaslow, Tout, Halle, Whittaker, et al., 2010) as well as by the K–12 teacher education literature (e.g., Boyd et al., 2009; NCATE, 2010; NRC, 2010). However, the connections between this persuasive body of knowledge and the realities of early childhood teacher education continue to be weak.

Field Experiences: Unmet Potential

Field experiences, including but not limited to end-of-program student teaching, are the most obvious vehicle to strengthen the skills that graduates will need for effective practice (e.g., La Paro, 2015). Yet, national surveys of faculty, administrators, and graduates of early childhood teacher preparation programs convey a picture of unmet promise (e.g., Chang et al., 2005; Maxwell, Lim, & Early, 2006; Ray, Bowman, & Robbins, 2006). Across studies, the data indicate that—despite the national recommendations summarized previously—field experiences tend to be too infrequent, sporadically available throughout students' programs, inadequately supervised, and often lacking in relevance to the settings and issues faced by early childhood professionals. Certainly, analyses of program descriptions and accreditation materials have identified some strongly skills-focused programs, but these kinds of programs continue to be rare and have not been carefully evaluated for their impact on skills and outcomes (e.g., Hyson, 2008; Hyson, Tomlinson, & Morris, 2009).

Despite the field experience expectations in accreditation standards such as NAEYC's (2011), many ECTE programs fail to place students in settings that reflect ethnic, economic, and ability diversity (Recchia, Beck, Esposito, & Tarrant, 2009). Furthermore, many early childhood teacher candidates fulfill student teaching requirements at their own workplace.

Although some may view such placements as a practical necessity, when student teachers stay in their own classrooms, it is difficult to expose them to new teaching methods and the kind of supervision and mentoring that are essential to implement practices introduced in their coursework (Whitebook et al., 2009).

Even if students are placed in other settings, as summarized in Hyson et al. (2012), there is little evidence that field experiences are meeting their needs to observe, implement, and receive feedback on effective practices. For example, consistent with the more general concerns in NCATE's (2010) report on clinical practice, a survey and interview study of baccalaureate ECTE programs in 40 states (Johnson, Fiene, McKinnon, & Babu, 2010) found that relatively few programs linked content topics directly with clinical practice/fieldwork. For example, students may have been learning about the principles of, and research on, effective literacy instruction (an example of an information-focused approach) but lacked in-depth, concurrent opportunities to observe and practice instructional skills (a skills-focused approach). Furthermore, faculty interviewed in the Johnson et al. study (2010) had major concerns about the absence of high-quality field placement sites and lack of knowledgeable field supervisors.

Using early childhood mathematics as another example, surveys show that relatively few programs link mathematics coursework with concurrent, aligned field experiences. A content analysis (Hyson, 2008) of 25 program reports submitted as part of the NCATE/NAEYC accreditation process showed that, although most provided mathematics education courses, fewer than half included any kind of mathematics-specific field experience. In theory, such experiences might include a content practicum in which students could 1) observe their master teacher's implementation of math curriculum; 2) design and implement some math activities consistent with the information they acquired in their math education course; and 3) assess the apparent effect of math activities on children's engagement and understanding. The evidence of limited opportunities to practice and receive feedback in mathematics teaching is similar to evidence from early childhood special education and infant/toddler teaching (Horm et al., 2013).

Other Missed Opportunities to Strengthen a Skills Focus

Of course, more and better field experiences are not the only way to strengthen a skills-focused emphasis in ECTE. In content courses, ECTE programs often rely primarily on information transmission, rather than closely connecting abstract information to concrete teaching skills through observations, demonstrations, and guided practice. For example, a course on early literacy might help students understand Vygotsky's zone of proximal development through readings and class discussion, without using class time for student observations or role plays about how to scaffold a child who is struggling with reading. As a result of the typical, strongly information-focused approaches to teacher education, many students continue to graduate lacking concrete skills and confidence in such areas as 1) understanding, preventing, and addressing challenging behaviors; 2) promoting the development of young children with disabilities; and 3) meeting the needs of young dual-language learners (Horm et al., 2013).

A TOOL TO STRENGTHEN KNOWLEDGE UTILIZATION IN EARLY CHILDHOOD EDUCATION: INSIGHTS FROM IMPLEMENTATION SCIENCE

As illustrated by these examples in just one area of the early childhood field, there continue to be major disconnects between what we know and what we do—that is, between knowledge and practice. In ECTE specifically, a major disconnect is between 1) the considerable evidence and strong recommendations about the value of skills-focused approaches to professional development in preservice and in-service settings and 2) the limited integration of these approaches into higher education programs. In brief, this question remains: Why has the evidence about skills-focused professional development not resulted in greater efforts to implement this approach in higher education? Implementation science has the potential to provide some answers, both for ECTE and for other areas of early care and education (Odom, 2009).

A relatively new and rapidly emerging field, implementation science's application to early care and education (Halle, Metz, & Martinez-Beck, 2013), has been marked by strong leadership from FPG's National Implementation Research Network (NIRN). A brief from the NIRN group defined the field this way:

> Implementation science is the study of the process of implementing programs and practices that have some evidence from the field to suggest they are worth replicating. It is the study of how a practice that is evidence-based or evidence-informed gets translated to different, more diverse contexts in the real world. (Metz et al., 2015, p. 1)

Many of the insights from the field of implementation science may help remove the barriers to, and improve the process of, successful knowledge utilization in ECTE.

Using Implementation Science to Improve Early Childhood Teacher Education

This section explores the possible uses of implementation science 1) to analyze barriers to implementation and 2) to identify drivers (processes that potentially improve competence and create favorable implementation environments, or what this chapter calls "conditions for success" in implementation), with the ultimate goal of promoting more effective utilization of research knowledge. Although these uses of implementation science can be put into place in many sectors of the ECE field, here the focus is on one especially daunting challenge: increasing the adoption of a more skills-focused approach to ECTE. The analysis draws primarily on the Metz et al. (2015) research brief, emphasizing four key insights:

1. Successful implementation takes into account the distinct stages of implementation and the activities important to each stage.

2. Successful implementation requires teamwork.

3. Successful implementation uses data and feedback loops to assess needs and track improvements.

4. Successful implementation requires infrastructure to support and sustain change over time.

Each of these insights is discussed with specific reference to ECTE's implementation of skills-based approaches to teacher preparation. Barriers that currently exist are identified and examples of "conditions for success" that can facilitate implementation are described.

Successful Implementation Takes Into Account the Distinct Stages of Implementation and the Activities Important to Each Stage
The first important insight is that effective implementation of evidence-based interventions or practices needs to occur in stages. Typically, these begin with an exploration stage and continue through the stages of installation, initial implementation, and full implementation. Research indicates that each stage has its own issues and needs, which must be addressed for effective implementation to occur (Metz et al., 2015). It is useful to consider these stage-related issues in relation to the barriers that face the task of implementing practice-focused approaches to ECTE, as well as what may be needed to optimize the drivers or conditions for successful implementation.

Barriers   For a number of reasons, in higher education the stages of the implementation process may proceed either too slowly or too rapidly. Academic departments are notorious for their glacially slow adoption of new approaches to their work. Under those conditions, a program may remain stuck for years at the exploration stage, never moving forward to install and implement new, evidence-based ideas.

In contrast, other programs may skip over the important exploration and installation stages, failing to take the time for iterative planning and phasing-in of new approaches (e.g., creating closer connections between content courses and field experiences, revising syllabi to increase opportunities for students to demonstrate and practice new teaching skills during class time). A new provost, a new state certification system, or legislative mandates may demand that higher education programs turn on a dime, moving immediately into full implementation. However, without building in time for familiarization, relationship building, and opportunities to experiment and improve, faculty and field staff may resent this kind of top-down change.

Both of these stage-related problems may lead to faculty resistance or, if faculty have been advocates for change, may lead to a sense of discouragement and hopelessness (Hyson et al., 2009).

Conditions for Success   For ECTE programs to implement more strongly skills-focused designs that reflect current research and recommendations on professional development, a well-planned, phased-in approach is essential. The evidence from implementation science can productively be used by faculty, administrators, and advocates to 1) develop explicit tasks and processes for each stage, 2) make a compelling case for deliberative steps toward full implementation, and 3) create conditions to reduce resistance and build a stronger commitment to change. The design of NAEYC's relatively new Early Childhood Associate Degree Accreditation System is a positive example that seems to promote thoughtful, staged implementation of program improvements. A deliberate self-study process is outlined and guided by a step-by-step accreditation handbook (NAEYC, 2011), with the self-study report describing both strengths in each area—including field experiences—and what the program is doing to build on strengths and address self-acknowledged challenges. The expected process and structure make it difficult for a program to rush this analysis.

Successful Implementation Requires Teamwork   Successful implementation is associated with the presence of carefully selected teams guiding the process (Metz et al., 2015). Implementation science has identified a number of characteristics of successful use of teams. Again, the example of implementing more skills-focused ECTE illustrates some current barriers as well as potential conditions for success.

Barriers   Staffing and time limitations are significant barriers to teamwork. Many early childhood programs have only one full-time faculty member; some programs are even staffed entirely by part-time adjunct instructors (e.g., Early & Winton, 2001; Whitebook & Austin, 2015). A related issue is time constraints; early childhood faculty typically teach more courses and have more advisees than faculty in other departments at the same institutions (Early & Winton, 2001), leaving minimal time for planning and implementing innovations. Additionally, the culture of higher education sometimes prioritizes individual rather than collective efforts by faculty, whether in teaching, research, or publication. Under these conditions, the prospect of teamwork may be daunting.

Conditions for Success   Despite these barriers, programs can move toward success by exploring innovative ways of establishing teams. For example, teams may be virtual as well as face-to-face. Many teacher education programs and individual faculty are increasingly using online instruction and other technologies, potentially linking faculty with one another as well as with their students. In contexts where only one faculty member represents an institution's early childhood program, implementation planning might proceed across institutions, with cross-departmental virtual teams. Such teams could, for example, jointly plan innovations that introduce more, and earlier, field experiences. Faculty at different institutions can also share online course syllabi and practicum guides, identify potential in-class skill building activities, and share successes and challenges to implementation.

Team roles may and should go beyond individual faculty or other within-institution personnel. Continuing with the ECTE example, to successfully implement a greater focus on teaching skills, team members might include school-based field experience personnel; alumni now working in ECE programs; district and state policymakers; those with histories of successful implementation of similar programs in other fields, such as nursing or mental health; or others with experience in and commitment to building new professionals' competence. Such a teaming strategy would be consistent with what NCATE recommended in its report on transforming teacher education through clinical practice (NCATE, 2010).

Successful Implementation Uses Data and Feedback Loops to Assess Needs and Track Improvements   Also essential to successful implementation—whatever the evidence-based innovation or intervention—is a well-designed, iterative data-gathering system that functions as a tool for continuous improvement (Metz et al., 2015). Considerable barriers exist in ECTE.

Barriers   The sheer lack of data on many aspects of ECTE poses a daunting barrier to implementing innovations, such as the skills-focused approaches recommended in the field. Although the body of research on child development and early learning is substantial and significant evidence exists on effective in-service professional development (e.g., Sheridan et al., 2009; Zaslow, Tout, Halle, Whittaker et al., 2010), the same is not the case for research on ECTE. Reviews of the status of ECTE research (Hyson et al., 2009; Horm et al., 2013) indicate that surveys have yielded rich descriptive data about variables, such as faculty characteristics and course content (e.g., Early & Winton, 2001; Whitebook & Austin, 2015). However, very few rigorous, large-sample investigations of innovations or variations in the provision of ECTE have been conducted, with many published studies being single-case descriptions of the implementation of promising initiatives (Horm et al., 2013; Hyson et al., 2012). Research with larger samples of institutions, and with emphasis on assessing outcomes for graduates and for children, is largely absent.

Furthermore, although higher education's mission emphasizes the generation and use of research knowledge, within ECTE programs—especially those that are small and have limited funds—there are often too few faculty with strong skills in research design and data analysis. An additional barrier is the tendency of academic publications to favor studies that describe unambiguously successful interventions rather than those that describe an uneven path toward implementation, although those stories may have equal value for the feedback loops and continuous improvement required for successful implementation (Metz et al., 2015).

Conditions for Success   As in other fields or in other areas of early child-hood research, ECTE will benefit from the creation of more research consortia. Such groups can pool expertise across institutions to focus on a critical issue (e.g., with the current example: interventions to strengthen the skill development focus of teacher preparation programs). A promising initiative is the Network of Infant Toddler Researchers (n.d.). With support from the Office of Planning, Research, and Evaluation, this new network links members from multiple institutions to share and try out new approaches to teacher preparation in the infant-toddler area, as well as to plan, conduct, and publish joint research and reports. The network includes specialized workgroups on preservice and in-service professional development and on data dissemination and use, which are both especially relevant here.

Successful Implementation Requires Infrastructure to Support and Sustain Change Over Time   Many efforts to implement evidence-based interventions have failed because they are not sustainable, often because of lack of supporting infrastructure. Studies of implementation have shown that one of the core elements of success is attention to long-term capacity building (Metz et al., 2015), including both individual competencies and institutional capacity. At the individual level, those engaged in implementation require knowledge, skills, and dispositions related to their own roles and to their work as teams. ECTE programs and their institutions need general capacity-building (across functions and parts of the programs and institutions) and the capacity to implement a specific intervention (in this chapter's example, to put specific skills-focused pedagogies in place within the program and to assess their effectiveness).

Barriers   Financial constraints constitute major barriers to both individual and institutional capacity-building efforts in higher education, and ECTE is no exception. In a national survey related to program improvement (Hyson et al., 2009), many faculty reported that budget constraints had placed on hold everything from new faculty hires to funds for professional travel. Many faculty also noted the lack of support for early childhood programs from higher administration as a significant barrier to improvement (Hyson et al., 2009). A survey of early childhood faculty members' math education experiences and issues found that many faculty acknowledged their own lack of capacity in teaching this content to undergraduates and wished for more professional development opportunities (Horm et al., 2013).

Conditions for Success   Fortunately, there are many examples of efforts to build the capacity of faculty and institutions to create conditions that nurture successful implementation, although at present the efforts are nowhere near at scale. Many of these innovations are closely associated with FPG's mission. For example, the online CONNECT modules provide faculty and other professional development providers with user-friendly resources to introduce students to key practices in early childhood special education and related areas (Buysse, Winton, Rous, Epstein, & Lim, 2012). Another example at the City University of New York, supported by the Foundation for Child Development, engaged faculty from all of the university's 2-year, 4-year, and graduate institutions in an open dialogue about the gaps between what they know from ECTE research and what they currently do in their programs. The dialogue not only built individual capacity but also led to concrete recommendations and action steps forwarded to upper administration (Dombro & Cleary, 2017). With support from Research Connections, faculty teaching modules have been designed to help early childhood instructors link their undergraduate students with how to find, reflect on, and use research on child development and early learning (Child Care and Early Education Research Connections, n.d.). Finally, the NAEYC's newly launched online "Higher Ed Community of Practice" for faculty across the United States and beyond is intended to build faculty capacity through mutual learning and knowledge exchange (NAEYC, 2017b). In this online community, faculty will be able to share their views on best practices, gain access to resources on topics of interest, and participate in dialogue with colleagues in early childhood teacher education.

Implementation Science as an Analytical Tool: Some General Recommendations

The preceding discussion has focused on the uses of implementation science as an analytical tool to help us understand one difficult question: What is needed in ECTE to remove barriers and create conditions for success in installing a more skills-focused approach in teacher preparation programs? Beyond this specific example, implementation science has great potential to explore implementation challenges in other aspects of early childhood teacher education, in-service professional development, and other areas of the field.

The concluding section of *Applying Implementation Science in Early Childhood Programs and Systems* (Halle et al., 2013) identified several strategies that should be useful in these tasks:

- Promote a broad understanding of implementation science's key concepts and tools, including understanding by teacher educators and other early childhood professionals, so that implementation science's central questions are asked routinely as programs are developed, put in place, and evaluated.

- Create outlets in which developers of interventions can share their processes of implementation and lessons learned along the way, providing others with valuable examples as they seek to implement a specific intervention.

- Identify resources and cost-effective approaches to capacity building at individual and institutional levels, always with the aim of creating conditions for long-term, sustainable implementation of practices known to be effective.

- Support current and future early childhood professionals in developing skills not only in working with children but also in successful teaming with other adults, collaboration, and thoughtful analysis—not just of whether new approaches "worked," but why or why not, as well as of what might be done to move toward more successful implementation.

CONCLUSION

As noted at the beginning of this chapter, effective utilization of knowledge within early care and education is not a straight or easy road. Rather, the obstacles to knowledge utilization are many: competing ideas about the nature of knowledge and about the value of specific bodies of knowledge and specific research methods; persistent disconnects between "knowledge" (evidence from research and professional recommendations) on the one hand and on-the-ground practices on the other hand. Drawing on insights from implementation science, barriers to effective implementation arise at every stage of the process—from inattention to a deliberative sequence of steps from initial exploration through full implementation, inadequate teamwork, insufficient use of data and feedback loops to support continuous improvement, and limited infrastructure or capacity to support sustainable change. However, this examination of the current state of affairs also reveals promising approaches to knowledge utilization, not yet taken to scale but able to provide examples to others.

In this chapter, I illustrated these general conclusions with one in-depth example—ECTE and the challenges posed by that field's uneven and slow integration of the "skills-focused" approaches recommended in national reports and supported by several bodies of relevant research. These challenges are by no means unique to ECTE, but lessons may be drawn from this sector to strengthen knowledge–practice connections across the broader early childhood field.

REFERENCES

Ackerman, D. J. (2008). Continuity of care, professional community, and the policy context: Potential benefits for infant and toddler teachers' professional development. *Early Education and Development, 19*(5), 753–772.

Aikens, N., & Akers, L. (2011). *Background review of existing literature on coaching: Final report.* Washington, DC: Mathematica Policy Research.

Artman-Meeker, K., Fettig, A., Barton, E., Penney, A., & Zeng, S. (2015). Applying an evidence-based framework to the early childhood coaching literature. *Topics in Early Childhood Special Education, 35*(3), 183–196.

Bloch, M., Swadener, B. B., & Canella, G. (Eds). (2014). *Reconceptualizing early childhood care and education.* New York, NY: Peter Lang.

Bornfreund, L. (2011). *Getting in sync: Revamping the preparation of teachers in preK, kindergarten, and the early grades.* Washington, DC: New America Foundation.

Boyd, D., Grossman, P., Lankford, H., Loeb, S., & Wyckoff, J. (2009). Teacher preparation and student achievement. *Educational Evaluation and Policy Analysis, 31*(4), 416–440.

Bredekamp, S. (Ed.). (1986). *Developmentally appropriate practice in early childhood programs serving children from birth to age 8.* Washington, DC: NAEYC.

Bredekamp, S., & Copple, C. (Eds.). (1997). *Developmentally appropriate practice in early childhood programs* (revised edition). Washington, DC: NAEYC.

Britto, P. R., Engle, P. L., & Super, C. M. (Eds.). (2013). *Handbook of early childhood development research and its impact on global policy.* London, UK: Oxford University Press.

Brock, L. L., & Curby, T. W. (2014). Emotional support consistency and teacher–child relationships forecast social competence and problem behaviors in prekindergarten and kindergarten. *Early Education and Development, 25*(5), 661–680.

Buysse, V., Winton, P. J., Rous, B., Epstein, D., & Lim, C.-I. (2012). Evidence-based practice: Foundation for the CONNECT 5-step learning cycle™ in professional development. *Zero to Three, 32*(4), 25–29.

Castro, D. C., Espinosa, L. M., & Paez, M. M. (2011). Defining and measuring quality in early childhood practices that promote dual language learners' development and learning. In M. Zaslow, I. Martinez-Beck, K. Tout, & T. Halle (Eds.), *Quality measurement in early childhood settings* (pp. 257–280). Baltimore, MD: Paul H. Brookes Publishing Co.

Castro, D. C., Páez, M. M., Dickinson, D. K., & Frede, E. (2011). Promoting language and literacy in young dual language learners: Research, practice, and policy. *Child Development Perspectives, 5*(1), 15–21.

Chang, F., Early, D. M., & Winton, P. J. (2005). Early childhood teacher preparation in special education at 2- and 4-year institutions of higher education. *Journal of Early Intervention, 27,* 110–124.

Child Care and Early Education Research Connections. (n.d.). *Faculty teaching modules.* Retrieved from http://www.researchconnections.org/childcare/modules

Copple, C., & Bredekamp, S. (Eds.). (2009). *Developmentally appropriate practice in early childhood programs serving children from birth through age 8* (3rd ed.). Washington, DC: NAEYC.

Dombro, A., & Cleary, S. (2017). *Raising the bar of quality in the preparation of early childhood educators: Bridging the gap between what we know and what we do.* New York: New York Early Childhood Professional Development Institute, City University of New York.

Early, D. M., Maxwell, K. L., Burchinal, M., Alva, S., Bender, R. H., Bryant, D., et al. (2007). Teachers' education, classroom quality, and young children's academic skills: Results from seven studies of preschool programs. *Child Development, 78*(2), 558–580.

Early, D. M., & Winton, P. J. (2001). Preparing the workforce: Early childhood teacher preparation at 2- and 4-year institutions of higher education. *Early Childhood Research Quarterly, 16,* 285–306.

Early Childhood Technical Assistance Center. (2015). *States' and territories' definitions of/criteria for IDEA Part C eligibility.* Retrieved from http://ectacenter.org/~pdfs/topics/earlyid/partc_elig_table.pdf

Farrell, A., Kagan, S. L., & Tisdall, E. K. M. (Eds.). (2016). *The Sage handbook of early childhood research.* London, UK: Sage Publications.

Foundation for Child Development. (2016). *A shared vision for transforming the workforce.* New York, NY: Foundation for Child Development. Retrieved from https://www.fcd-us.org/shared-vision-transforming-workforce

Gilliam, W. S. (2005). *Prekindergarteners left behind: Expulsion rates in state prekindergarten systems.* New Haven, CT: Yale University Child Study Center.

Gilliam, W. S. (2016). *Early childhood expulsions and suspensions undermine our nation's most promising agent of opportunity and social justice.* Issue brief. Princeton, NJ: Robert Wood Johnson Foundation.

Goffin, S. G. (2015). *Professionalizing early childhood education as a field of practice: A guide to the next era.* Washington, DC: National Association for the Education of Young Children.

Halle, T., Metz, A., & Martinez-Beck, I. (Eds.). (2013). *Applying implementation science in early childhood programs and systems.* Baltimore, MD: Paul H. Brookes Publishing Co.

Hamre, B. K., Pianta, R. C., Downer, J. T., DeCoster, J., Mashburn, A. J., Jones, S. M., et al. (2013). Teaching through interactions: Testing a developmental framework of teacher effectiveness in over 4,000 classrooms. *The Elementary School Journal, 113*(4), 461–487.

Horm, D., Hyson, M., & Winton, P. (2013). Research on early childhood teacher education: Evidence from three domains and recommendations for moving forward. *Journal of Early Childhood Teacher Education, 34,* 95–112.

Hyson, M. (2008). *Preparing teachers to promote young children's mathematical competence.* Unpublished report to National Research Council's Committee on Early Childhood Mathematics. Washington, DC: National Research Council.

Hyson, M., Horm, D. M., & Winton, P. J. (2012). Higher education for early childhood educators and outcomes for young children: Pathways toward greater effectiveness. In R. Pianta, L. Justice, S. Barnett, & S. Sheridan (Eds.), *Handbook of early education* (pp. 553–583). New York, NY: Guilford Press.

Hyson, M., Tomlinson, H. B., & Morris, C. (2009). Quality improvement in early childhood teacher education: Faculty perspectives and recommendations for the future. *Early Childhood Research & Practice, 11*(1). Retrieved from http://ecrp.uiuc.edu/v11n1/index.html

Institute of Medicine (IOM) & National Research Council (NRC). (2015). *Transforming the workforce for children birth through age 8: A unifying foundation.* Washington, DC: National Academies Press.

Johnson, J., Fiene, R., McKinnon, K., & Babu, S. (2010). *A study of ECE pre-service teacher education at major universities in 38 PreK states.* Final Report to the Foundation for Child Development. State College: The Pennsylvania State University.

Katz, L. G. (1996). Child development knowledge and teacher preparation: Confronting assumptions. *Early Childhood Research Quarterly, 11,* 135–146.

La Paro, K .M. (2015). Field experiences in the preparation of early childhood teachers. In L. Couse & S. Recchia (Eds.), *Handbook of early childhood teacher education* (pp. 209–223). New York, NY: Routledge.

Lascarides, V. C., & Hinitz, B. F. (2011). *History of early childhood education.* London, UK: Routledge.

Lawrence, S., Smith, S., & Banerjee, R. (2016). *Preschool inclusion: Key findings from research and implications for policy.* New York, NY: National Center for Children in Poverty, Columbia University Mailman School of Public Health.

Lubeck, S. (1996). Deconstructing "child development knowledge" and "teacher preparation." *Early Childhood Research Quarterly, 11*(2), 147–157.

Mackenzie, N., & Knipe, S. (2006). Research dilemmas: Paradigms, methods, and methodology. *Issues in educational research, 16*(2), 193–205. Retrieved from http://www.iier.org.au/iier16/mackenzie.html

Maxwell, K., Lim, C.-I., & Early, D. M. (2006). *Early childhood teacher preparation programs in the United States: National Report.* Chapel Hill, NC: University of North Carolina, Frank Porter Graham Child Development Institute.

McCartney, K., & Phillips, D. A. (Eds.) (2006). *The Blackwell handbook of early childhood development.* Malden, MA: Blackwell Publishing.

Metz, A., Naoom, S. F., Halle, T., & Bartley, L. (2015). *An integrated stage-based framework for implementation of early childhood programs and systems* (OPRE Research Brief. OPRE 201548). Washington, DC: Office of Planning, Research, and Evaluation, Administration for Children and Families, U.S. Department of Health and Human Services.

Morrison, G. (2012). *Early childhood education today* (13th ed.). New York, NY: Pearson.

National Association for the Education of Young Children (NAEYC). (2011). *Early childhood associate degree accreditation: Accreditation handbook.* Retrieved from https://www.naeyc.org/ecada/files/ecada/AccreditationHandbook.pdf

National Association for the Education of Young Children (NAEYC). (2018). *Power to the profession: Overview.* Retrieved from https://www.naeyc.org/our-work/initiatives/profession/overview

National Association for the Education of Young Children (NAEYC). (2017a). *NAEYC early childhood higher education directory.* Retrieved from https://degreefinder.naeyc.org/

National Association for the Education of Young Children (NAEYC). (2017b). *Higher ed community of practice.* Retrieved from http://hello.naeyc.org/communities/community-home?CommunityKey=46ae962d-e888-4a55-8e46-b42fc260eee7

National Center on Quality Teaching and Learning. (2014). *What do we know about coaching? Literature review.* Seattle, WA: National Center on Quality Teaching and Learning. Retrieved from https://eclkc.ohs.acf.hhs.gov/sites/default/files/pdf/pbc-what-do-we-know.pdf

National Council for Accreditation of Teacher Education. (NCATE). (2010). *Transforming teacher education through clinical practice: A national strategy to prepare effective teachers.* Washington, DC: Author. Retrieved from http://www.ncate.org/Public/ResearchReports/NCATE Initiatives/ BlueRibbonPanel/tabid/715/Default.aspx

National Early Childhood Technical Assistance Center. (2011). *The importance of early intervention for infants and toddlers with disabilities and their families.* Washington, DC: NECTAC. Retrieved from http://www.nectac.org/~pdfs/pubs/importanceofearlyintervention.pdf

National Institute of Early Education Research. (2018). *The state of preschool 2017.* New Brunswick, NJ: Author. Retrieved from http://nieer.org/state-preschool-yearbooks/yearbook2017

National Institute of Child Health and Human Development & National Council for the Accreditation of Teacher Education. (2006). *Child and adolescent development research and teacher education: Evidence-based pedagogy, policy, and practice.* Washington, DC: Author.

National Research Council. (2010). *Preparing teachers: Building evidence for sound policy.* Washington, DC: National Academies Press.

Network of Infant Toddler Researchers. (n.d.). *Network of Infant Toddler Researchers (NITR).* Retrieved from https://www.acf.hhs.gov/opre/research/project/network-of-infant-toddler-researchers-nitr

Neuman, S. B., & Dickinson, D. K. (Eds.) (2010). *Handbook of early literacy research.* New York, NY: Guilford.

Nilsen, P. (2015). Making sense of implementation theories, models, and frameworks. *Implementation Science, 10,* 53. Retrieved from https://implementationscience.biomedcentral.com/articles/10.1186/s13012-015-0242-0

Norris, D. J., Horm, D., & McMullen, M. B. (2015). Research in review: Teacher interactions with infants and toddlers. *Young Children, 70*(5), 84–91.

Odom, S. L. (2009). The ties that bind: Evidence-based practice, implementation science, and outcomes for children. *Topics in Early Childhood Special Education, 29,* 53–61.

Pianta, R. (Ed.). (2012). *Handbook of early childhood education.* New York, NY: Guilford Press.

Pianta, R. C., Hitz, R., & West, B. (2010). *Increasing the application of developmental sciences knowledge in educator preparation: Policy issues and recommendations.* Washington, DC: National Council for Accreditation of Teacher Education.

Ray, A., Bowman, B., & Robbins, J. (2006). *Preparing early childhood teachers to successfully educate all children: The contribution of four-year undergraduate teacher preparation programs.* Chicago, IL: Erikson Institute.

Recchia, S. L., Beck, L., Esposito, A., & Tarrant, K. (2009). Diverse field experiences as a catalyst for preparing high quality early childhood teachers. *Journal of Early Childhood Teacher Education, 30*(2), 105–122.

Ryan, S., & Gibson, M. (2015). Preservice early childhood teacher education. In L. Couse & S. Recchia (Eds.), *Handbook of early childhood teacher education* (pp. 195–201). New York, NY: Routledge.

Saracho, O. N., & Spodek, B. (Eds.). (2012). *Handbook of research on the education of young children* (3rd ed.). New York, NY: Routledge.

Schmit, S., & Matthews, H. (2013). *Better for babies: A study of state infant and toddler child care policies.* Washington, DC: Center for Law and Social Policy.

Sheridan, S. M., Edwards, C. P., Marvin, C. A., & Knoche, L. L. (2009). Professional development in early childhood programs: Process issues and research needs. *Early Education and Development, 20*(3), 377–401.

Spodek, B. (Ed.). (1993). *Handbook of research on the education of young children.* New York, NY: Macmillan.

Spodek, B., & Saracho, O. N. (2005). (Eds.). *Handbook of research on the education of young children* (2nd ed.). Mahwah, NJ: Lawrence Erlbaum Associates.

Stott, F., & Bowman, B. (1996). Child development knowledge: A slippery base for practice. *Early Childhood Research Quarterly, 11*(2), 169–183.

Straus, S., Tetroe, J., & Graham, I. D. (Eds.). (2013). *Knowledge translation in health care: Moving from evidence to practice* (2nd ed.). London, UK: BMJ Books.

Washington, V. (2008). *Role, relevance, reinvention: Higher education in the field of early care and education.* Boston, MA: Wheelock College.

Whitebook, M., & Austin, L.J.E. (2015). *Early childhood higher education: Taking stock across the states.* Berkeley, CA: Center for the Study of Child Care Employment, University of California Berkeley.

Whitebook, M., Austin, L. J. E., Ryan, S., Kipnis, F., Almaraz, M., & Sakai, L. (2012). *By default or by design? Variations in higher education programs for early care and teachers and their implications for research methodology, policy, and practice. Executive Summary.* Berkeley, CA: Center for the Study of Child Care Employment, University of California, Berkeley.

Whitebook, M., Gomby, D., Bellm, D., Sakai, L., & Kipnis, F. (2009). *Preparing teachers of young children: The current state of knowledge, and a blueprint for the future. Executive Summary.* Berkeley, CA: Center for the Study of Child Care Employment, Institute for Research on Labor and Employment, University of California at Berkeley.

Yoshikawa, H., Weiland, C., Brooks-Gunn, J., Burchinal, M., Espinosa, L., Gormley, W. T., et al. (2013). *Investing in our future: The evidence base on preschool.* New York, NY: Foundation for Child Development. Retrieved from http://www.srcd.org/sites/default/files/documents/washington/mb_2013_10_16_investing_in_children.pdf

Zaslow, M., Tout, K., Halle, T., & Starr, R. (2010). Professional development for early educators: Reviewing and revising conceptualizations. In S. B. Neuman & D. Dickinson (Eds.), *Handbook of early language and literacy development* (Vol. 3, pp. 425–434). New York, NY: Guilford.

Zaslow, M., Tout, K., Halle, T., Whittaker, J. V., & Lavelle, B. (2010). *Toward the identification of features of effective professional development for early childhood educators: Literature review.* Washington, DC: U.S. Department of Education Office of Planning, Evaluation and Policy Development, Policy and Program Studies Service.

9

Stuck in Place

A Brief History of Early Childhood Education Policy and Prospects for Expansion

Ron Haskins

The Abecedarian Project played a seminal role in creating the view now held by most parents, researchers, and policy makers that early childhood programs are one of the most effective ways to boost the development of children from disadvantaged families and improve their chances of achieving economic success as adults. As this view strengthened over the years, with a powerful boost from the emergence of brain science (Calderone, 2014), the number of government-sponsored early childhood programs and the amount of spending have grown from virtually nothing before the War on Poverty in the 1960s to three major and several more modest programs and around $38 billion in government spending in 2015 (see Fig. 9.1, p. 201). This growth in programs and spending reflects an impressive change in public perception and public policy, which in turn reflects a host of developments over the past half century, including the influential Abecedarian (Ramey, Sparling, & Ramey, 2012) and Perry Preschool (Schweinhart, 2004) early childhood programs.

The growth in the regard for the efficacy of early childhood programs and in public spending on early childhood has been driven primarily by two engines. The first is the combination of the theoretical literature on how and why high-quality preschool programs boost development and the

The author thanks Nathan Joo for data analysis and fact checking and Emily Bowden and Elizabeth Racine for help with the manuscript. The author is also indebted to Karen Lynch of the Congressional Research Service for extensive help with calculating spending on the nation's child care and development programs.

Some of the text under the heading "The Growth of Spending and Prospects for Additional Growth" was taken from Haskins, R. (2017). Financing early childhood programs. In K. Dodge (Ed.), *The current state of scientific knowledge on pre-kindergarten effects.* Washington, DC: Brookings Institution.

empirical literature showing that high-quality programs, such as Abecedarian and the Perry Preschool, can in fact boost development and have positive long-term impacts on life chances.

The second engine is the growth in the number of families that need child care, caused primarily by huge increases in the percentage of mothers with young children who are employed. The percentage of working mothers with children ages 0–4 years skyrocketed from approximately 26% in 1968 to more than 60% in 2016—an increase of approximately 135%. Nearly all working families, especially single-mother families, need help caring for their children. As the promise of financial help with child care for working families by both presidential candidates Hillary Clinton (2016) and Donald Trump (Sullivan & Costa, 2016) during the 2016 campaign demonstrated, the issue of government support for child care sometimes reaches the level of presidential politics. If that presidential campaign was any indication, both Republican and Democratic voters are attracted to candidates who promise to increase funding for child care.

These two engines are often conflated. When policy makers discuss legislation to increase funds for child care, part of the debate addresses regulations that apply to the quality of child care provided by facilities that qualify for funds. The primary way this desire for quality gets expressed is through state regulations driven by federal requirements. In the most recent reauthorization of the Child Care and Development Block Grant in 2014, for example, there was an important strengthening of mandatory state regulations regarding the quality of care (Office of Child Care, 2014). Granted, a major motivation for regulations is to establish a floor below quality requirements because of the concern that some child care is so bad that it poses a danger to children's health and safety (Cohn, 2013). Still, the debate over regulations and standards is usually accompanied by sweeping statements about how good child care can boost children's development. The line between programs designed primarily to provide child care and programs designed to boost children's development is not always clear.

My goal in this chapter is to review the remarkable growth in early childhood programs—both those intended primarily to provide child care for working parents and those intended to boost child development. It is useful to review this growth and to make educated guesses about the prospects for further growth in programs and in public spending because the issues of child safety and child development are vital to the future of the nation. Similarly, the issues of fighting poverty and promoting economic mobility by ensuring the healthy growth and development of all the nation's children are of lasting importance. My major conclusion is that, despite the remarkable growth in the public's view that high-quality early childhood and preschool programs are needed and valuable and despite the growth in spending on these programs, the prospects for continued growth in public spending are modest and are probably greater at the state than federal level.

GROWTH OF MAJOR EARLY CHILDHOOD PROGRAMS

As early childhood and Head Start historian Maris Vinovskis (2005) has shown, before the advent of Head Start, few people thought that babies could learn much. In fact, the belief that intelligence was fixed by genes and was immutable may have been the dominant view. However, two important books published in the 1960s—*Experience and Intelligence* by J. McVicker Hunt in 1961 and *Stability and Change in Human Characteristics* by Benjamin Bloom in 1964—opened a vista of learning by babies, toddlers, and preschool children. As these two books became known to scholars and many early childhood programs were launched around the country beginning as early as the 1950s, the view that babies and children were malleable and that early experience shaped their development grew among both scholars and the public, including politicians.

By the 1960s, the ideas that the environments of low-income and minority children are deficient and that early childhood programs could improve their environments and thereby boost their intellectual and social development, and even have long-term effects on life success, became popular and have remained the dominant views today. (See Chapter 1 for the emergence of similar ideas in the 19th and early 20th century.)

I turn now to a review of how the nation, through actions by both the federal and state governments, converted the idea that early childhood programs could boost the development of all children, but especially the disadvantaged, into public policy and large national programs. The motivation of the public and policy makers to support child development programs during the preschool years was augmented by a growing desire to help families with working mothers pay for child care. Four specific programs—Head Start, state pre-K programs, the Child Care and Development Block Grant (CCDBG), and the child care spending by the Temporary Assistance for Needy Families (TANF) program—are given special attention, as is the ill-fated Brademas-Mondale bill, which would have greatly boosted the federal commitment to high-quality care in the early 1970s. That proposal was enacted by Congress on a bipartisan basis but was killed by President Nixon, who implemented the conservative strategy of standing athwart history, yelling "stop!" But after the veto of the Brademas-Mondale bill, the nation barely paused in its rush toward more programs and more spending on early childhood programs. After reviewing these four major programs, I provide a brief overview of five additional billion-dollar (or nearly billion-dollar) programs that subsidize child development or child care. Having shown an impressive commitment by federal and state governments to early childhood policy, programs, and spending, I end the chapter by considering the possibility that the growth trend will continue.

Head Start

From the perspective of those who favor a major federal role in boosting the development of low-income children, it would be difficult to exaggerate the importance of Head Start, which began in 1965 as one of the main forces in President Lyndon Johnson's War on Poverty. Federal support for child care was provided during World War II by the Lanham Act, primarily because of the number of mothers employed in defense industries, but the Lanham Act was terminated soon after the war (Herbst, 2017). Two decades later, Head Start opened the door to a government (especially federal) commitment to the care and development of young children—a commitment that has probably not yet run its course.

Careful historical research by Vinovskis (2005; Zigler & Muenchow, 1992) revealed a fascinating story about the origins of Head Start. Vinovskis found that members of Congress, especially Republicans, were championing early childhood education before the Johnson administration proposed Head Start as part of the War on Poverty. During the summer of 1964, the noted scholar of early childhood, Urie Bronfenbrenner of Cornell University, had testified in House hearings on the Economic Opportunity Act of 1964. Bronfenbrenner argued that the administration's focus on adolescents and young adults over age 16 years was a mistake and that the time of life when intervention programs could have great impact on children was during the preschool period. Sargent Shriver, who headed the War on Poverty for Johnson and who had previously not included preschool programs among his weapons in the War on Poverty, decided in late 1964 that preschool might be a good bet after all. He had visited an exemplary early childhood program conducted by the well-known early childhood scholar Susan Gray at Vanderbilt University and came away impressed.

Shriver was serious enough about having an early childhood program that he appointed a Head Start Planning Committee that, given the pending opportunity to start something big, met eight times in January and February of 1965 (Vinovskis, 2005). Known as the Cooke Committee, members included early childhood gurus Urie Bronfenbrenner of Cornell University, Edward Zigler of Yale University, and Robert Cooke of Johns Hopkins University, who chaired the committee. Of the committee's recommendations, issued in February 1965, two stand out. First, because the committee was composed mostly of researchers, it should not be surprising that they recommended that the administration begin the federal venture into early childhood with a small number of early childhood programs, which would be carefully studied and then expanded as knowledge accumulated about staffing, curriculum, parent involvement, and other program characteristics. This advice was contrary to Johnson's and Shriver's goal of establishing a major program that had constituencies who could protect the program in the future. In his State of the Union address to the U.S. Congress on January 4, 1965, Johnson had announced his intention to establish the biggest and most important education initiative in the history of federal policy, an initiative that would include preschool. In a subsequent message to Congress, Johnson announced that the administration would sponsor a large-scale summer program called Head Start, which would be run by Shriver's Office of Economic Opportunity. After an impressive if hurried effort by the administration, Head Start kicked off with a summer program in 1965 that enrolled more than 550,000 children at a cost of nearly $100 million (approximately $760 million in 2016 dollars). Although enrollment in Head Start programs (including Early Head Start, which began in 1994), fell back to about 330,000 in 1977, it grew in fits and starts to exceed 550,000 in 1990, 820,000 in 1998, and 900,000 in 2001. In 2015, enrollment stood at nearly 945,000, having exceeded 900,000 every year after 2000. Thus, enrollment in Head Start started high and continued to increase.

A second notable recommendation by the Cooke Committee was that Head Start should be a comprehensive program, meaning that it should aim to provide or arrange for medical care, nutrition, family involvement, and social and intellectual development. Over the years, there has been tension between being comprehensive and focusing on learning of the type that would prepare children for doing well in school (typically measured by reading and math tests). This debate on goals continues today, although Head Start has increasingly focused on, and been held accountable for, school readiness.

After more than a half century of expansions in early childhood programs, Head Start is still the most expensive of the early childhood programs (see Table 9.1, p. 200). According to the Office of Head Start (2016), in 2015 the program cost $8.3 billion. The program is widely admired and nearly everyone agrees that it produces immediate impacts on children's development and school readiness, but there is controversy about whether these impacts on development last into third grade, let alone adolescence and adulthood (Deming, 2009; Garces, Thomas, & Currie, 2002).

A 2016 review of Head Start by Sara Mead and Ashley LiBetti Mitchell (Haskins, 2016) showed that the trend toward greater emphasis on education and school readiness is intensifying. The Head Start reauthorization of 1998 required the program to develop education performance standards and strengthened the requirements on teacher credentials. The 2007 reauthorization increased these requirements by, for example, requiring half of Head Start teachers to have at least an associate degree by 2011 and half to have at least a bachelor's degree by 2013. This focus on the credentials of teachers reflects the concern of Congress that Head Start quality varies greatly across programs and too many programs produce mediocre results. (See Chapter 4 for a discussion comparing teacher credentials with a focus on teacher training and competencies.)

The 2007 reauthorization also contained arguably the most important reform in Head Start's history and provided a forceful indication that Congress was concerned about Head Start quality. Since the beginning of the program in 1965, grantees had been given permanent grant awards, meaning that local sponsors were exempt from losing their grant unless they committed serious infractions that came to the attention of the Department of Health and Human Services (HHS). The 2007 reauthorization ended this somewhat lax system and created a new system in which grants were given for what the legislation referred to as a 5-year "designation" period. At the end of that period, the grantee's program would be assessed and the grantees who did not pass the assessment would have their grant put up for recompetition, meaning other organizations could compete for this same funding.

Congress also required HHS to convene an advisory committee to propose a system of assessing Head Start programs every 5 years. HHS quickly appointed the committee, which completed its report in one year and made recommendations for what is now called the Designation Renewal System (DRS; Secretary's Advisory Committee, 2008).[1] Based on the Committee's recommendations as well as ideas of its own, in September 2010, the HHS under President Barack Obama published the particulars of its DRS, sought public comment, and then published the official DRS in November 2011 (Congressional Research Service, 2013).

Over the first three rounds of the DRS, about a quarter of Head Start grantees failed the review and had to recompete for their grant awards. Nearly 20% ended up losing their grants and approximately 7% of all Head Start grants went to new providers because of the new accountability system. The major reason more projects have not changed hands is that there are too few entities that compete for the grants. Thus, the sound approach of replacing failing Head Start programs with better programs that may have greater impacts on children's development is not working as well as it could because there are not enough organizations competing to capture the Head Start funds to conduct high-quality programs (Mead, LiBetti, & Mitchell, 2016).

Head Start is a venerable program that has served millions of children and families, but it does not produce consistently positive results (Bloom & Weiland, 2015). In addition, the only random assignment evaluation that was national in scope showed impressive immediate impacts, but these impacts faded in the early elementary grades (Puma et al., 2012). This finding, combined with the results from several years of the DRS, show that Head Start needs to find ways to improve its consistency and increase its long-term impacts. Many of the programs are good, but like nearly every other social intervention program, Head Start has inconsistent impacts across its nearly 1,600 programs and may not produce long-term impacts.

The concluding paragraph of the masterful review of Head Start from Mead and LiBetti Mitchell (2016) is worth quoting at length:

---

[1]Ron Haskins, the author of this chapter, was a member of the Designation Renewal Committee.

Over its 50-year history, Head Start has improved the lives of millions of children and their families, and it continues to improve school readiness for our nation's most at-risk children. But Head Start needs additional changes. Policymakers must be willing to raise expectations for Head Start quality and outcomes, set clear priorities, find fair and accurate ways to measure performance and results, and explore ways to better integrate Head Start with state and local preschool programs. These changes will be difficult, but they are necessary to maximize Head Start's impact for children and families. (p. 27)

The Adventures of the Brademas-Mondale Bill

As is true of so much of Johnson's Great Society, Head Start represented an expansion of federal responsibility for a vast sector of American life, in this case the education of low-income children. Congress clearly supported the principle of providing federal support for public schools because it passed the historic Elementary and Secondary Education Act of 1965 that provided support for public education at the K–12 level. Congress also, at least implicitly, indicated it would support federal spending on preschool programs because it appropriated funds for Head Start year after year beginning in 1966. But Congress did not enact legislation that authorized early childhood programs, leaving some doubt about the level of support for these programs in Congress. Surprisingly, President Richard Nixon relit the fire for early childhood education by delivering the following message to Congress in 1969: "So crucial is the matter of early growth that we must make a national commitment to providing all American children an opportunity for healthful and stimulating development during the first five years of life." Despite this call for action, which could serve as the battle cry for the entire early childhood movement, the Nixon administration did not have a legislative agenda prepared to ensure "healthful and stimulating development" for children. However, Democrats in Congress decided to take advantage of Nixon's call for a national commitment and quickly introduced legislation to create such a program.

More specifically, Walter Mondale in the U.S. Senate and John Brademas in the House of Representatives introduced bills in 1971 calling for a national program that provided funds, either to states or local nonprofit and community-based organizations, to provide high-quality early childhood programs (Steiner, 1976). The Mondale version of the bill would have authorized appropriations of $1.2 billion (more than $7 billion in 2016 dollars) in the first year, increasing to $5 billion (more than $20 billion in 2016 dollars) in the fifth year. Both bills explicitly aimed to promote child development to help children, as the Brademas bill put it, "attain their full potential." Clearly, both bills would have committed the federal government to playing a major role in promoting child development during the preschool years. The amount of funding promised, even by today's standards, was very large.

Lobbying groups, including the American Federation of Labor and Congress of Industrial Organizations, the National Association for the

Education of Young Children, the League of Women Voters, the Day Care and Child Development Council of America, the National League of Cities–U.S. Conference of Mayors, the National Welfare Rights Organization, and many other organizations, had formed a coalition to support early childhood education in general and the Brademas and Mondale bills in particular. As enacted in 1971 after hearings, committee markups, floor votes, and a successful House–Senate conference committee, the Brademas-Mondale bill would have authorized up to $2 billion (nearly $11.9 billion in 2016 dollars) in the initial year with the promise of more later. The money would go not to states, but to community organizations, local governments, and other entities that would subsequently form the backbone of lobbying groups to protect and even expand the new program, much in the manner of Head Start. Equally important, the funds were specifically aimed at promoting the development of children from low-income families. In other words, Brademas-Mondale would have created a national program, with the funds controlled by hundreds or even thousands of community and local government organizations around the nation for the purpose of stimulating the development of children from low-income families (Steiner, 1976).

In a surprise development, President Nixon, who had previously informed Congress and the nation that he supported "a national commitment to providing all American children an opportunity for healthful and stimulating development during the first five years of life" (Nixon, 1969), vetoed the legislation with what could well have been the most controversial and misleading veto message of his administration. Several features of the bill provided reasonable targets for a veto, especially its cost and the way the program's funds would have been administered. However, the major argument of the veto was that the bill would change American culture by "committing the vast moral authority of the National Government to the side of communal approaches to child rearing against the family-centered approach" (Steiner, 1976).

Many people considered this veto message over the top—another example in a long history of preferring home care by mothers over care for children outside the home—but it is worth noting how wrong this justification for Nixon's veto turned out to be. A nation with millions of working parents and a growing number of single mothers needed expanding child care capacity. In addition, there was strong pressure for single mothers on welfare to work; but, if they did not have child care, these mothers would never attain financial independence. It followed that the nation would need public programs that supported "communal" forms of child care for welfare mothers, something that in fact the nation has had since at least the mid-1970s. Even so, before and during the 1970s, many conservatives argued that a mother's place was in the home. However, they were destined to lose the debate as more and more mothers entered the labor force. The main questions shifted from whether support should be provided to who would control the child care funds, how much child care cost, who had the right to sponsor the programs, what the quality standards would be, and who would enforce these standards. The Nixon veto may have temporarily delayed the expansion of federal legislation on child care and child development, but the movement toward government-sponsored child care was just getting started.

The State Pre-K Movement

The federal government is far from the only player in the early childhood movement. State pre-K refers to educational programs, primarily for 4-year-olds, that are organized and paid for by states. By 2016, a total of 43 states and the District of Columbia had such programs that enrolled nearly 1.5 million children (Barnett et al., 2017). Of the 44 programs, 34 (nearly 80%) admitted only children whose families met a state definition of low income. The major goal of most state programs is to increase school readiness by helping 4-year-olds obtain the skills needed to perform well in reading and math when they reach kindergarten. States also frequently argue that their programs aim to increase nonacademic skills, such as social and emotional skills. A major aim of nearly all the state programs is to reduce the gap in reading, math, and other school-related skills between children from low-income families as compared with children from families with higher income (Reardon, 2011). This education goal is intended both to reduce poverty for these children when they are grown and to reduce the large and growing gap in income between children from advantaged and disadvantaged families that increasingly plague the nation (Haskins & Sawhill, 2009).

Although there is no widely agreed-upon explanation of why states began to mount their pre-K programs, Elizabeth Rose (2010) argued that the well-known *Nation at Risk* report of 1983 was an important stimulus for school systems to adopt the view that they could and should play a role in ensuring that children from low-income families are ready for school. This commitment was especially apparent after the National Education Summit at Charlottesville, Virginia, in 1989, which was attended by 49 of the 50 governors and the first President Bush. The summit produced bipartisan and unanimous agreement on six goals for the nation's education systems (Klein, 2014). Goal 1 stated that, "By the year 2000, all children will start school ready to learn." States evidently took this goal to heart and began establishing or expanding their own pre-K programs for 4-year-olds, especially those from low-income families, to ensure that they would be ready to learn at kindergarten entry.

By the time of the first state preschool yearbook from the National Institute for Early Education Research in 2003, 40 states had pre-K programs that enrolled over 700,000 children, primarily 4-year-olds; in 2008, 38 states had pre-K programs that enrolled just over 1 million 4-year-olds (Barnett, Epstein, Friedman, Boyd, & Hustedt, 2008); and in 2016, 43 states and Washington, D.C., had programs that enrolled 1.28 million 4-year-olds (Barnett et al., 2017). The National Institute for Early Education Research yearbooks, published annually since 2003, provide extensive information about the characteristics of the pre-K program in every state, including performance on quality standards and state spending, which was $7.4 billion in 2016 (Barnett et al., 2017). Given the rise in the number of states with pre-K programs and the magnitude of state spending, there can be no question that the state pre-K programs rapidly developed to occupy a primary place in the early childhood movement.

An especially fortunate feature of state pre-K programs is the large (and in some cases, high-quality) research literature on the individual programs. (For a list of most of the studies, see Phillips et al., 2017, pp. 14–15). These studies have led to considerable controversy, especially the results of the large-scale, random assignment study conducted on the Tennessee Voluntary Preschool program. The Tennessee program, like every other research study of state pre-K programs, produced immediate impacts at the end of the program that showed superior performance on academic tests and teacher ratings by children who attended the program as compared with those who did not. The controversy over the Tennessee program began when the control group not only caught up with the program group but surpassed it on both test scores and teacher ratings in the early elementary school years. This outcome—and especially the excellent and even provocative writing about the results and their meaning by the well-known researchers who conducted the study, Dale Farran (who started her career working in the Abecedarian program) and Mark Lipsey (Farran & Lipsey, 2015, 2016) of Vanderbilt University—caused something of an uproar in the pre-K world (Haskins & Brooks-Gunn, 2016).

Farran and Lipsey (2015) argued that the claims made by many researchers, editorial page writers, the Obama administration, and many others about state pre-K programs' beneficial impacts on low-income children are not fully justified and that the entire edifice on which popular support for preschool programs rests is much weaker than the experts claim. They question even the definition of pre-K because the versions being implemented across the nation differ widely in teacher–student ratios, curricula, ages of children, parents' involvement, hours of operation, sponsorship, and many other dimensions. In other words, we have nothing like a national pre-K model that makes programs similar across states and no common definition of the term, making it impossible to argue that pre-K programs work. Furthermore, if a given pre-K program produces positive impacts, those impacts might not generalize to other pre-K programs that differ in important ways. Farran and Lipsey (2016) have also argued that the studies of pre-K's long-term effects do not meet high standards for rigorous research; that the results are inconsistent across studies; and that the results do not support the claims often made for the success of pre-K.

The reactions to the Tennessee study varied greatly, but many well-known researchers criticized both the study and its findings. Nobel Prize winner James Heckman (2016) of the University of Chicago, for example, wrote on his web site that the Tennessee study used a "flawed methodology" that was "corrupted" by noncompliance with the intended random assignment design and that the press release issued with the study "exaggerated" its findings and quality.[2]

A policy brief (Haskins & Brooks-Gunn, 2016) argued that one appropriate reaction to the Tennessee report and the subsequent, often intense response to the report was to have the body of research on pre-K impacts examined by a group of top scholars of early childhood education and to issue a consensus statement about what we know about pre-K from the research. Subsequently, a group of 10 distinguished scholars of preschool education was formed and met twice in day-long discussion sessions and talked often by phone to reach final agreement on the Consensus Statements (Phillips et al., 2017).[3] Of the six consensus statements on pre-K research reached by the group, two are directly related to this chapter. First, every research study of scaled-up pre-K programs shows that the programs have immediate impacts at the end of the program year as measured by the typical measures of intellectual readiness for school. Second, the evidence on long-term impacts is too sparse to permit broad conclusions. This consensus statement is consistent with the Farran and Lipsey argument that the numerous claims by researchers and others that scaled-up pre-K produces impressive long-term impacts on development or school performance are not well supported by the research literature.

Summarizing the importance of the state pre-K movement while maintaining consistency with the pre-K consensus statement requires careful threading. The major goal of the pre-K movement—to better prepare children from disadvantaged families for schooling—is one of the major goals of the nation's social policy. The assumption of responsibility for achieving this worthy educational goal for children has created a new and important chapter in the nation's support for early childhood education. Furthermore, the emphasis on program evaluation and research by many state pre-K programs is exactly the way most experts think social policy should be monitored and improved.

Despite these desirable characteristics of the state pre-K movement, it seems reasonable to conclude that the movement has run up against the sin-

---

[2]The full randomly assigned sample has now been reported and the results closely replicate those of the sample Heckman criticized so harshly. See Lipsey, M., Farran, D. C., & Durkin, K. (2017, March). State test scores and retention data for the TNVPK full randomized sample in 3rd grade. In D. C. Farran (Chair), *New insights from the Tennessee Voluntary Pre-K Program: Full sample results, school, and neighborhood effects.* Symposium presented at the annual meeting of the Society for Research in Educational Effectiveness, Washington, DC

[3]The group included Deborah Phillips of Georgetown University, Mark Lipsey of Vanderbilt University, Ken Dodge of Duke University, Ron Haskins of the Brookings Institution, Daphna Bassok of the University of Virginia, Margaret R. Burchinal of the University of North Carolina, Greg J. Duncan of the University of California at Irvine, Mark Dynarski of the Brookings Institution, Katherine A. Magnuson of the University of Wisconsin, and Christina Weiland of the University of Michigan).

gle biggest problem faced by most programs designed to attack the nation's social and educational problems—namely, the difficulty of producing long-term impacts at scale. As the consensus statement recommended, finding the effectiveness factors that can produce long-term impacts such as good curriculums, coaching, and classroom management skills and then learning to replicate those on a large scale should now be a major focus of state pre-K programs. In addition, adjusting public school early elementary school programs to take advantage of the new level of school readiness students who attended pre-K bring to kindergarten entry should be a focus of practice and research. Following these two steps could lead to a substantial improvement in the pre-K movement's ability to increase school readiness and produce impacts on progress in the early elementary grades and beyond.

The Child Care and Development Block Grant and the Temporary Assistance for Needy Families Program

The history traced previously in this chapter shows that there are two distinct goals of the nation's early childhood policy: child care and child development. Since the 1960s, these goals have become increasingly intertwined as the nation has become more aware of the large differences in school readiness between children from disadvantaged and advantaged families and the difficulty of ameliorating those differences. Still, Congress has authorized several programs for which the goal is clearly to help Americans pay for child care, with a special emphasis on helping low-income parents. In these programs, there is much less emphasis on quality to promote child development.

Other than the World War II Lanham Act, the first federal ventures into paying for child care were associated with the old Aid to Families with Dependent Children program, the cash welfare program started during the New Deal in 1935. In 1967, Congress enacted the Work Incentive Program, which aimed to encourage mothers on welfare to work (Committee on Finance, 1970). The legislation included a provision that provided child care for mothers who were in work or training. This modest program was later replaced with additional provisions designed to provide child care to welfare mothers who were in work or training programs. The welfare-related programs were relatively limited programs and had child care funds only for families on welfare or at risk of falling into welfare. However, in 1990, after several years of debate, Congress created the Child Care and Development Block Grant with funding for low-income families outside welfare, although the child care programs associated with Aid to Families with Dependent Children also continued.

In 1996, the nation's child care programs were overhauled as part of the welfare reform legislation. The 1996 child care reforms repealed several child care programs, created new programs associated with welfare, and simplified and expanded the CCDBG, which remained separate from welfare. The major intent of the new CCDBG was to greatly simplify administration of child care by the states. The new CCDBG had one set of programs rules, one target population, one lead state agency, and two federal funding authorizations. The two federal funding authorizations were necessitated by the fact that two congressional committees in the House and two in the Senate—Ways and Means and Education and the Workforce in the House and Finance and Health, Education, Labor, and Pensions (HELP) in the Senate—had held jurisdiction of child care programs under previous law and none of the committees wanted to get out of the child care business. Most congressional committees operate under the dictum that committees should never give up program jurisdiction. Consequently, the CCDBG now has four funding sources, a stream of mandatory funding under jurisdiction of Ways and Means in the House and Finance in the Senate and a stream of appropriated funding under jurisdiction of Education and the Workforce in the House and HELP in the Senate.

In addition to this funding, there are two other sources of funding for the CCDBG. Under the 1996 legislation, states were required to provide matching funds to qualify to receive funds from the CCDBG. Second, states were allowed to transfer funds from the TANF block grant (which provided states with about $16.5 billion annually) into the CCDBG. These funding provisions have resulted in the CCDBG having combined funding of between $8.6 and $8.9 billion in nominal dollars every year since 2010 (Lynch, 2016). States are also allowed to spend TANF funds directly out of the TANF block grant on child care. In 2015, states used this flexibility to spend about $1.2 billion of their TANF dollars directly on child care without transferring the funds to the CCDBG. Despite all this funding, less than 20% of the families eligible for CCDBG subsidies actually receive any support for their purchase of child care because not enough money is available to support all eligible families. This major shortfall is one of the most obvious and important inequities in federal and state policy designed to help low-income families: Some families receive a subsidy for their child care expenses, whereas other qualified families do not. States have great flexibility in deciding who gets the subsidy, although most states spend most of their funds on lower-income families according to their own definition of "lower income."

In designing the reforms of the CCDBG in 1996, Republicans were intent on minimizing federal standards. The basic concept of the 1996 reforms was to give states as much money as possible with streamlined administrative procedures and minimum regulatory standards and to leave decisions about how the money would be spent to states, with the proviso that states spend their funds on families with incomes below 85% of state median income ($47,400 in the median household in the median income state in 2015). Although Republicans agreed, in a compromise with Democrats, to include health and safety standards for facilities that received CCDBG funds, the standards were minimal.

However, the reauthorization of the CCDBG in 2014 brought important changes in the philosophy that states should make most of the decisions on regulations and other matters associated with child care (Lynch, 2016; Office of Child Care, 2014). Specifically, the federal government increased health and safety standards and enforcement, created a set of stiff requirements for criminal background checks of child care providers, strengthened the requirements for consumer education, and included new requirements designed to boost the quality of care. The quality requirements were augmented by a substantial increase in block grant funds that had to be spent by states on improving quality. The 2014 reauthorization more than doubled the percentage of block grant funds that had to be spent on quality improvement, from 4% to 9%. In addition, states are required to spend an additional 3% on quality improvements in programs for infants and toddlers. Thus, the 2014 reauthorization actually tripled the quality set-aside, from 4% to 12%.

These CCDBG changes in regulations imposed on states by the federal government represent a more activist role for the federal government's involvement in child care. Whether this trend toward increased federal impact on child care—especially of encouraging states to improve quality so that day care will have greater impacts on child development—will be expanded in the future remains to be determined. The current philosophy of the relative powers of the federal government and the states seems to be that the federal government will play a direct role in designing and operating Head Start and the CCDBG, leave control of the pre-K program to states and localities, and give states great flexibility in the allocation of TANF dollars.

Other Programs

The close examination of the three major early childhood programs (Head Start, state pre-K, and the CCDBG) plus the TANF program does not exhaust the early childhood programs that have been enacted and funded by Congress. According to the Government Accountability Office (2017), 50 programs are authorized to spend funds on various forms of child care. No overview of federal programs would be complete without at least mentioning five of the remaining programs that spend at least $1 billion (or nearly $1 billion) per year:

- The Child and Adult Care Food Program provides $3.3 billion annually to subsidize meals and snacks for children in child care facilities.

- The 21st Century Community Learning Centers program pays for after-school and summer care for children, mostly in public schools or community-based organizations, at a cost of about $1.2 billion per year.

- The Individuals with Disabilities Education Act (PL 101-476) has two provisions that provide states with nearly $.8 billion in 2015 to pay for care for disabled infants, toddlers, and preschoolers.

- The Child and Dependent Care Tax Credit, a provision in the tax code designed to help working parents pay for child care, allows parents to use tax liability to subsidize the cost of child care of up to $3,000 per child but a maximum of $6,000 per year. The amount of the credit ranges from 35% of child care expenses for parents with adjusted gross incomes up to $15,000 and 20% for parents with adjusted gross incomes over $43,000. The credit is not refundable, which means that only parents with federal tax liability can claim the credit. In 2015, the credit cost $4.5 billion.

- At a cost of about $0.9 billion per year, the tax code also has a provision called the Dependent Care Assistance Program, which allows working parents to exclude up to $5,000 in child care expenses from their income for purpose of computing their taxable income. This provision has the effect of removing up to $5,000 of income on which parents must pay both income taxes and payroll taxes.

THE GROWTH OF SPENDING AND PROSPECTS FOR ADDITIONAL GROWTH

From the perspective of 1965, when Head Start leaped almost full blown from the brows of Lyndon Johnson, Sergeant Shriver, and the Cooke Committee (Gillette, 2010), the early childhood movement has continued to thrive at both the federal and state levels. As shown in Table 9.1, there are now 10 programs (or 12, if all three versions of TANF spending are counted separately) with spending that approaches $1 billion per year or more (often much more). The total spending on these 10 programs was more than $36.8 billion in 2015. Few of these 10 programs appear to face the risk of elimination or even substantial cuts (the 21st Century Community Learning Centers could be an exception), but a more important question is whether the growth in spending will continue. After all, there are many prominent scholars, elected officials, and members of the public who believe that preschool education could play a vital role in reducing poverty and economic inequality in America.

We can gain a clue about future spending on early childhood by inspecting Figure 9.1, which reports total spending on the major early childhood programs for every year between 1965 and 2015. Spending growth was more or less continuous until 2011. Then, between 2012 and 2015, spending was much flatter than in previous years—actually declining in two years. By 2015, spending was only slightly above where it had been in 2011. This trend in total spending on early childhood is not encouraging.

To gain a more complete understanding of the likelihood of increased spending by the federal government and the states, we need a broader perspective on the overall fiscal condition of the federal budget and the budgets of state governments in recent years. Any attempt to increase government spending on any given area of policy has a better chance of success, other factors being equal, if government revenues are rising and deficits are under control.

Table 9.1.   Early childhood spending on major and other programs, FY 2015

Program	FY 2015 $(millions)
Major programs	
Head Start (and Early Head Start)[a]	$8,286
State Pre-K[b]	$6,200
Child Care and Development Block Grant (CCDBG) (excluding TANF transfers):[c]	
➢ Federal spending	$4,937
➢ State match	$2,200
Temporary Assistance for Needy Families (TANF):	
➢ Direct TANF Spending	$1,250
➢ TANF transfer to CCDBG discretionary[d]	$1,320
➢ TANF "Excess" state MOE child care	$1,965
Other programs	
Child and adult care food program[e]	$3,307
21st-century learning centers[f]	$1,152
Individuals with Disabilities Education Act[g]	$792
Child and dependent care tax credit (tax code)[h]	$4,500
Dependent care assistance program (tax code)[i]	$900
TOTAL[j]	$36,808

[a] "Head Start Program Facts Fiscal Year 2015," by Office of Head Start, 2015, Administration for Children & Families.

[b] "The State of Preschool 2015," by W. S. Barnett et al., 2016, National Institute for Early Education Research.

[c] CCDBG and TANF data provided courtesy of Karen Lynch. Table prepared by CRS based on CCDF expenditure data, plus Office of Family Assistance data for TANF-direct expenditures.

[d] Adapted from CCDF allocation data and "TANF Financial Data – FY 2015," by the Office of Family Assistance, 2016, U.S. Department of Health and Human Services.

[e] Adapted from "Child and Adult Care Food – Participation, Meals, and Costs," by the U.S. Department of Agriculture Food and Nutrition Service, 2017, U.S. Department of Agriculture.

[f] Adapted from "21st Century Community Learning Centers: Providing Local Afterschool and Summer Learning Programs for Families," by Afterschool Alliance.

[g] IDEA Part B, Sec. 619 funding: "Preschool Grants for Children with Disabilities," by the U.S. Department of Education, 2016. IDEA Part C funding: "Early Intervention Program for Infants and Toddlers with Disabilities," by the U.S. Department of Education, 2016.

[h] Adapted from "Credit for Child and Dependent Care Expenses," by the U.S. Department of Treasury, 2016.

[i] Adapted from "Employer Provided Child Care Exclusion/Employer Provided Child Care Credit," by the U.S. Department of Treasury, 2016.

[j] This total only counts major programs and thus does not cover the following additional programs: TANF Transfers to Social Services Block Grant spent on child care ($24 million), Title XX Grants (Social Services Block Grant) spent on child care ($6 million), estimated spending on preschool from Education for the Disadvantaged: Title 1, Part A ($29 million), Maternal, Infant, and Early Childhood Home Visiting ($40 million), and Preschool Development Grants ($250 million).

Figure 9.2 shows Office of Management and Budget (OMB, 2015) data on federal revenues, outlays, and deficits between 1980 and 2015. Although revenues (receipts) fell precipitously during the Great Recession, from 17.9% of gross domestic product (GDP) in 2007 to 14.6% of GDP in both 2009 and 2010, by 2015 revenues had fully recovered to 18.3% of GDP, but spending has been greater than revenues every year since 2002, yielding substantial deficits and adding greatly to the nation's debt. Moreover, both the Congressional Budget Office (CBO) and OMB, two major sources of reliable budget data in the nation's capital, project deficits as far into the future as estimates have been made by both agencies. CBO (2017, p. 5) presents a stark picture

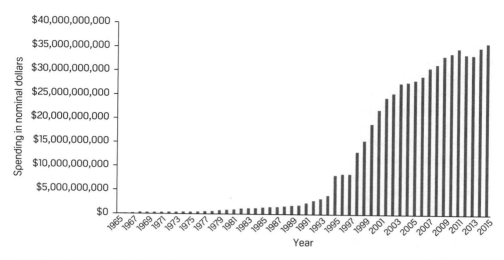

Figure 9.1. Total early childhood spending on major and other programs for fiscal years from 1965 to 2015. The following programs are included: Head Start, Early Head Start, state pre-K, Child and Development Block Grant, Temporary Assistance for Needy Families, Child and Adult Care Food Program, 21st Century Community Learning Centers, Individuals with Disabilities Education Act, Child and Dependent Care Tax Credit (tax code), and Dependent Care Assistance Program (tax code). (*Sources:* Afterschool Alliance, U.S. Department of Education, 2016; National Institute for Early Education Research, 2016; Office of Family Assistance, U.S. Department of Health and Human Services, 2016; Office of Head Start, 2015; U.S. Department of Agriculture, 2017; U.S. Department of Treasury, 2016.)

of the long-term debt problem facing the country, concluding that three decades from now, "debt held by the public is projected to be nearly twice as high, relative to GDP, as it is this year—a higher percentage than any previously recorded in the nation's history."

Congress and two presidents have done very little to reduce the deficit since reaching a modest compromise deficit reduction plan in 2014, usually referred to as the Murray-Ryan Budget Deal (Weisman & Baker 2013)—and

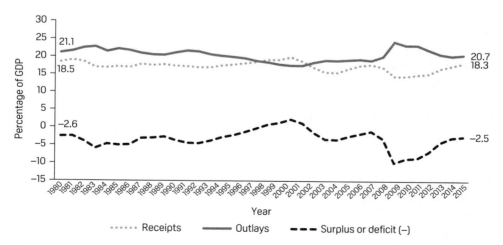

Figure 9.2. Federal receipts, outlays, and surpluses or deficits as percentages of the gross domestic product, 1980–2015. (*Source:* Office of Management and Budget, Historical Tables, Table 1.2: Summary of Receipts, Outlays, and Surpluses or Deficits (–) as Percentages of GDP: 1930–2021. Reprinted with permission from the Brookings Institution and Duke Center for Child and Family Policy.)

that deal did virtually nothing to reduce the long-term deficit. In a word, Congress is ignoring the growing debt, as is President Donald Trump. In fact, they have passed many pieces of legislation that have increased the long-term debt. By contrast, in earlier years, Congress made substantial cuts in spending and modest increases in taxes; the caps Congress imposed on appropriated spending (about one-third of the federal budget) are still tightening and causing reduced spending on many programs. Moreover, both President Trump and congressional Republicans have proposed drastic cuts in spending, including cuts in children's programs. Thus, the federal budget picture is less than favorable for any group that wants to increase spending on early childhood.

However, Congress has shown in recent years that it is not above using budget tricks to avoid limits on new spending if it decides new spending is in order. Moreover, President Trump, who has proposed extensive cuts in social programs, supports expansions of day care programs; the proposals he offered during the campaign were extremely expensive (although most of the benefits would go to families with high incomes because, like the current Child and Dependent Care Tax Credit, most low-income families have either zero or modest tax liability against which to claim the credits and deductions that President Trump supports). At an estimated $115 billion over 10 years, his various proposals to increase support for child care are shocking to some (Batchelder, Maag, Huang, & Horton, 2017). Furthermore, it is difficult to believe that the Republican majority in the 115th Congress (2017–2018) or any other Congress would support spending more than $10 billion a year on new child care programs.

In a development that surprised almost everyone, the 2018 budget agreement enacted in February 2018 contained generous funding for child care (Adams, 2018). The budget provided $5.8 billion over the next two years for the Child Care and Development Block Grant, which can only be spent on children from low-income families. This sum amounts to the biggest increase in the program's history. One piece of legislation does not signal a trend, and it seems unlikely that further increases will occur in subsequent years. But with Democrats now in the majority in the House after the 2018 elections, the looming fights over social spending in general and child care in particular will be fascinating to watch.

Despite the recent increase in child care spending, the long-term trends in federal spending on children's programs (not just child care and child development programs) show that spending was flat in the years between 2012 and 2015 and is now declining as a percentage of both all federal expenditures and the nation's GDP. Budget analysts at the Urban Institute have been keeping track of federal spending on children using rigorous and creative methods (Edelstein, Hahn, Isaacs, Steele, & Steuerle, 2016). They found that, between 1960 and 2010, federal spending on children as a share of all federal spending increased in most years and overall increased from 3.2% to 10.7% of federal spending. By contrast, between 2010 and 2015, spending on children as a share of all federal spending declined to 9.9%. The Urban

Institute researchers project that by 2026, the children's share will decline further to just 7.7%. Unless there are changes in the underlying laws that determine spending on children, which the previous brief review of actions on the federal budget suggests are unlikely, the Urban Institute's projection of continuing decline in federal spending on children will be correct. The decline is baked into the cake. Meanwhile, spending on Social Security, Medicare, and Medicaid for the elderly will grow substantially, indicating clearly that the elderly take precedence over children in the allocation of federal dollars (Haskins, 2017).

Turning to the fiscal situation of states, one of the most remarkable characteristics of state budgets is their dependence on federal grants. Total state revenues grew from around 8% to 11% of GDP between 1977 and 2011 before falling to around 10% in 2012 and 2013. This decline represents the largest decline in state revenues in the past 35 years. Federal grants to states rose from approximately 2% of GDP in the 1980s to approximately 3% in the 1990s and the 2000s. Then, federal grants jumped to nearly 4% of GDP as the federal government tried to make up for the fall in state tax revenues that struck nearly every state during the Great Recession. However, federal grants fell back to their prerecession level by 2013. States now get approximately 30% of their revenue from federal grants. Given the level of the federal debt, this figure seems unlikely to increase very much. The overall budget situation of states is not as bad as that of the federal government, in large part because most states have constitutions that prohibit deficit spending (although this limitation on state spending is sometimes observed in the breach). Most states, especially Illinois, Pennsylvania, New Jersey, and Kentucky, have even more serious budget problems than might at first appear because of the long-term obligations of their state pensions. One study estimates that the amount of money states and localities contribute to their pension systems over the next 30 years will have to increase by 2.5 times or by approximately 14% of the total revenue projected to be generated over this period by state and local governments. This level of funding would require a tax increase of $1,385 per household per year (Novy-Marx & Rauh, 2012).

Despite the very tight condition of state budgets, 43 states plus Guam and the District of Columbia have initiated pre-K programs, and many states have managed to increase their spending on their pre-K program in at least some years. State total spending on pre-K increased at a healthy pace until 2010, when it leveled off and then declined—primarily as a result of historic declines in state revenues during the Great Recession, then the falloff in federal grant dollars starting in 2012. During the 7 years between 2004 and 2011, state funds for pre-K rose from about $3.3 billion to $5.9 billion in 2015 dollars. Funding then fell for 2 years before increasing to $6.2 billion in 2015 (Barnett et al., 2017). It can be hoped that many states, despite their budget issues, can keep increasing their spending on pre-K programs. In any case, the prospects for additional spending on early childhood seem better at the state level than the federal level.

CONCLUSION

Both the states and the federal government, mostly on a bipartisan basis, have come to the view that early childhood programs are essential. Compared to a time when few Americans knew anything about preschool programs and when we had little research to go on, we now have many programs at the state and federal levels that spend $1 billion or more on early childhood services, as well as a blizzard of research about the impacts of early childhood programs. More importantly, there is now almost universal agreement that the nation has experienced a cultural shift toward women's paid employment outside the home and that this shift has become a permanent characteristic of American culture. Consequently, given the high cost of child care and the low income of millions of parents, there is widespread agreement that the government should help parents pay for child care.

Since the early 1960s, there has also been something like a cultural shift in our understanding of child development. We now see infants and preschool children as active learners, but with the caveat that the home and neighborhood environments of children play a vital role in helping them learn. Because millions of children have home and neighborhood environments that constrain their development, a part of the cultural shift regarding development is that high-quality early childhood environments, which have been created by many early childhood programs across the country, can compensate for the home and neighborhood constraints experienced by so many children. The result is that most parents, researchers, policy makers, and members of the public think that providing quality preschool experiences to these children from low-income families is an essential ingredient in the nation's goal of reducing poverty and promoting equal opportunity.

We face two problems in delivering on this goal. First, as shown here, the financial circumstances at both the federal and state level are in disarray. Spending on children at the federal level has already stopped growing and, as a percentage of GDP, has even declined. Meanwhile, spending on the elderly continues to skyrocket. Because of little or no action from a series of pusillanimous Congresses and presidents, the federal budget disaster continues to grow worse. It is difficult to believe that the reduction in spending on children has not been influenced by both the out-of-control spending on the elderly and the growing national debt. The financial situation in many states is also alarming, but on balance many states can afford to continue their increased spending on early childhood, especially their pre-K programs.

Although early childhood advocates try to squeeze federal and state governments for more resources, there is a second problem for researchers and program developers. If we accept the consensus statement discussed in this chapter, which states that there is abundant evidence of short-term impacts of state pre-K programs on preschool children's test scores and classroom preparation but mixed evidence on long-term impacts (thus preventing one from drawing broad conclusions), we have to admit that our field has a lot of work to do in increasing the long-term impacts of our programs. If we show that early childhood programs can produce long-term impacts when programs are implemented at scale, our case for increased spending will be greatly strengthened for the day when the prospects for increased funding by government are better.

REFERENCES

Adams, G. (2018). *A historic boost to child care funding means states can start to realize the potential of the Child Care and Development Block Grant.* Washington, DC: Urban Institute. Retrieved from https://www.urban.org/urban-wire/historic-boost-child-care-funding-means-states-can-start-realize-potential-child-care-and-development-block-grant.

Barnett, S. W., Epstein, D. J., Friedman, A. H., Boyd, J. S., & Hustedt, J. T. (2008). *The state of preschool 2008: State preschool yearbook.* New Brunswick, NJ: The National Institute for Early Education Research. Retrieved from http://nieer.org/state-preschool-yearbooks/state-preschool-2008

Barnett, S. W., Friedman-Krauss, A. H., Gomez, R. E., Horowitz, M., Weisenfeld, G. G., Brown, K. C., et al. (2016). *The state of preschool 2015: State preschool yearbook.* New Brunswick, NJ: The National Institute for Early Education Research. Retrieved from http://nieer.org/wp-content/uploads/2016/05/Yearbook_2015_rev1.pdf

Barnett, S. W., Friedman-Krauss, A. H., Weisenfeld, G. G., Horowitz, M., Kasmin, R., & Squires, J. H. (2017). *The state of preschool 2016: State preschool yearbook.* New Brunswick, NJ: The National Institute for Early Education Research. Retrieved from http://nieer.org/state-preschool-yearbooks/yearbook2016

Barnett, S. W., Robin, K. B., Hustedt, J. T., & Schulman, K. L. (2003). *The state of preschool 2003: State preschool yearbook.* New Brunswick, NJ: The National Institute for Early Education Research. Retrieved from http://nieer.org/state-preschool-yearbooks/state-preschool-2003

Batchelder, L. L., Maag, E., Huang, C., & Horton, E. (2017). *Who benefits from President Trump's child care proposals?* Washington, DC: Tax Policy Center.

Bloom, B. (1964). *Stability and change in human characteristics.* New York, NY: Wiley.

Bloom, H., & Weiland, C. (2015, March). *Quantifying variation in Head Start effects on young children's cognitive and socio-emotional skills using data from the National Head Start Impact Study.* New York, NY: MDRC.

Calderone, J. (2014, November 6). 10 big ideas in 10 years of brain science. *Scientific American.* Retrieved from https://www.scientificamerican.com/article/10-big-ideas-in-10-years-of-brain-science

Clinton, H. (2016, May 20). Child care now costs more than rent: Here's how to fix this crisis. *Washington Post.* Retrieved from https://www.washingtonpost.com/opinions/hillary-clinton-child-care-now-costs-more-than-rent-heres-how-to-fix-this-crisis/2016/05/20/9055a200-1dd6-11e6-b6e0-c53b7ef63b45_story.html

Committee on Finance, U.S. Senate. (1970). *Staff data with respect to modification of the work incentive program and related provisions (91st Congress, 2nd session).* Retrieved from https://www.finance.senate.gov/imo/media/doc/162.pdf

Congressional Budget Office. (2017). *An update to the budget and economic outlook: 2017–2027.* Retrieved from https://www.cbo.gov/publication/52370

Congressional Research Service. (2013, August 14). *Head Start: Designation renewal system* (Report No. R43171). Retrieved from https://www.everycrsreport.com/reports/R43171.html

Deming, D. (2009). Early childhood intervention and life-cycle skill development: Evidence from Head Start. *American Economic Journal of Applied Economics, 1*(3): 111–134.

Edelstein, S., Hahn, H., Isaacs, J., Steele, E., & Steuerle, C. E. (2016). *Kids' Share 2016: Federal expenditures on children through 2015 and future projections.* Washington, DC: Urban Institute.

Farran, D. C., & Lipsey, M. W. (2015). *Expectations of sustained effects from scaled up Pre-K: Challenges from the Tennessee study* (Evidence Speaks Reports, Vol 1, No. 3). Washington, DC: The Brookings Institution.

Farran, D. C., & Lipsey, M. W. (2016). Spotlight—Pre-kindergarten interventions: Evidence for the benefits of state prekindergarten programs: Myth and misrepresentation. In R. Haskins (Ed.), *Behavior Science & Policy, 2*(1), 9–18.

Garces, E., Thomas, D., & Currie, J. (2002). Longer-term effects of Head Start. *American Economic Review, 92*(4): 999–1012.

Gillette, M. (2010). *Launching the War on Poverty: An oral history* (2nd ed). Oxford, UK: Oxford University Press.

Government Accountability Office. (2017, July). *Early learning and child care: Agencies have helped address fragmentation and overlap through improved coordination.* Washington, DC: Author.

Haskins, R. (2017). The most important non-issue in the 2016 campaign. In M. E. O'Hanlon (Ed.), *Brookings big ideas for America* (pp. 83–89). Washington, DC: Brookings Press.

Haskins, R., & Brooks-Gunn, J. (2016, Fall). *Trouble in the land of early childhood education?* Princeton, NJ: The Future of Children.

Haskins, R., & Sawhill, I. (2009). *Creating an opportunity society.* Washington, DC: Brookings Press.

Heckman, J. J. (2016). *Vanderbilt Pre-k Study: You get what you pay for.* Retrieved from https://heckmanequation.org/resource/vanderbilt-pre-K-study-you-get-what-you-pay-for

Herbst, C. M. (2017). Universal child care, maternal employment, and children's long-run outcomes: Evidence from the U.S. Lanham Act of 1940. *Journal of Labor Economics, 35*(2), 519–564.

Hunt, J. M. (1961). *Intelligence and experience.* New York, NY: Ronald Press.

Individuals with Disabilities Education Act (IDEA) of 1990, PL 101-476, 20 U.S.C. §§ 1400 et seq.

Institute of Medicine. (2000). *From neurons to neighborhoods: The science of early childhood development.* Washington, DC: National Academies Press.

Klein, A. (2014, September 23). Historic summit fueled push for K–12 standards. *Education Week.* Retrieved from http://www.edweek.org/ew/articles/2014/09/24/05summit.h34.html

Lynch, K. E. (2016a, November 22). *CCDBG Act of 2014: Key provisions and implementation status* (CRS Report No. RL30785). Retrieved from https://www.everycrsreport.com/reports/RL30785.html

Lynch, K. E. (2016b, November 22). *Child care entitlement to states* (CRS Report No. IF10511). Retrieved from http://greenbook.waysandmeans.house.gov/sites/greenbook.waysandmeans.house.gov/files/IF10511%20-%20Child%20Care%20Entitlement%20to%20States.pdf

Mead, S., & LiBetti Mitchell, A. (2016). Spotlight—Pre-kindergarten interventions: Reforming Head Start for the 21st century: A policy prescription. In R. Haskins (Ed.), *Behavior Science & Policy, 2*(1).

Nixon, R. (1969, February 19). *Special message to the Congress on the nation's antipoverty programs.* Retrieved from http://www.presidency.ucsb.edu/ws/?pid=2397.

Novy-Marx, R., & Rauh, J. D. (2012). *The revenue demands of public employee pension promises* (Working paper No. 18489). Washington, DC: National Bureau of Economic Research.

Office of Child Care. (2014, December). *Reauthorization of the Child Care and Development Fund (CCDF): An exciting new era for child care.* Retrieved from https://www.acf.hhs.gov/sites/default/files/occ/occ_reauthorization_webinar.pdf

Office of Head Start. (2015). *Head Start program facts fiscal year 2015.* Retrieved from https://eclkc.ohs.acf.hhs.gov/about-us/article/head-start-program-facts-fiscal-year-2015

Office of Management and Budget. (2015). *Budget of the U.S. government: Historical tables: Fiscal year 2016.* Washington, DC: Office of the President.

Phillips, D. A., Lipsey, M. W., Dodge, K. A., Haskins, R., Bassok, D., Burchinal, M. R., et al. (2017). *Puzzling it out: The current state of scientific knowledge on pre-kindergarten effects: A consensus statement.* Washington, DC: Brookings Institution.

Puma, M., Bell, S., Cook, R., Heid, C., Broene, P., Jenkins, F., et al. (2012). *Third grade follow-up to the Head Start Impact Study: Final report* (OPRE Report 2012-45). Washington, DC: Office of Planning and Evaluation.

Ramey, C. T., Sparling, J. J., & Ramey, S. L. (2012). *Abecedarian: The ideas, the approach, and the findings.* Los Altos, CA: Sociometrics Corporation.

Reardon, S. F. (2011). The widening academic achievement gap between the rich and the poor: New evidence and possible explanations. In R. Murnane & G. Duncan (Eds.),

Whither opportunity? Rising inequality and the uncertain life chances of low-income children. New York, NY: Russell Sage Foundation Press.

Rose, E. (2010). *The promise of preschool: From Head Start to universal pre-kindergarten.* New York, NY: Oxford University Press.

Schweinhart, L. J. (2004). *The High/Scope Perry Preschool Study through age 40: Summary, conclusions, and frequently asked questions.* Ypsilanti, MI: High/Scope Press. Retrieved from http://www.highscope.org/file/Research/PerryProject/3_specialsummary%20col%20 06%2007.pdf

Secretary's Advisory Committee on Re-designation of Head Start Grantees. (2008). *A system of designation renewal of Head Start grantees.* Washington, DC: Office of Planning and Evaluation.

Steiner, G. Y. (1976). *The children's cause.* Washington, DC: Brookings Institution.

Sullivan, S., & Costa, R. (2016, September 13). Donald Trump unveils child-care policy influenced by Ivanka Trump. *Washington Post.* Retrieved from https://www.washington post.com/news/post-politics/wp/2016/09/13/donald-trump-joined-by-ivanka-trump-to-outline-child-care-policy/?utm_term=.d9acd830f1cd

Vinovskis, M. A. (2005). *The birth of Head Start: Preschool education policies in the Kennedy and Johnson administrations.* Chicago, IL: University of Chicago Press.

Weisman, J., & Baker, P. (2013, December 18). Budget deal offers a reprieve from Washington paralysis. *The New York Times,* pp. A1.

Zigler, E., & Muenchow, S. (1992). *Head Start: The inside story of America's most successful educational experiment.* New York, NY: Basic Books.

10

From Research to Effective Policy
and Practice in Early Care and Education

Lessons from Frank Porter Graham's 50 Years of Research

W. S. Barnett

The early childhood education field faces a major challenge in translating research into effective policy and practice on a large scale. Research has promised not just immediate impacts on learning and development, but also long-term gains in intelligence, achievement, and social and economic success for disadvantaged populations that decrease inequality and grow the economy. However, most large-scale public programs have fallen short in both the magnitude and persistence of their effects (Haskins & Brooks-Gunn, 2016). One state's preschool program appears to harm children in the long run, despite some features that support provision of quality early education (Lipsey, Farran, & Hofer, 2017). This chapter draws lessons from work by researchers from the Frank Porter Graham Child Development Institute (FPG) and from related studies that help us to understand the challenge and how it might be better addressed.

BACKGROUND

The three preceding chapters in this section by Craig Ramey, Marilou Hyson, and Ron Haskins each focused on a different area of research that is relevant to the translation of research into policy and practice. In Chapter 7, Ramey described the progress of a decades-long program of research designed to build developmental science to provide a stronger basis for policy and practice. In Chapter 8, Hyson focused on problems in moving from research to practice via policy, as well as the contributions of implementation science to a better understanding of those problems and how they can be overcome. In Chapter 9, Haskins analyzed trends in federal and state policy with specific attention to the key determinants of spending over time and success at scale.

Before delving into how these chapters can help early childhood policy succeed at scale, it is useful to describe this challenge in more detail. The early childhood field has been remarkably successful in demonstrating the potential of early childhood education to improve learning and development over the life course (Yoshikawa et al., 2013). In a large body of applicable research, a number of small-scale studies stand out for their findings that programs made remarkable differences in children's development and subsequent educational, social, and economic success. Such programs promised better outcomes for the individuals who participated and for society generally by decreasing inequality and improving productivity and quality of life. Economic analyses found that benefits consistently exceeded costs by a wide margin (Ramon et al., 2017).

However, large-scale public preschool programs have not consistently produced the results expected from the small-scale research. Typically, large-scale public programs have been found to produce much smaller initial impacts with little or no persistent impacts (Haskins & Brooks-Gunn, 2016). In a recent meta-analysis, the average effect size in studies conducted after 1980 was just 0.16 (Duncan & Magnuson, 2013). Findings in several large-scale randomized trials of public preschool programs have been particularly disappointing. Even the exceptions found to produce some persistent gains had results that were less consistently positive than expected (e.g., Huizen, Dumhs, & Plantenga, 2017). Benefit-cost estimates for large-scale public programs have been correspondingly less favorable (Huizen et al., 2017).

DESIGNING EVIDENCE-BASED POLICY

In Chapter 7, Ramey described a long-term program of research designed to inform the rationale for investing in early childhood development, as well as specific aspects of policy and program design. This research program has been strongly theory based and has followed a progression from Abecedarian to the Carolina Approach to Responsive Education (CARE) Project to the Infant Health and Development Program (IHDP) that expanded the range of program approaches and contexts beyond that of the original study. This research simultaneously focused on two goals of program provision—education and child care—rather than keeping these siloed, while controlling for contributions to child development from nutrition, health, and social services. These are key studies that inform contemporary understanding of the malleability of cognitive development and the consequences of nonparental child care.

Together with studies of such other programs as the Perry Preschool and Chicago Child Parent Centers, the Abecedarian program generated a vision and aspirations for early childhood programs to profoundly improve the cognitive development and life courses of children in poverty. Large gains have been expected in general cognitive abilities and academic outcomes including achievement, grade repetition, special education, and educational attainment. To these results can be added the long-term gains found in other domains, including decreased delinquency and crime, increased employment and earnings, and improved indicators of adult health.

As noted earlier, large-scale public programs have not delivered the same results. For multiple reasons, they should not have been expected to deliver the same results. From Chapter 7, it should be clear that such expectations are inconsistent with the evidence from the full program of research that followed from the initial Abecedarian study—and from similar efforts by others. The findings of the oldest and most commonly cited studies, including Abecedarian, should never have been considered representative of what could be accomplished more generally. Subsequent research on Abecedarian and other programs has provided lessons about the ways in which outcomes can be expected to vary with person, process, and context that suggest much more modest expectations for large-scale public programs.

Generalization and Seminal Studies as Outliers

Reproducibility—the production of similar results from similar programs using similar procedures with similar populations in similar circumstance—has become recognized as an important problem in research generally (Drummond, 2009). Medical science has found that carefully controlled studies have difficulty reproducing prior findings (Ioannidis, 2005). Educational research has a similar, if less dire, problem (Makel & Plucker, 2014).

Some of the differentials between outcomes in the best-known small-scale studies and large-scale public programs may be an artifact of the process through which some studies become successes. Most early studies were small and weakly powered. Large numbers of outcome measures were analyzed without preselection of tested relationships or adjustments for the number of comparisons. Studies that luck favored with larger outcomes were more likely to "succeed" in publication, funding for follow-up, and acclaim (Pashler & Wagenmakers, 2012).

Sample selection in the oft-cited small-scale studies also contributed to favorable results that increased their probability of being survivors. Both Abecedarian and Perry selected children who were at exceptionally high risk of poor cognitive outcomes. The samples also may have unintentionally differed from the general disadvantaged population in ways that influenced outcomes. Grade repetition and special education placement in the Abecedarian control group were around 50%, which is a much higher level than for children in poverty generally. An even more extraordinary 80% of the Abecedarian families reported a smoker in the home (Ramey, 1979). Could the 10 hours per day, 5 days per week that the children spent in the program for the first 5 years of their lives have improved health and development by reducing exposure to secondhand smoke?

The Chicago Child–Parent Center raises another version of this concern (Reynolds, 2000). Its sample was not selected for study based on risk. However, treatment and comparison groups were created when some neighborhoods and not others succeeded in getting the city to continue the program. This situation suggests that the two groups differ from each other, if not from the broader population, in their context. Could the local contexts of all three of the seminal studies have been unique in unknown ways that contributed to higher-than-usual levels of success?

The concerns raised here are among the more important reasons that studies such as IHDP were conducted (Ramey et al., 1992). However, the results of IHDP and other such studies have received much less attention than studies in the earlier wave. Also, relatively little attention has been paid to what has been learned about the ways in which outcomes varied within later studies such as IHDP, perhaps because policy advocacy eschews such complications. For example, Ramey, Sparling, and Ramey (2012) reported that IHDP results differed dramatically by parental education level. Such heterogeneity in outcomes has implications for future research, as well as the use of research to inform policy. However, parental education level has not been a focus for sample selection in many studies, nor has it often been considered as a key eligibility criterion for services. Of course, studies that have examined this particular variable have not led to simple conclusions; neither Head Start nor Early Head Start randomized trials provide confirmation of larger persistent gains for children whose parents had lower levels of education within a narrower socioeconomic range (e.g., Puma et al., 2012; Vogel, Xue, Moiduddin, Kisker, & Carlson, 2010).

Generalization in the Context of Change

The normative experiences of young children—including those in poverty—have changed dramatically since the time of the seminal studies of early childhood program impacts (Magnuson & Waldfogel, 2016). Control-group children in the oldest studies were primarily in parent care, but over time participation in some form of early care and education has become much more common. Nearly half of control group children in the national Head Start Impact Study attended another preschool program (Bloom & Weiland, 2015). In a recent study of Boston's prekindergarten program, two thirds of the control group were in nonparental care, with 57% in other preschool programs (Weiland & Yoshikawa, 2013). We should expect effects to differ as a result. For example, Feller, Grindal, Miratrix, and Page (2016) found larger effects of Head Start for children who would have otherwise been home with their parents than for those who would have been in another preschool program.

Generally, the broader contexts in which children and families live have in most ways changed for the better. Abecedarian is better designed than many other studies to withstand some of this challenge because it provided nutrition, health care, and social services to treatment and control groups—a path that might be taken by more studies today. Access to health care has improved, as has health care itself, reducing the potential health benefits from preschool program participation. The air and water are cleaner and children are less exposed to such environmental toxins as lead, even though some well-known environmental problems remain. Children and families are much more likely to receive other services, such as home visiting, which can lead to improvements in home environments. Parents have more education today; furthermore, across all income levels, parents engage in more learning activities with their young children than in years past (Bassok, Finch, Lee, Reardon, & Waldfogel, 2016). The percentage of children born to teenage mothers is much lower. Parents are less likely to smoke during and after pregnancy.

There are other demographic changes with implications that are less obvious. Most families in the older seminal studies were African American. Between 1980 and 2015, the percentage of Hispanic children nearly tripled to approximately 25% (Child Trends Data Bank, 2016). Today, the majority of enrollees in some state pre-K programs are dual-language Spanish speakers (Barnett et al., 2017). The enrollment of young children with special needs in preschool programs has increased (Barnett et al., 2017). The percentage of children in single-parent households has increased. The consequences of these demographic trends overall are difficult to assess with precision, but most of them may be expected to have reduced the average impact of preschool programs on child outcomes.

The Context for Learning and Development Over Time

Ramey and the other developers of the most successful small-scale programs were greatly concerned about the education of children after leaving their preschool programs. They created special follow-on programs and studied them in ways that shed some light on how later education relates to sustained gains. Subsequent research has revealed that primary schools vary greatly in the achievement levels attained by children in poverty (Fahle & Reardon, 2017). Yet, the extent and ways in which the persistence of preschool effects depend on children's K–12 experiences are still not well understood. Increased support in recent decades for children who fall behind (e.g., through smaller classes or extra instruction) may have decreased the long-term disadvantages of children who did not attend preschool programs (Akerhielm, 1995). Some have found that preschool gains are more likely to be sustained if students subsequently have better, or better aligned, educational experiences (Swain, Springer, & Hofer, 2015). Others have found largely null results for a host of early elementary school structural and process features in promoting sustained gains from preschool programs (Jenkins et al., 2015).

Although we may not yet know if key elements of post-preschool education can be identified that promote lasting gains, schools have changed in ways that could have influenced the potential for lasting gains from preschool. For example, the accountability movement may have led to a greater focus on helping children at the bottom of the achievement distribution to catch up, thus increasing the resources schools devote to these children compared to earlier years. In the other direction, the accountability movement has led some districts to move their least qualified teachers into the untested early grades, where end-of-year state achievement tests are not given; this action could lower the quality of teaching in the early grades compared to years past (Grissom, Kalogrides, & Loeb, 2017). These changes leave us without a clear answer to the question of how differences in K–12 policy and practice over time and across districts affect the long-term results we should expect from early childhood programs today and in the future. It also leaves us uncertain about how we might improve the conditions for success.

POLICY CHALLENGES FOR ACHIEVING EVIDENCE-BASED SUCCESS AT SCALE

In Chapter 9, Ron Haskins provided an extremely useful and admirably concise description of the evolution of federal and (to a lesser extent) state early childhood policy. Primarily through budget data, he told us where we are and the path that we have taken to get here. With a somewhat generous definition of major public programs supporting early childhood programs, he calculated a total expenditure of $36 billion per year. Not all these expenditures (I include here tax "expenditures" in the forms of credits and deductions) support preschool-age children because many of them fund child care for children up to age 13 years.

Haskins attributed the rise to this level of expenditure and the ways that it has been directed over the past half century primarily to two major factors. One is research on early childhood development that demonstrated the potential for adversity to damage development and for early childhood programs of a variety of types to buffer and support development. The second factor is the growth in maternal employment and the concomitant increase in the need for and use of nonparental care generating a political demand from this constituency. The importance of this political demand can be seen in the composition of government funding, with nearly two thirds focused on child care and relatively little child care funding dedicated to quality that would enhance child development.

Nevertheless, the weak political support for early childhood programs is evident in the overall level of funding. Although $36 billion is by many standards a very large number, it is a tiny fraction of total government spending, which is about $7 trillion annually. Spending for early childhood programs is just 0.5% of government expenditures. Funding for child care is so limited relative to its express goals that less than 20% of the eligible population receives federally and state funded direct child care subsidies.

In Chapter 9, Haskins is pessimistic about the potential for a positive change in the overall early childhood funding picture. Current spending levels benefited from a substantial rise beginning near the end of the 20th century, but this level plateaued shortly before the Great Recession. This pattern suggests that the plateau in recent years is not a temporary response to the recession's impact on government budgets. One key factor may be the end of increasing rates of maternal employment (Hipple, 2016). However, Haskins also concluded that long-term trends in government revenue and spending—most notably rising demands for spending on an older population—create tremendous pressure for a reduction in the percentage of government spending that goes to early childhood. This trend is already evident.

These big picture elements matter for reasons explicated by Minervino (2014). Political will and adequate funding are essential elements for producing success at scale. Most public programs have not been funded at the level of the successful small-scale models. The federal Head Start and child care subsidy programs offer strong lessons in this regard. As research has strengthened the case that high quality, intensity, and duration are necessary for success, Congress has modified program requirements and allocated additional resources to quality. Yet, despite progress, spending remains far short of what is required to replicate successful models, as Haskins documented. Funding has never approached the levels needed to serve all those eligible for major federal early childhood programs; as a result, agencies experience scarcity and a pull between quality and quantity that also promotes dysfunction from siloed services. Head Start essentially has been a child development program for children of parents who do not work, while child care subsidies support work but do little to support—and may sometimes even harm—children's development (Herbst & Tekin, 2016).

DESIGN FAILURE: A SUMMARY

Together, Chapters 7 and 9 provide strong reasons to moderate expectations for the outcomes of today's programs, as well as lessons about how outcomes might be improved. To begin with, current programs should not be expected, even in theory, to reproduce at scale the effects of the small-scale programs studied in the past, even if the programs themselves were to be reproduced exactly. In addition, the political will has not existed at the federal level or in most states or localities to create large-scale programs that have the features of successful models.

The failure of most large-scale public programs to replicate the features of successful models is a design flaw that can be attributed to this lack of political will. The Perry Preschool, Chicago, and Abecedarian programs had well-paid, well-educated teachers with strong supervision and high teacher-to-child ratios (Hanushek, 2015). Abecedarian and Perry Preschool, for example, had much better prepared and supported teachers and much better ratios of teachers to children than is standard practice today. Most children attended these programs for multiple years—nearly 5 years for Abecedarian. The vast majority of state pre-K program enrollments are for 1 year at age 4 years (Barnett et al., 2017). Most children enrolled in Head Start attend for no more than 1 year (Caronongan, Moiduddin, West, & Vogel, 2014). In short, large-scale public programs have not been designed to replicate the features of the small-scale programs that were extensively studied and furthermore have not been funded at levels that would permit replication of those programs (Hanushek, 2015). Even allowing for reduced expectations regarding outcomes for all the reasons discussed previously, no one should expect to produce similar results from dissimilar programs. Yet, evidently, this is what policy makers, the public, and, too often, researchers expect.

IMPLEMENTATION FAILURE

In Chapter 8, Marilou Hyson provides another perspective on the limited impact of research on policy and practice with respect to both design and implementation. Her chapter goes beyond the question of influence to the challenge of achieving sustained change at scale. Several of her examples are instances of design failure that are best explained by the political realities set out by Haskins in Chapter 9. Punitive discipline for preschool children in the form of suspension and expulsion occurs almost entirely in private-sector programs that are poorly funded and have poorly prepared teachers; it is quite rare in public preschool programs. Similarly, the poor quality of infant and toddler care can be directly traced to inadequate funding for the adults working in those programs. These might best be characterized not as the result of failures to access knowledge, but as failures of the will to spend money on what is known. The failure of state policies to reflect knowledge about dual-language learning may be somewhat less related to willingness to spend public dollars and more to larger political issues relating to multilingualism and immigration, but such policies also require added funding.

However, Hyson also pointed out that there are reasons to expect research to have limited influence on policy and practice beyond a very limited willingness to devote scarce resources to early childhood programs and policies. Virtually all policy-relevant research is contested within the academy so that even the early childhood field does not agree on what constitutes the evidence base for policy and practice. Moreover, the application of research to policy and practice often is far from straightforward given the complexity of the systems that contribute to early childhood learning and development. In addition, it is difficult for research to provide sufficient precision to override differences of opinion about the value of specific policy and practice decisions. Much of the time, some study can be found that justifies almost any opinion. Sometimes prominent researchers advocate diametrically different approaches to policy and practice, too often based on small slices of the evidence base. Research syntheses seek to address these problems by summarizing the evidence; however, in early childhood, the number of rigorous studies devoted to synthesizing the details of policy and practice remains too small to offer policy makers and practitioners detailed guidance from this approach. These conditions lead to deeper, difficult questions. What types of research can usefully inform policy and practice? How much of this research do we need? What other forms of evidence may be needed to inform policy and practice? How does the field acquire and use this evidence?

The research program Ramey described in Chapter 9 might be characterized as the classic approach to rigorous research to inform policy. It begins with a strongly framed question that is a test of a broad general theory, in this case about the modifiability of intelligence over the life course. It also tests a specific, well-defined program. In this classic approach, randomized trials are used to isolate the effects of a specific intervention and, ideally, other influences on the outcomes of interest are controlled or equalized across groups. Neither families nor teachers choose policies or practices because these are defined for study within the experiment. The next steps in this approach are to investigate how outcomes vary with modifications of the program, population, and the context. Considerable emphasis is placed on fidelity of implementation of the model during each study and in replication.

Another example of the classic approach to policy and practice informing research in early childhood is the set of studies conducted on the Nurse–Family Partnership (NFP) over several decades (Olds et al., 2014). The NFP intervention has specially trained nurses visit first-time expectant mothers prenatally through the second year of life. Positive outcomes for children include fewer injuries, less abuse and neglect, and improved child mental health and achievement (Olds et al., 2014). The NFP program of research has benefited from more extensive funding than comparable interventions in education, perhaps because it is viewed as health research. The variations in outcomes across NFP studies with person, process, and context (e.g., some outcomes are limited to unmarried mothers and others to mothers with low psychological resources, nurses are more effective than paraprofessionals, and differences by location; Olds, 2016) suggest that much more research on specific programs than is typical in early intervention is needed to usefully inform policy.

The example explored in depth by Hyson in Chapter 8—namely, practice-focused professional development—points to an even greater challenge: the likelihood that no amount of randomized trial research will provide a sufficiently strong basis for sustained successful implementation of evidence-based policy and practice. The essential reason that led me to this conclusion is the extent to which details matter, and the right details are too idiosyncratic to be identified by traditional research programs—what I previously referred to as the "classic" approach (Murnane & Nelson, 1984). As noted previously, not only does the effectiveness of specific practices vary by person and context at any given time, but the characteristics of the population served, service providers, and the proximal and distal physical, social, and economic environments change over time. In sum, there is not likely to be one right way to develop a highly effective early childhood workforce, nor is there one right way for all of them to teach young children—at least not at the level of specificity that they need for their day-to-day work. From this perspective, departures from fidelity are not failures of practice but necessary adaptations for success.

The view articulated here suggests that success in sustaining effective policy and practice requires the development of information systems for policy and practice that routinely collect and use data for continuous improvement based on trial and error (e.g., Manzi, 2012). From this perspective, evidence-based success at scale requires a profound shift from the classic model of research that is conducted apart from policy and practice— a model in which researchers develop recommendations that are then to be implemented by policy makers and practitioners—to one of research embedded in practice that generates information to directly and continuously inform policy makers and practitioners. This alternative vision of the research to practice process requires ongoing dialogue and partnership among research, policy, and practice. It also implies very high levels of knowledge, skills, and authority for practitioners.

The approach to research aiming to improve policy and practice as embedded in policy and practice rather than independent of policy and practice is aligned with the three *"core elements"* for successful knowledge implementation that Hyson's Chapter 8 sets out. These are teamwork, data gathering for continuous improvement, and building capacity for sustainability. However, from the embedded research as continuous improvement perspective the paradigm changes to one where data gathering and capacity building are not separate activities of researchers, policy makers, and practitioners but the product of the teamwork of these groups working together. With this teamwork the translation of research to practices does not require intermediaries to link the three groups. This approach to research informing policy and practice does require transcending the traditional boundaries of each partner in the team, for example with researchers becoming more engaged outside the academy and practitioners becoming more engaged in the study of their practice.

The difficulties of the suggested transformation in the relationship that links research to policy and practice are considerable. Each resides in institutions that resist change. Each would have to acknowledge much more uncertainty about the best paths forward than they do now, and this acknowledgement entails considerable risk. What would happen to public support for spending on early childhood programs if all the uncertainties were widely acknowledged, even by advocates? Is that the equivalent of unilateral disarmament in the political world? However, without testing this proposition, how can the field be sufficiently open to evidence-based change to make real progress in improving program effectiveness? The feasibility of the new approach to research suggested above depends on the answers to these questions.

HOW CAN RESEARCH IMPROVE PROGRAM EFFECTIVENESS?

The first part of this chapter identified inappropriate expectations, failures of both design and implementation, and gaps in knowledge and knowledge development as explanations for the disappointing results of many large-scale public programs. To what extent can we move forward by making better use of the knowledge we have while pursuing more? The sections that follow offer recommendations regarding the use of existing research and directions for future research with respect to program design and implementation, specifically focusing on structural quality, curriculum, and process quality.

Structural Quality

Research has failed to find much association between the structural features of early childhood programs that drive costs—duration, teacher qualifications, and class size or ratio—and program effectiveness (Hanushek, 2015). Some have concluded from this finding that what the field calls "structural quality" matters little. However, the small-scale programs in the United States that proved effective in the long term lasted 2 or more years, hired well-educated teachers (with bachelor's degrees or higher) and paid them well, and had higher ratios of teachers to children than is common in large-scale programs (Schweinhart, 2007). From this set of common program features of successful models, one might conclude that much of the research since the older studies has taken a wrong turn somewhere. One possible wrong turn is the assumption in most studies that these program characteristics and other program features (e.g., staff compensation, class size, duration) are independent. From case studies of large-scale public programs with evidence of effectiveness, Minervino (2014) concluded that structural program features were interdependent, and that effectiveness depended on a collection of essential elements that includes contextual elements such as political will, structural features, and supports for practice—none of which was sufficient on its own.

If Minervino (2014) is correct, quantitative research would be more successful if it sought to reverse-engineer program design by identifying the common features of programs that were highly effective. For example, the average estimated effects of a teacher having a 4-year degree, specialized training in early childhood, and experience is quite small (Early et al., 2007).

From this finding, some have concluded that teacher preparation does not matter. However, the only examples of programs that have produced large gains like those in the small-scale studies all had highly qualified teachers (Kelley & Camilli, 2007). This latter outcome has led others to conclude that the requirement of a 4-year degree is necessary, but not sufficient, for highly effective education of young children at scale and that the content of this degree matters greatly (National Research Council, 2015).

Some researchers and policy makers have concluded that in-service training of preschool educators is a more cost-effective approach to improving teacher quality than preservice preparation. However, the success of such an approach depends on the ability to fully reproduce the results of the small-scale experiments with the best results in large-scale public provision of training, which is essentially another version of the outlier problem. A meta-analysis found in-service training to have larger, positive effects on teacher skills than did credentials, but the results were noticeably weaker for multisite training in large-scale programs than in small-scale studies (Fukkink & Lont, 2007). Consistent with this outcome, a recent randomized trial of state-provided intensive professional development at scale focused on language and literacy failed to find significant impacts on teachers with or without substantial in-class coaching (Piasta et al., 2017). Another multisite professional development study had null findings with respect to child outcomes (Pianta et al., 2017).

If new experimental studies of the impacts of structural features of programs are to be useful, such studies will have to recognize that structural features are highly interdependent, including staff compensation, working conditions, preservice qualifications, experience, in-service professional development, and supervision. This conclusion suggests testing constellations of stronger features against weaker features over a substantial time period. To test the effects of sustained differences in program structure, researchers will have to confront the question of how randomized trials might be conducted with long-term commitments to the resources required to pay for more expensive sets of program features.

New approaches to nonexperimental research on structural features are also likely to be required. One approach is to stagger change in policy geographically or to otherwise vary the timing with which policy changes are implemented. Grant programs for quality improvement offer another opportunity to systematically vary program structure and evaluate the impacts. Cross-state comparisons might be particularly useful as a way of comparing very different structural constellations, but the results of such comparisons would be much more informative if there were comparable assessments that could serve as pre- and posttests. We might follow the example of other countries by implementing birth cohorts or other studies that collect nationally representative data on child development, which could provide the data required for such studies to be rigorous (e.g., Feinstein, 2003).

Curriculum

What should be taught in preschool and how should it be taught? Clearly, the answer to this question is only partly dependent on evidence because values play a dominant role in such decisions. For example, the National Association for the Education of Young Children (2009) has advanced a framework of developmentally appropriate practices (first published in the 1980s and updated regularly since then), which emphasizes the following: 1) there are known sequences in which children gain specific concepts, skills, and abilities; 2) familiarity with these sequences should inform teacher's practices; 3) good teaching is intentional and goal oriented; and 4) teachers must know where each child is relative to classroom learning goals to be intentional about helping individual children progress. This framework is informed by evidence, but it also reflects a particular set of values. Moreover, within this broad framework, there is still ample room for disagreement about content and the balance among activities (e.g., Pyle & Danniels, 2017).

Key disagreements about preschool curriculum arise from both differences in interpreting the research and differences in values. The specification of a preschool curriculum requires trade-offs. Intentional teaching, especially direct instruction, can be seen to promote more efficient learning at a cost. For example, intentional teaching "produces an inductive bias that constrains children's hypothesis space for better and for worse: in promoting rapid and efficient learning of target material, pedagogical instruction necessarily limits the range of hypotheses children consider" (Bonawitz et al., 2011, p. 323). From this perspective, disagreements about the balance of activities and approaches in a curriculum are disagreements about benefits and costs, which reflect differences of opinion and values regarding different child outcomes.

Recently, some scholars have advocated for domain-specific curricula that follow insights into children's developmental trajectories in each domain and offer a specific scope and sequence individualized to each child (e.g., "Goldilocks" activities that are not too hard but not too easy for a child's current skill level) over broad, whole-child curricula (Weiland, 2016). By contrast, whole-child curricula are viewed as encompassing all domains of children's learning; they offer activities that children tend to find engaging but leave the scope and sequencing up to individual teachers. Domain-specific curricula have outperformed whole-child curricula with respect to improving achievement test scores in rigorous trials (Phillips et al., 2017). However, a limitation is that few rigorous trials with global curriculum are included in these reviews. Furthermore, the outcome measures are short term and do not include many aspects of learning and development (e.g., creativity, empathy, habits, dispositions) that are valued by parents and practitioners.

Debates about curriculum take place in the context of a history of strong assertions for and against direct instruction. A strong case can be made that direct instruction is associated with greater achievement (Camilli, Vargas, Ryan, & Barnett, 2010). It can also be argued that direct instruction's gains are not worth the costs in other domains (Schweinhart & Weikart, 1997). Rigorous studies cast doubt on the strongest claims for and against direct instruction and indicate a need for more research to make more nuanced distinctions of differences among curricula and the balance of activities provided (Lillard et al., 2013). It is particularly troubling that preschool special education, which might be thought to make more use of direct instruction, has been found to be associated with worse outcomes for children in literacy and mathematics at kindergarten (Sullivan & Field, 2013). How should policy makers and practitioners use the evidence to guide their decisions?

Curriculum also has been an important topic in debates about how to best support gains from preschool in the primary grades. There is a long history of complaints that schools resist adopting the curricular approaches that were found to be effective in studies specifically designed to investigate how best to sustain gains for disadvantaged children after preschool (e.g., Binder & Watkins, 2013). Debates regarding primary school curriculum content and methods, the extent to which teaching should be scripted, and the need for coaching to guide teachers continue to be explored in research (e.g., Snow & Matthews, 2016).

Curriculum effects may be implicated in a possible interaction between preschool effects on the assignment of children—particularly disadvantaged children—to special education and child outcomes (O'Connor & Fernandez, 2006). Children without clearly identified specific disabilities have been found to have worse long-term educational outcomes when placed in special education, with most of the negative effects observed by age 9 years (Morgan, Frisco, Farber, & Hibel, 2010). Early childhood programs might secure part of their long-term gains by helping children avoid special education. Negative long-term outcomes found by a recent randomized trial of Tennessee's pre-K program occurred within the context of higher special education placement rates for children who had attended the preschool program (Lipsey et al., 2017).

Perhaps research provides its most useful guidance regarding curriculum at a higher level. One finding that seems to have stood the test of time is that "programs with specific objectives and strategies to achieve them" are more effective in achieving their specific objectives (Bissell, 1972, p. 68). Specificity with respect to objectives and strategies is found to increase effectiveness, not just for achievement but also for social and emotional development (Schindler et al., 2015). This outcome might be said to only make it painfully obvious that children are unlikely to learn what they are not taught, but it is useful guidance that could change practice.

Ultimately, the field is left with many unanswered questions about the short- and long-term impacts of alternative curricular approaches. If randomized trials comparing these alternatives are to provide better information, they will need to advance over past studies by accomplishing the following: 1) allowing more time for teachers to learn complex approaches well; 2) expanding outcome measures to include creativity, intrinsic motivation to learn, and a wide array of dispositions, habits, attitudes, and beliefs; and 3) ensuring that follow-up is long enough to identity persistent and not just short-term impacts (Graue, Hatch, Rao, & Oen, 2007). Moreover, gaining the knowledge needed and securing its widespread adoption in practice may require less research using the classic approach, but more research embedded in continuous improvement processes that learn through trial and error, including planned systematic variations within and across local programs.

PARENT INVOLVEMENT

Small-scale programs found to have large impacts often, but not always, had extensive emphasis on parent involvement (Bronfenbrenner, 1974; Weikart, 1967; Reynolds, 2000). This was also true of some approaches that were less effective (Bronfenbrenner, 1974). A common expectation was that parents who had developed the capacity and inclination to be more engaged with their children's learning and schools would play a major role in sustaining children's gains after they entered primary schools (e.g., Bronfenbrenner, 1974). Yet, systematic reviews of preschool program impacts have found little association between parent involvement activities and child outcomes (Camilli et al., 2010; Grindal et al., 2016). The mixed findings could be due to limitations of research or variations in implementation. Some suggest that preschool programs providing home visits produced larger effects on child development, but home visiting is a mode or location of service rather than a type of intervention (Grindal et al., 2016). For example, home visits in the Perry Preschool were devoted to child-focused communication with parents and one-to-one tutoring by the teacher, which suggests that the home visit impact was not entirely transmitted through parents (Weikart, 1967).

Process Quality

Preschool program impacts most directly depend on the experiences they provide to children and families. The structural features discussed previously can be regarded as resources available to generate those experiences. Such resources can be used more or less well, and the fields of educational administration and implementation science both can be considered to be devoted to understanding how resources are used to produce activities. Even curriculum is a tool that is employed with differential expertise from one program and classroom to another. A variety of measures have been developed to directly assess the quality of experiences that preschools provide to children (Tout et al., 2010). Most large-scale public programs do not score highly on these measures, and scores are particularly low on the scales most directly related to achievement (e.g., Keys et al., 2013).

Despite their greater proximity to child outcomes, process quality measures do not capture all that we would wish to know about quality, and they are only modestly related to children's learning and development (Burchinal, Kainz, & Cai, 2014; Keys et al., 2013). Some studies suggest thresholds for substantive gains at higher levels of quality (e.g., Burchinal, Vandergrift, Pianta, & Mashburn, 2010). Other studies found no relationships and raised questions about both technical and practical problems with process quality measures (Gordon, Fujimoto, Kaestner, Korenman, & Abner, 2013). Domain-specific measures of quantity have been found to have higher correlations with domain specific measures of child progress (Votruba-Drzal & Miller, 2016). Even these findings are complicated because the quality measures found to perform best vary with the research methodology used (Auger, Farkas, Burchinal, Duncan, & Vandell, 2014; for the primary grades, see Bacher-Hicks, Chin, Kane, & Staiger, 2017). Again, traditional research contributes to the understanding of policy and practice, but a tremendous amount of uncertainty remains that may require another approach, as discussed in the following section.

Research for Continuous Improvement

The field has made undeniable progress through experimental research. However, relative to the needs for information to guide policy and practice, the accumulated knowledge remains modest. Although greater investments in traditional research would be productive, a need exists for new approaches to informing continuous improvement that extends beyond the classroom walls. Although essential to success, what happens inside the classroom is not exclusively determined within its walls (Coburn, 2003). Broader policies and practices of the educational system (e.g., high rates of teacher instability due to turnover and shifting assignments, allocation of poorly performing teachers to untested grades) that are not specific to early childhood education can be important determinants of young children's experiences within the classroom (Boruch et al., in press). Leadership also is likely to be an important determinant of preschool classroom quality (Aubrey, Godfrey, & Harris, 2013). If research is to advance our understanding of how to produce stronger results at scale, it will have to move beyond the classroom to centers, schools, districts, and even states (Bronfenbrenner, 2009).

CONCLUSIONS REGARDING RESEARCH AT SCALE

From the brief review here and in Chapter 8, it is evident that we need new approaches to research that explicitly focus on learning how to scale up and sustain effective programs. Coburn (2003) recommended an approach that would lead to greater knowledge about four interrelated dimensions: 1) depth of implementation including adoption of pedagogical principles; 2) sustainability over many years; 3) spread of norms, beliefs, and principles; and 4) ownership by teachers and administrators throughout a system. In early childhood, Reynolds et al. (2017) have embarked on such an approach with a program of research in which multiple studies replicate the child–

parent centers in multiple sites, with particular attention to factors that may contribute to larger and lasting gains. They have laid out in detail how to conduct such a study and developed an array of tools for measuring implementation at scale. Their methods might usefully be applied to other models and at a truly large scale—citywide or statewide. Researchers might also employ those methods and tools to reverse-engineer high quality at scale, asking what it is that differentiates systems that produce consistently high levels of success for disadvantaged students at scale over many years (e.g., Kirp, 2015).

More generally, the field can develop its own implementation science, as some researchers at FPG and elsewhere have done to focus on systemic sustained change (Halle, Metz, & Martinez-Beck, 2013). In the past, the early childhood field has devoted most of its attention to the problem of implementation at the level of the individual classroom as influenced by individual teachers, curriculum, and professional development (Dunst, Trivette, & Raab, 2013). The problem of sustained improvement in quality at scale has been conceptualized as producing fidelity of implementation at the classroom level systemwide, with the hope for a key to sustaining that fidelity over the long term through the use of a Quality Rating and Improvement System (QRIS) (Connors & Morris, 2015). As suggested earlier, a focus on fidelity may not be the best way to conceptualize the problem. If adaptation and change are more important than fidelity, what policy makers and practitioners need to accomplish for continuous improvement is feedback more akin to that provided by a GPS than by a QRIS—real-time information on where they are and the direction they are heading with respect to who is actually served, the experiences they provide to children (and parents), and the learning and development of those children. This continuous flow of information is needed at multiple levels, from the classroom to the capitol.

Finally, policy makers, practitioners, and researchers should find new ways to collaborate in studying the implementation and impacts of systemic efforts to produce large and persistent gains at scale. A starting place for this could be new conversations regarding the questions and research agenda that policy makers and practitioners wish to have answered at both the macro level (e.g., political will, governance, finance, preparation of the workforce, data systems, and accountability) and micro level (e.g., the details of how best to teach specific children). In addition, the sheer amount of information required if, as seems likely, the answers vary significantly across and within populations and contexts requires a shift toward a reliance on highly knowledgeable and skilled practitioners to interpret data they and others collect, with the support of administrators and analysts embedded in the organizations that design and implement policy and practice. Such an approach is a supplement rather than a substitute for the traditional approach, but it is not supplement at the margin. Rather, this new approach needs to be the primary way in which policy and practice improve. This approach need not mean a decline in the use of systematic experiments, because these can be embedded within typical practice. Indeed, such an approach might do much to reduce the haphazard changes in policy and practice that have dominated the field. Implementation of these new research approaches to inform practice will require major changes in the ways in which everyone in early childhood thinks about their roles in generating and using data to improve policy and practice. As Bob Marley said, "None but ourselves can free our minds."

REFERENCES

Akerhielm, K. (1995). Does class size matter? *Economics of Education Review, 14*(3), 229–241.

Aubrey, C., Godfrey, R., & Harris, A. (2013). How do they manage? An investigation of early childhood leadership. *Educational Management Administration & Leadership, 41*(1), 5–29.

Auger, A., Farkas, G., Burchinal, M. R., Duncan, G. J., & Vandell, D. L. (2014). Preschool center care quality effects on academic achievement: An instrumental variables analysis. *Developmental Psychology, 50*(12), 25–59.

Bacher-Hicks, A., Chin, M. J., Kane, T. J., & Staiger, D. O. (2017). *An evaluation of bias in three measures of teacher quality: Value-added, classroom observations, and student surveys* (No. w23478). Cambridge, MA: National Bureau of Economic Research.

Barnett, W. S., Friedman-Krauss, A. H., Squires, J. H., Weisenfield, G. G., Horowitz, M., & Kasmin, R. (2017). *The state of preschool 2017: State preschool yearbook.* New Brunswick, NJ: National Institute for Early Education Research.

Bassok, D., Finch, J. E., Lee, R., Reardon, S. F., & Waldfogel, J. (2016). Socioeconomic gaps in early childhood experiences: 1998 to 2010. *AERA Open, 2*(3), 2332858416653924.

Bassok, D., & Galdo, E. (2016). Inequality in preschool quality? Community-level disparities in access to high-quality learning environments. *Early Education and Development, 27*(1), 128–144.

Binder, C., & Watkins, C. L. (2013). Precision teaching and direct instruction: Measurably superior instructional technology in schools. *Performance Improvement Quarterly, 26*(2), 73–115.

Bissell, J. S. (1972). *Planned variation in Head Start and Follow Through.* Washington, DC: Department of Health, Education, and Welfare.

Bloom, H. S., & Weiland, C. (2015). Quantifying variation in Head Start effects on young children's cognitive and socio-emotional skills using data from the National Head Start Impact Study. New York, NY: MDRC.

Boruch, R., Merlino, F. J., Bowdon, J., Baker, J., Chao, J., Park, J. E., et al. (in press). In search of terra firma: Administrative records on teachers' positional instability across subjects, grades, and schools and the implications for deploying randomized controlled trials. *Journal of Research on Educational Effectiveness.*

Bonawitz, E., Shafto, P., Gweon, H., Goodman, N. D., Spelke, E., & Schulz, L. (2011). The double-edged sword of pedagogy: Instruction limits spontaneous exploration and discovery. *Cognition, 120*(3), 322–330.

Bronfenbrenner, U. (1974). Is early intervention effective? *Day Care and Early Education, 2*(2), 14–18.

Bronfenbrenner, U. (2009). *The ecology of human development.* Cambridge, MA: Harvard University Press.

Burchinal, M. R., Kainz, K., & Cai, Y. (2014). How well do our measures of quality predict child outcomes? A meta-analysis and coordinated analysis of data from large-scale studies of early childhood settings. In M. Zaslow (Ed.), *Reasons to take stock and strengthen our measures of quality* (pp. 11–31). Baltimore, MD: Paul H. Brookes Publishing Co.

Burchinal, M., Vandergrift, N., Pianta, R., & Mashburn, A. (2010). Threshold analysis of association between child care quality and child outcomes for low-income children in pre-kindergarten programs. *Early Childhood Research Quarterly, 25*(2), 166–176.

Camilli, G., Vargas, S., Ryan, S., & Barnett, W. S. (2010). Meta-analysis of the effects of early education interventions on cognitive and social development. *Teachers College Record, 112*(3), 579–620.

Caronongan, P., Moiduddin, E., West, J., & Vogel, C. A. (2014). *Children in Early Head Start and Head Start: A profile of early leavers. Baby FACES and FACES 2009 Research Brief* (OPRE Report 2014-54). Washington, DC. Office of Planning, Research, and Evaluation, Administration for Children and Families, U.S. Department of Health and Human Services.

Child Trends Databank. (2016). *Racial and ethnic composition of the child population.* Retrieved from https://www.childtrends.org/?indicators=racial-and-ethnic-composition-of-the-child-population

Coburn, C. E. (2003). Rethinking scale: Moving beyond numbers to deep and lasting change. *Educational Researcher, 32*(6), 3–12.

Connors, M. C., & Morris, P. A. (2015). Comparing state policy approaches to early care and education quality: A multidimensional assessment of quality rating and improvement systems and child care licensing regulations. *Early Childhood Research Quarterly, 30,* 266–279.

Drummond, C. (2009). *Replicability is not reproducibility: Nor is it good science.* Presented at the Twenty-Sixth International Conference on Machine Learning: Workshop on Evaluation Methods for Machine Learning IV, Montreal, Quebec, Canada. Retrieved from http://ww.csi.uottawa.ca/~cdrummon/pubs/ICMLws09.pdf

Duncan, G. J., & Magnuson, K. (2013). Investing in preschool programs. *The Journal of Economic Perspectives, 27*(2), 109–132.

Dunst, C. J., Trivette, C. M., & Raab, M. (2013). An implementation science framework for conceptualizing and operationalizing fidelity in early childhood intervention studies. *Journal of Early Intervention, 35*(2), 85–101.

Early, D. M., Maxwell, K. L., Burchinal, M., Alva, S., Bender, R. H., Bryant, D., et al. (2007). Teachers' education, classroom quality, and young children's academic skills: Results from seven studies of preschool programs. *Child Development, 78*(2), 558–580.

Fahle, E. M., & Reardon, S. F. (2017). *How much do test scores vary among school districts? New estimates using population data, 2009–2015* (CEPA Working Paper No. 17-02). Palo Alto, CA: Stanford Center for Education Policy Analysis, Stanford University.

Feinstein, L. (2003). Inequality in the early cognitive development of British children in the 1970 cohort. *Economica, 70*(277), 73–97.

Feller, A., Grindal, T., Miratrix, L., & Page, L. C. (2016). Compared to what? Variation in the impacts of early childhood education by alternative care type. *The Annals of Applied Statistics, 10*(3), 1245–1285.

Fukkink, R. G., & Lont, A. (2007). Does training matter? A meta-analysis and review of caregiver training studies. *Early Childhood Research Quarterly, 22*(3), 294–311.

Gordon, R. A., Fujimoto, K., Kaestner, R., Korenman, S., & Abner, K. (2013). An assessment of the validity of the ECERS-R with implications for measures of child care quality and relations to child development. *Developmental Psychology, 49*(1), 146.

Graue, E., Hatch, K., Rao, K., & Oen, D. (2007). The wisdom of class-size reduction. *American Educational Research Journal, 44*(3), 670–700.

Grindal, T., Bowne, J. B., Yoshikawa, H., Schindler, H. S., Duncan, G. J., Magnuson, K., et al., (2016). The added impact of parenting education in early childhood education programs: A meta-analysis. *Children and Youth Services Review, 70,* 238–249.

Grissom, J. A., Kalogrides, D., & Loeb, S. (2017). Strategic staffing? How performance pressures affect the distribution of teachers within schools and resulting student achievement. *American Educational Research Journal, 54*(6), 1079–1116.

Halle, T., Metz, A., & Martinez-Beck, I. (Eds.). (2013). *Applying implementation science in early childhood programs and systems.* Baltimore, MD: Paul H. Brookes Publishing Co.

Hanushek, E. A. (2015). The preschool debate: Translating research into policy. In I. G. Ellen, E. L. Glaeser, E. A. Hanushek, M. E. Kahn, & A. M. Renn (Eds.), *The next urban renaissance: How public-policy innovation and evaluation can improve life in America's cities* (pp. 25–40). New York, NY: Manhattan Institute for Policy Research.

Haskins, R., & Brooks-Gunn, J. (2016). Trouble in the land of early childhood education. *Future of Children: Policy Brief.* Retrieved from http://www. e3va. org/wp-content/uploads/2016/11/FOC-POLICY-BRIEF-Fall-2016-V2.pdf

Herbst, C. M., & Tekin, E. (2016). The impact of child-care subsidies on child development: Evidence from geographic variation in the distance to social service agencies. *Journal of Policy Analysis and Management, 35*(1), 94–116.

Hipple, S. (2016). Labor force participation: What has happened since the peak? *Monthly Labor Review*. Washington, DC: U.S. Bureau of Labor Statistics.

Huizen, T., Dumhs, L., & Plantenga, J. (2017). The costs and benefits of investing in universal preschool: Evidence from a Spanish reform. *Child Development*. Advance online publication.

Ioannidis, J. P. A. (2005). Why most published research findings are false. *PLOS Medicine* 2(8), e124.

Jenkins, J., Watts, T. W., Magnuson, K., Clements, D., Sarama, J., Wolfe, C., et al. (2015). *Preventing preschool fadeout through instructional intervention in kindergarten and first grade*. Retrieved from http://inid.gse.uci.edu/ files/2011/03/Jenkinsetal_Fadeout_SREE.pdf

Kelley, P., & Camilli. G. (2007). *The impact of teacher education on outcomes in center-based early childhood education programs: A meta-analysis*. New Brunswick, NJ: National Institute for Early Education Research.

Keys, T. D., Farkas, G., Burchinal, M. R., Duncan, G. J., Vandell, D. L., Li, W., et al. (2013). Preschool center quality and school readiness: Quality effects and variation by demographic and child characteristics. *Child Development, 84*(4), 1171–1190.

Kirp, D. L. (2015). *Improbable scholars: The rebirth of a great American school system and a strategy for America's schools*. Oxford, UK: Oxford University Press.

Lillard, A. S., Lerner, M. D., Hopkins, E. J., Dore, R. A., Smith, E. D., & Palmquist, C. M. (2013). The impact of pretend play on children's development: A review of the evidence. *Psychological Bulletin, 139*(1), 1–34.

Lipsey, M. W., Farran, D. C., & Hofer, K. G. (2017). *State test scores and retention data for the TNVPK full randomized sample in 3rd grade*. Retrieved from https://www.sree.org/ conferences/2017s/program/download/abstract/2057_intro.pdf

Magnuson, K., & Waldfogel, J. (2016). Trends in income-related gaps in enrollment in early childhood education: 1968 to 2013. *AERA Open, 2*(2), 2332858416648933.

Makel, M. C., & Plucker, J. A. (2014). Facts are more important than novelty: Replication in the education sciences. *Educational Researcher, 43*(6), 304–316.

Manzi, J. (2012). *Uncontrolled: The surprising payoff of trial-and-error for business, politics, and society*. New York, NY: Basic Books.

Minervino, J. (2014). *Lessons from research and the classroom: Implementing high-quality pre-K that makes a difference for young children*. Seattle, WA: Bill & Melinda Gates Foundation.

Morgan, P. L., Frisco, M. L., Farkas, G., & Hibel, J. (2010). A propensity score matching analysis of the effects of special education services. *The Journal of Special Education, 43*(4), 236–254.

Murnane, R. J., & Nelson, R. R. (1984). Production and innovation when techniques are tacit: The case of education. *Journal of Economic Behavior & Organization, 5*(3–4), 353–373.

National Research Council. (2015). *Transforming the workforce for children birth through age 8: A unifying foundation*. Washington, DC: National Academies Press.

O'Connor, C., & Fernandez, S. D. (2006). Race, class, and disproportionality: Reevaluating the relationship between poverty and special education placement. *Educational Researcher, 35*(6), 6–11.

Olds, D. (2016). Building evidence to improve maternal and child health. *The Lancet, 387*(10014), 105–107.

Olds, D. L., Holmberg, J. R., Donelan-McCall, N., Luckey, D. W., Knudtson, M. D., & Robinson, J. (2014). Effects of home visits by paraprofessionals and by nurses on children: Follow-up of a randomized trial at ages 6 and 9 years. *JAMA Pediatrics, 168*(2), 114–121.

Pashler, H., & Wagenmakers, E. (2012). Editors' introduction to the special section on replicability in psychological science a crisis of confidence. *Perspectives on Psychological Science, 7*(6), 528–530.

Phillips, D. A., Lipsey, M. W., Dodge, K. A., Haskins, R., Bassok, D., Burchinal, M. R., et al. (2017). *Puzzling it out: The current state of scientific knowledge on pre-kindergarten effects, a consensus statement*. Washington, DC: Brookings Institution.

Pianta, R., Hamre, B., Downer, J., Burchinal, M., Williford, A., LoCasale-Crouch, J., et al. (2017). Early childhood professional development: Coaching and coursework effects on indicators of children's school readiness. *Early Education and Development, 19*, 1–20.

Piasta, S. B., Justice, L. M., O'Connell, A. A., Mauck, S. A., Weber-Mayrer, M., Schachter, R. E., et al. (2017). Effectiveness of large-scale, state-sponsored language and literacy professional development on early childhood educator outcomes. *Journal of Research on Educational Effectiveness, 10*(2), 354–378.

Puma, M., Bell, S., Cook, R., Heid, C., Broene, P., Jenkins, F., et al. (2012). *Third grade follow-up to the Head Start Impact Study final report* (OPRE Report # 2012-45). Washington, DC: Administration for Children and Families, U.S. Department of Health and Human Services.

Pyle, A., & Danniels, E. (2017). A continuum of play-based learning: The role of the teacher in play-based pedagogy and the fear of hijacking play. *Early Education and Development, 28*(3), 274–289.

Ramey, C. T. (1979). *The Abecedarian Approach to social competence: Cognitive and linguistic intervention for disadvantaged preschoolers.* Chapel Hill, NC: Frank Porter Graham Child Development Center, University of North Carolina.

Ramey, C. T., Bryant, D. M., Wasik, B. H., Sparling, J. J., Fendt, K. H., & La Vange, L. M. (1992). Infant Health and Development Program for low birth weight, premature infants: Program elements, family participation, and child intelligence. *Pediatrics, 89*(3), 454–465.

Ramey, C. T., Collier, A., Sparling, J. J., Loda, F.A., Campbell, F.A., Ingram, D.L., et al. (1974). *The Carolina Abecedarian Project: A longitudinal and multidisciplinary approach to the prevention of developmental retardation.* Bethesda, MD: National Institute of Child Health and Human Development.

Ramey, C. T., Sparling, J. J., & Ramey, S. L. (2012). *Abecedarian: The ideas, the approach, and the findings.* Los Altos, CA: Sociometrics Corporation.

Ramon, I., Chattopadhyay, S. K., Hahn, R., Barnett, W. S., & the Community Preventive Services Task Force. (2017). *Early childhood education to promote health equity: A community guide economic review.* Atlanta, GA: Centers for Disease Control and Prevention, Community Guide Branch.

Reynolds, A. J. (2000). *Success in early intervention: The Chicago Child-Parent Centers.* Lincoln, NE: University of Nebraska Press.

Reynolds, A. J., Hayakawa, M., Ou, S. R., Mondi, C. F., Englund, M. M., Candee, A. J., et al. (2017). Scaling and sustaining effective early childhood programs through school–family–university collaboration. *Child Development, 88*(5), 1453–1465.

Reynolds, A. J., Ou, S. R., Mondi, C. F., & Hayakawa, M. (2017). Processes of early childhood interventions to adult well-being. *Child Development, 88*(2), 378–387.

Schindler, H. S., Kholoptseva, J., Oh, S. S., Yoshikawa, H., Duncan, G. J., Magnuson, K. A., et al. (2015). Maximizing the potential of early childhood education to prevent externalizing behavior problems: A meta-analysis. *Journal of School Psychology, 53*(3), 243–263.

Schweinhart, L. J. (2007, December). *How to take the High/Scope Perry Preschool to scale.* Presented at the National Invitational Conference of the Early Childhood Research Collaborative. Minneapolis, MN: University of Minnesota.

Schweinhart, L. J., & Weikart, D. P. (1997). The High/Scope preschool curriculum comparison study through age 23. *Early Childhood Research Quarterly, 12*(2), 117–143.

Snow, C. E., & Matthews, T. J. (2016). Reading and language in the early grades. *The Future of Children, 26*(2), 57–74.

Sullivan, A. L., & Field, S. (2013). Do preschool special education services make a difference in kindergarten reading and mathematics skills? A propensity score weighting analysis. *Journal of School Psychology, 51*(2), 243–260.

Swain, W. A., Springer, M. G., & Hofer, K. G. (2015). Early grade teacher effectiveness and pre-K effect persistence. *AERA Open, 1*(4), article 2332858415612751.

Tout, K., Starr, R., Soli, M., Moodie, S., Kirby, G., & Boller, K. (2010). *Compendium of quality rating systems and evaluations: The child care quality rating system (QRS) assessment.* Washington, DC: Administration for Children & Families.

Vogel, C. A., Xue, Y., Moiduddin, E. M., Kisker, E. E., & Carlson, B. L. (2010). *Early Head Start children in grade 5: Long-term follow-up of the Early Head Start Research and Evaluation Study sample.* Washington, DC: Administration for Children and Families, U.S. Department of Health and Human Services.

Votruba-Drzal, E., & Miller, P. (2016). Reflections on quality and dosage of preschool and children's development. *Monographs of the Society for Research in Child Development, 81*(2), 100–113.

Weikart, D. P. (1967). *Preschool intervention: A preliminary report of the Perry Preschool Project.* Ann Arbor, MI: Campus Publishers.

Weiland, C. (2016). Launching Preschool 2.0: A road map to high quality public programs at scale. *Behavioral Science & Policy, 2*(1), 37–46.

Weiland, C., & Yoshikawa, H. (2013). Impacts of a prekindergarten program on children's mathematics, language, literacy, executive function, and emotional skills. *Child Development, 84*(6), 2112–2130.

Yoshikawa, H., Weiland, C., Brooks-Gunn, J., Burchinal, M., Espinosa, L. M., Gormley Jr., W. T., et al. (2013). *Investing in our future: The evidence base on preschool education*. Ann Arbor, MI: Society for Research in Child Development.

IV

Theme C: Children With Disabilities and Their Families

To this point, sections and chapters have focused on factors that may create developmental vulnerabilities for some children, the developmental and educational disparities that exist for this population of children, and early childhood education programs that may reduce such disparities. The authors also have spoken about the strengths of children who demographically fall into life circumstances that create such vulnerabilities. In the current section, the authors turn their attention to children and youth who have identified disabilities, such as intellectual disabilities, autism spectrum disorder, fragile X syndrome, and developmental delays. Programs addressing the characteristics and needs of this group of children with disabilities and their families have long been a focus for FPG, beginning as far back as the Carolina Institute for Early Education for the Handicapped that Jim Gallagher led in the late 1970s and 1980s and the Technical Assistance Development Systems that Pat Trohanis led during the same time period. These projects and others at FPG were part of a national movement to establish programs and practices that practitioners could use in their work with children and youth with identified disabilities and their families, as well as to provide the technical assistance nationally to support improvement in early intervention and early childhood special education services that could led to positive life outcomes.

In Chapter 11, Judith Carta and Patricia Snyder profile this history of research and lessons learned along the way. They characterize the research happening in three phases. In phase 1, researchers concentrated on learning how to change behavior of children—that is, specific interventions and practices that led to improvements in children's learning and development. Demonstrations that children with disabilities could make significant progress led to phase 2 research, which focused on using research about interventions and practices to build programs that practitioners could then use in their work with children having disabilities. Carta and Snyder describe 11 valuable lessons learned from these last 50 years of research. They then turn their addition to the future, proposing the next phase of research that addresses research opportunities and challenges that lie ahead, with recommendations about the lines of research that needed to be continued and strengthened in the future.

In Chapter 12, Pamela J. Winton focuses on professional development in early intervention/early childhood special education (EI/ECSE) and its implications for early childhood education. She begins by describing the strengths of the EI/ECSE workforce, attributing these strengths to a strong federal policy that supported professional development, the development of research-based practice guidelines, family partnerships, interdisciplinary collaborations, and inclusion. Although many strengths exist, Winton also notes significant challenges for future professional development efforts. These include ongoing fragmentation between IDEA Part C (early intervention) and Part B (preschool) programs, the lack of a parallel history and system of professional development in early childhood education, a lack of agreed-upon "best" approaches to professional development, and the relatively small amount of effort that currently goes into research on professional development practices. She concludes with a number of promising directions for the future.

Social policy is the foundation for research and professional development related to disabilities. In Chapter 13, Rud Turnbull reviews the evolution of legislation and litigation that has guided policy formation and implementation for individuals with disabilities over the last 50-plus years. He begins the chapter with a personal acknowledgement of contributions by FPG leaders and their impacts on policy. From a comprehensive review of legislation and litigation, he identifies a number of core concepts related to policy as well as key themes reflected in those concepts. He then uses those core concepts to identify constitutional, administrative, and ethical principles. Among the ethical principles, he highlights the importance of dignity as the central focus for programs and the outcomes they seek to achieve for children and youth with disabilities.

In Chapter 14, Sam Odom discusses the common themes that emerged across chapters, as well as potential direction for future research. In the areas of research, professional development, and social policy, the authors consistently saw the federal government's roles in education as one essential influence. The authors also emphasized individualization, collaboration across disciplines, inclusion, and family involvement as key features of EI/ESCE. In looking forward, Odom drew from the professional literature and proposed current research themes that may emerge in the future. These included results from biomedical research (i.e., neuroscience, genetics) that may eventually provide valuable information that could affect program practices. Rapid advances in technology and the expanding research base aided by the evolution of the field of information science may well have a major impact. The changing demographics in the United States as well as the changing structure of families will undoubtedly affect the EI/ECSE practices in the future. Last, the field of implementation science has already emerged as a significant influence on many human services programs and is quite likely to influence the quality and provision of services in the future.

11

Fifty Years of Research on Children With Disabilities and Their Families

From Changing Behaviors to Transforming Lives

Judith Carta and Patricia Snyder

The outlook for young children with disabilities and their families has undergone a monumental shift over the last 50 years. Federal and state policies have shaped the development of services, model practices, the field of early childhood special education, and its professional organization, the Division for Early Childhood. This chapter describes how programs and services for young children with disabilities have evolved from changing behaviors to transforming lives. We will outline select historical events and policies that were foundational for the field and provided the impetus for contemporary services, programs, and practices (Hebbeler, Smith, & Black, 1991; McLean, Sandall, & Smith, 2016). The primary focus of the chapter is to describe and illustrate how research has been the intellectual engine that has driven progress in enhancing outcomes for young children with disabilities and their families. We outline two major phases of research across the last 50 years and describe the types of questions that researchers sought to answer in each phase. In addition, we provide a snapshot of some of the key lessons learned in each phase, as well as describe the ways in which research improved service delivery and helped to inform policy for children with disabilities. We end with thoughts about the opportunities and challenges that lie ahead.

PUTTING 50 YEARS OF RESEARCH INTO PERSPECTIVE

What can 50 years of research accomplish? As we gathered together in Chapel Hill, North Carolina, to celebrate the golden anniversary of the Frank Porter Graham Child Development Institute (FPG) and its many contributions to improving the quality of life for individuals with disabilities and their families, it was informative to reflect on how a half century of research in other areas has changed our lives. In Kitty Hawk, another part of the great state of North Carolina, on December 17, 1903, the Wright brothers launched the age of aviation with the first successful human-crewed flight. With 50 years of research and development, aviation advanced at warp speed. More than 50 million people were being transported yearly on the world's passenger airlines, and fleets of jet fighters were routinely being used in the Korean War. In medicine, in 1955—the year Jonas Salk developed a vaccine to prevent polio—approximately 29,000 individuals were afflicted with polio. Fifty years later, with widespread use of Salk's vaccine, the number of polio cases worldwide dropped by 96%, or to about 1,200 cases per year. In technology, the first general purpose computer, the 30-ton Electronic Numerical Integrator and Computer (ENIAC), was developed in 1947. Heralded by the press as the "Giant Brain" (Goncalves, 2016), it could perform calculations 1,000 times faster than existing electromechanical machines. Fifty years later, in 1997, IBM designed the supercomputer, which could carry out about 1.3 trillion calculations per second (*Computer History Museum,* 2018).

What is life like 50 years later for children and youth with developmental disabilities? Many children are attending neighborhood schools, accessing the general curriculum, and achieving academic success. For example, between 1998 and 2017, National Assessment of Educational Progress (U.S. Department of Education, 2018) data indicate that basic reading proficiency has increased among students with disabilities from 25% to 32%. Great strides have been made in early intervention and early childhood special education. Data reported from the Individuals with Disabilities Education Improvement Act (IDEA; PL 108-446) reveal that between 1997 and 2017, twice as many children between the age of birth and 2 years received Part C early intervention services (Lazara, Danaher, & Detweiler, 2018). In this same time period, 23% more preschool-aged children were able to receive

Therefore, 50 years of research in engineering, medicine, and technology have created massive changes in our society and in how we function on a daily basis. Just as these changes have taken place in a half century, giant leaps have taken place in research to enhance the quality of lives of persons with developmental disabilities and their families. It is instructive to go back about 50 years and reflect on what life was like in 1967 for persons with disabilities, including young children with disabilities. In the United States at the end of June 1967, state institutions were home to 194,650 persons with significant disabilities, which was the highest total in history (Scott, Larkin, & Larson, 2008). The focus in these institutions was on providing individuals with basic needs (food, clothing, and shelter). In many states, laws specifically excluded children with disabilities, particularly those who had not attained a mental age of 5 years, from attending public schools (Yell, Rogers, & Rogers, 1998).

Part B early childhood special education services. For older students with disabilities, vast improvements have been made in educational services for high school and postsecondary students. Between 1998 and 2017, graduation rates increased by 16%. Furthermore, between 2000 and 2010, enrollment in postsecondary programs increased from 15% to 32% for individuals with disabilities (U.S. Department of Education, 2010).

Increasingly, adults with developmental disabilities are living within their communities. Since the landmark legislation in the 1960s (see Chapter 13), most individuals with intellectual disabilities no longer live in state institutions or nursing homes but instead live in small residential settings in the community, supported living apartments, or individually in homes. In fact, the number of people with intellectual disabilities living in homes either rented or owned by themselves doubled between 1998 and 2011 (Larson, Lakin, & Hill, 2013). Moreover, when living in community-based settings, these individuals are generally found to fare much better than those in large institutions and show improvements in areas of adaptive skills such as communication, social skills, self-care, community living skills, and academic skills (Lifshitz, Merrick, & Morad, 2008).

HISTORICAL POLICY EVENTS THAT OPENED THE DOOR TO CHANGE

The world for persons with disabilities took dramatic turns in the last 50 years. Changes of that magnitude occur only when major shifts in policy occur at the national level. In the United States, as the civil rights movement took shape, disability advocates joined forces with other minority groups to demand equal access, equal treatment, and equal opportunity for persons with disabilities. A number of laws were enacted that provided new educational, vocational, and living opportunities for members of the disability community (see Chapter 13). An important law that opened the door to early intervention for children birth to age 5 years with disabilities was the Handicapped Children's Early Education Assistance Act of 1968 (PL 90-538). This program initiated the first funding for experimental programs for young children with disabilities and sparked the first research demonstrating exemplary practices for young children with disabilities and their families. The establishment of a network called "First Chance" enabled the creation of program models, supported their replication across the country, and launched the field of early childhood special education. For more than 30 years, programs funded as part of the Handicapped Children's Early Education Program (HCEEP), which later became the Early Education Program for Children with Disabilities, have supported demonstration, outreach, and research projects, as well as state implementation grants, in-service training projects, research institutes, and technical assistance to support practices for young children with or at risk for disabilities from birth through age 8 years and their families (Snyder, Bishop, & McLaughlin, 2017).

Other important laws that opened the door to services and supports for young children with disabilities and their families include the following:

- The Economic Opportunity Amendments of 1972 (PL 92-424) mandated that at least 10% of the children enrolled in Head Start programs be children with disabilities.

- The Education for All Handicapped Children Act (PL 94-142) mandated a free and appropriate education in the least restrictive environment for all children with disabilities between the ages of 6 and 21 years. Preschool incentive grants encouraged states to begin serving children with disabilities from 3 through 5 years of age.

- The Education of the Handicapped Act Amendments of 1986 (PL 99-457) required states and schools receiving federal dollars to provide services to young children with disabilities in a preschool setting. It specifically set aside funding to expand services from the Education for All Handicapped Children Act of 1975 to children ages 3 through 5 years who needed special education (20 U.S.C. Secs. 1400). It established the early intervention program for infants and toddlers (Part H, now Part C) in recognition of the need to promote the development of the youngest children to minimize the effects of disability and reduce the potential for developmental delays in this group of children.

Taken together, these policies have provided the foundation for services and supports provided to young children with or at risk for disabilities, their families, and the personnel who support them. In addition, many of these policies have been repeatedly amended over the past 50 years and reflect findings from research focused on the effectiveness of early intervention for positively influencing children's developmental and learning trajectories, for enhancing family capacity and competence to support the development and learning of their young children, and for preventing the development of secondary disabilities.

RESEARCH AS A DRIVER OF CHANGE

Complementing the policy changes driving initiatives that influenced the lives of children with developmental disabilities and their families were changes in the directions of research and development that were shaping the field of early intervention and early childhood special education. Research in the field can be defined in three major phases. The first phase, in which opportunities and access to public education were first being developed and expanded, was expressed by these types of questions: 1) can interventions be designed to systematically change children's behavior and 2) can interventions result in long-term meaningful outcomes for children with developmental disabilities?

The primary focus in this first phase of research was answering questions about the efficacy of early intervention, often referred to as first-generation research (Guralnick, 1993). Research in this phase was success-ful in answering important policy and scientific questions about the over-all effectiveness of early intervention, despite the fact that intervention approaches and samples of the studies were quite dissimilar (Guralnick & Bennett, 1987). The body of research conducted during this phase con-cluded that the programs serving young children with disabilities gener-ally produced positive effects (Casto & Mastropieri, 1986). This first phase of research paved the way for the passage of the Education of the Handicapped Act Amendments of 1986, which included mandatory preschool programs for young children with disabilities and an early intervention program for infants and toddlers with disabilities.

The focus for the second phase of research in the field has been on devel-oping, validating, and evaluating interventions or practices. In this phase, an important emphasis has been expanding the evidence by examining spe-cific interventions or practices; focusing on what works best for whom; and examining the child characteristics, family characteristics, and program features that moderate or influence children's outcomes (Guralnick, 1993). This phase of research has addressed "second-generation" research ques-tions. The third phase of research and the challenge that lies ahead is in learning about effective ways to scale up evidence-based interventions or practices associated with improved outcomes for children with disabilities and their families, as well as identifying promising approaches for support-ing practitioners and families in their implementation of the effective inter-ventions or practices (Snyder et al., 2018).

In the following sections, we highlight examples of research conducted during each of these three phases to illustrate how 50 years of research has helped the field move from learning how to change behavior to transform-ing lives.

Phase 1: Learning How to Change Behavior

In the 1960s and early 1970s, as access to services and supports increased with the passage of federal legislation, the field was challenged to demon-strate that children's behavior could be systematically changed. During this era, many researchers were using principles from applied behavior analysis to demonstrate they could teach individuals with disabilities specific behav-iors (Jacobson & Holburn, 2004). This pioneering work challenged existing myths regarding the educability of individuals with intellectual disabilities, including young children with disabilities. Researchers demonstrated that principles from behavior analysis could be applied to teach adaptive skills such as feeding, toileting, dressing, and language skills, and to reduce or eliminate problem behaviors. For example, many early studies showed that teachers or parents could reduce children's negative behaviors (e.g., isolate behavior, excessive scratching) by withholding their attention from children when they engaged in those behaviors (Allen & Harris, 1966). Similarly, they could increase certain behaviors, such as children's social interactions, when they attended to children when they engaged in sustained play with peers (Hart, Reynolds, Baer, Brawley, & Harris, 1968).

Increasing evidence demonstrated the effectiveness of applied behavior analysis and associated behavioral techniques for helping individuals with disabilities learn new skills or eliminate challenging behaviors (see Lerman, LeBlanc, & Valentino, 2015). Informed by mounting evidence from phase 1 research, these behavioral approaches were incorporated into many programs and practices within the program, shifting the focus from custodial to habilitation. In addition, during this phase, researchers began to examine features of the environment that influenced behavior and learning (e.g., Rogers-Warren & Warren, 1977) and to describe the importance of context for understanding behavior in terms of both broad ecological factors (e.g., Bronfenbrenner, 1979) and variables more proximal to the child's and family's immediate social and physical environments (e.g., Hart & Risley, 1974).

Phase 2: Developing and Replicating
Effective Programs for Young Children With Disabilities

The phase 1 research showed children with disabilities could learn, which was one of the factors that led to federal investment in the development of model programs for preschoolers with special needs under the HCEEP program. Because there were so few services for young children with disabilities in the United States in 1968, demonstrations of effective models were needed to showcase how interventions for young children with disabilities could be delivered and promote successful outcomes. Besides establishing model programs, the goals of this program were to stimulate research on new interventions or practices, explore the possibilities of early education models for young children with disabilities, and disseminate successful models (Kennedy & McDaniels, 1982).

Throughout its history, more than 800 model programs and replications were funded across the United States. These programs resulted in a large body of knowledge showing that carefully designed programs could result in important outcomes for young children with disabilities and their families. For example, infants and toddlers with Down syndrome could be taught basic skills (Hayden & Haring, 1976) and show growth on these skills that approximated typical development (Hanson & Schwarz, 1978). The Portage Home Visiting Program demonstrated that parents could be taught to teach their children through a systematic sequence of skills (Shearer & Shearer, 1972). Several projects revealed that children with disabilities could be taught in "mainstream" or "integrated" classrooms alongside typically developing peers (Allen, Benning, & Drummond, 1972), and both they and their peers would make developmental progress (Bricker & Bricker, 1976). The success of these model demonstration programs has been documented through their positive impact on children's outcomes (see Stock et al., 1976), as well as their ability to sustain themselves when federal funding ended

(Hebbeler et al., 1991). An evaluation of the projects in 1982 indicated that 80% of them were able to obtain funding to continue operating at the end of their HCEEP funding. For example, in 2018, the Regional Intervention Project (Strain & Timm, 2001) established in 1969 at George Peabody College (now Vanderbilt University) and the Learning Experiences-Alternative Program (LEAP) program (Strain & Cordisco, 1993) established in 1981, both with HCEEP funding, have expanded and been replicated across many sites nationally and internationally.

Another program that substantially contributed to the expansion of state-of-the-art knowledge of programs and practices for teaching young children with special needs and supporting their families were the Outreach Projects funded by the Bureau of Education for the Handicapped in 1972. Outreach projects provided support for the dissemination of effective HCEEP demonstration projects to service providers and state planners across the United States (Garland, Black, & Jesien, 1986). An evaluation of the Outreach Projects (Littlejohn Associates, 1982) reported that the HCEEP Outreach program was responsible for expanding the reach of effective early intervention models to over 100,000 children after 10 years of implementation. Moreover, despite the fact these projects were not funded to do research, they were able to generate efficacy data that were educationally and statistically significant (White, Mastropieri, & Casto, 1984). Through the Outreach Projects, programs for children from birth to age 5 years were able to expand to every state in the United States and 25 foreign countries, as well as generate curricula and train personnel in the developing field of early childhood special education (Casto, 1985). Besides expanding services to children and families, the HCEEP Outreach Program provided early lessons on how to replicate and sustain successful models that predated the emergence of the field of implementation science (Metz & Bartley, 2012).

One additional federal investment during this period related to early investment was the First Chance Network (DeWeerd & Cole, 1976). The First Chance Network established an early community of practice among HCEEP model demonstration and outreach projects and provided a vehicle for interaction among individuals and programs focused on early intervention and early childhood special education. The national First Chance Network, as well as local offshoots, became a force for shaping state and federal policy related to the early education and intervention for children with disabilities and also helped spark the development of the Division for Early Childhood (DEC) of the Council for Exceptional Children (Garland et al., 1986). As a repository for the growing body of knowledge generated from the HCEEP projects and from research being conducted in the field, the official journal of the Division for Early Childhood, the *Journal of the Division for Early Childhood* (now known as the *Journal of Early Intervention*) was founded in 1979 and published under the editorship of Merle B. Karnes.

During the same time that the model demonstration and outreach projects were generating new knowledge about how to organize service delivery for young children with disabilities, the Bureau of Education for the Handicapped also funded research institutes under the auspices of HCEEP (McLean et al., 2016). Starting in 1977 and continuing until 1998, a total of 14 research institutes were funded to generate new knowledge and practices related to young children with disabilities and their families. These institutes focused on areas such as mainstreaming and inclusion, assessment practices and approaches for identifying and intervening with children at risk for disabilities, practices for improving children's transitions between settings (e.g., preschool to kindergarten, infant-toddler program to preschool), and service utilization (examining how states were implementing IDEA with respect to young children and their families). These institutes were the innovation engines that advanced the knowledge base with regard to evidence-based interventions or practices, training, and policy. Because these institutes also included funding for graduate students, they became the training ground for the next generation of scholars in this new area of early intervention and early childhood special education.

The evolution to the second phase of research began as researchers started to address second-generation questions to advance knowledge about which early intervention/early childhood special education interventions or practices worked best for which children and families, and under what conditions. During this second phase of research, a transition occurred when funding for special education research was moved to the National Center for Special Education Research (NCSER) within the Institute of Education Sciences. NCSER was established in December 2004 and began funding research under the early intervention and early learning in special education topic area in 2006. According to the NCSER web site, this is the only topic area among all Institute of Education Sciences research centers that supports research on infants and toddlers.

Lessons Learned During Phase 2   Building on lessons learned during phase 1 research studies and those lessons accrued as part of phase 2 research, a number of key principles have been generated that inform the way services and supports are delivered to young children with disabilities and their families. Although the following is not an exhaustive list, it includes many of the important lessons learned from five decades of research:

1. *We know how to teach new behavior to children with developmental delays and prevent/reduce challenging behaviors by understanding the environmental variables that cause or maintain them* (Baer, Wolf, & Risley, 1968). An important tenet of early intervention is that children's developmental trajectories are shaped by their histories of interactions with persons and events within their environments (Bijou, 1966). According to this principle, children with developmental delays act as they do not because of a specific condition, but because they have a "limited repertoire of behavior shaped by events that constitute [their] history" (Bijou, 1966, p. 2). Therefore, intervention for a specific child with a developmental delay or a specific behavioral concern

should be based not on an assessed mental state, but on the critical relationships the child has with the environment (Sidman, 1960). In this way, an intervention can change a child's developmental or learning trajectory by intervening in interactions that appear to impede development or learning.

2. *We know that children's interests and preferences are the foundations for their learning and are the key for individualizing instruction* (Hart & Risley, 1974). A large number of studies document the intuitively obvious principle that children will be more likely to engage with people and materials and learn when instruction is focused on activities in which they are most interested. Children's active participation or engagement in preferred learning activities has been demonstrated to promote child development and learning in areas such as language (Dunst, Jones, Johnson, Raab, & Hamby, 2011) and early literacy (Whitehurst & Lonigan, 1998). According to Whitehurst and Lonigan (1998, p. 854), "A child who is interested in literacy is more likely to facilitate shared reading interactions, notice print in the environment, and spend more time reading once he or she is able."

3. *We know that children learn through active engagement, so interventionists should arrange the environment and interact with children in ways that increase children's active engagement* (McWilliam & Bailey, 1995). A wealth of studies underscores the importance of active engagement as a predictor of later academic or social outcomes. Although early educators typically arrange their classroom environments and organize activities to provide ongoing opportunities for children to engage in a variety of tasks and to interact socially with peers and teachers, research shows that not all children have these experiences across all classrooms and not all activities across a classroom day set the stage for children's active engagement (Kontos & Keyes, 1999). Research shows the importance of focusing on active engagement because it has been shown to be a significant predictor of school readiness. Children who spend more time actively engaged in classroom activities and show greater levels of persistence and independence in these activities are more likely to demonstrate higher academic performance in school years than peers who engage less often and less positively with activities in preschool (Fantuzzo, Perry, & McDermott, 2004). Furthermore, research suggests that positive task or activity engagement may act as a protective factor for children with challenging behaviors (Dominguez & Greenfield, 2009). These and other studies underscore the importance to early educators that they should intentionally organize activities and routines to engage each child and provide ample learning opportunities during these activities and routines that provide challenges and allow each child to demonstrate independence, mastery, and persistence.

4. *We know that responsive caregiving is fundamental to promoting children's learning and development* (Kaiser et al., 1996). Responsiveness is one of the most studied behaviors of parents, teachers, and caregivers of young children. This construct of caregiving has been identified across various research paradigms and theories as providing a critical foundation for

children's learning and their interactions with others (Bornstein & Tamis-LeMonda, 1989). Responsiveness is characterized by a style of interaction that links caregivers' attention and warmth to a child's behaviors and interests. A wealth of descriptive studies have demonstrated that adults' responsive interactions are positively related to children's positive developmental trajectories in the social-emotional domain (Kim & Mahoney, 2004), early language domain (McDuffie & Yoder, 2010), and cognitive domain (Landry, Smith, Swank, & Miller-Loncar, 2000). Several intervention approaches have been developed that teach caregivers a responsive style of interaction, such as Relationship-Focused Intervention (Mahoney & Perales, 2005), the Play and Learning Strategies program (Landry & Smith, 1996), and Enhanced Milieu Teaching (Kaiser 1993). The extensive body of literature documenting the effectiveness of these strategies when used within families' daily routines (e.g., Woods, Kashinath & Goldstein, 2004) or in classrooms make them an important set of interventions for enhancing children's outcomes (Kong & Carta, 2013).

5.   *We know that families are essential in promoting their child's development. Families will be more likely to provide children with development-enhancing opportunities if the well-being of the entire family is supported* (Turnbull et al., 2007). One of the most significant lessons from the past 50 years of research on individuals with disabilities is the principle that the family system is the primary nurturing context for young children with disabilities (Odom & Wolery, 2003). In the first half of the 20th century, parents were advised to place their young children in residential facilities. This recommendation was replaced with the knowledge that children with disabilities will be most likely to develop like peers who are typically developing when they live in their communities with their families. A major area of research has focused on describing the types of information and support families need (Bailey, Blasco, & Simeonsson, 1992) and the relationships between family support and child outcomes (Dunst & Espe-Scherwindt, 2016). Researchers have carefully defined and studied practices associated with "family-centered services" and the role professionals should play in ensuring that services are responsive to families' strengths and needs (Dunst & Trivette, 2010). Another large area of research has focused on helping parents learn how to promote the development of their child with a disability (Machalicek, Lang, & Raulston, 2015). Significant bodies of research have been generated for supporting parents to promote their children's learning in the areas of communication (Roberts & Kaiser, 2011), social-emotional development (Sanders, Kirby, Tellegen, & Day, 2014), and behavioral skills (Strain & Timm, 2001).

6.   *We know that children's learning is most likely to generalize to real-life situations when instruction occurs in everyday activities and routines* (Snyder et al., 2015; Snyder et al., 2018). The research is strong that children's learning is enhanced when it occurs within activities and routines that contain meaningful social and material interactions compared with teaching in the

absence of meaningful social and material engagement (Kuhl, 2007). Across developmental and early intervention research, empirical studies have documented that when children are taught within socially engaged situations, they receive opportunities to learn about the social landscape around them (Schreibman et al., 2015). Teaching that occurs in a child's everyday activities and routines with familiar caregivers is able to foster learning and generalization of skills because it capitalizes on the quality of relationship between the child and caregiver, the emotional valence of interactions with familiar adults and peers, and the learning situation. Daily activities and routines are powerful contexts for young children to learn new skills because they are functional, predictable, and often occur numerous times throughout the day (Woods et al., 2004).

   7.   *We know that a child's learning goals should be individualized and determined by a team that includes parents* (Neisworth & Bagnato, 2000). A core tenet of early intervention and early childhood special education is that the diversity of young children within early intervention and early special education programs argues for the importance of the individualization of children's learning goals (Wolery, 2000). To determine the specific developmental and academic skills that should be the focus of a specific child's program, individualized assessment across multiple domains is essential (Bagnato, McLean, Macy, & Neisworth, 2011). Involvement of parents or other family members in the team assessment process is also critical for making important decisions regarding a child's individualized program. Indeed, IDEA of 2004 requires early intervention and early childhood special education programs to include parents on any team whose purpose is to make decisions about children's individualized programs (i.e., either their individualized family service program or their individualized education program).

   8.   *We know that children's learning goals should be continuously informed by ongoing assessment of their progress* (Greenwood, Carta, & McConnell, 2011). When children's progress is monitored on a frequent and ongoing basis, a team can use information from progress-monitoring assessments to gauge the effectiveness of teaching, to develop and adjust children's individualized learning goals, and to adjust instruction to meet children's individualized needs. For children who are not responding adequately to their current instructional/intervention program, practitioners should increase instructional intensity, adopt a different type of intervention or practice, or adjust the learning goal. Research has documented that when progress monitoring is implemented, practitioners and families make more informed instructional decisions, children learn more quickly because they are more likely to be receiving appropriate instruction, and communication is enhanced between families and professionals about children's progress (Fuchs & Fuchs, 2006).

   9.   *We know that adults can mediate and promote children's learning by implementing evidence-based instructional practices* (e.g., Cook & Odom, 2013). Early intervention and early childhood special education has a growing body of

evidence-based practices that can guide teachers, parents, and other caregivers in the way they arrange instruction for young children with disabilities. A practice is considered to be evidence-based when it has been documented to be effective in several rigorous studies conducted across multiple settings (Cook & Odom, 2013). While practitioners can use "evidence-based practices" as a starting place in their search for effective practices, an important caveat is that even those instructional strategies documented as effective may not be effective with all children. That is, practitioners have to regularly monitor an individual child's progress and make changes in instructional strategies to meet the needs of the individual learner (e.g., Strain & Dunlap, 2006). Important starting points for locating evidence-based practices relevant to early intervention/early childhood special education can be found in the recommended practices of the Division for Early Childhood (2014) of the Council for Exceptional Children and the What Works Clearinghouse (2013).

10. *We know that promoting children's learning requires intentional teaching specific to individualized learning goals* (Snyder et al., 2018). Reviews of the quality of early education programs that seek to identify the "active ingredients" of programs increasingly point to intentional or embedded teaching that is structured around engaging and preferred activities and routines as one of the most important classroom features that is most strongly associated with children's learning outcomes, especially when carried out by sensitive, responsive teachers (Diamond, Justice, Siegler, & Snyder, 2013). When teachers systematically engage children by talking and modeling within activities structured to engage specific children by building and extending on their interests and intentionally embed learning opportunities in children's individualized goals, these types of learning interactions maximize children's learning.

11. *We know that children with and without disabilities experience positive outcomes in inclusive settings* (Odom & Diamond, 1998). A paradox exists around the concept of inclusion and early education. For more than 30 years, numerous studies and reviews of research have documented that inclusion is an effective early childhood practice that results in children participating in, belonging to, and forming positive social relationships when inclusion is carried out in school and community settings (Odom, Buysse, & Soukakou, 2011). An important finding reported by many researchers is that the effectiveness of inclusion for promoting childhood outcomes relies on the quality of the early education program within which inclusive practices take place (Odom & Bailey, 2001). Another determinant of how well inclusion works is the use of evidence-based practices, such as embedded learning opportunities (Horn & Banerjee, 2009; Snyder et al., 2018) and peer-mediated intervention (Robertson, Green, Alper, Schloss, & Kohler, 2003). Despite the wealth of knowledge about the effectiveness of inclusion for promoting a variety of outcomes for children with and without disabilities, little progress has been made in advancing inclusion in practice. Annual reports from the U.S.

Department of Education (2016) show that only 42% of preschool-aged children had received special education in a regular early education setting—an increase of only 5.7% in the last 27 years.

Phase 3: Research Opportunities and Challenges That Lie Ahead in the Next 50 Years

Although research has resulted in a growing number of evidence-based practices with considerable promise to improve both short-term and long-term outcomes for children, a challenge is that these practices are still not in wide-scale use. For example, if more than half of young children with special needs are still *not* receiving education in inclusive settings, then many children are not benefiting from the peer-mediated evidence-based interventions that were so carefully developed through decades of research. Clearly, much more work needs to be done to ensure that interventions or practices demonstrated to be efficacious are implemented with fidelity by practitioners and families in authentic contexts, have positive effects on children, and can transform the lives of individuals with disabilities, their families, and the practitioners who support them. Opportunities and challenges remain in areas such as knowledge translation, scale-up, and sustainability of what research identifies as effective or evidence-based practices.

Besides learning how research on interventions or practices can have broader and more sustained impact and affect greater numbers of children and families, new programs of research are needed to address barriers that currently prevent the field from knowing what interventions work best for which individuals and under what conditions. Adaptive interventions and the use of adaptive intervention designs hold promise for helping to address these types of research questions (Snyder et al., 2018) For example, practitioners need to know how to tailor interventions based on child or family responses to the intervention or how to adapt interventions based on child and family cultural or linguistic factors. Similarly, we need greater understanding about how to tailor interventions and deliver them with the precision and intensity required to meet a child's or family's needs.

A focus on implementation means studying specified sets of activities that are designed to put into practice an activity or program (evidence-based practices) of known dimensions (Metz & Bartley, 2012). Phase 3 research will need to address complex questions about which strategies are efficacious for supporting practitioners or families to implement, as well as which evidence-based interventions or practices work for which children and under what conditions. Informed by implementation science, which involves understanding processes and procedures that promote or impede the transfer and adoption and use of evidence-based practices in real-world contexts (Kelly & Perkins, 2014), implementation research should dominate phase 3 research in the coming years. Implementation research will need to focus on the study of competency, organizational, and leadership variables associated with the fidelity of implementation of evidence-based practices in authentic contexts. To respond to the opportunities and challenges listed previously, support will be needed to continue and strengthen the following lines of research:

1.   *Research leading to a greater understanding of efficacious professional development practices and how they can be implemented with fidelity.* Our knowledge of the processes of professional development in early intervention and early childhood and how they affect practitioners' knowledge and skills is still quite limited (see Chapter 12). Research is needed to build a body of evidence about forms of professional development, the underlying mechanisms that influence change in practitioners, and how they affect both proximal and distal outcomes (i.e., effects on interventionists and the children and families they serve) (Snyder, Hemmeter, & Fox, 2015). More empirical studies are needed to understand how the various forms of professional development help to promote new levels of understanding and how individuals translate that new knowledge into skillful practice.

2.   *Research focusing on ways to ensure that practitioners sustain high-fidelity implementation of evidence-based practices.* A growing body of research across multiple fields (health, mental health, and education) has documented the importance of implementation of evidence practices with fidelity (Durlak & DuPre, 2008). Although there is a growing body of research describing how implementation works in community settings, relatively little research has studied implementation in early education and early intervention (Franks & Schroeder, 2013). Specifically, research should focus on the factors associated with training on specific evidence-based practices, continuous quality improvement, and the leadership, organizational, and system-level policies that support sustained, high-quality implementation.

3.   *Development and validation of practices that fit the language and culture of children and families.* Our understanding of what works for which children and under what conditions must consider children from diverse language and cultural backgrounds. Research must address the fact that the "new mainstream" includes a diverse range of cultures and children born in and outside of the United States to parents who are both natives and immigrants (Fortuny, Hernandez, & Chaudry, 2010). New research must be carried out to tailor evidence-based practices to meet the needs of these children and their families, as well as to develop or adapt interventions to incorporate the strengths of their cultures.

4.   *Developing more effective ways of identifying and providing the appropriate levels of intervention and services to children and families as quickly as possible.* A fundamental principle of early intervention/early childhood special education is the need to find children and families who require additional support, determine the types and intensity of supports needed, and then implement and evaluate the effectiveness of these supports. Although millions of children have been the recipients of individualized early interven-

tion and early childhood special education services, too many children who would benefit from greater levels of instruction or intervention are missed completely or receive services that could be described as "too little" and "too late." Response to Intervention and Multi-Tiered Systems of Support (Carta & Miller Young, 2018) offer frameworks that have helped to speed the delivery of appropriate levels of effective instruction to young children. Although a foundation for applying this framework to young children has been developed in the last 10 years (Carta et al., 2015), much more research is needed to develop new screening and progress monitoring measures, decision-making models employing benchmarks that help practitioners identify children needing extra support, evidence-based professional development models that help sustain implementation of these approaches, and the most effective methods to engaging families in these tiered models.

CONCLUSIONS

Looking back over 50 years, it is clear that research in the field has made a major contribution to improving the quality of life for young children with disabilities and their families. Investments by the federal government in programs of model demonstration, outreach, and research and the dedication of individuals and investigative groups to pursue important and relevant research questions have led to improved interventions and practices, procedures for training practitioners, strategies for engaging and supporting families, measures for ensuring that interventions are producing desired results, and programs that incorporate all of these features and result in enhanced quality of life. In addition, research has been used to inform and advance both policies and recommended practices in the field. Despite impressive progress over the past 50 years, many questions remain unanswered. The next generation of researchers have a strong foundation to address the opportunities and challenges that remain. They should use the knowledge and wisdom of the field to date to conduct the next generation of research, which will advance young children's developmental and learning trajectories and transform their lives, as well as those of their families.

REFERENCES

Allen, K. E., Benning, P. M., & Drummond, W. T. (1972). Integration of normal and handicapped children in a behavior modification preschool: A case study. In G. Semb (Ed.), *Behavior analysis and education* (pp. 127–141). Lawrence, KS: University of Kansas.

Allen, K. E., & Harris, F. R. (1966). Elimination of a child's excessive scratching by training the mother in reinforcement procedures. *Behaviour Research and Therapy, 4,* 79–84.

Baer, D. M., Wolf, M. M., & Risley, T. R. (1968). Some current dimensions of applied behavior analysis. *Journal of Applied Behavior Analysis, 1,* 91–97.

Bagnato, S., McLean, M., Macy, M., & Neisworth, J. T. (2011). Identifying instructional targets for early childhood via authentic assessment: Alignment of professional standards and practice-based evidence. *Journal of Early Intervention, 33,* 243–253.

Bailey, D. B., Blasco, P. M., & Simeonsson, R. J. (1992). Needs expressed by mothers and fathers of young children with disabilities. *American Journal on Mental Retardation, 97,* 1–10.

Bijou, S. W. (1966). Theory and research in mental (developmental) retardation. *Psychological Record, 13,* 95–110.

Bornstein, M. H., & Tamis-LeMonda, C. S. (1989). Maternal responsiveness and cognitive development in children. In M. H. Bornstein (Ed.), *New directions for child development: No. 43. Maternal responsiveness* (pp. 49–61). San Francisco, CA: Jossey-Bass.

Bricker, W. A., & Bricker, D. D. (1976). The Infant, Toddler, and Preschool Research and Intervention Project. In T. D. Tjossem (Ed.), *Intervention strategies for high risk infants and young children* (pp. 545–572). Baltimore, MD: University Park Press.

Bronfenbrenner, U. (1979). *The ecology of human development: Experiments by nature and design.* Cambridge, MA: Harvard University Press.

Carta, J. J., Greenwood, C. R., Atwater, J., McConnell, S. R., Goldstein, H., & Kaminski, R. (2015). Identifying preschool children for higher tiers of language and early literacy instruction within a Response to Intervention framework. *Journal of Early Intervention, 36,* 281–291.

Carta, J. J., & Miller Young, R. (2018). *Multi-tiered systems of support for young children: Driving change in early education.* Baltimore, MD: Paul H. Brookes Publishing Co.

Casto, G. (1985). *Common outreach indicators* (Outreach series paper no. 1). Chapel Hill, NC: University of North Carolina.

Casto, G., & Mastropieri, M. A. (1986). The efficacy of early intervention programs: A meta-analysis. *Exceptional Children, 52,* 417–424.

Computer History Museum. (2018). *Timeline of computer history.* Retrieved from http://www.computerhistory.org/timeline/1997/

Cook, B. G., & Odom, S. L. (2013). Evidence-based practices and implementation science in special education. *Exceptional Children, 79,* 135–144.

DeWeerd, J., & Cole, A. (1976). Handicapped children's early education program. *Exceptional Children, 43,* 155–157.

Diamond, K. E., Justice, L. M., Siegler, R. S., & Snyder, P. A. (2013). *Synthesis of IES research on early intervention and early childhood education* (NCSER 2013-3001). Washington, DC: Institute of Education Sciences, U.S. Department of Education.

Division for Early Childhood. (2014). *DEC recommended practices in early intervention/early childhood special education 2014.* Retrieved from http://www.dec-sped.org/recommended practices

Dominguez, X. D., & Greenfield, D. (2009). Learning behaviors mediating the effects of behavior problems on academic outcomes. *NHSA Dialog, 12,* 1–17.

Dunst, C. J., & Espe-Sherwindt, M. (2016). Family-centered practices in early intervention. In B. Reichow, B. Boyd, E. Barton, & S. Odom (Eds.), *Handbook of early childhood special education* (pp. 37–56). New York, NY: Springer.

Dunst, C. J., Jones, T., Johnson, M., Raab, M., & Hamby, D. W. (2011). Role of children's interests in early literacy and language development. *CELLreviews, 4*(5), 1–18. Retrieved from http://www.earlyliteracylearning.org/cellreviews/cellreviews_v4_n5.pdf

Dunst, C. J., & Trivette, C. M. (2010). Family-centered help giving practices, parent-professional partnerships, and parent, family and child outcomes. In S. L. Christenson & A. L. Reschley (Eds.), *Handbook of school-family partnerships* (pp. 362–379). New York, NY: Routledge.

Durlak, J. A., & DuPre, E. P. (2008). Implementation matters: A review of research on the influence of implementation on program outcomes and the factors affecting implementation. *American Journal of Community Psychology, 41,* 327–350.

Economic Opportunity Amendments of 1972. Public Law 92-424, 92nd Congress, H. R. 12350, September 19, 1972.

Education for All Handicapped Children Act of 1975, PL 94-142, 20 U.S.C. §§ 1400 *et seq.*

Education of the Handicapped Act Amendments of 1986, PL 99-457, 20 U.S.C. §§ 1400 *et seq.*

Fantuzzo, J., Perry, M. A., & McDermott, P. (2004). Preschool approaches to learning and their relationship to other relevant classroom competencies for low-income children. *School Psychology Quarterly, 19,* 212–230.

Fortuny, K., Hernandez, D. J., & Chaudry, A. (2010). *Young children of immigrants: The leading edge of America's future.* Retrieved from http://www.urban.org/research/publication/young-children-immigrants-leading-edge-americas-future

Franks, R. P., & Schroeder, J. (2013). Implementation science: What do we know and where do we go from here? In T. Halle, A. Metz, & I. Martinez-Beck (Eds.). *Applying implementation science in early childhood programs and systems* (pp. 5–20). Baltimore, MD: Paul H. Brookes Publishing Co.

Fuchs, D., & Fuchs, L. S. (2006). Introduction to responsiveness-to-intervention: What, why, and how valid is it? *Reading Research Quarterly, 4,* 93–99.

Garland, C., Black, T., & Jesien, G. (1986). *The future of outreach: A DEC position paper.* Unpublished manuscript. Reston, VA: CEC Division for Early Childhood.

Goncalves, S. (2016). *Tech throwback: Army signs contract to develop ENIAC "giant brain."* Retrieved from https://www.wirelessdesignmag.com/blog/2016/05/tech-throwback-army-signs-contract-develop-eniac-giant-brain

Greenwood, C., Carta, J., & McConnell, S. (2011). Advances in measurement for universal screening and progress monitoring of young children. *Journal of Early Intervention, 33,* 254-267.

Guralnick, M. J. (1993). Second generation research on the effectiveness of early intervention. *Early Education and Development, 4,* 366–378.

Guralnick, M. J., & Bennett, F. C. (Eds.). (1987). *The effectiveness of early intervention for at-risk and handicapped children.* New York: Academic Press.

Handicapped Children's Early Education Act of 1968, PL 90-538, 20 U.S.C. §§ 621 *et seq.*

Hanson, M. J., & Schwarz, R. (1978). Results of a longitudinal intervention program for Down syndrome infants and their families. *Education and Training of the Mentally Retarded, 13,* 403–407.

Hart, B. M., Reynolds, N. J., Baer, D. M., Brawley, E. R., & Harris, F. R. (1968). Effect of contingent and non-contingent social reinforcement on the cooperative play of a preschool child. *Journal of Applied Behavior Analysis, 1,* 73–76.

Hart, B., & Risley, T. R. (1974). Using preschool materials to modify the language of disadvantaged children. *Journal of Applied Behavior Analysis, 7,* 243–256.

Hayden, A. H., & Haring, N. G. (1976). Early intervention for high risk infants and young children: Programs for Down Syndrome children. In T. D. Tjossem (Ed.), *Intervention strategies for high risk infants and young children* (pp. 573–608). Baltimore, MD: University Park Press.

Hebbeler, K. M., Smith, B., & Black, T. L. (1991). Federal early childhood special education policy: A model for the improvement of services for children with disabilities. *Exceptional Children, 58,* 104–112.

Horn, E., & Banerjee, R. (2009). Understanding curriculum modifications and embedded learning opportunities in the context of supporting all children's success. *Language, Speech, and Hearing Services in Schools, 40,* 406–415.

Individuals with Disabilities Education Improvement Act (IDEA) of 2004, PL 108-446, 20 U.S.C. §§ 1400 *et seq.*

Jacobson J. W., & Holburn, S. (2004). History and current status of applied behavior analysis in developmental disabilities. In J. L. Matson, R. B. Laud, & M. L. Matson (Eds.) *Behavior modification for persons with developmental disabilities: Treatments and supports* (pp. 1–32). Kingston, NY: National Association for the Dually Diagnosed.

Kaiser, A. P. (1993). Parent-implemented language intervention: An environmental system perspective. In A. Kaiser & D. Gray (Eds.), *Enhancing children's communication: Research foundations for intervention, Vol. 2* (pp. 63–84). Baltimore, MD: Paul H. Brookes Publishing Co.

Kaiser, A. P., Hemmeter, M. L., Ostrosky, M. M., Fischer, R., Yoder, P., & Keefer, M. (1996). The effects of teaching parents to use responsive interaction strategies. *Topics in Early Childhood Special Education, 16,* 375–406.

Kelly, B., & Perkins, D. F. (Eds.). (2014). *Handbook of implementation science for psychology in education.* Cambridge, UK: Cambridge University Press.

Kennedy, M. M., & McDaniels, G. L. (1982). Informing policy makers about programs for handicapped children. In J. Travers & R. Light (Eds.), *Evaluating early childhood demonstration programs* (pp. 163–186). Washington, DC: National Academies Press.

Kim, J., & Mahoney, G. (2004). The effects of mother's style of interaction on children's engagement. *Topics in Early Childhood Special Education, 24,* 31–38.

Kong, N., & Carta, J. (2013). Research synthesis of studies on responsive interaction intervention for children with or at risk for developmental delays. *Topics in Early Childhood Special Education, 33,* 4–17.

Kontos, S., & Keyes, L. (1999). An ecobehavioral analysis of early childhood classrooms. *Early Childhood Research Quarterly, 14,* 35–50.

Kuhl, P. (2007). Is speech learning "gated" by the social brain? *Developmental Science, 10,* 110–120.

Landry, S. H., & Smith, K. E. (1996). *Playing and learning strategies—I.* Houston, TX: University of Texas–Houston Health Science Center.

Landry, S. H., Smith, K. E., Swank, P., & Miller-Loncar, C. (2000). Early maternal and child influences on children's later independent cognitive and social functioning. *Child Development, 71,* 358–375.

Larson, S., Lakin, C., & Hill, S. (2013). Behavioral outcomes of moving from institutional to community living for people with intellectual and developmental disabilities. *Research and Practice for Persons with Severe Disabilities, 37,* 235–246.

Lazara, A., Danaher, J., & Detwiler, S. (2018). Chapel Hill: The University of North Carolina, FPG Child Development Institute, Early Childhood Technical Assistance Center. Retrieved from http://ectacenter.org/~pdfs/growthcomppartc-2018-04-17.pdf.

Lerman, D. C., LeBlanc, L. A., & Valentino, A. L. (2015). Evidence-based application of staff and caregiver training procedures. In J. L. Ringdahl & T. S. Falcomata (Eds.), *Clinical and organizational applications of applied behavior analysis* (pp. 321–351). San Diego, CA: Academic Press.

Lifshitz, H., Merrick, J., & Morad, M. (2008). Health status and ADL functioning of older persons with intellectual disability: Community residence versus residential care centers. *Research in Developmental Disabilities, 29,* 301–315.

Littlejohn Associates. (1982). *An analysis of the impact of the handicapped children's early education program* (contract no. 300-81-0061). Washington, DC: Author.

Machalicek, W., Lang, R., & Raulston, T. J. (2015). Training parents of children with intellectual disabilities. *Current Developmental Disorders Reports, 2*(2), 110–118.

Mahoney, G., & Perales, F. (2005). Relationship-focused early intervention with children with pervasive developmental disorders and other disabilities: A comparative study. *Developmental and Behavioral Pediatrics, 26*(2), 77–85.

McDuffie, A., & Yoder, P. (2010). Types of parent verbal responsiveness that predict language in young children with autism spectrum disorder. *Journal of Speech, Language, and Hearing Research, 53*(4), 1026–1039.

McLean, M., Sandall, S., & Smith, B. J. (2016). A history of early childhood special education. In B. Reichow, B. Boyd, E. Barton, & S. Odom (Eds.), *Handbook of early childhood special education* (pp. 3–19). London, UK: Springer.

McWilliam, R. A., & Bailey, D. B. (1995). Effects of classroom social structure and disability on engagement. *Topics in Early Childhood Special Education, 15,* 123–147.

Metz, A., & Bartley, L. (2012). Active implementation frameworks for program success: How to use implementation science to improve outcomes for children. *Zero to Three, 32*(4), 11–18.

Morgan, P. L., Farkas, G., Cook, M., Strassfeld, N. M., Hillemeier, M. M., Pun, W. K., et al. (2018). Are Hispanic, Asian, Native American, or language-minority children overrepresented in special education? *Exceptional Children, 84,* 261–279.

Neisworth, J. T., & Bagnato, S. J. (2000). Recommended practices in assessment. In S. Sandall, M. McLean, & B. Smith (Eds.), *DEC recommended practices in early intervention/early childhood special education* (pp. 17–27). Longmont, CO: Sopris West.

Odom, S. L., & Bailey, D. B. (2001). Inclusive preschool programs: Ecology and child outcomes. In M. Guralnick (Ed.), *Early childhood inclusion: Focus on change* (pp. 253–276). Baltimore, MD: Paul H. Brookes Publishing Co.

Odom, S. L., Buysse, V., & Soukakou, E. (2011). Inclusion for young children with disabilities: A quarter century of research perspectives. *Journal of Early Intervention, 33,* 344–356.

Odom, S. L., & Diamond, K. E. (1998). Inclusion of young children with special needs in early childhood education: The research base. *Early Childhood Research Quarterly, 13,* 3–25.

Odom, S. L., & Wolery, M. (2003). A unified theory of practice in Early Intervention/Early Childhood Special Education. *Journal of Special Education, 37,* 164–173.

Roberts, M. Y., & Kaiser, A. P. (2011). The effectiveness of parent-implemented language intervention: A meta-analysis. *American Journal of Speech-Language Pathology, 20*, 180–199.

Robertson, J., Green, K., Alper, S., Schloss, P. J., & Kohler, F. (2003). Using peer-mediated intervention to facilitate children's participation in inclusive child care activities. *Education & Treatment of Children, 26*, 182–197.

Rogers-Warren, A., & Warren, S. F. (Eds.). (1977). *Ecological perspectives in behavior analysis*. Baltimore, MD: University Park Press.

Sanders, M. R., Kirby, J. N., Tellegen, C. L., & Day, J. J. (2014). The Triple P-Positive Parenting Program: A systematic review and meta-analysis of a multi-level system of parenting support. *Clinical Psychology Review, 34*, 337–357.

Schreibman, L., Dawson, G., Stahmer, A. C., Landa, R., Rogers, S. J., McGee, G. G., et al. (2015). Naturalistic developmental behavioral interventions: Empirically validated treatments for autism spectrum disorder. *Journal of Autism and Developmental Disorders, 45*, 2411–2428.

Scott, N., Lakin, C., & Larson, S. A. (2008). The 40th anniversary of deinstitutionalization in the United States: Decreasing state institutional populations, 1967–2007. *Intellectual and Developmental Disabilities, 46*, 402–405.

Shearer, M. S., & Shearer, D. E. (1972). The Portage Project: A model for early childhood education. *Exceptional Children, 39*, 210–217.

Sidman, M. (1960). *Tactics of scientific research*. New York, NY: Basic Books.

Snyder, P. A., Bishop, C. C., & McLaughlin, T. (2017). Frameworks for guiding program focus and practices in early intervention. In J. M. Kauffman, D. P. Hallahan, and P. C. Pullen (Eds.), *Handbook of special education* (2nd ed., pp. 865–881). New York, NY: Routledge.

Snyder, P., Hemmeter, M. L., & Fox, L. (2015). Supporting implementation of evidence-based practices through practice-based coaching. *Topics in Early Childhood Special Education, 35*, 133–143.

Snyder, P., Hemmeter, M. L., McLean, M., Sandall, S., McLaughlin, T., & Algina, J. (2018). Effects of professional development on preschool teachers' use of embedded instruction practices. *Exceptional Children, 84*, 213–232.

Snyder, P. A., Rakap, S., Hemmeter, M. L., McLaughlin, T. W., Sandall, S., & McLean, M. E. (2015). Naturalistic instructional approaches in early learning: A systematic review. *Journal of Early Intervention, 37*, 69–97.

Stock, J. R., Wnek. L. L., Newborg, J. A., Schenck, E. A., Gable, J. R., Spurgeon, M.S., et al. (1976). *Evaluation of the Handicapped Children's Early Education Program (HCEEP) (contract no. OEC-0-14-0402)*. Columbus, OH: Battelle Memorial Institute.

Strain, P. S., & Cordisco, L. (1993). The LEAP preschool model: Description and outcomes. In S. Harris & J. Handleman (Eds.), *Preschool education programs for children with autism* (pp. 224–244). Austin, TX: Pro-Ed.

Strain, P. S., & Dunlap, G. (2006). *Recommended practices: Being an evidence-based practitioner*. Tampa, FL: University of South Florida, Louis de la Parte Florida Mental Health Institute, Center for Evidence-based Practice: Young Children with Challenging Behavior.

Strain, P., & Timm, M. (2001). Remediation and prevention of aggression: An evaluation of the Regional Intervention Program over a quarter century. *Behavior Disorders, 26*, 297–313.

Turnbull, A. P., Summers, J. A., Turnbull, R., Brotherson, M. J., Winton, P., Roberts, R., et al. (2007). Family supports and services in early intervention: A bold vision. *Journal of Early Intervention, 29*, 187–206.

U.S. Department of Education. (2010). *Thirty-five years of progress in educating children with disabilities through IDEA*. Washington, DC: Office of Special Education and Rehabilitative Services.

U.S. Department of Education. (2016). *Early childhood education*. Washington, DC: Institute of Education Sciences, What Works Clearinghouse. Retrieved from http://ies.ed.gov/ncee/wwc/topic.aspx?sid=4

U.S. Department of Education, Institute of Education Sciences, National Center for Education Statistics, National Assessment of Educational Progress (NAEP), (2018). 1992–2017 Reading Assessments.

What Works Clearinghouse. (2013). *Social skills training intervention report*. Washington, DC: U.S. Department of Education, Institute of Education Sciences. Retrieved from http://whatworks.ed.gov

White, K. R., Mastropieri, M., & Casto, G. (1984). An analysis of special education early childhood projects approved by the Joint Dissemination Review Panel. *Journal of the Division for Early Childhood, 9*(1), 11–26.

Whitehurst, G., & Lonigan, C. (1998). Child development and emergent literacy. *Child Development, 69,* 848–872.

Wolery, M. (2000). Recommended practices in child-focused interventions. In S. Sandall, M. McLean, & B. Smith (Eds.), *DEC recommended practices in early intervention/early childhood special education* (pp. 29–37). Denver, CO: Division of Early Childhood.

Woods, J., Kashinath, S., & Goldstein, H. (2004). Children's communication outcomes. *Journal of Early Intervention, 26,* 175–193.

Yell, M. L., Rogers, D., & Rogers, E. L. (1998). The legal history of special education: What a long, strange trip it's been. *Remedial and Special Education, 19,* 219–228.

12

The Early Intervention/Early Childhood Special Education Workforce
Professional Development Issues and Future Directions

Pamela J. Winton

The message from decades of intervention research is unequivocal: High-quality early intervention for children ages birth to 5 years who are at risk because of environmental, developmental, and/or health factors has a lifelong impact on health and well-being (Campbell et al., 2014). These findings, along with research on the importance of early influences on the developing brain (National Research Council, 2000), have stimulated the growth of government-supported federal and state early childhood programs for children aged 0 to 5 years (Epstein & Barnett, 2012; Kagan & Kauerz, 2012). A linchpin to the quality of early childhood programs is the availability of a competent, confident workforce (Martinez-Beck & Zaslow, 2006) that is adequately prepared and supported to implement evidence-based practices associated with improving positive outcomes for all young children (Hamre, Downer, Jamil, & Pianta, 2012). Unfortunately, national survey data indicate that the early childhood education (ECE) workforce, including those graduating from degree programs in which a primary stated mission is preparing early intervention/early childhood special educators (Chang, Early, & Winton, 2005; Early & Winton 2001; Maxwell, Lim, & Early, 2006; Ray, Bowman, & Robbins, 2006), is far from prepared to provide the types of ongoing multiple learning experiences throughout the day that young children need. This is especially true for children with disabilities, who need support to grow, learn, and reach their highest potential (Hyson, Horm, & Winton, 2012).

The author would like to acknowledge Shuting Zheng, doctoral student at the University of North Carolina, for help with copyediting this manuscript.

255

Multiple factors have contributed to the current status of the early childhood workforce and the challenges it faces in adequately serving young
children with disabilities. These include fragmentation of the professional
development (PD) system; lack of accountability and quality of those providing PD and how it is delivered; the uneven quality of the workforce because
of the lack of uniform training, teacher licensure/certification requirements,
and compensation; and the absence of a well-developed research base on
effective approaches to preparing and supporting the workforce (Hamre
et al., 2012; Hyson et al., 2012; Winton, Snyder, & Goffin, 2016). These challenges, in part, reflect the legacy of diverse funding streams and administrative homes for early childhood service delivery.

Despite these challenges, a case can be made that one of the unacknowl-
edged strengths within the broad ECE workforce is the early intervention/
early childhood special education (EI/ECSE) sector. The purpose of this
chapter, in keeping with the forward focus aim of the book, is to examine
how the origins of the field of EI/ECSE have shaped and contributed to the
current strengths and challenges facing the workforce and future PD directions to ensure positive outcomes for children with disabilities and their
families.

THE ORIGINS OF THE EARLY INTERVENTION/
EARLY CHILDHOOD SPECIAL EDUCATION WORKFORCE

EI/ECSE is a relatively young field whose earliest practitioners came from
and/or were influenced by psychology, child and human development,
mental health, and other fields (see McLean, Sandall, & Smith, 2016 for
more information on the history of the field). It is composed of multiple
disciplines, meaning that sources of knowledge, standards for practice, and
policy guidelines are rich and varied. The field is undergirded by decades
of research on effective intervention strategies for children with disabilities (see Chapter 11); legislative safeguards that protect the rights of young
children with disabilities and their families, with a particular emphasis
on family partnerships and inclusion (see Chapter 13); and federal investments in infrastructure support designed to advance knowledge to enhance
lives of young children with disabilities and their families (Gallagher, 2000;
Trohanis, 2008). Certain features of these historical origins have had an
enduring impact on the strengths and challenges of the EI/ECSE workforce
and its future potential.

STRENGTHS OF THE EARLY INTERVENTION/
EARLY CHILDHOOD SPECIAL EDUCATION WORKFORCE

The strengths of the EI/ECSE workforce have been influenced by multiple
factors. As alluded to above, they include the historic presence of federal
infrastructure support for the workforce; the decades-long presence of

research-based practice guidelines; the integral role of families as leaders, advocates, and participants in the delivery of PD; and the way in which the values and legislative support within EI/ECSE on interdisciplinary and inclusive service delivery models has shaped the structure of personnel preparation programs and the content and delivery of PD.

Federal Infrastructure Support

From its inception and due to the efforts of the pioneers who framed the earliest special education legislations, the field of EI/ECSE has benefited from infrastructure support (e.g., research, policy, professional development, technical assistance) designed to ensure the quality of the direct services for children with disabilities (Gallagher, 2000; McLean et al., 2016; Trohanis, 2008). During those early days of policy development, recognition that the success of the societal changes being instigated in policy depended upon support for a competent workforce have had an enduring impact on the availability and educational level of the EI/ECSE workforce. Federal discretionary grant funding from the U.S. Department of Education, Office of Special Education Programs (OSEP) historically and currently is available to Institutions of Higher Education (IHEs) to prepare EI/ECSE staff. Annually, OSEP awards approximately $2.5 million in new grants for personnel preparation (Kavulic, 2017; U.S. Department of Education, 2018). These grants provide support to personnel seeking degrees primarily at the graduate level in special education, early intervention, or related services. The availability of loan-free stipends and tuition has served as a recruitment tool for building a highly qualified workforce with individuals likely to have a bachelor's degree or higher (U.S. Department of Education, 2012).

Federal discretionary funding has also supported multiple national technical assistance centers over the last three decades. Their primary mission has been to develop products, provide PD to the workforce, and provide technical assistance to states for implementing early childhood programs and services as specified in the Individuals with Disabilities Education Act (IDEA) of 2004 (PL 108-446) (Bruder, 2016; Gallagher, 2000; Kavulic, 2017; Trohanis, 2008). These federal investments in infrastructure for preparing and supporting the workforce have contributed to the quality and availability of EI/ECSE practitioners, leaders, and PD resources.

Research-Based Practice Guidelines

The legacy of intervention research and its practical applications (see Chapter 11) contributed to the development of a set of recommended practices that provided guidance for the relatively new field of EI/ECSE (Odom & McLean, 1996). The Division for Early Childhood (DEC) of the Council for Exceptional Children has spearheaded these efforts and, with funding from OSEP at points in its history, completed four revisions of these recommended practices over the last 25 years.

Several features of the most recently revised recommended practices (Division for Early Childhood, 2014) make this resource particularly relevant at this point in time for EI/ECSE and the broader field of ECE. The 66 practices are organized into eight topical areas focused on practitioners and leaders working with children ages 0–5 years who have or are at risk for developmental delays and disabilities. They extend beyond children who are eligible for IDEA services, which is important because of the emphasis within the broader early childhood field on individualizing for all children. They represent the breadth of the topic area in that, within each topical area, there are multiple practices. They are observable; that is, they describe with specificity the actions practitioners take to support children and families. They are not disability specific; they are practices associated with functional child and family outcomes in domains that are relevant for children, regardless of their particular label or disability. They can be delivered in all settings, including natural/inclusive environments.

The examples provided with the practices illustrate how the practices might be implemented by different types of early childhood practitioners working in different settings. They build on, but do not duplicate, practice standards for typical early childhood settings, such as the National Association for the Education of Young Children (NAEYC) Developmentally Appropriate Practices. By building on foundational practices that provide a baseline for quality, they provide guidance to practitioners for individualizing for children and families based on needs, preferences, and interests, which makes them a valuable resource for practitioners in all early childhood settings (e.g., Head Start, Early Head Start, child care, pre-K). The practices are supported by research, as well as the values and experiences of the field. In addition, systematic, iterative, and rigorous processes and tools have been developed to locate, appraise, and synthesize evidence on the practices in an ongoing fashion so that the practices are updated on a regular basis. One more important feature of the 2014 revision of the DEC recommendations is that the set of practices are now free, publicly accessible, and downloadable along with sets of professional development resources designed to support implementation of the practices. DEC is making a systematic effort to share the practices and resources to support their implementation across all early childhood sectors.

In addition to the DEC Recommended Practices (2014), OSEP funded the National Professional Development Center on Autism Spectrum Disorder (n.d.) to identify evidence-based practices and related free professional resources for teachers, therapists, and technical assistance providers who work specifically with individuals aged birth to 22 years who have autism spectrum disorders. Resources include detailed information on how to plan, implement, and monitor specific evidence-based practices. Additional support from OSEP is supporting the ongoing updating of the practices as new evidence emerges from the field.

Family Partnerships

The role that families historically played in advocating for policy changes and the recognition of the central and enduring impact of families on children's development contributed to the emergence of family-centered early intervention and family partnerships being integral to service delivery for EI/ECE. The legacy of the strong values base along with a solid research base demonstrating the benefits of family partnerships (Dunst & Espe-Sherwindt, 2016) led to family content being infused within professional development (Brotherson, Summers, Bruns & Sharp, 2007). Approaches for delivering PD have included families serving as co-instructors, co-facilitators, or mentors in preservice and in-service contexts (Capone, Hull, & DiVenere, 1997; Winton & DiVenere, 1995). To date, there are no rigorous evaluation data demonstrating the positive impact of family involvement in PD on learner outcomes. However, anecdotal information and qualitative studies (Turnbull, Turnbull, Erwin, & Soodak, 2006) suggest that learning directly from families about their perspectives on service delivery, professional relationships, and parenting a child with disabilities raises practitioners' awareness and builds understanding. The DEC (2014) recommended practices include a topic area devoted to families, with an emphasis on family–professional collaboration, family capacity-building, and family-centered practices. A plethora of professional development resources related to family partnerships have been developed over the years, often through federal project funding from OSEP. (Examples of PD resources are available at https://eclkc.ohs.acf.hhs.gov/children-disabilities). Knowledge and use of these resources and practice standards are a strength that the EI/ECSE workforce brings to the overall ECE workforce.

Interdisciplinary Collaboration

The recognition that the needs of young children with disabilities and their families, especially infants and toddlers, are best addressed by an interdisciplinary approach (Bailey, Palsha, & Huntington, 1990) has shaped the content and structure of professional development for EI/ECSE (Kilgo & Bruder, 1997). The emphasis on an interdisciplinary approach to service delivery was reinforced by the passage of the Education of the Handicapped Act Amendments of 1986 (PL 99-457), which extended the requirement for states to provide services for children with disabilities down to preschoolers and established incentives for states to provide services for children ages birth through 2 years. The competitive, discretionary grants for personnel preparation programs from the U.S. Department of Education's OSEP began to include funding priorities for IHE programs that were interdisciplinary in terms of faculty and students. In addition, in the early 1990s, OSEP funded the Carolina Institute for Research on Infant Personnel Preparation, an interdisciplinary research consortium. The members of this institute developed discipline-specific (Crais, 1991; Hanft, Burke, Cahill, Swenson-Miller, & Humphry, 1992; Sparling, 1992) and interdisciplinary training curricula (Winton, 1992) focused on family content for preservice coursework and a set of agreed-upon interdisciplinary competencies for early intervention (Bailey et al., 1990). These interdisciplinary competencies became the foundation for standards that still guide the field of EI/ECSE today (Bruder, 2016). In addition, content related to teaming and collaboration among disciplines became recognized as an important component of professional development (Guillen & Winton, 2015; Kilgo & Bruder, 1997; Sexton, Snyder, Lobman, Kimbrough, & Matthews, 1997). In fact, teaming/collaboration is one of eight key topic areas in the current DEC recommended practices, thus providing guidance for programs, practitioners, and PD providers.

Inclusion

The values, research, and legislative support for inclusion as a service delivery approach in supporting children with disabilities and their families has made an impact on PD for EI/ECSE and the broader ECE workforce. Regulations within IDEA (2004) stipulate that services and supports for preschoolers be provided in the least restrictive environment for preschoolers and in natural environments for infants and toddlers. Inclusion also has substantial research support (Odom et al., 2004) and is a core value for the field of EI/ECSE (DEC/NAEYC, 2009). The recognition that inclusion is unlikely to be an effective strategy without ECE teachers able to implement inclusion as intended has increased the focus within the EI/ECSE sector on raising the quality of the overall ECE workforce. In the early 1990s, teacher education programs were challenged to make changes in their structure to reflect the continued movement toward inclusion (Miller, 1992). This led to the emergence of blended programs in which some IHEs merged ECE and EI/ECSE programs that had previously been administratively housed in separate departments. Even though data on the effectiveness of these programs is scant, the approach has endured over time with a number of early childhood teacher education programs engaging faculty from different disciplinary backgrounds and enrolling students prepared to work in inclusive settings (Bruder, 2016; Grisham-Brown & Hemmeter, 2017). It is now generally understood that "*all* young children, whether officially identified as having a disability or not, benefit from well-planned, intentional, learning opportunities throughout the day that respond to their developmental, linguistic, cultural, and individual characteristics" (Hyson & Winton, 2017, p. xii).

The implications for PD in the inclusion movement are significant. There has been an increased focus on blended practices or practices that can be used to address the needs of all children in inclusive settings (Grisham-Brown & Hemmeter, 2017). One of the parameters in the revision of the DEC (2014) recommended practices is that the practices are broadly applicable across all early childhood sectors and can be implemented in inclusive settings and natural environments (DEC, 2015), thus contributing not only to the PD of the EI/ECSE workforce but also providing important practice guidance to the broader ECE field. In addition, OSEP has supported the development of PD resources focused on inclusion (e.g., The Center to Mobilize Early Childhood Knowledge, also known as the CONNECT Project) for which one of the primary beneficiaries has been the ECE workforce (Buysse, Winton, Rous, Epstein, & Lim, 2012; Winton, Buysse, Rous, Lim, & Epstein, 2013). The adage "a rising tide lifts all boats" is apt in describing these investments in the quality of the broader ECE workforce as part of the effort of improving the likelihood that young children with disabilities receive high-quality services and supports in natural environments and inclusive settings.

These five factors have defined how the field of EI/ECSE has evolved. It now consists of an interdisciplinary mix of professional disciplines, with a strong values base for family partnerships, collaboration, and inclusion. Undergirding the field is a solid body of research on intervention and teaching strategies for individualizing practice to meet the unique needs of young children with disabilities. In addition, the EI/ECSE workforce has benefited from a legacy of federal support for preparation, professional development, technical assistance, and product development. The EI/ECSE workforce has much to offer the broader ECE workforce in terms of these strengths.

CHALLENGES RELATED TO THE EARLY INTERVENTION/ EARLY CHILDHOOD SPECIAL EDUCATION WORKFORCE

Despite a strong history, the EI/ECSE workforce faces interrelated challenges. Some of these challenges ironically co-exist as strengths, signifying areas where work in the past both informs and provides a platform for future efforts in the area of professional development.

Ongoing Fragmentation

The fragmentation challenges mentioned in the introduction of this chapter are decades long and have proven difficult to eliminate. The tapestry of programs that support young children age birth to 5 years originated at different points in time under different auspices with different primary missions that addressed emerging national and federal priorities salient at the time. For instance, the Part C early intervention and 619 preschool programs funded by OSEP were designed to improve the lives of young children with disabilities (0–5 years) and their families. The primary focus of Head Start and Early Head Start has historically been young children living in poverty and their families; child care programs emerged as an industry devoted to helping parents of young children with employment needs and demands.

All of these programs have the shared mission of providing overall support to young children and their families. There are numerous examples of ways in which programs within these different sectors collaborate and leverage resources. For example, in 1972, Head Start became the first major public early childhood program providing services to young preschool children in inclusive settings through a legislative mandate that required 10% of total enrolled children to be identified as having a disability.

There is, however, much more work to be done to address the lost opportunities for collaboration because of turf and tradition, especially with regard to delivering professional development and workforce support. For example, Head Start disability coordinators report that one of the biggest challenges they face in serving children with identified or suspected disabilities is collaboration with their local education agencies (Winton & Lim, 2017). Specific problems included referrals not being addressed in a timely manner and children not getting services for which they qualify. The bottom line is families of young children (0–5 years) who need EI/ECSE services, family support, and child care as a comprehensive package do not necessarily care about the intricacies of funding streams and the complications of different sets of standards. They want and deserve a seamless set of services and support that are predictable and consistently of high quality.

Early Intervention/Early Childhood Special Education Leadership in Early Care and Education Systems-Building

A challenge related to fragmentation is how EI/ECSE workforce issues can best be addressed within the broader early childhood systems building efforts, which began under federal initiatives such as the Race to the Top–Early Learning Challenge and Preschool Development and Expansion grants to states. The recognition of the importance of the early years and the accompanying expansion of publicly supported early childhood programs (Epstein & Barnett, 2012; Kagan & Kauerz, 2012) have the potential to benefit young children with disabilities in many ways. The increasing number of public preschool programs potentially could provide more inclusive options for the growing number of children who are eligible for services under IDEA (Zablotsky, Black, & Blumberg, 2017). The strengthening of training requirements for early childhood teachers as part of the overall early childhood systems-building efforts provides an impetus for teachers to obtain degrees and for PD opportunities that could build the capacity of the workforce for meeting the needs of all children in inclusive settings.

Although data on the overall impact of improving the quality of pre-K programs are promising (National Institute for Early Education Research, 2017), there is little information about the extent to which these federal and state initiatives directly addressed the needs of the workforce to improve quality for children with disabilities and their families. A survey of the

42 states with a Quality Rating and Improvement System (Horowitz & Squires, 2014) indicated that only a few states have made direct efforts to address quality improvements for children with disabilities. This is not surprising given an analysis of the 35 Race to the Top-Early Learning Challenge state applications (Stoney, 2012), in which children with disabilities were not mentioned anywhere in the report. These data call into question the extent to which Part C, Section 619, Parent Training and Information Centers, EI/ECSE faculty, and EI/ECSE PD and technical assistance leaders are involved in state systems-building efforts. If the strengths of the EI/ECSE workforce and PD infrastructure are not integrated into early childhood systems-building efforts, individuals making decisions about budget allocations and policies are likely to overlook the needs of children with disabilities. This integration requires leaders with a deep understanding of their own sector's strengths, as well as an appreciation for the strengths of other sectors and challenges to integrating the sectors (e.g., Head Start and Early Head Start, Part C, Section 619, child care, pre-K) that fall under the broad umbrella of early childhood education.

Lack of Agreed-Upon National Professional Development Guidance

Although the DEC (2014) recommended practices have been described in this chapter as a valuable resource for the broad field of ECE, one cannot assume that these practices are known and valued by early childhood sectors outside of EI/ECSE in spite of DEC's efforts to make them widely available and free for download. As has been stated previously and reported on in more detail in other publications (Bruder, 2016; Goffin, 2015; Winton & West, 2011), one of the challenges for the broad field of early childhood is the absence of agreed-upon national personnel standards and competences for the early childhood workforce.

Winton and West (2011) identified the many challenges in changing the status quo. Early childhood teachers work in a variety of settings and, depending upon the type of setting, they are likely to have different requirements for the level of education, competency expectations, and wages and compensation. Different national early childhood organizations (e.g., NAEYC, DEC) have developed standards and related competencies; these standards and competencies are not aligned across organizations, with evidence-based practice, or with demographic changes in the early childhood populations being served.

States are taking varied approaches to developing state competencies, certifications, and licensures for EI/ECSE and ECE staff, rather than following national standards, with requirements varying from state to state. There are no agreed-upon measures to assess teacher competencies or practices. In addition to the lack of national standards and practice guidance, there are different sets of child outcome frameworks used by different sectors. For instance, to document progress in addressing child and family outcomes under OSEP's Results-Driven Accountability (Vinh, Lucas, Taylor, Kelley, &

Kasprzak, 2014), EI/ECSE uses an outcomes framework provided by OSEP (Early Childhood Technical Assistance Center, 2016). In contrast Head Start/ Early Head Start staff use the Head Start Early Learning Outcomes Framework (Office of Head Start, 2010) and the Head Start Parent, Family & Community Engagement Outcome Framework (Office of Head Start, 2011). There are also competing PD frameworks across sectors. EI/ECSE use a framework developed by the Early Childhood Technical Assistance Center (Early Childhood Technical Assistance Center, 2015), whereas general early childhood sectors (e.g., child care, Head Start/Early Head Start) often look to a framework developed by the Professional Development Workforce Center (2014) to guide their PD planning. The lack of agreed-upon frameworks, standards, competencies, and practice guidance for early childhood PD is a barrier that has been difficult to breach.

The Status of Professional Development Research and the Gap Between Research and Practice

Two additional workforce challenges are related to the rigor of the research on effective preparation and the gap between what we know about effective PD and the reality of PD delivery. The research on effective preservice preparation for the EI/ECSE workforce is characterized by survey research and a large number of descriptive studies of single IHE programs or courses (Bruder, 2016; Hyson et al., 2012). There is little rigorous experimental research on preservice training, thus making it difficult to identify the essential features of effective preparation programs (Hyson et al., 2012).

There is a more rigorous and growing body of research on the effective approaches for delivering job-embedded PD to EI/ECSE and ECE practitioners if the PD goal is to enhance early childhood teachers' abilities to implement research-based practices with fidelity (e.g., Hemmeter, Snyder, Fox, & Algina, 2016; Snyder, Hemmeter, & Fox, 2015; Snyder et al., 2017). In fact, in 2016, the National Center on Special Education Research (2018) of the Institute for Education Science limited the focus of their request for research proposals to research on professional development. At this writing, there were 28 research projects under the category "Professional Development for Teachers and School-Based Service Providers."

The literature on professional development in EI/ECSE has been reviewed in other publications (Bruder, 2016; Diamond, Justice, Siegler, & Snyder, 2013; Dunst, 2015; Snyder, Hemmeter & McLaughlin, 2011; Winton et al., 2016) and suggests that effective approaches include some essential features. Practices that are the focus of the PD need to be explicitly defined and demonstrated. Practitioners should have multiple job-embedded opportunities over time to learn and implement the practices with explicit feedback on their performance. In addition, improvements in practitioners' implementation of practices should be monitored over time to document intended outcomes for children and families.

Unfortunately, what we know about effective PD delivery is not the norm for how PD for the EI/ECSE workforce is delivered (Bruder, Mogro-Wilson, Stayton, & Dietrich, 2009). National survey data from the state agencies with responsibilities for supporting the EI/ECSE workforce indicate that workshops are the predominate approach to PD (Bruder et al., 2009). This is the case even though it is commonly accepted that workshops by themselves are not likely to be effective in increasing practitioners' use of recommended practices consistently and with fidelity. In fact, additional survey data reported by Bruder (2016) indicate that state Part C and Part B (619) coordinators have concerns about the number of specialists available who have the needed professional development in working with infants, toddlers, and preschoolers with disabilities. This suggests that simply having a degree, which is often a proxy for quality, does not guarantee competency in working with young children with disabilities.

Uneven Quality of Professional Development Providers

A corollary challenge is the unknown qualifications and characteristics of those coaches, mentors, supervisors, technical assistance providers, and trainers with responsibilities for providing the PD and support to the early childhood workforce (Winton et al., 2016). Their titles vary and they work under different agency auspices (e.g., Head Start, state pre-K, early intervention), even though they are likely to intersect in some of the same local early childhood programs, especially those serving children with disabilities in inclusive settings. It is generally assumed that effective coaches have knowledge and skills related to early childhood, as well as knowledge and skills in adult learning and effective PD delivery approaches. However, there are no agreed-upon competencies, licensure, or certification requirements and often little systematic PD to support their learning and growth in their roles. In addition, the absence of systematic attention across agencies to the distribution of PD providers, such as coaches, in relationship to the need for their services has the potential to create duplications of effort as well as gaps in terms of those who receive their services.

In summarizing the strengths and challenges of the EI/ECSE workforce and the PD to support it, a few points are worthy of note. The legacy of applied intervention research and accompanying practice guidelines have contributed to a culture of practicality and an emphasis on a practice-focused approach to preparation and ongoing support for the workforce. However, without agreed-upon competencies, practice standards, tools, and strategies for measuring teachers' application of practices with fidelity and without shared outcome frameworks to measure whether the practices were effective at achieving desired goals, it is difficult to determine if professional development is effective. The interdisciplinary origins of EI/ECSE and the focus on inclusion and family partnerships have provided richness and diversity to the workforce. However, the diversity is accompanied by challenges brought about by the lingering fiefdoms of early childhood sectors whose boundaries are difficult to soften.

EMERGING AND PROMISING EFFORTS
TO ADDRESS WORKFORCE CHALLENGES

Despite the challenges previously noted, there are emerging and promising efforts addressing the fragmentation of efforts and implementation of research-based approaches to PD.

Federal Cross-Sector Collaboration
on Professional Development Guidance

Several federal efforts hold promise for providing cross-sector national PD guidance for state and local communities, thus addressing the fragmentation of PD support for the workforce. In recognition that there are certain key topics that are best addressed through cross-sector systems-building efforts, the U.S. Department of Health and Human Services and the U.S. Department of Education (2015, 2017) have collaboratively developed and issued joint policy statements on inclusion and family engagement. The statements include a recommendation for jointly sponsored and implemented cross-sector PD to ensure that resources are leveraged and used efficiently and that issues related to collaboration and partnership are fully explored from multiple perspectives. In addition, the Office of Head Start within the Department of Health and Human Services has reaffirmed the ongoing commitment to serving children with disabilities in collaboration with local agencies through their guidance to local Head Start and Early Head Start programs. The Head Start Program Performance Standards (Office of Head Start, 2016) clarified the 2007 Head Start Act in strengthening the linkages between Head Start/Early Head Start and state and local Part B (preschool) and Part C (infant and toddler) programs. The standards maintain requirements for programs to coordinate and collaborate with local agencies responsible for implementing IDEA services to ensure appropriate referral, evaluation, service delivery, and transition. To maximize collaboration, the Head Start Program Performance Standards require interagency agreements with local education agencies and Part C agencies that specify points of intersection and collaboration. The standards also require coordinated approaches to both PD and disabilities, thus encouraging local Head Start/Early Head Start to coordinate with local EI/ECSE programs and professionals. The emphasis within EI/ECSE on competences and practices related to collaboration and teaming, as described previously, mean that the EI/ECSE workforce has a potential leadership role in building stronger partnerships with Head Start/Early Head Start programs, especially in response to the challenges to collaboration with local education agencies identified by Head Start Disability Coordinators.

National Professional Organization
Collaboration on Professional Development Guidance

Another promising direction focuses on activities jointly supported by early childhood professional organizations that represent different membership constituencies. A seminal event was the development by DEC and NAEYC (2009) of a joint position statement on inclusion, which provided an agreed-upon definition, desired outcomes, and essential features of early childhood inclusion. The joint position statement on inclusion, coupled with the Joint Policy Statement on Inclusion (U.S. Department of Health and Human Services & U.S. Department of Education, 2015), has provided the broad early childhood field with a unified vision, mission, and recommendations for implementing early childhood inclusion and undergirds collaborative activities across ECE and EI/ECSE in support of young children with disabilities. One of the essential features of high-quality inclusion identified in the joint position statement on inclusion was the importance of professional development.

In addition to the joint position statement on inclusion, DEC and NAEYC are collaborating with 13 other national early childhood organizations in a foundation-funded initiative entitled Power to the Profession, which builds upon the work of leading scholars (Goffin & Washington, 2007) and the recommendations from the National Academy of Science report *Transforming the Workforce for Children Birth through Age 8: A Unifying Foundation* (Institute of Medicine & National Research Council, 2015). In recognition that a central challenge for the field of ECE is its lack of unity, the purpose of the initiative is to harness the collective energies of the various early childhood professional membership organizations to create a unified early childhood profession with an accepted set of core components. These include a shared purpose, a common identity, unifying frameworks, and agreement on the unique responsibilities, characteristics, and ethics of their members (NAEYC, n.d.).

The initiative is ongoing and organized into a set of eight interactive decision cycles. In its current cycle, the initiative is using a rigorous and systematic process involving experts and validation from the field to develop an agreed-upon set of national personnel standards and competencies that define the expectations of the workforce, which is an essential feature of any profession (Goffin, 2015). These standards and competencies will provide a foundation for preparation, support, accreditation, and licensing to replace the multiple state and national standards that currently exist. The Power to the Profession initiative has promise for raising the quality of the workforce and increasing the public's recognition that supporting the development of young children requires qualified and well-compensated professionals equal to that of educators and specialists working with older children and adults. Because the process is inclusive of all sectors, it could be transformative in terms of acknowledging the unique role, contributions, and strengths of the EI/ECSE sector to the overall quality of the workforce. In future cycles, it is hoped that some of the additional fragmentation challenges, such as developing competencies and standards for the burgeoning number of individuals serving in the important role of PD providers and workforce supporters (e.g., trainers, coaches, mentors, supervisors), will be addressed, as well as the challenges of multiple frameworks for outcomes and PD planning.

Solutions to the Research-to-Practice Gap

As stated previously, emerging research has identified that if the desired outcome of PD is implementation of practices with fidelity in work settings, then more complex experiential strategies are essential features of high-quality PD. This research (Hemmeter et al., 2016; Snyder et al., 2015; Snyder et al., 2017) is shaping the emergence of job-embedded models of professional development, such as practice-based coaching, to support implementation of practices shown to be effective in supporting the development and learning of young children with disabilities. For instance, the Head Start Program Performance Standards (Office of Head Start, 2016) require that all Head Start/Early Head Start programs must implement a research-based coaching strategy that includes observation and feedback/modeling to support education staff in effective teaching practices. In recognition that not all education staff can receive intensive coaching, it is recommended that those not being coached receive other forms of research-based PD. Although programs can use any research-based coaching strategy they choose, the Office of Head Start has invested in practice-based coaching for several years and has free resources available.

For those planning and funding PD, it is important to consider how the coaching strategy to PD being supported by the Office of Head Start aligns with state and federal coaching strategies being supported by IDEA-funded programs. The issue of some inclusive early childhood programs having multiple coaches providing support to teachers and children and other programs having none is highly possible in the context of the fragmentation issues that plague the field. In addition, PD interventions such as coaching are expensive to develop, sustain, and scale up to the extent that they reach a large number of early childhood programs. Coaching and other intensive approaches need to be developed and delivered as part of an integrated continuum of research-based PD that addresses the individual learning needs and desired outcomes for learners being sought, from simple awareness levels to more intense implementation of practices in job settings (Winton et al., 2016).

FUTURE DIRECTIONS

The strengths of EI/ECSE are numerous. They include a highly qualified EI/ECSE workforce guided by a set of research-based, field-validated recommended practices and possessing values and skills for building partnerships and collaborating with others in inclusive settings. In addition, the power of family voices to advocate for change is part of the legacy that EI/ECSE can offer the broader ECE field in order to influence the public, who, in turn, are likely to influence those with the power, money, and authority to fund initiatives and programs that lead to positive changes benefiting young children with disabilities and their families. The EI/ECSE workforce is well positioned to play a leadership role in a new unified early childhood profession.

The Chinese symbol for change (consisting of two characters: one for opportunity, the other for risk) is an apt expression for the current climate for young children with disabilities and their families and the EI/ECSE workforce that support them. Bipartisan federal and state support for early education, which grew at an unprecedented pace over the last decade, may continue. Within that overall expansion, there is promise that the support available to the growing number of young children with identified disabilities will continue to expand in terms of options and quality; the EI/ECSE workforce who implement IDEA services will be supported in their growth and development as valued professionals; and EI/ECSE leaders will be in the forefront of early childhood systems-building efforts. Building on recommendations from Winton et al. (2016), what follows are suggestions to EI/ECSE leaders for making this promising situation become reality.

Advocate for and Conduct Rigorous Research on Effective Professional Development Strategies

The research on effective PD approaches and the impact that research is having on policy is an important step in improving the quality of PD available to the workforce; however, there is more work to be done to understand and implement promising PD approaches like practice-based coaching and how this strategy logically builds on less intensive research-based PD strategies. As noted, the Institute of Education Sciences is currently making strides in that area. A number of future research questions are important for planning and funding PD (Winton et al., 2016). Should practice-based coaching focus on a large set of practices, such as those that comprise the child-focused DEC recommended practices in the areas of environmental, interaction, and instruction, or should the focus be on a small number of domain-specific practices? What levels of coaching intensity are needed for practitioners to implement practices over time with fidelity? Is there a threshold for coaching intensity beyond which practice improvements are small and not worthy of the investment? What are the criteria for choosing which teachers have the greatest need for coaching? What are the strategies for evaluating practice-based coaching as part of an effective continuum of research-based PD? With the growing role of technology in PD delivery, what are the most effective ways to use technology to build awareness, knowledge, skills, and application of practices in job-embedded settings?

Seek Support and Professional Development to Develop Knowledge and Skills of Early Intervention/Early Childhood Special Education Leaders

A question for the current EI/ECSE leadership is how to utilize the strengths of EI/ECSE (e.g., the culture of collaboration and skills of teamwork, the power of family voices, the tools and products focused on research-based inclusive practices) to support the early childhood systems-building efforts in ways that also recognize and align them with the strengths and contributions of other early childhood sectors. EI/ECSE leaders will need support to acknowledge, appreciate, and lead inclusive efforts to integrate the best of each of the early childhood sectors into a coherent whole, in which individual and unique contributions are maintained and aligned for efficiency and effectiveness. They may draw such support from lessons learned through implementation science (Fixsen, Naoom, Blasé, Friedman, & Wallace, 2005; Metz & Bartley, 2012). This includes distributing leadership across a team of leaders, which include those with technical skills for managing daily operations and details and those with adaptive skills for leading groups in strategic thinking and problem solving. It requires leaders with skills in planning and gaining support for dedicated local and state implementation teams communicating regularly, efficiently, and clearly horizontally across sectors and vertically from local to state levels, as well as collecting and using data to inform progress in practice implementation. It requires a long-term commitment of time across a number of years to reach full implementation of a set of practices. Politicians often operate within the context of short-term fixes and funding cycles with little interest in long-term investments or in issues such as children with disabilities that affect a small proportion of their voting constituents.

Adopt and Promote the Development of a Comprehensive and Unified Professional Development Framework

One of the challenges to PD systems building is the somewhat fragmented approach that is taken, whereby different sectors rely on different frameworks to plan PD. In their proposal for a unified PD framework, Winton et al. (2016) expanded on an earlier framework (Hyson et al., 2012) that could provide a starting point for developing a unified comprehensive framework embraced by all sectors. In this framework, the starting point is the desired child and family outcomes that are the focus of PD, and its centerpiece is agreed-upon practices with the strongest evidence for achieving those outcomes. The PD delivery methods reflect research on a continuum of effective PD strategies inclusive of both in-service and preservice contexts and the individualized needs of learners within those contexts. Heeding the lessons from the science of implementation that bringing about improvements at the level of practice change requires more than professional development (Fixsen et al., 2005; Metz & Bartley, 2012), the framework acknowledges the importance of infrastructure supports (e.g., policies, data systems, resources), which in the case of the broad field of ECE means understanding and integrating different sets of policies, data systems, and resources. A simplified version of the framework is included in the position statement on personnel standards in early childhood special education from the DEC (2017).

A unified framework for PD that acknowledges the importance of a continuum of research-based PD delivery based upon the needs of individual learners and situated within the context of needed infrastructure support makes sense and has been proposed in the literature over decades (McCollum & Catlett, 1997; Winton et al., 2016). Yet, the deeply entrenched current early childhood PD systems—each one with its own funding stream, standards for practice, accreditation and licensing structure, and target audience—has made an integrated "common-sense" approach to PD infrastructure and delivery difficult to achieve. Initiatives such as the Power to the Profession, if successful, are important for developing some of the building blocks for an integrated PD system. However, it will take a concerted national and federal effort committed over time to build a unified PD system for the early childhood profession, to generate support for continued efforts to conduct research on PD interventions, and to ensure that research-based PD interventions are widely available to support the workforce. The ultimate beneficiaries of such a PD system are the children with disabilities and their families who depend upon competent, confident practitioners with whom to work in partnership in inclusive settings and natural environments to ensure the best possible outcomes for their children and themselves.

REFERENCES

Bailey Jr, D. B., Palsha, S. A., & Huntington, G. S. (1990). Preservice preparation of special educators to serve infants with handicaps and their families: Current status and training needs. *Journal of Early Intervention, 14,* 43–54.

Brotherson, M. J., Summers, J. A., Bruns, D. A., & Sharp, L. M. (2007). Family-centered practices: Working in partnership with families. In P. J. Winton, J. A. McCollum, & C. Catlett (Eds.), *Practical approaches to early childhood professional development: Evidence, strategies, and resources* (pp. 53–80). Washington, DC: Zero To Three.

Bruder, M. B. (2016). Personnel development practices in early childhood intervention. In B. Reichow, B. Boyd, E. Barton, & S. Odom (Eds.), *Handbook of early childhood special education* (pp. 289–333). New York, NY: Springer.

Bruder, M. B., Mogro-Wilson, C. M., Stayton, V. D., & Dietrich, S. L. (2009). The national status of in-service professional development systems for early intervention and early childhood special education practitioners. *Infants and Young Children, 22,* 13–20.

Buysse, V., Winton, P. J., Rous, B., Epstein, D., & Lim, C.-I. (2012). Evidence-based practice: Foundation for the CONNECT 5-step learning cycle™ in professional development. *Zero to Three, 32*(4), 25–29.

Campbell, F., Conti, G., Heckman, J. J., Moon, S. H., Pinto, R., Pungello, E., et al. (2014). Early childhood investments substantially boost adult health. *Science, 343*(6178), 1478–1485.

Capone, A., Hull, K. M., & DiVenere, N. J. (1997). Parent-professional partnership in preservice and inservice education. In P. J. Winton, J. A. McCollum, & C. Catlett (Eds.), *Reforming personnel preparation in early intervention: Issues, models, and practical strategies* (pp. 435–452). Baltimore, MD: Paul H. Brookes Publishing Co.

Chang, F., Early, D., & Winton, P. (2005). Early childhood teacher preparation in special education at 2- and 4-year institutions of higher education. *Journal of Early Intervention, 27,* 110–124.

Crais, E. R. (1991). *A practical guide to embedding family-centered content into existing speech-language pathology coursework.* Chapel Hill, NC: Carolina Institute for Research on Infant Personnel Preparation, Frank Porter Graham Child Development Center, University of North Carolina.

Diamond, K. E., Justice, L. M., Siegler, R. S., & Snyder, P. A. (2013). *Synthesis of IES research on early intervention and early childhood education (NCSER 2013–3001).* Washington, DC: U.S. Department of Education, Institute of Education Sciences, National Center for Special Education Research. Retrieved from http://ies.ed.gov/ncser/pubs/20133001/pdf/20133001.pdf

Division for Early Childhood. (2014). *DEC recommended practices in early intervention/early childhood special education.* Retrieved from http://www.dec-sped.org/recommendedpractices

Division for Early Childhood. (2015). *DEC recommended practices: Enhancing services for young children with disabilities and their families* (DEC Recommended Practices Monograph Series No. 1). Los Angeles, CA: Author.

Division for Early Childhood. (2017). *Personnel standards in early childhood special education.* Retrieved from http://www.dec-sped.org/position-statements

Division for Early Childhood and the National Association for the Education of Young Children. (2009). *Early childhood inclusion: A joint position statement of the Division for Early Childhood (DEC) and the National Association for the Education of Young Children (NAEYC).* Chapel Hill, NC: Frank Porter Graham Child Development Institute, The University of North Carolina.

Dunst, C. (2015). Improving the design and implementation of in-service professional development in early childhood intervention. *Infants and Young Children, 29,* 210–219.

Dunst, C. J., & Espe-Sherwindt, M. (2016). Family-centered practices in early childhood intervention. In B. Reichow, B. Boyd, E. Barton, & S. Odom (Eds.), *Handbook of early childhood special education* (pp. 37–55). New York, NY: Springer.

Early Childhood Technical Assistance Center. (2015). *System framework for Part C & Section 619: Personnel/workforce.* Chapel Hill, NC. Author. Retrieved from http://ectacenter.org/sysframe/component-personnel.asp

Early Childhood Technical Assistance Center. (2016, July). *Outcomes for children served through IDEA's early childhood programs: 2014-15.* Retrieved from http://ectacenter.org/eco/assets/pdfs/childoutcomeshighlights.pdf

Early, D. M., & Winton, P. J. (2001). Preparing the workforce: Early childhood teacher preparation at 2- and 4-year institutions of higher education. *Early Childhood Research Quarterly, 16,* 285–306.

Education of the Handicapped Act Amendments of 1986, PL 99-457, 20 U.S.C. §§ 1400 *et seq.*

Epstein, D. J., & Barnett, W. S. (2012). Early education in the United States: Programs and access. In R. Pianta, L. Justice, S. Barnett, & S. Sheridan (Eds.), *Handbook of early childhood education* (pp. 3–21). New York, NY: Guilford Press.

Fixsen, D. L., Naoom, S. F., Blase, K. A., Friedman, R. M., & Wallace, F. (2005). *Implementation research: A synthesis of the literature.* Tampa, FL: University of South Florida, Louis de la Parte Florida Mental Health Institute, The National Implementation Research Network. Retrieved from http://www.fpg.unc.edu/~nirn/resources/detail.cfm?resourceID=31

Gallagher, J. J. (2000). The beginnings of federal help for young children with disabilities. *Topics in Early Childhood Special Education, 20*(1), 3–6.

Goffin, S. (2015). *Professionalizing early childhood education as a field of practice: A guide to the next era.* New York, NY: Teachers College Press.

Goffin, S. G., & Washington, V. (2007). *Ready or not: Leadership choices in early care and education.* New York, NY: Teachers College Press.

Grisham-Brown, J., & Hemmeter, M. L. (2017). *Blended practices for teaching young children in inclusive settings.* Baltimore, MD: Paul H. Brookes Publishing Co.

Guillen, C., & Winton, P. (2015). Teaming and collaboration: Thinking about how as well as what. In *DEC recommended practices: Enhancing services for young children with disabilities and their families* (pp. 99–108). Los Angeles, CA: Division for Early Childhood.

Hamre, B. K., Downer, J. T., Jamil, F. M., & Pianta, R. C. (2012). Enhancing teachers' intentional use of effective interactions with children: Designing and testing professional development interventions. In R. Pianta, L. Justice, S. Barnett, & S. Sheridan (Eds.), *Handbook of early childhood education* (pp. 3–21). New York, NY: Guilford Press.

Hanft, B., Burke, J., Cahill, M., Swenson-Miller, K., & Humphry, R. (1992). *Working with families: A curriculum guide for pediatric occupational therapists.* Chapel Hill, NC: Frank Porter Graham Child Development Institute, University of North Carolina.

Hemmeter, M. L., Snyder, P. A., Fox, L., & Algina, J. (2016). Evaluating the implementation of the Pyramid Model for promoting social-emotional competence in early childhood classrooms. *Topics in Early Childhood Special Education, 36,* 133–146.

Horowitz, M., & Squires, J. (2014). *QRIS and inclusion: Do state QRIS standards support the learning needs of all children?* New Brunswick, NJ: Center on Enhancing Early Learning Outcomes. Retrieved from http://ceelo.org/wp-content/uploads/2014/11/ceelo_fast_fact_qris_inclusion.pdf

Hyson, M., Horm, D. M., & Winton, P. J. (2012). Higher education for early childhood educators and outcomes for young children: Pathways toward greater effectiveness. In R. Pianta, L. Justice, S. Barnett, & S. Sheridan (Eds.), *Handbook of early childhood education* (pp. 553–583). New York, NY: Guilford Press.

Hyson, M. & Winton, P. (2017). Forward. In J. Grisham-Brown & M. L. Hemmeter (Eds.), *Blended practices for teaching young children in inclusive settings* (2nd ed). Baltimore, MD: Paul H. Brookes Publishing Co.

Individuals with Disabilities Education Improvement Act (IDEA) of 2004, PL 108-446, 20 U.S.C. §§ 1400 *et seq.*

Institute of Medicine & National Research Council. (2015). *Transforming the workforce for children birth through age 8: A unifying foundation.* Washington, DC: National Academies Press.

Kagan, S. L., & Kauerz, K. (Eds.). (2012). *Early childhood systems: Transforming early learning.* New York, NY: Teachers College Press.

Kavulic, M. (2017). *From pilot to permanent: A case study of the institutionalization of a grant-funded transition program for individuals with intellectual disabilities in a public research institution in the midwest of the United States* (Doctoral dissertation). Retrieved from https://etd.ohiolink.edu/!etd.send_file?accession=kent1491735132473102&disposition=inline

Kilgo, J. L., & Bruder, M. B. (1997). Creating new visions in institutions of higher education: Interdisciplinary approaches to personnel preparation in early interveion. In P. Winton, J. McCollum, & C. Catlett (Eds.), *Reforming personnel preparation in early intervention: Issues, models, and practical strategies* (pp. 81–102). Baltimore, MD: Paul H. Brookes Publishing Co.

Martinez-Beck, I., & Zaslow, M. (2006). Introduction: The context for critical issues in early childhood professional development. In M. Zaslow & I. Martinez-Beck (Eds.), *Critical issues in early childhood professional development* (pp. 1–16). Baltimore, MD: Paul H. Brookes Publishing Co.

Maxwell, K., Lim, C.-I., & Early, D. M. (2006). *Early childhood teacher preparation programs in the United States: National report.* Chapel Hill, NC: University of North Carolina, Frank Porter Graham Child Development Institute. Retrieved from http://fpg.unc.edu/sites/fpg.unc.edu/files/resources/reports-and-policy-briefs/NPC_National_Report_2006.pdf

McCollum, J. A., & Catlett, C. (1997). Designing effective personnel preparation for early intervention: Theoretical frameworks. In P. Winton, J. McCollum, & C. Catlett (Eds.), *Reforming personnel preparation in early intervention: Issues, models, and practical strategies* (pp. 105–126). Baltimore, MD: Paul H. Brookes Publishing Co.

McLean, M., Sandall, S., & Smith, B. (2016). A history of early childhood special education. In B. Reichow, B. Boyd, E. Barton, & S. Odom (Eds.), *Handbook of early childhood special education* (pp. 3–20). New York, NY: Springer.

Metz, A., & Bartley, L. (2012). Active implementation frameworks for program success: How to use implementation science to improve outcomes for children. *Zero to Three, 32*(4), 11–18.

Miller, P. S. (1992). Segregated programs of teacher education in early childhood: Immoral and inefficient practice. *Topics in Early Childhood Special Education, 11*(4), 39–52.

National Association for the Education of Young Children (NAEYC). (n.d.). *Overview: Power to the profession.* Retrived from https://www.naeyc.org/our-work/initiatives/profession/overview

National Center on Child Care Professional Development Workforce Center. (2014). *Strengthening the early childhood and school-age workforce: A tool to improve workplace conditions, compensation, and access to professional development.* Washington, DC: Author. Retrieved from https://childcareta.acf.hhs.gov/sites/default/files/public/strengtheningworkforce_tool.pdf

National Center on Special Education Research. (2018). *Search funded opportunities and grants: Professional development.* Washington, DC: Institute of Education Sciences. Retrieved from https://ies.ed.gov/funding/grantsearch/index.asp

National Institute for Early Education Research. (2017). *The state of preschool 2016: State preschool yearbook.* New Brunswick, NJ: National Institute for Early Education Research. Retrieved from http://nieer.org/wp-content/uploads/2017/05/YB2016_StateofPreschool2.pdf

National Professional Development Center on Autism Spectrum Disorder. (n.d.). *AFIRM: Autism focused intervention resources and modules.* Chapel Hill, NC: The University of North Carolina, Frank Porter Graham Child Development Institute. Retrieved from http://autismpdc.fpg.unc.edu/npdc-resources

National Research Council. (2000). *How people learn: Brain, mind, experience, and school: Expanded edition.* Washington, DC: National Academies Press.

Odom, S., & McLean, M. (1996). *Early intervention/early childhood special education: Recommended practices.* Austin, TX: Pro-Ed.

Odom, S. L., Vitztum, J., Wolery, R., Lieber, J., Sandall, S., Hanson, M. J., et al. (2004). Preschool inclusion in the United States: A review of research from an ecological systems perspective. *Journal of Research in Special Educational Needs, 4*(1), 17–49.

Office of Head Start. (2010). *The Head Start child development and early learning framework: Promoting positive outcomes in programs serving children 3–5 years old.* Washington, DC: Author. Retrieved from https://eclkc.ohs.acf.hhs.gov

Office of Head Start. (2011). *The Head Start parent, family and community outcomes framework: Promoting family engagement and school readiness, from prenatal to age 8.* Washington, DC: Author. Retrieved from https://eclkc.ohs.acf.hhs.gov/pdguide/media/resource_files/PFCEFramework.pdf

Office of Head Start. (2016). *Head Start program performance standards (HSPPS).* Washington, DC: Author. Retrieved from http://eclkc.ohs.acf.hhs.gov/hslc/hs/docs/hspss-final.pdf

Ray, A., Bowman, B., & Robbins, J. (2006). *Preparing early childhood teachers to successfully educate all children: The contribution of four-year undergraduate teacher preparation programs. Final report to the Foundation for Child Development.* Retrieved from http://www.erikson.edu/wp-content/uploads/Teachered.pdf

Sexton, D., Snyder, P., Lobman, A. S., Kimbrough, P. M., & Matthews, K. (1997). A team-based model to improve early intervention programs: Linking preservice and inservice. In P. Winton, J. McCollum, & C. Catlett (Eds.), *Reforming personnel preparation in early intervention: Issues, models, and practical strategies* (pp. 495–526). Baltimore, MD: Paul H. Brookes Publishing Co.

Snyder, P. A., Hemmeter, M. L., & Fox, L. (2015). Supporting implementation of evidence-based practices through practice-based coaching. *Topics in Early Childhood Special Education, 35,* 133–143.

Snyder, P., Hemmeter, M. L., & McLaughlin, T. (2011). Professional development in early childhood intervention: Where we stand on the silver anniversary of PL 99-457. *Journal of Early Intervention, 33*(4), 357–370.

Snyder, P., Hemmeter, M. L., McLean, M., Sandall, S., McLaughlin, T., & Algina, J. (2017). Effects of professional development on preschool teachers' use of embedded instruction practices. *Exceptional Children, 84,* 213–232.

Sparling, J. W. (1992). *A guide to embedding family information in an entry-level physical therapy curriculum.* Chapel Hill, NC: Carolina Institute for Research on Infant Personnel Preparation, Frank Porter Graham Child Development Center, University of North Carolina at Chapel Hill.

Stoney, L. (2012, February). *Unlocking the potential of QRIS: Trends and opportunities in the Race to the Top–Early Learning Challenge applications.* Retrieved from http://ow.ly/jYEFs

Trohanis, P. L. (2008). Progress in providing services to young children with special needs and their families: An overview to and update on the implementation of the Individuals with Disabilities Education Act (IDEA). *Journal of Early Intervention, 30,* 140–151.

Turnbull, A., Turnbull, R., Erwin, E. J., & Soodak, L. C. (2006). *Families, professionals and exceptionality: Positive outcomes through partnership and trust* (5th ed.). Upper Saddle River, New Jersey: Pearson/Merrill/Prentice Hall.

U.S. Department of Education. (2012). *31st annual report to Congress on the implementation of Individuals with Disabilities Education Act, 2009.* Alexandria, VA: Author.

U.S. Department of Education. (2018). *Office of Special Education Programs discretionary grants database.* Retrieved from https://publicddb.osepideasthatwork.org

U.S. Department of Health and Human Services & U.S. Department of Education. (2015). *Policy statement on inclusion of children with disabilities in early childhood programs.* Retrieved from http://www2.ed.gov/policy/speced/guid/earlylearning/joint-statement-full-text.pdf

U.S. Department of Health and Human Services & U.S. Department of Education. (2017). *Policy statement on family engagement from the early years to the early grades.* Retrieved from https://www.acf.hhs.gov/ecd/family-engagement

Vinh, M., Lucas, A., Taylor, C., Kelley, G., & Kasprzak, C. (2014, August). *SSIP phase I roadmap.* Retrieved from http://ectacenter.org/~pdfs/calls/2014/ssip/ SSIP_Phase_I_Roadmap_081914.pdf

Winton, P. (1992). *Working with families in early intervention: An interdisciplinary preservice curriculum* (2nd ed.). Chapel Hill, NC: Carolina Institute for Research on Infant Personnel Preparation, Frank Porter Graham Research Center.

Winton, P., Buysse, V., Rous, B., Lim, C., & Epstein, D. (2013). CONNECTing evidence-based practice and teacher research: Resources for early childhood faculty and instructors. *Voices of Practitioners, 8*(2), 1–7.

Winton, P. J., & DiVenere, N. (1995). Family-professional partnerships in early intervention personnel preparation: Guidelines and strategies. *Topics in Early Childhood Special Education, 15*(3), 296–313.

Winton, P., & Lim, C.-L. (2017, December). *Issues and strategies for Head Start/LEA collaboration.* Presentation at the Head Start Region II Disability Institute. New Brunswick, NJ.

Winton, P. J., Snyder, P., & Goffin, S. G. (2016). Beyond the status quo: Rethinking professional development for early childhood teachers. In L. Couse & S. Recchia (Eds.), *Handbook of early childhood teacher education* (pp. 54–68). New York, NY: Routledge.

Winton, P. J., & West, T. (2011). Early childhood competencies: Sitting on the shelf or guiding professional development? In C. Howes & R. Pianta (Eds.), *Foundations for teaching excellence: Connecting early childhood quality rating, professional development, and competency systems in states* (pp. 69–92). Baltimore, MD: Paul H. Brookes Publishing Co.

Zablotsky, B., Black, L. I., & Blumberg, S. J. (2017). *Estimated prevalence of children with diagnosed developmental disabilities in the United States, 2014–2016. NCHS Data Brief, 291,* 1-7. Hyattsville, MD: National Center for Health Statistics.

13

Disability Law and Policy

Core Concepts and the Ethical Principles of Family, Dignity, and Community

Rud Turnbull

In this chapter, I describe and analyze disability policy related to young children and their families who are affected by disabilities. I also prescribe and advocate research on how (if at all) policy and practice do and should confer dignity on young children and their families. This chapter will challenge readers who are not well versed in public policy because it deals with policy in rather granular detail, then introduces concepts and analytical frameworks that organize and explain policy. Accordingly, and contrary to the customary third-person voice, I write in the first-person. I believe that if I address you, the reader, as if we were conversing with each other in a seminar, I may be able to explain policies and their meanings more clearly.

I organized this chapter into eight major topics. The first two parts of the chapter are descriptive. I begin by commenting on the role of families and professionals, especially the Kennedy family and the professionals at the Frank Porter Graham Institute (FPG). This section of the chapter gives a brief nod to history. In the second part of the chapter, I identify six major strands of federal policy. Here, I organize the policies according to the general areas of child and family development that federal policy intends to support.

The next four parts of the chapter are analytical. In the third part of the chapter, I describe the core concepts expressed in those policies and the relationship of the concepts to the strands. Here, I move from description to analysis, where the analysis describes the essence of the policies. In the fourth part, I organize the core concepts according to the overarching constitutional, ethical, and administrative principles they express. Here, I move away from a rather narrow analysis, from what each policy has at its core to how each belongs to a much larger taxonomy. In the fifth part, I discuss law as a form of behavior modification and social engineering. Here, I remind the reader exactly what the law, as a tool for organizing society, seeks to do, for that understanding of the essential purpose of law clarifies the policies and the several ways in which I have analyzed and organized them. In the sixth part, I describe law and its role in advancing the ethical principles of community and dignity. Here, I move from one level of analysis to a more encompassing level of analysis.

Having been descriptive (first and second parts) and then analytical (third through sixth parts), I come to the seventh part. Here, I propose a research initiative related to dignity. Finally, I close by referring to Jay Turnbull (1967–2009). Jay was our son—Ann's and mine. He had an intellectual disability, rapid-cycling bipolar disorder, and autism. He was our best professor, for he taught us—and now through him I teach you—about policy, community, and dignity.

In this chapter, I am as concerned with describing policy as I am with arguing that law alone—policy alone—is a necessary but insufficient foundation for the present and future of those children and their families. To respond to that insufficiency, I propose that disability policy, especially as it affects young children with disabilities and their families, is a fertile field for research and practice about dignity.

FAMILIES, PASSIONATE INSIDERS, AND THE FRANK PORTER GRAHAM INSTITUTE

Let us begin with a bit of history, for history enlivens the descriptions and analyses that follow. Indisputably, much of contemporary federal policy has its origins in a single family—that of President John F. Kennedy. Early in his short term in office and influenced greatly by the fact that his sister Rosemary had what was then called "mental retardation," he established the President's Panel on Mental Retardation in 1961. The panel's mandate was to identify what was known about, and what must be done in, three major areas. Those areas were science, practice, and policy, as each affects the health, education, general welfare, and rights of people with intellectual disabilities and their families. The foundations of the many federal laws that I describe in this chapter originated in two eras—first, in the enactment and expansion of the Social Security program that Congress authorized during President Franklin D. Roosevelt's early term in office (it should not pass without noting that he himself had a physical disability) and, second, in President Kennedy's New Frontier programs and then President Lyndon Johnson's Great Society initiatives. Indeed, the Social Security Act, enacted in 1935 in President Roosevelt's first term in office, has been the "home" of many of the Kennedy-Johnson programs to benefit young children and their families. Also, many of the laws that postdate the Kennedy-Johnson eras reflect the legal and ethical precepts that those disability-sensitive presidents—Roosevelt, Kennedy, and Johnson—brought to bear.

It should not be forgotten that passionate insiders—people with disabilities, family members of people with disabilities, leaders in organizations whose missions included educating and persuading policy makers, and professionals who were in key federal government roles—were, like the Kennedys, vital advocates for federal policy (Turnbull & Turnbull, 1996; Turnbull, Shogren, & Turnbull, 2011). Of the many who were "insiders," two were associated with FPG: Jim Gallagher and Barbara Smith.

Before becoming FPG's director, Dr. Gallagher served as the director of federal special education services. That was an insider role, if there ever was one. Dr. Gallagher had a deep understanding of the challenges families face when they have a child with special needs, as well as the challenges the children themselves face. Based on this understanding, he proposed the concept of an individualized education program for children with disabilities. Congress adopted that idea when it enacted the federal special education law, the Education for All Handicapped Children Act of 1975 (PL 94-142), requiring state and local education agencies to develop an individualized education program for every student of school age and, later under the title of the Individuals with Disabilities Education Act (IDEA) of 2004 (PL 108-446), an individualized family services plan for infants and toddlers.

Dr. Smith had been a special education teacher before becoming one of Dr. Gallagher's doctoral students and student research assistant at FPG. She soon became a member and then a leader within the Council for Exceptional Children. In that role, she was a leading advocate for IDEA's infant-and-toddler provisions and a ferocious scholar-advocate who knew what had to be done and never relented in her advocacy for Congress to enact Part C (early childhood) rights.

Two passionate FGP insiders carried on the Kennedy legacy and, together with other insiders, advanced the Kennedy initiatives in early education in ways that the Kennedy family could not have anticipated but that it certainly would have applauded. The power of knowledge grows when combined with the power to change policy.

SIX STRANDS OF FEDERAL POLICY

Having briefly described some of the history of the policies, I now describe the general fields of research and practice, related to human development, that policies have supported. I characterize these fields as "strands," where that word refers to the elements (of policy) that are interwoven to create a complex whole (Mish, 1990). This part of the chapter is descriptive, too.

There are six strands of federal policy related to young children and their families who are affected by disabilities. Some of the policies in these strands affect only those children and families; accordingly, they are specialized and exceptional. Other policies affect all children and families; accordingly, they are generic and universal.

Health

When did Congress first concern itself with young children with disabilities and their families? Trohanis (2008), the first director of the national technical assistance network in early education and disabilities at FPG, asserted that the federal role began when Congress enacted the Social Security Act of 1935 (PL 74-271). He is undoubtedly correct because Congress amended the statute with the Social Security Amendments of 1965 (PL 89-97) to provide for Medicare (for elderly people), Medicaid (for children and adults with disabilities), and Maternal and Child Health (prevention and treatment for mothers and their children). In 1967, Congress again amended the Social Security Act (PL 90-48) to authorize a program of Early and Periodic Screening, Diagnosis, and Treatment of childhood disabilities. Other important health-related policies include the following (with dates of enactment or most recent reauthorizations):

- Balanced Budget Act of 1997 (PL 105-33), which created the State Child Health Insurance Program (SCHIP), authorizing federal support for low-income children through primary and preventive care; the statutory authority for SCHIP is under Title XXI of the Social Security Act

- The Child Health Act of 1967, which was Title III of the Social Security Act Amendments of 1967 (PL 90-48), provided integrated treatment for children with co-occurring conditions

- The Children's Health Act of 2000 (PL 106-310), which authorized research and programs in the field of developmental disabilities

- The Mental Health Parity Act of 1996 (PL 104-204), which required employers to cover mental health treatment as much as they cover physical health treatment

- The Patient Protection and Affordable Care Act (PL 111-148; commonly known as "Obamacare") of 2010, amended by the Tax Reform and Jobs Act of 2017 (PL 115-97), which further ensured families and young children with disabilities have access to federally assisted health care

Education

In 1963, Congress enacted the Mental Retardation Facilities and Community Mental Health Centers Construction Act (PL 88-164), which created federally assisted research and training centers, including FPG. Two years later, Congress enacted the Elementary and Secondary Education Act of 1965 (PL 89-10), authorizing federal assistance to state and local education agencies. In the same year, it also amended Title I of that Act, authorizing federal assistance to state-operated schools and programs for children with disabilities (PL 89-313).

The Elementary and Secondary Education Act (amended in 2015 by the Every Student Succeeds Act, PL 114-95) soon became for education what the Social Security Act was for health care. Congress amended it to create the Handicapped Children's Early Education Act of 1968 (PL 90-538) and soon thereafter to create the Handicapped Children's Early Education Program of 1970 (PL 91-230). These programs authorized federal assistance for research, model and demonstration programs, and training.

In response to federal court decisions requiring the education of all handicapped children, Congress enacted the Education of the Handicapped Act Amendments of 1974 (PL 93-380), followed by the truly frontier-busting Education for All Handicapped Children Act of 1975 (PL 94-142). That law now has a new name, IDEA, and was reauthorized most recently in 2004 (PL 108-446).

Although not strictly an education law (because it addresses children's health and has family-engagement components), Head Start was enacted in 1965 during President Johnson's administration to serve children ages 3 to 5. Since 1972, it has set aside a 10% quota to serve children with disabilities. In 1994, Early Head Start was funded to serve children from birth to age 3 years with the same 10% inclusive provision (42 U.S.C. Secs. 9837(a) and 9840).

Four other strands of policy also relate to young children generally and to those with disabilities particularly. I list the major federal statutes related to each. Many of these statutes also authorize federal funding so that states may plan and develop statewide systems of service. For example, that is precisely the purpose of the Developmental Disabilities Assistance and Bill of Rights Act Amendments of 2000 (PL 106-402).

Child Welfare

Important policies that benefit children and their families include the following:

- Head Start and Early Head Start not only provide education services as noted previously, but also provide federal assistance to state and local programs for health and family engagement. Together, these two programs address needs for children from birth to age 5 years.

- The Child Abuse Prevention and Treatment Act of 1974 (PL 93-247) and the Child Abuse Prevention, Adoption and Family Services Act of 1988 (PL 100-294) use federal funding to protect children, especially those born with disabling anomalies, against abuse, including in health care facilities.

- The Adoption Assistance and Child Welfare Act of 1980 (PL 96-272) and its major amendments, the Adoption and Safe Families Act of 1997

(PL 105-89), the Foster Care Independence Act of 1999 (PL 106-169), and the Promoting Safe and Stable Families Act Amendments of 2001 (PL 107-133) collectively provide federal assistance to state and local child welfare agencies.

- The Children's and Communities' Mental Health Systems Improvement Act of 1991 provided for grants to public and private agencies to provide individualized community-based mental health and wraparound services for children and their families.

- Title XX of the Social Services Amendments of 1974 (PL 93-647) provided federal assistance for state and local social service programs to prevent institutionalization and support families.

Family Support

Policies that provide cash assistance to families in poverty who have children or adult members with disabilities:

- Title XIX of the Social Security Amendments of 1965 authorized federal assistance through Medicaid to support families to keep their members at home and avoid institutionalization through home-and-community based programs.

- Supplemental Security Income, another Social Security program, provides direct financial support to families and individuals with disabilities who meet federal poverty standards.

Antidiscrimination

Policies that prohibit discrimination based solely on the fact that the person has, has a record of, or is regarded as having a disability include the following:

- IDEA (see previous, under "Education") protects against discrimination in education and grants all children with disabilities the right to a free appropriate public education.

- Section 504 of the Rehabilitation Act of 1973 (PL 93-112) prohibits discrimination in federally assisted programs.

- The Americans with Disabilities Act (ADA) of 1990 (PL 101-336) prohibits discrimination by private and public entities.

- The Fair Housing Act of 1968 (Title VIII of the Civil Rights Act of 1968, PL 90-284) prohibits discrimination in housing.

Technology

The following policy aims to increase, augment, or prevent declines in a person's functions:

- The Technology-Related Assistance for Individuals with Disabilities Act of 1988 (PL 100-407) assisted states with developing technology-related assistance and extended the availability of that technology to individuals with disabilities and their families.

CORE CONCEPTS OF DISABILITY POLICIES

In the introduction to this chapter, I stated that these various policies can be understood through two perspectives: their history and their purpose to support people with disabilities and their families. History and purpose are the foundations for analysis. In this section, I begin the first of several analyses of the policies. The first analysis reveals the core concepts of the policies. What are the core concepts of policy, and why should we be concerned with them? To answer the question, it is necessary to begin by defining "concept" and "core."

The word *concept* means "something conceived in the mind"; it is "an abstract or generic idea generalized from specific instances" (Mish, 1990). The word *core* refers to that which is a "central and often foundational" part of another thing (Mish, 1990). Thus, a core concept is a foundational part of disability policy. Why should we be concerned with them? Because they are the indicators by which we know whether policy has been, is, or will be well justified. If former, present, or future policy does not conform in one way or another with one or more of the core concepts, then an individual should be most skeptical about the wisdom of that nonconforming policy, it may well be deviant and not stand the test of history, past and future.

To identify, define, and exemplify the core concepts of disability policy, my colleagues and I analyzed all major disability-related federal statutes, all decisions of the U.S. Supreme Court, and all precedent-setting decisions of other federal courts (Turnbull, Beegle, & Stowe, 2001). Altogether, we analyzed more than 80 such statutes and decisions. We then conducted focus groups and interviews with federal, state, and local policy experts. These were the people involved in making policy in Congress and state legislatures; implementing it in federal, state, and local executive branches; and benefiting from it individually or as leaders of family or professional associations. Collectively, these individuals represented both federal and state perspectives across two branches of government and perspectives of the advocacy and "consumer" communities. In addition, we conducted interviews with 24 family, legislative, administrative, or professional association staff members who had expertise on federal policy. We also interviewed 20 disability policy researchers via focus groups or individual interviews, 47 individuals having a state-local perspective in two different states, and 17 health-policy experts. In all, 108 individuals complemented our analyses of statutes and case law.

Significantly, the statutes and case law affected individuals and their families without respect to age (newborns through adulthood), nature of disability (physical, sensory, intellectual, and emotional/behavioral), extent of disability (requiring only minimal support to extensive, life-preserving support), and place of life (home, community, hospital, or institutional residence). Of particular importance for this chapter, our research included policies directly affecting newborns, infants and toddlers, young children, and their families.

I have continued to analyze policy according to the core concepts. No federal statute or decision by the Supreme Court gives me reason to delete from or add to the list of core concepts. That is not to say that some statutes or decisions conform more or less perfectly with one or more of the core concepts.

Defining the Core Concepts

The following list briefly defines each of the 18 core concepts:

- *Antidiscrimination:* The right not to experience discrimination and the right to participate (which are negative and positive rights, respectively)

- *Individualized and appropriate services:* Supports tailored to meet a person's specific needs, memorialized by individual service/support plans

- *Classification:* The determination of eligibility—who gets what, why, and under what criteria and procedures

- *Capacity-based services:* Supports that build on a person's capacities, even as they ameliorate the person's needs

- *Autonomy:* The right of the person to make choices about one's life

- *Empowerment and participatory decision making:* The right of the person to effectively participate in deciding what supports to receive and how they are delivered

- *Service coordination and collaboration:* Intra-agency and interagency activity to ensure individualized and capacity-based services and to ensure accountability

- *Protection from harm:* The right of the person to freedom from abuse, neglect, exploitation, or other danger while in state custody or under state supervision

- *Liberty:* The right of the person to physical freedom from restraint, custody, or confinement

- *Privacy and confidentiality:* The right of the person to a zone/area of private action and to confidentiality of personally identifiable oral and written information

- *Integration:* The right to be in a community and activities of the person's choice

- *Productivity and contribution:* A person's genuine opportunity to income-producing or otherwise contributory work and participation in employment or other activity

- *Family integration and unity:* Preservation of the nuclear or extended family

- *Family-centeredness:* Services and supports that target the person and the family collectively and the family explicitly

- *Cultural responsivity:* Services and supports that deliberately take into account a person's or family's ethnicity, race, language, and cultural and spiritual values

- *Accountability:* Fiscal, legal, programmatic/professional, and electoral accountability for predetermined outcomes

- *Professional and system capacity development:* The creation, maintenance, and expansion of individual and agency professional capacities to implement assigned duties

- *Prevention and amelioration:* Primary, secondary, and tertiary interventions with respect to a person's disabilities

A reader of this chapter may be tempted to regard each core concept as distinct from and not directly or even indirectly related to any other core concept. The reader would be wrong to understand the core concepts that way. They overlap. For example, the core concept of *antidiscrimination* connects to the core concept of *integration;* when a person experiences discrimination, the person is apt to be excluded from participating in a program or place. Conversely, protection from discrimination enhances integration. Likewise, the core concept of *integration* makes it possible for a person to enjoy the consequences of yet another core concept, namely, *productivity and contribution.* Similarly, the core concept of *autonomy* (the freedom and capacity to choose) is a form of the core concept of *liberty;* it is also the precursor of the core concept of *empowerment and participatory decision making.*

Connecting the Core Concepts to Six Strands of Policy: Discovering Six Themes Related to the Nature of Purpose of Policies

Given that the core concepts are both separate from, yet overlap, each other, how might both their separateness and overlapping be understood? It is by finding what each concept has in common with the other concepts. What they have in common is that they express six themes. Just as the policies themselves are interwoven strands of research and practice related to human development, so what they express are themes, where "themes" refers to specific and distinctive qualities, characteristics, or concerns (Mish, 1990). (I ask the reader to excuse me for mixing two different metaphors of strands and themes; these mixed metaphors do, however, have this advantage: They are distinct from each other and they help me explain my analyses.)

The themes describe the policies according to the essential nature and purpose of each—namely, to support individuals and their families with respect to their health, education, and child welfare, and with respect to their needs for family support, antidiscrimination, and technology. Herein, I italicized the core concepts so that they may be more easily identified.

These are the themes about who gets what, why, and under what criteria for eligibility:

- *Antidiscrimination:* Prohibitions of discrimination based solely on disability; Section 504 and the ADA

- *Classification:* Establishing eligibility criteria for rights or entitlements; all health and child welfare programs

These are the themes about the roles of the person and providers:

- *Individualization and appropriate services:* Specially tailored interventions to meet education and health needs; IDEA, Head Start and Early Head Start [Improving Head Start for School Readiness Act of 2007; PL 110-134], Children's and Communities Mental Health Systems Improvement Act, Child Health Act, and Early Periodic Screening, Detection, and Treatment

- *Capacity-based services:* Interventions that acknowledge and build on strengths of a recipient of service; IDEA, Head Start, and Early Head Start

- *Empowerment and participatory decision making:* Opportunities and rights of a person affected by a policy or program to decide whether and how to participate under a policy or in a program; IDEA, Developmental Disabilities Act, Supplemental Security Income, and Title XIX (Medicaid home and community-based services)

- *Service coordination and collaboration:* Intra-agency and interagency activities; Developmental Disabilities Act, Technology-Related Assistance for Individuals with Disabilities Act of 1988, Child Health Act, and Children's and Communities' Mental Health Systems Improvement Act

These are the themes about a person's freedom—issues about "negative liberty/freedom from":

- *Protection from harm while in state custody:* Safeguards of one's health; Child Abuse Prevention and Treatment Act

- *Liberty and protection from confinement:* Safeguards against unwarranted confinement: ADA, Section 504 of the Rehabilitation Act

- *Autonomy:* Freedom to choose; Title XIX (Medicaid home and community-based services) (positive liberty)

- *Privacy and confidentiality:* Freedom to control information about oneself; Family Educational Rights and Privacy Act of 1974 (PL 93-380), Affordable Care Act (positive liberty)

Theme about a person's opportunities—"positive liberty" and "freedom from":

- *Integration:* Presence in places and programs; ADA, IDEA

- *Productivity and contribution:* The roles one may play for one's own sake or for others' sakes

Theme about the effect of disability on families:

- *Family integration and unity:* Maintaining an intact family; Adoption and Safe Families Act

- *Family centeredness:* Services that benefit a family; Part C (early education) of IDEA

- *Cultural responsiveness:* Services that take into account a person's or family's theological, philosophical, cultural, linguistic, or other traits; Part C of IDEA

Theme about service systems:

- *Accountability:* Legal, financial, and professional-programmatic techniques to ensure that services are provided as intended; Developmental Disabilities Assistance and Bill of Rights Act

- *Professional and system capacity-development:* Assurances that professionals and the systems they operate do the jobs they are intended to do; IDEA Part B (children ages 3–5 years) and Part C (infants, birth through age 2 years)

- *Prevention and amelioration:* The worth and efficacy of services themselves; Child Abuse Prevention and Treatment Act

In this section, I have defined the core concepts of disability policy. I then connected those core concepts to the six strands of policy that I described in the previous section. Finally, I identified the themes that the policies and strands share. These three analyses—core concepts, connecting strands, and common themes—are complex; they demand that a reader hold several similar but different analyses in mind, all at one time. Is there a way to simplify that task and, simultaneously, enrich these analyses? Yes, there is, as I describe in the next section.

ORGANIZING THE CORE CONCEPTS
ACCORDING TO THEIR OVERARCHING PRINCIPLES

I began this chapter by describing briefly the history of policy. I then described the major strands of policy. Next, I moved from description to analysis and argued that there are core concepts and common themes to the policies. In this section, I enlarge that analysis.

Believing that these core concepts can be understood collectively as expressing certain overarching principles, two of us (Turnbull & Stowe, 2001a) then organized these 18 core concepts into three overarching principles, each of which has three components. The first two principles—the constitutional and ethical principles—prescribe "what" to do; the third principle, administrative, prescribes "how" to accomplish the "what." After each of the three principles, I list some of the core concepts related to that principle. The principles and their related core concepts are as follows:

- Constitutional principles
  - Life
  - Liberty
  - Equality
- Ethical principles
  - Dignity
  - Family as foundation
  - Community
- Administrative principles
  - Capacity
  - Individualization
  - Accountability

All statutes and decisions of courts must conform to, or at least not be inconsistent with, constitutional doctrine and principles. Relying on that fundamental precept of law, my colleague and I organized the core concepts according to the three constitutional principles that emerged from our analyses:

These are the constitutional principles and related core concepts:

- Life (sanctity and quality of life): The core concepts include *antidiscrimination, prevention,* and *protection from harm.*

- Liberty (physical and psychological): The core concepts include *autonomy, empowerment and participatory decision making,* and *privacy and confidentiality.*

- Equality (equal opportunity): The core concepts include *anti-discrimination, integration,* and *productivity and contribution.*

Constitutional principles alone do not fully suffice as a taxonomy for the core concepts. That is so because constitutional principles can be understood to express mores and norms—really, ethical principles—that are embedded in our country's ethos, in our collective sense of what is right and wrong as we consider how to respond to people and families affected by disability. Therefore, my colleague and I organized the core concepts according to what seemed to us to be the three ethical principles that are both coherent with the constitutional principles and expressed in discourse about disability policy.

The ethical principles and related core concepts:

- Dignity (inherent value): The core concepts include *autonomy* and *empowerment and participatory decision making.*

- Family as foundation (family as the core unit of society): The core concepts include *family unity and integrity, family centeredness,* and *cultural responsiveness.*

- Community (physical presence and sense of belonging): The core concepts include *anti-discrimination, integration,* and *productivity and contribution.*

The constitutional and ethical principles express what policy should seek; they are aspirational, hortatory, and idealistic. They express what kinds of people we collectively want to be and how we want policy to nurture us to be those kinds of people. They do not, however, tell us what structures we should create to ensure that we realize our ideals through our service delivery systems. The "structures"—who does what with/for/to whom, when, where, and how—are expressed by three administrative principles and their related core concepts.

The administrative principles and related core concepts:

- Capacity (personal and system capacity): The core concepts related to personal capacity include *autonomy* and *participatory decision making and empowerment,* and the core concepts related to system capacity include *coordination and collaboration* and *professional and system capacity development.*

- Individualization (specially designed services): The core concepts include *individualized appropriate services* and *person capacity development.*

- Accountability (legal, programmatic, and fiscal): The core concepts include *coordination and collaboration* and *accountability.*

These core concepts and three overarching principles have not changed since our work in 2001. I have tracked federal statutes and Supreme Court case law for the last 18 years and concluded that these give no reason to amend, add to, or delete from the list of core concepts or to change the overarching principles. If anything, amendments to Individuals with Disabilities Education Act in 1997 and 2004 strengthen such core concepts as *autonomy, integration/inclusion* (the doctrine of the "natural environment" and "least restrictive environment"), and *protection from harm* through positive behavioral supports.

Further, Congress's comprehensive health care law (Patient Protection and Affordable Care Act, "Obamacare"), even as amended (weakened) by the Tax Cuts and Jobs Act of 2017 (PL 115-97), reflects the core concept of *anti-discrimination* (protection against discrimination because of preexisting health conditions). The Court's decisions interpreting the concept of *protec-*

tion from harm by prohibiting capital punishment of individuals with intellectual disability (*Atkins v. Virginia*, 2002; *Moore v. Texas*, 2017) and the concept of *individualized and appropriate services* by interpreting IDEA's principle of appropriate education (*Endrew F. v. Douglas County School District RE-1*, 2017) underscore the "coreness" of those concepts. *Endrew F.* does more than strengthen the IDEA principle of appropriate education; when read to find whether there is an ethical basis for the decision, one discovers that the case proclaims that an appropriate education—one that ensures academic progress—dignifies a student (Turnbull, Turnbull, & Cooper, 2018). Dignity is an ethical overarching principle.

LAW AS BEHAVIOR MODIFICATION AND SOCIAL ENGINEERING: ADVANCING THE ETHICAL PRINCIPLES OF COMMUNITY AND DIGNITY

In the introduction to this chapter, I wrote that, having described history and the six strands of the policies, I would then analyze them according to their core concepts and their overarching principles. I have just completed those two analyses. I also wrote that, next, I would explain how law and policy affect individuals and families affected by disability and why they do so. Here, I intend to clarify the "how" and "why" of law and policy—the means ("how") and purposes ("why") of law and policy. Simply analyzing law and policy is not enough. What must then occur is to connect the analysis to the lives of people and families affected by disability.

Law as a Means: How Law Consists of Behavior Modification and Social Engineering

Law is a type of behavior modification. It modifies the behavior of government with the governed, declaring rights and duties and boundaries of permissible and impermissible action—government-to-person behavior. It also modifies the behavior of the governed with each other—person-to-person behaviors. Thus, for example, various federal laws prohibit discrimination based solely on disability (ADA), thereby ensuring inclusion of persons with disabilities in education (IDEA of 2004) and their communities of choice (*Olmstead v. L.C.*, 1999). Other law safeguards the governed from harm while in state custody (*Youngberg v. Romeo*, 1982). Still other law compels the state to offer individually beneficial services for children and adults and their families and to provide means to make the services accountable (Adoption Assistance and Child Welfare Act of 1980; Child Health Act of 1967; Child Abuse Prevention and Treatment Reform Act of 1978 [PL 95-266]; Children's and Communities Mental Health Systems Improvement Act of 1991; Early Periodic Screening, Diagnosis, and Treatment [Medicaid, 1967]; Promoting Safe and Stable Families Program [2001]).

Law is also a type of social engineering (Pound, 1933). It engineers (creates the structures for and arranges) the relationships people have with each other in their private lives and that they have with their governments in their lives as citizens. It declares rights and duties; it sets the boundaries of acceptable and unacceptable behavior.

Thus, law declares, for example, that *autonomy*—the freedom to choose one's relationships with others (*Loving v. Virginia*, 1967, striking down a state's antimiscegenation statute that prohibited interracial marriage; *Lawrence v. Texas*, 2003, striking down a state's sodomy statute; *Obergefell v. Hodges*, 2015, upholding a state's law permitting same-sex marriage) or over one's life (*Washington v. Glucksburg*, 1997, sustaining a state's prohibition of assisted suicide; and *Vacco v. Quill*, 1997, permitting a state to distinguish between assisted suicide by prohibiting it and the right to refuse lifesaving medical intervention by allowing a person to make that choice)—is a "freedom to" (a positive liberty) that government is justified in preserving. Similarly, *privacy and confidentiality* (Family Educational Rights and Privacy Act of 1974) is a "freedom to" (positive liberty) that is worth preserving.

Law as a Means: How Law Advances the Ethical Principle of Community

It is one thing to describe law as a means of shaping our relationships with our governments and with each other. It is quite another to explain how and why law's behavior-shaping role is important in order for us to understand disability policy. To help us understand that, I briefly review the recent history of disability law and then I offer two theories to explain the law.

History The American civil rights revolution began with the Supreme Court's holding in *Brown v. Board of Education* (1954) that discrimination in education based solely on race violates the equal protection guarantee of the 14th Amendment. That holding was the doctrinal basis for the Court's later holdings, relying also on the 14th Amendment, that limit the following:

- The power of parents to institutionalize their children with disabilities (*Parham v. J.R.*, 1979)

- The power of the local governments to exclude people with disabilities from residential zones (*City of Cleburne v. Cleburne Living Center*, 1985)

- The power of state governments to prevent people with disabilities from living in communities (*Olmstead v. L.C.*, 1999)

Just as race was a constitutionally impermissible basis for state segregation, so too was disability. Trait—unchangeable and unchosen trait—does not justify discrimination and segregation. Two theories explain why law, as a means, makes a difference for individuals with disabilities and their families—why law matters.

The "Why" of Law Having explained how law works (the law as means), I now state three reasons why the law works as it does.

1. *The Theory of Compelled Confrontation.* These cases and their complementary statutes—IDEA of 2004, Section 504 of the Rehabilitation Act of 1973, and ADA—compelled those of different abilities (and often different races) to confront each other in schools. The purpose of the compelled confrontation was and still is to permit those who differ from others in intrinsically unchangeable ways to discover what, if anything, they have in common with each other (Burt, 1995). Compelled confrontation becomes, then, a way not only to find interpersonal commonalities but also thereby to discover how one may be "in community with" a person in a certain place and status. *Antidiscrimination* law fosters *integration* and integration comes to mean inclusion in education and in other dimensions of life in our communities.

2. *The Theory of Distinctions and Differences.* The theory of compelled confrontation was not the only construct that prompted a discourse about inclusion and integration. Another theory did likewise. That theory asks whether the distinctions that differentiate some of us from others do or should make a difference and, if so, what kind and how great a difference (Minow, 1990). Granted, an ordinary function of law is to draw distinctions for various purposes (e.g., who is guilty in criminal law, who is liable in civil law). However, it is that very act of drawing distinctions that tends to separate us from one another, to make us blind to what we have in common with each other, and to impede our opportunities, perhaps even our desires, to be in community with each other.

3. *Leading Us Toward Each Other.* My argument here is that the core concepts of *disability policy*—especially antidiscrimination and integration—are utterly consistent with the theories of compelled confrontation and distinctions without a difference. The core concepts of *antidiscrimination* and *inclusion* lead us toward each other. They bring us into common places and relationships with each other. They give us insight into how we can be in community with each other, how we can and should confront our differences, and how we can and should acknowledge but then disregard our differences in order to celebrate our common traits and desires.

These core concepts are more than legal and constitutional in nature. They also are the foundations for the overarching ethical principles of community and dignity. *Antidiscrimination* promotes community; *inclusion* offers an avenue for finding the dignity in each other. Indeed, these two core concepts and the two principles of dignity and community ask us to try to see others as being more like than unlike ourselves. We cannot do that unless we are compelled to come face to face with each other and to acknowledge that we ascribe distinctions and practice separation where similarity and community might otherwise obtain (Minow, 1990).

The law eschews discrimination; it favors integration and inclusion; it seeks the common ground and places where distinctions do not make a difference. It becomes thereby an engine for cultural reformation. It reveals itself as a form of behavior modification, as a technique of social engineering. Furthermore, it has powerful roles to play related to the dignity—or lack of dignity—that those without disabilities ascribe to those with disabilities. What is more, as members of communities ascribe dignity to a person and family or as they stigmatize the person and family as not being worthy of dignity, the members of these communities create, or fail to create, ethical communities.

LAW AS ADVANCING DIGNITY AND CREATING ETHICAL COMMUNITIES: REFORMNG OUR CULTURE

I have just briefly explained sophisticated analyses of how law modifies our behavior and engineers our movement toward each other. Why do these analyses and theories matter? The answers appear if we ask more pointed questions: How do they apply particularly to young children with disabilities and their families? How do they especially apply in publicly supported infant and toddler programs (IDEA, Part C, Sections 1431 *et seq.*), in early education (IDEA, Part B, Sections 1419 *et seq.*), and in elementary, middle, and secondary school programs (for children with disabilities ages 6–21 years, IDEA Part B, Sections 1400 *et seq.*)? If we can answer those pointed questions, we then can answer the broader question: Why do the analyses and theories of compelled confrontation and differences/similarities matter? The short answer is that they matter because they affect individuals and communities alike. They do so (or do not do so) by dignifying people with disabilities and their families, by creating ethical communities, and by reforming our culture.

Infants and Toddlers, Students, and Their Environments: Their Communities

To begin to answer these questions about ascribed dignity and ethical communities, it is appropriate to use infants and toddlers and their service programs as examples. To that end, I begin with the laws and policies affecting them, starting with IDEA.

Part C declares that services for the infant and toddler and family are to be delivered in the child's natural environment (20 U.S.C. Secs. 1436(d) (4)). It defines the natural environment as consisting of two different places: 1) the child's home and 2) community settings in which children without disabilities participate (20 U.S.C. Sec. 1432(4)(G)). That second environment is a place where many programs for the child and family occur. However, it is more than that: It is a place of inclusion and integration, a community unto itself, a small community within the larger community of the entities and programs that constitute inclusive education. Those learning communities are, of course, embedded within much larger communities—villages, towns, cities, and states that constitute our America.

What happens in the "natural environment" of infants and toddlers, in the preschool programs for young children, in the elementary through secondary programs of our country's schools? Note that this question extends beyond the environments of infants and toddlers. It expands to all education environments. By further extension, the question includes all environments in which adults with and without disabilities interact, or might interact, with each other. My focus, now, goes from the particular to the general, from the early years of one's life to all subsequent years.

Early Education: Two Kinds of "Learning"

With respect to infants and toddlers and then older children, learning is a consequence of education. IDEA identifies the learning for infants and toddlers as that which develops their physical, cognitive, communication, social-emotional, and adaptive capacities (20 U.S.C. Sec. 1432(4)(C)). IDEA identifies learning for older children as that which fosters their cognitive, emotional/behavioral, functional, and development capacities (20 U.S.C. Sec. 1414(a)–(d)) and enables them to make progress (augment these capacities) in and as a result of being in school (*Endrew v. Douglas County RE-1*, 2017).

Still another kind of learning occurs, however. It is learning about each other; it is education about how we differ from but also are like each other (Turnbull, Brotherson, Czyzewski, Esquith, & Otis, 1983). In that kind of learning, we are taught, and teach each other, whether to assign value to those who differ from us by reason of disability; whether to esteem them for what they can do and struggle to do; and whether to value them not just for their valor, but also and especially for their inherent dignity of being— simply being—among us, of being included with us, of being integrated into our lives and learning environments.

Knowing, Valuing, and Dignifying

Let me put it a different way, and to make my point not just as it relates to schools but to all environments: Compelled to confront each other, and integrated so we may find what distinguishes us from and connects us to each other, we begin to learn how to value each other. That act of valuing has profound implications for those of us who have or will have, or are regarded or will be regarded as having, a disability.

Both IDEA (civil rights and education law) and ADA (purely civil rights law) introduce that concept of value when they declare that disability is a natural consequence of the human condition that in no way diminishes a person's rights. Consider the meaning of the phrase "natural consequence." It means that disability is natural, normal, not aberrant, and not abhorrent; it is not, as a matter of law, a reason for shunning, devaluing, and, consequently, discriminating. Here, IDEA and ADA make a statement about the human condition in context—in the context of education and other public domains of American life.

The statement favors confrontation—not a hostile facing-off against each other, but at least a benign act of looking at each other and discovering what makes us different from and yet also like each other. This act of confrontation allows us to declare commonality, not difference; it enables us to abjure discrimination; and, implicitly, it calls us to value the person who has (or who we may regard as having) a disability. That calling, that beckoning to our sense of decency, proclaims that those of us who have a disability are worthy in and of ourselves to be in schools and in public places, with those of us who do not now and may never have a disability. That calling esteems those of us with disabilities; it dignifies us by respecting us for who we are, not for what we might do with education and accommodations or for what we might become with services and supports. Less able does not mean less worthy (Turnbull, 1976). In other words, "natural consequence" points us toward communities where dignity is not just apparent, but advanced. Whether schools or other public environments, these communities are—or, more accurately, should be—places that dignify those of us who cannot do all that others can do without support and accommodations.

Am I being utopian? Yes, there are reasons to believe that. Am I denying the dystopian aspects of our schools and communities? Yes, also. However, consider this: The integration mandates of IDEA and ADA—the inclusive education and the natural and least restrictive environments that both require—are not just about education in the sense of developing a child's cognitive, emotional/behavioral, functional, and developmental talents. They are about ascribing value to those with disabilities, shaping the personhood of those students, recognizing that disability is in large part a social construct, and then amending the construct so that "natural consequence" flows easily into "welcomed into." They are about changing the culture of our schools and communities.

THE DIGNITY PROJECT

If my analyses of the core concepts, overarching principles, means (law as behavior analysis and social engineering) and ends (community and dignity) are sound, then it is appropriate to propose action. I propose action that I call "the dignity project."

Federal policy, as enacted in statutes, and constitutional doctrine and federal statutes, as interpreted by the Supreme Court, specify who has what duties to other people. The "who/duty/other" specifications are expressed by the core concepts and their three overarching principles. One of the ethical principles is dignity. I now turn my attention to that principle and to its relationship with children and families affected by disability. Here, I state my central thesis—namely, that dignity demands our attention as we carry out research and create and implement policy.

Researching Dignity

Our schools, where confrontation is compelled and distinctions are nominally relegated to not making a difference, can indeed be places where educators deliberately advance dignity and community, especially when they apply positive behavioral supports (Turnbull & Turnbull, 2001; Turnbull, 2017). My concern is whether the larger research community of which the Frank Porter Graham Child Development Institute is a part has sufficiently concerned itself with the concepts of dignity and community as they exist, do not exist, and should exist in our schools. In our intensive efforts to improve school accountability for outcomes, have we lost sight of other functions of education—namely, that education is (or can be) the means for conferring dignity on those with disabilities and for creating sites of learning that are also ethical communities and places where dignity and commonality are found, advanced, and celebrated? Perhaps, but perhaps not.

Doing Enough?

Surely in the field of special education and disability policy and services, researchers have done magnificently in investigating, developing, and applying positive behavioral supports in lieu of punishments; of teaching self-determination instead of creating learned helplessness; and of strengthening cognitive and behavioral capacities so that secondary education leads to equal postsecondary opportunities, including full participation, independent living, and economic self-sufficiency, which are the bedrocks of our national disability policy (IDEA Sec. 1400; ADA).

Have we done enough? Have we purposefully gone beyond that work? Undoubtedly, some of us have. However, is dignity an explicit part of our national disability policy? No. One may search IDEA and ADA and other law to find dignity as an explicit concern of Congress and the Court. Except for cases involving public institutions and centers for those with disabilities (*Wyatt v. Stickney*, 1971) or capital punishment (*Atkins v. Virginia*, 2002), one will not find that dignity—the personhood ascribed by society and expressed by law—is a central concern of the law. It is rarely explicit; it is almost always implicit. That fact is insufficient. Statutes and decisions may change the law, but unless they are explicit about their purpose to change culture also, they will always be insufficient to that end.

Permit me to conclude by quoting myself (Turnbull, 2017). Speaking to the audience convened by the U.S. Department of Education to celebrate the 40th anniversary of the enactment of IDEA at a ceremony held in the White House in Washington, in August, 2015, I said the following:

> Our second challenge (in education, the first being to improve outcomes) is to ensure that our schools are the foundations for more than rights and education. They must be the places where a new culture is birthed, raised, and matured. This new culture occurs in what is best called ethical communities. This culture acknowledges the abilities of people with disabilities. It honors their liberty to lead self-determined lives. This culture creates ethical communities.

So, the new IDEA will say not just that disability is a natural consequence of our human condition and therefore an expected presence in our communities. No, the new IDEA will proclaim that those with disabilities are welcome and will be treated with dignity in every one of our communities.

IDEA now and forever should memorialize a foundational American creed: our differences, whether based on race, ethnicity, cultural heritage, sexuality, age, and disability—yes, especially disability—should not separate, should not segregate, us from each other. Each of us is less able than someone else, in one way or another; all of us have different lineages, different abilities, and different limitations. But none of us is therefore less worthy: each of us who has a disability must be welcomed and dignified.

Doing More!

What might educators do to acknowledge the desirability—nay, the necessity—of ethical communities and human dignity? It would be to construct and lead a national program on the relationship of the science of education and the ethic of dignity in school and community. Call it The Dignity Project.

Research is needed on how general and special educators, school administrators, related service providers, children and their families, and community members affiliated in various ways with schools can understand and advance dignity of those with disabilities. The questions will be those a cub reporter is taught to ask: who, what, when, where, why, and how is dignity brought to life in our schools? The answers (some of which we must know already but have yet to catalogue) should shape what we do in education, for they will shape who we are and how we confront those who differ from us and find our commonalities.

LEARNING FROM JAY TURNBULL

I now come to the end of this chapter, but I dare not end it without a personal note. Please bear with me.

The core concepts of law and policy will be well and alive more than they are now when our ethics attend to dignity and community, and when we construct our culture to acknowledge not just that disability is a natural consequence of the human condition, but also that disability is a welcome condition in our communities. That is not to say that we should not use all of our knowledge to ameliorate disability's effects. Rather it is to say that what is natural and permanent—the fact of disability—enriches us and our communities.

That lesson about enrichment is what my son taught me—that man-child who had intellectual disability, autism, and rapid cycling bipolar disorder (Turnbull, 2011). On his gravestone, Ann and I have inscribed three words, under his name and dates of birth and death (1964 and 2009). They are: *Our Best Professor.*

To have had a truly rich life and to have participated in the reform of our laws and policies and thus our communities is the path I have taken, with my wife Ann and my daughters Amy and Kate. That kind of life arose directly from being Jay's father and was the result of what he taught me.

If you, the reader, have learned anything from this chapter and intend to act about the dignity of the lives of people and families affected by disability, you too will have been Jay's student and will become, as we in his family have become, an advocate for dignity through education. You then may say that Jay has been your professor, too.

REFERENCES

Adoption Assistance and Child Welfare Act of 1980, PL 96-272, 45 U.S.C. §§ 620, 629 and 670 *et seq.*

Adoption and Safe Families Act of 1997, PL 105-89, 42 U.S.C. §§ 620 *et seq.*

Americans with Disabilities Act (ADA) of 1990, PL101-336, 42 U.S.C. §§ 12101 *et seq.*

Atkins v. Virginia, 536 U.S. 304 (2002).

Balanced Budget Act of 1997, PL 105-33, 111 Stat. 251.

Brown v. Board of Education, 437 U.S. 483 (1954).

Burt, R. (1995). *The court in conflict.* Cambridge, MA: Harvard University Press.

Child Abuse Prevention, Adoption, and Family Services Act of 1988, PL 100-294, 42 U.S.C. §§ 5101 *et seq.*

Child Abuse Prevention and Treatment Reform Act of 1978, PL 95-266, 42 U.S.C. §§ 5106a.

Child Health Act of 1967, PL 90-48, 42 U.S.C. §§ 290bb.

Children's Health Act of 2000, PL 106-310, 42 U.S.C. §§ 108 *et seq.*

Children's and Communities' Mental Health Improvement Act of 1991, 42 U.S.C. §§ 290ff *et seq.*

City of Cleburne v. Cleburne Living Center, 473 U.S. 432 (1985).

Community Mental Health Act of 1963, PL 88-164, 77 Stat. 282.

DeShaney v. Winnebago, 489 U.S. 189 (1982).

Developmental Disabilities Assistance and Bill of Rights Act Amendments of 2000, PL 106-402, 42 U.S.C. §§ 6000 *et seq.*

Education for All Handicapped Children Act of 1975, PL 94-142, 20 U.S.C. §§ 1400 *et seq.*

Education of the Handicapped Act Amendments of 1974, PL 93-380, 88 Stat. 576.

Elementary and Secondary Education Act of 1965, PL 89-10, 20 U.S.C. §§ 241.

Endrew F. v. Douglas County School District RE-1, 580 U.S. ___ (No. 15-827, decided March 22, 2017).

Fair Housing Act of 1968 (Title VIII of the Civil Rights Act of 1964), PL 88-352, 42 U.S.C. §§ 3601 *et seq.*

Family Educational Rights and Privacy Act (FERPA) of 1974, PL 93-380, 20 U.S.C. §§ 1232g *et seq.*

Foster Care Independence Act of 1999, PL 106-169, 42 U.S.C. §§ 673 and 677.

Handicapped Children's Early Education Act of 1968, PL 90-538, 20 U.S.C. §§ 621 *et seq.*

Improving Head Start for School Readiness Act of 2007, PL 110-134, 42 U.S.C. §§ 9801, 9831, 9837, 9840 *et seq.*

Individuals with Disabilities Education Act (IDEA) of 1990, PL 101-476, 20 U.S.C. §§ 1400 *et seq.*

Individuals with Disabilities Education Improvement Act (IDEA) of 2004, PL 108-446, 20 U.S.C. §§ 1400 *et seq.*

Lawrence v. Texas, 539 U.S. 558 (2003).

Loving v. Virginia, 388 U.S. 1 (1967).

McLean, M., Sandall, S. R.., & Smith, B. J. (2016). A history of early childhood special education. In B. Reichow, B.A. Boyd, E. E. Barton, E. E., & S. L. Odom, S. L. (Eds.). *Handbook of early childhood special education* (pp. 3–20). Geneva, Switzerland: Springer.

Mental Health Parity Act of 1996, PL 104-204.

Mental Retardation Facilities and Community Mental Health Centers Construction Act of 1963, PL 88-164, 42 U.S.C. §§ 2670 *et seq.*

Minow, M. (1990). *Making all the difference: Inclusion, exclusion, and American law*. Ithaca, NY: Cornell University Press.

Mish, F. C. (1990). *Webster's ninth new collegiate dictionary*. Springfield, MA: Merriam-Webster.

Moore v. Texas, 581 U.S. ___ (2017).

Obergefell v. Hodges, 409 U.S. 810 (2015).

Olmstead v. L.C., 527 U.S. 581 (1999).

Parham v. J. R., 442 U.S. 584 (1979).

Patient Protection and Affordable Care Act of 2010, PL 111-148, 124 Stat. 119-1025, 42 U.S.C. §§ 18001 *et seq.*

Pound, R. (1933). A comparison of ideal of law. *Harvard Law Review, 47*, 1.

Rehabilitation Act of 1973, PL 93-112, 29 U.S.C. §§ 701.

Social Security Act Amendments of 1967, PL 90-48, 42 U.S.C. §§ 1396d *et seq.*

Social Security Act of 1935, PL 74-271, 42 U.S.C. §§ 301 *et seq.*

Social Security Amendments of 1965, PL 89-97, 42 U.S.C. §§ 401 *et seq.*

Social Services Amendments of 1974, PL 93-647.

Technology-Related Assistance for Individuals with Disabilities Act of 1988, PL 100-407, 29 U.S.C. §§ 2201 *et seq.*

Troxell v. Granville, 530 U.S. 57 (2000).

Trohanis, P. L. (2008). Progress in providing services to young children with special needs and their families: An overview and update on the implementation of the Individuals with Disabilities Education Act (IDEA). *Journal of Early Intervention, 30*(2), 140–151.

Turnbull, A., & Turnbull, R. (2001). Right science and right results: Lifestyle change, positive behavior support, and human dignity. *Journal of Positive Behavior Support, 13*(2), 69–77.

Turnbull, H. R., Brotherson, M. J., Czyzewski, M. J., Esquith, D. S., & Otis, A. K. (1983). A policy analysis of the doctrine of the "least restrictive education" of handicapped children. *Rutgers Law Journal, 14*(3), 489–540.

Turnbull, H. R., Shogren, K. A., & Turnbull, A. P. (2011). Evolution of the parent movement: Past, present, and future. In J. M. Kauffman & D. P. Hallahan (Eds.), *Handbook of special education* (pp. 639–653). Geneva, Switzerland: Routledge.

Turnbull, H. R., & Turnbull, A. P. (1996). The synchrony of stakeholders: Lessons from the disability rights movement. In S. L. Kagan & N. E. Cohen (Eds.). *Reinventing early care and education* (pp. 290–308). San Francisco, CA: Jossey-Bass.

Turnbull, R. (1976). Report of the Parents' Committee: Families in crisis, families at risk. In T. Tjossem (Ed.). *Intervention strategies for high risk infants and children* (pp. 765–769). Baltimore, MD: University Park Press.

Turnbull, R. (2011). *The exceptional life of Jay Turnbull: Disability and dignity in America, 1967–2009*. Amherst, MA: White Poppy Press.

Turnbull, R. (2013). Quality of life: Four under-considered intersections. *International Public Health Journal, 6*(4).

Turnbull, R. (2017). Education, ethical communities, and personal dignity. *Intellectual Disability, 55*(2), 110–111.

Turnbull, R., Beegle, G., & Stowe, M. S. (2001). The core concepts of disability policy affecting families who have children with disabilities. *Journal of Disability Policy Studies, 12*(3), 133–143.

Turnbull, R., & Stowe, M. (2001a). Five models for thinking about disability: Implications for policy. *Journal of Disability Policy Studies, 12*(3), 198–205.

Turnbull, R., & Stowe, M. S. (2001b). A taxonomy for organizing the core concepts according to their underlying principles. *Journal of Disability Policy Studies, 12*(3), 177–197.

Turnbull, R., Turnbull, A., & Cooper, D. (2018). The Supreme Court, Endrew, and the appropriate education of students with disabilities: Gains and losses. *Exceptional Children, 84*(2), 124–140.

Vacco v. Quill, 521 U.S. 793 (1997).

Washington v. Glucksberg, 521 U.S. 702 (1997).

Wyatt v. Stickney, 325 F. Supp. 781 (M.D. Ala., 1971).

Youngberg v. Romeo, 457 U.S. 307 (1982).

14

Looking Forward

Research and Practice in Programs for Children and Youth With Disabilities and Their Families

Samuel L. Odom

S ince its inception, the Frank Porter Graham Child Development Institute (FPG) has had an emphasis on children who are developmentally vulnerable and their families. Reflecting the zeitgeist of the 1960s, FPG and other "Mental Retardation Research Centers" (now known as Intellectual and Developmental Disabilities Research Institutes) focused on the prevention of what was then called mental retardation (now intellectual disability) due primarily to poverty and environment. This prevention effort provided enriched learning environments in early child care settings and led to the Abecedarian Project, which became a signature project for FPG (see Chapter 7).

Early in its history, FPG's emphasis expanded in two ways, in large part because of the appointment of Dr. James Gallagher as Director. First, Dr. Gallagher broadened the research activities to include young children with established disabilities (e.g., developmental delays, autism spectrum disorders), children with gifted intellectual abilities, and the families of each (Gallagher, 1975). Second, Dr. Gallagher was committed to the idea that the science generated by FPG and other researchers in the field should not lie fallow in research journal articles but be disseminated in ways that would inform practice. The emphasis was enacted through technical assistance and professional development activities (Gallagher, Danaher, & Clifford, 2009). The chapters in this section have strongly documented the research in early intervention, professional development, and social policy foundations that underlie current practice and services for children and youth with disabilities and their families. In this chapter, I briefly summarize several themes that these chapters share. Then based on this summary, I suggest additional themes that will likely influence research, professional development, and policy in the future.

THEMES ACROSS CHAPTERS

The chapters in this section, by Carta and Snyder (Chapter 11), Winton (Chapter 12), and Turnbull (Chapter 13), focus on research, professional development, and social policy, respectively, as they relate to children and youth with developmental disabilities and their families. Although each chapter focuses on a different topic, the chapters share five common themes: the federal role in supporting services, individualization, collaboration across disciplines, inclusion, and the essential role of families. Each of these themes are discussed below.

Federal Role in Education

A consistent theme across chapters was the role the U. S. government played, through both legislation and litigation, in supporting the evolution of services for children and youth with disabilities and their families. Here again, Dr. Gallagher's presence was influential. Previous to his directorship at FPG he was the Director of the Bureau for the Education of the Handicapped in the U.S. Department of Education and was pivotal in the creation of the Handicapped Children's Early Education Program activities. As Turnbull describes, beginning with the first federal mandate of the Education for All Handicapped Children Act of 1975 (PL 94-142), which required states to provide a free and appropriate public education for students with disabilities, and then the extension of the mandate to include preschool-age children and discretionary support for infants and toddlers through early intervention in the Education of the Handicapped Act Amendments of 1986 (PL 99-457), the federal government placed a requirement on states to adhere to common standards of educational services. Both Chapters 11 and 12 note that federal legislation also provided discretionary funds for research and professional development. Without these federal initiatives, an inconsistent patchwork of services would now exist across states, much of the research that is the foundation for current practices would not have been funded, and we would have a much more poorly trained workforce than currently exists. In Chapter 12, Winton suggests that the recent history of early childhood education, in which a federal mandate did not occur, serves as a natural contrast. For example, most U.S. states have funded pre-K programs. When examining these programs, it is apparent that the quality, reach (i.e., accessible for all young children), funding, and professional training requirements of teachers of those programs vary substantially among states. Examples of the considerable variations in these state programs are described in the annual *State of Preschool* reports published by the National Institute for Early Education Research (Friedman-Kraus et al., 2018). Clearly, the federal government has had an important and positive impact on early education for children with and without disabilities.

Individualization

In an era when the medical community has discovered the importance of individualized or personalized medicine (Academy of Medical Sciences, 2015), it is noteworthy that such "personalization" has long been an essential element of services for children and youth with disabilities and their families. In Chapter 13, Turnbull clearly described that the early legislation (PL 94-142 and PL 99-457) required an individual education plan be established based on the assessment of children's strengths and needs. Such individualization necessitates a workforce that is trained to identify those individual needs and to support learning in inclusive, naturally occurring contexts. Furthermore, as Carta and Snyder noted in Chapter 11, research now provides the field with tools for individually monitoring learning and growth in an ongoing, dynamic fashion, such that teachers can modify programs when progress does not occur, and alternatively can document when a goal has been achieved and move on to other goals (e.g., Buzhardt et al., 2010).

Collaboration Across Disciplines

Programs that foster the development and learning of children and youth with disabilities work best when there is collaboration across disciplines such as special education, early childhood and general education, speech and language pathology, occupational therapy, physical therapy, and psychology. This theme of collaboration is tied to the previous theme noting the federal role in early education and special education, in that such collaboration is required by law, as Turnbull noted in Chapter 13. In addition, the involvement of specific disciplines in a child's program is dictated by the needs of the child and the family, suggesting the individualization theme. In Chapter 12, Winton proposed that professional development within and across disciplines should include skills needed for establishing collaborative relationships, and research from a range of disciplines is necessary to inform practices that foster children's development and learning. Indeed, as we learn more from neuroscience about brain function, as technology evolves, and as our society becomes increasingly diverse, the need to draw from and share knowledge across multiple disciplines will become even more important. I return to these issues in subsequent sections.

Inclusion

The importance of inclusion for children and youth with disabilities in programs involving same-age peers without disabilities (and indeed, in society at large) is a common theme across chapters. In Chapter 13, Turnbull noted that federal laws require educational services be provided in the "least restrictive environments," which for most children with disabilities are inclusive settings. Part C of the Individuals with Disabilities Education Improvement Act also specifies that early intervention services must occur in the "natural environment," which is often defined as the home but also includes early child care settings involving other young children who are typically developing. Turnbull moved this discussion forward by invoking the concept of "dignity" as a goal for individuals with disabilities, in which children and youth are treated with respect as well as supported as full members of their community and society.

In Chapter 12, Winton also noted that joint policy statements from major professional organizations (e.g., the Division for Early Childhood [DEC] and the National Association for the Education of Young Children [NAEYC]) and federal agencies (e.g., the U.S. Departments of Education and Health and Human Services) specify the need for children with disabilities to be placed in inclusive settings. For this to occur successfully, she emphasized the critical need for training the early childhood education and early childhood special education workforces on strategies to support children with disabilities in inclusive settings. In addition, in Chapter 11, Carta and Snyder specifically highlighted the research that documents the benefits of inclusion for children with and without disabilities, as well as strategies for providing intentional teaching in routine activities in such inclusive early childhood education settings.

Families

From infancy to young adulthood (and beyond), family contexts are the greatest sources for caregiving, security, and learning for children and youth with disabilities. Early on, policy makers reflected the central role of family by specifying that family members had to be a part of the individualized education plan process. Policy makers emphasized this point even more strongly in Part C of IDEA, with the required development of the individual family service plan, which is the cornerstone of early intervention services. In addition to describing this legislation in Chapter 13, Turnbull highlighted other regulations, such as through Social Security and Medicaid, that are designed to support families of children and youth with disabilities and also noted the role family members sometime played in the ligation that shaped social policy. To directly engage families in programs for their children and youth with disabilities, a workforce trained to work with families is needed, which Winton highlighted in Chapter 12. In addition, in Chapter 11, Carta and Snyder noted the critical developmental influence on children of the broader family context, styles of responsive caregiving, and family members' involvement in intentional teaching in natural routines and activities. I return to this topic of families in a subsequent section.

REFLECTIONS ON FUTURE TRENDS

In 1988, two audacious young professors (Odom & Warren, 1988) published their predictions about the state of early childhood special education and early intervention in the year 2000. Although our predictions anticipated some of the changes to come and some that are still reflected in the themes just described (i.e., inclusion, collaboration, families), the world is quite different 30 years later. Influences are now present that did not exist when early intervention and early childhood special education emerged in the 1970s and 1980s, and these influences have implications for future directions in the field. In this section, I speculate on those potential influences and future directions.

Biomedical Research

Over the course of his career, Bronfenbrenner modified his early ecological theory of child development (Bronfenbrenner, 1979) that emphasized the context for development to a theory that emphasized the central role of proximal processes in development and the relevance of personal characteristics as well as context (Bronfenbrenner & Morris, 2006). With this change, he recognized the importance of the biological characteristics of the child (e.g., genetics, health) and the changing nature of the biosystem across time (Rosa & Tudge, 2013). Indeed, our better understanding of how biology affects development holds greater promise than any time in our history. Rapid advances in the measurement of brain activity of young children are leading to a plethora of neuroscience studies about the structure and function of the brain (e.g., Haartsen, Jones, & Johnson, 2016). The most immediate relevance has been in the search for biomarkers that might predict patterns of future development, serve as indicators of risk, and lead to early identification and intervention (Symons & Roberts, 2013). For example, in the area of autism spectrum disorders, several research groups have identified abnormalities in early brain development, such as extra-axial fluid and enlarged brain volume (Shen et al., 2013) and overgrowth on the cortical surface area of the brain (Hazlett et al., 2017) as very early predictors of a later diagnosis of autism. Building on the early gaze pattern and visual preference research conducted by Jones and Klin (2013), members of Dawson's laboratory (Murias et al., 2018) are examining early gaze preferences as a potential early biomarker. Although to date the search for biomarkers has not risen to the level of clinical efficacy, this research may hold promise for our future ability to identify the risk of disability earlier and potentially provide earlier intervention than currently possible (Murphy, 2018).

Similarly, for years there has been a great deal of excitement about the potential for discovering elements of or processes involving brain architecture (Institute of Medicine, 2000), but the immediate relevance for actual practices for children and youth with disabilities and their families has yet to be realized. Learning from the history of the past is important. There was a time when "scientific intervention practice" was based on assumptions of how the brain works, which led to therapy and instructional programs like "patterning techniques" (Doman, 1974) and the perceptual-motor instructional approach to remediate learning disabilities (Kephart, 1960), which are now largely discounted because of their ineffectiveness (Von Tetzcher et al.,

2013; Kavale & Forness, 2000). Even today, programs purported to be based on brain science but that have little evidence of efficacy continue to be used (Bruer, 2015). Although the rapid pace of neuroscience research has not yet yielded the type of information relevant for intervention and instructional programming, the hope for the future is that it will yield important findings.

Genetics research is a second feature of biomedical science that may also hold promise for children and youth with disabilities and their families. Again, the medical community is placing great faith in genetics to lead the way to precise and personalized medical care, which to date has been unprecedented (Lu, Goldstein, Angrist, & Cavalleri, 2014). In fact, such successes in genetic research have been found in the treatments of some diseases, such as cancer (Garraway, Verweij, & Ballman, 2013). Newborn genetic screenings can indicate or predict the possibility of a disability occurring, which can assist family members in making future plans. Also, genetic conditions, such as fragile X syndrome (in boys) or Angelman syndrome, can sometimes indicate that a great deal of support will be needed for the child throughout his or her life. Like neuroscience, the genetics research has moved at a rapid, even lightning, pace. Yet, in terms of early intervention and special education practices that could be informed by genetics to promote development and learning by young children and youth with disabilities, as with neuroscience, the potential lies well into the future.

Technology

In terms of education for children and youth with disabilities, the impact of technology has come to fruition and its potential continues into the future in possibly unanticipated ways. More than 30 years ago, the impact of technology on the education of children and youth was similar to where biomedical research (just discussed) is today—holding great promise but with little current impact (Strain & Odom, 1985). Today, technology permeates nearly every aspect of our lives, with its application to early intervention and education being no exception. In fact, applications have become so extensive that an adequate review is beyond the space limitations of this chapter. Therefore, only a few aspects of where the impact of technology is now occurring and will extend into the future will be mentioned, with the first being early identification and assessment.

Early developmental assessment programs are now computerized/web-based. They can identify when children's development differs substantially for typical trajectories, as well as provide ongoing developmental monitoring when children are identified and intervention has begun. The Indicators of Growth and Development is a primary example of just such a program (Buzhardt et al., 2010). Other efficacious screening tools, such as the current *Ages and Stages* questionnaire (Squires & Bricker, 2009), now have computerized assessments options (San Antonio, Fenick, Shabanova, Levanthall, & Weitzman, 2014). Building on the eye-tracking paradigm noted previously,

Dawson (2018) reported that her team is developing an eye-tracking assessment that can be delivered through a smartphone, administered by a parent, and may eventually be able to screen very young children (as early as 6 months) who are at risk for developing autism spectrum disorders or other developmental delays.

Practitioners have used computer-assisted instruction for many years, especially for academic instruction (McClellan, 2013). Although traditional computers and monitors are still a valid pedagogical instructional delivery tool (depending on the software), the form of technology and its potential for instruction expanded exponentially (Dell & Newton, 2011). In many classrooms now, smart whiteboards allow students to actively manipulate images on the screen through touch and movement, and easily accessible audio recordings allow children independent (or teacher-guided) access to literacy experiences. The *Story Friends* program that Goldstein et al. (2016) developed to promote vocabulary acquisition and comprehension is a primary example of such a program that has evidence of efficacy. The intervention employs repeated story reading and dialogic reading instructional techniques embedded in interesting story content. Children listen to and follow a themed set of storybook experiences that build on their interests and are increasingly layered with instructional content.

The availability of immediate video recording and playback through smartphones and tablets has moved into common practice in many early intervention programs and classrooms. For home-based early intervention programs that have evidence of efficacy, it is now common for practitioners to show examples of other parents using a particular technique for working with their child (e.g., a certain way to promote joint attention or turn-taking), for the parent to try using the technique while a home visitor is video recording the parent and child, and then for the home visitor and parent to discuss the parent's use of the technique and their child's response (Schertz, Odom, Baggett, & Sideris, 2018). Similarly, video modeling—a technique in which the teacher shows a student on a smartphone or tablet a video example of a behavior or skill to be learned—has one of the strongest sets of empirical supports (Odom et al., 2015); with current smartphone and tablet technology, it is now practical for use in many programs (Plavnick, 2012). Relatedly, the collection of work samples, which were once confined to paper-and-pencil formats, can now be captured by smartphones/tablets on video or photographs. Such examples can provide powerful evidence to parents of their children's progress (although this does not replace the collection of data to monitor children's progress). For children with severe communication challenges, specialized augmentative communication devices were once the only alternative available (e.g., Murphy, 1986). Again, with advances in tablet technology and software design, many augmentative communication programs can run on regular iPads or other tablets (Lorah, 2018), with these devices being much more normalized and socially acceptable than previous specialized devices.

Last, the potential of technological advances for professional development is considerable. Content and information now appears on computerized modules that previously were conveyed just through print media. The DEC recommended practices are a primary example. Over the more than 25 years of their history, these practices have primarily appeared in edited books (Odom & McLean, 1996) or procedural manuals (Sandall, McLean, & Smith, 2001). Currently, free interactive computer modules are available that describe each of the practices (Division for Early Childhood, 2018). Through their National Center to Mobilize Early Learning, Winton, Buysse, and Rous (2015) developed a set of online modules designed to promote teachers' use of eight practices that support the inclusion of children with disabilities in early childhood programs. For children with autism spectrum disorders, investigators with the AFIRM project (Sam, Cox, & Odom, 2018) have designed 27 online learning modules that convey practical information about implementation of evidence-based practices, with these modules having been accessed, at this writing, by over 45,000 new users from around the world. It is important to note that online learning modules such as these can effectively introduce instructional practices and provide some guidance for implementation, but usually practitioners require coaching and feedback about the actual use of the practice in their program to use the practice with fidelity (Odom, 2009). Such coaching feedback might be provided in person, but it also can occur remotely through real-time webcam observations of instructional sessions (Vernon-Feagans, Kainz, Hedrick, Ginsberg, & Amendum, 2013) or by video recording instructional sessions and receiving feedback at a later time (Hadden & Pianta, 2006). Given the increasing ease of use and refinement of coaching techniques, the frequency of using videos and real-time webcam observations is likely to increase in the future.

Expanding Research Base and Information Science

The societal phenomena of increased availability and access to information is certainly reflected in the current early intervention and education practices for children and youth with disabilities. Thirty years ago, reviewing the research base for early intervention (Odom & Karnes, 1988) was a reasonable task. The major scholarly research was conducted through hours spent in the library, reading photocopied articles, taking notes on notecards, scrolling through ERIC microfilms and, if lucky, word processing on a desktop computer. There were only two journals whose primary focus was on early intervention and early childhood special education (the *Journal of Early Intervention* and *Topics in Early Childhood Special Education*), making it relatively easy to conduct a review of the research in these areas.

Since that time, the volume of research and professional literature has expanded exponentially. Fortunately, the knowledge synthesis process has changed substantially as well. The capability of searching the literature through powerful search engines (e.g., ERIC, EBSCO, PSYCH-INFO) and the online access to journal articles has created a great capacity for accessing and synthesizing the literature. With this capacity came the need for systemization. The field of information science (Yan, 2011) has emerged primarily from the library science discipline to provide guidance. International standards now exist for conducting systematic reviews of the literature and meta-analyses (e.g., PRISMA; Moher, Liberati, Tetzlaf, Altman, & the PRISMA Group, 2009). As we move forward, there is an increasing trend—and even a requirement in some cases—for researchers to register their research studies before they begin, make data from their research studies publicly available, and even make their findings available to the public before journal publication. However, this latter practice does raise concerns because peer review has always been the safeguard against faulty research information entering the public domain.

In addition, the advance of popular (e.g., Facebook, Instagram, Snapchat) and professional (e.g., Linked In, Research Gate) social networking systems has increased the flow of information, with this expected to continue to increase in the future. This trend has been and will continue to be used in the future by creating support groups among parents of children with disabilities (DeHoff, Staten, Rodgers, & Denne, 2016) and also among professionals (Arora, 2014). These are potentially positive features of the technology revolution.

With the increased access to information through social media and other sources, a concern exists about the validity of information conveyed over the Internet. Since science became the mode for making decisions about patient care in medicine (and the social services) and the experiment being the mechanism through which science is generated, peer review has been the process through which the quality of science is evaluated. This process for disseminating scientific information is slow, yet without it there is concern about the flow of unvetted information. For example, pseudo-scientific practices such as "facilitated communication" and now "rapid prompting method" became wildly popular without having any scientific basis of efficacy and, in fact, sometimes having deleterious effects. From researchers' perspectives, the safeguards of scientific review must underlie practices and, as Turnbull noted in Chapter 13, evidence-based practices are now written into current legislation.

Changing Demographics: Race, Ethnicity, and Family Structure

In Chapter 2, Iruka described the changing ethnic and racial demographic in the United States. I briefly return to that theme in this chapter because changing demographics will influence the nature of early intervention and special education for children and youth with disabilities in the future. In a quarter century, the non-Hispanic White population in the United States will no longer be the demographic majority (Colby & Ortman, 2015). With this change will come the even more intense need to instill a cultural sensitivity into our educational and intervention practices for children and youth with disabilities. The most obvious accommodation will be ensuring that children who are dual-language learners receive instruction that is meaningful (i.e., in their home language) and that schools can communicate with families in their home language (see Chapter 4). However, a complication for some locations is the prevalence of a large set of home languages, making it difficult to provide the kinds of services that families need. Understanding and being responsive to the cultural values of the families and communities when designing programs have always been (Odom & McLean, 1996) and continue to be (Division for Early Childhood, 2018) central tenets of recommended practices for young children with disabilities, and this emphasis will only increase in future.

Two other points are relevant. First, the early intervention/early childhood special education workforce is largely White, non-Hispanic, and female. As Winton noted in Chapter 12, recruiting individuals into the workforce who look and sound like the children and families for whom they are providing services (and are well trained) is an important future direction. Second, one feature of cultural sensitivity is including symbolic representation within the program or classroom (e.g., pictures on the wall, cultural objects, books). For example, in literacy activities having stories that include characters with disabilities *and* from culturally diverse communities will increase in importance as the diversity of the country continues to change (e.g., see The Making Friends Program; Favazza, Ostrosky, & Mouzourou, 2016).

As racial and ethnic heterogeneity increases in U.S. society, the issue of overassignment of children of color to special education is likely to be a recurring theme. Disproportionality in assignment to special education services based on race and ethnicity has been a major issue for the field since the 1960s (Dunn, 1968). School systems and special education programs have been criticized for the overrepresentation of minority youth, especially African American youth, in special education (Skiba, Poloni-Staudinger, Gallani, Simmons, & Feggins-Azziz, 2006). Contrary to earlier research, more recent reviews of research studies about the disproportionality of children from five racial/ethnic groups suggest that children from these groups are actually underrepresented in special education—that is, proportionally fewer children are receiving services than non-Hispanic White children (Morgan et al., 2017, 2018). As Skiba, Artiles, Kozleski, Losen, and Harry (2016) noted, the issue of proportionality is important and also more complex than single or cumulative statistical estimates because assignment to special education varies substantially across districts, socioeconomic class, and cultural groups.

A point missed in these discussions is what I will call attitudinal *valence*. That is, the positive or negative attitude about proportionality is dictated by the attributional lens through which it is viewed. As noted, some attribute assignment of minority students to special education as a form of segregation based on race/ethnicity, whereas others see assignment to special education as a way of better meeting the educational and developmental needs of children and youth, thus enhancing their potential for participation in society. The increased cultural heterogeneity will indeed push these issues further into the forefront in the future.

A last related issue concerns political context and access to special education services. At this writing, increasingly assertive enforcement of immigration regulations and deportation of families and children who are undocumented may well affect utilization of special education services. Although all children of immigrant families are entitled by federal law to educational services (U.S. Department of Education, 2014), children with identifiable disabilities whose family members are undocumented or even may have been born in the United States may not access early intervention and/or special education services because of fear of deportation. This distrust of the government may well extend to members of the same ethnic communities, even if they have formal authorization to be in the country. As we look to the future and increased diversity of the student population, school systems and advocacy groups will be challenged by the task of ensuring that *all* children with disabilities receive the special education services they need to support their success in school and society.

In this section, I have spoken of cultural values as if they were the same for all members of a racial, linguistic, or ethnic group. However, cultural values are almost always translated through the family (and also by peer groups for older children and youth). It has been recognized for a while that many families no longer fit the 1950s-stereotyped concept of the two-parent plus children nuclear family (although this is still the case and should be respected in some families) (National Academies of Science, Engineering, and Medicine, 2016). Single-parent and blended families are now a common phenomenon. In some cultures, it is common for grandparents and other extended family members as well as the nuclear family to live together in the same household. For families in which the parents do not speak English, older children who are fluent in English sometimes become the translator for the families. The elaboration and diversification of the family structure in U.S. society is likely to increase in the future with the increased acceptance (both legally and attitudinally in society) of same-sex marriages and gender identity. Special education teachers and programs have had to be responsive to societal changes over the years, and the increased diversity in family structure and makeup will require ongoing flexibility and responsivity to families.

Emerging Field of Implementation Science

In human services, disciplines sometimes emerge out of necessity. For example, the professionalization of program evaluation, at least as it pertains to education, emerged in the 1960s when the number of federal programs for children increased and there was a need to determine their effects (Hogan, 2007). The information science discipline emerged to deal with increased information availability (Yan, 2011). A similar evolution exists for the emerging discipline of implementation science, which has substantial implications for the future. With the new millennium, researchers identified practices and programs that had scientific evidence of efficacy (Odom et al., 2005), which led to an increased awareness in the field of education and human services of the long lag between scientifically based knowledge and its use in practice (Odom, 2009).

With the intention of enhancing practitioners' use of scientifically based instructional and intervention practices, similar movements emerged under different names (e.g., dissemination science, diffusion theory, improvement science, implementation science). For this discussion, I focus on implementation science. Originating in the health services field (Bauer, Damschroder, Hagedorn, Smith, & Kilbourne, 2015), implementation science also has been broadly applied to social services, including early intervention and special education (Cook & Odom, 2013), and has been increasingly operationalized (Lyons et al., 2018). A variety of implementation science models have been proposed. Many have a systems orientation (Ghate, 2015), a stage-like quality (e.g., moving from exploration to adoption to initial implementation to full implementation; Fixsen, Blase, Metz, & Van Dyke, 2013), and a recognition that adaptation will be a common feature of implementation (Aarons et al., 2012).

The implications of implementation science for the future have already begun to be felt. The implementation process begins with the identification and specification of practices or programs that have scientific evidence of efficacy (i.e., the "what" of the program). To successfully implement a new program in an early intervention or special education system, a system first must be ready for change. Tools are available that assess such readiness (Shea, Jacobs, Esserman, Bruce, & Weiner, 2014). Critical components include leadership support (Lyons et al., 2018), with this leadership coming most often from the top (e.g., a supervisor's initiative), but it also may emerge from other sources (e.g., teachers as a group, parents as a group). Often, an external change agent is brought in to introduce practices or programs (Fixsen et al., 2013). Single workshop trainings, which were the modal form of training in the past and unfortunately are still prevalent, will most likely not result in practitioners' use of new practices. Ongoing coaching, consultation, and/or performance feedback are essential for supporting the "uptake" of new innovative early intervention and special education practices in these programs. For example, Odom, Cox, and Brock (2013) used an implementation science framework to promote the adoption by 12 states of a professional development program to promote practitioners' use of evidence-based practices for students with autism. Implementation science is now of primary interest to leaders and policy makers in many fields as we continue to focus on closing the gap between research and practice. It will strongly influence our research and professional development efforts in the future.

CONCLUSION

Research, professional development, and policy initiatives emanating from FPG and colleagues in the field have been very much about advancing knowledge that would have a positive impact on children and youth with disabilities. The authors of chapters in this section captured well the breadth of knowledge generated in the past, which extends into current practice and remains relevant for children and families with disabilities. They all touched on themes about the role of the federal government, the importance of individualization, the necessity of collaboration among members of different disciplines, the goal of inclusion, and the essential involvement of families. In the previous section of this chapter, I proposed additional themes that will affect early intervention and special education for children and youth with disabilities, including biomedical research, the impact of technology, the acceleration of information and need for information science, the emergence of implementation science, and the changing demographics of the United States, while also returning to the theme of families. As we look to the future, being aware of all these influences may better prepare us, as a profession, to build programs that truly enhance the lives of children and youth with disabilities and their families.

REFERENCES

Aarons, G. A., Green, A. E., Plainkas, L. A., Self-Brown, S., Whitaker, D. J., Lutzker, J. R., et al. (2012). Dynamic adaptation process to implement an evidence-based child maltreatment intervention. *Implementation Science, 7*, 1–9.

Academy of Medical Sciences. (2015). *Stratified, personalised or P4 medicine: A new direction for placing the patient at the centre of healthcare and health education.* London: Author. Retrieved from https://acmedsci.ac.uk/download?f=file&i=32644

Arora, D. (2014). How to use social media for professional development. *Social Media Today.* Retrieved from https://www.socialmediatoday.com/content/how-use-social-media-professional-development

Bauer, M. S., Damschroder, L., Hagedorn, H., Smith, J., & Kilbourne, A. M. (2015). An introduction to implementation science for the non-specialist. *BioMed Central Psychology, 3*(1), 1–32.

Bronfenbrenner, U. (1979). *The ecology of human development: Experiments by nature and design.* Cambridge, MA: Harvard University Press.

Bronfenbrenner, U., & Morris, P. A. (2006). The bioecological model of human development. In W. Damon & R. Lerner (Eds.), *Handbook of child psychology: Theoretical models of human development* (pp. 793–828). New York, NY: Wiley.

Bruer, J. T. (2015). Research base for improved classroom learning: Brain vs. behavior? *Evidence Speaks Report, Vol. 1, #9.* Washington, DC: Brookings Institute. Retrieved from https://www.brookings.edu/wp-content/uploads/2016/07/Download-the-paper-4.pdf

Buzhardt, J., Greenwood, C. R., Walker, D., Carta, J., Terry, B., & Garrett, M. (2010). A web-based tool to support data-based early intervention decision making. *Topics in Early Childhood Special Education, 29*, 201–213.

Colby, S. L., & Ortman, J. M. (2015). Projections of the size and composition of the U.S. Population: 2014 to 2060. *Current Population Reports, P25-1143.* Washington, DC: U.S. Census

Bureau. Retrieved from https://census.gov/content/dam/Census/library/publications/2015/demo/p25-1143.pdf

Cook, B., & Odom, S. L. (2013). Evidence-based practices and implementation science in special education. *Exceptional Children, 79,* 135–145.

Dawson, G. (2018, May). *Paradigm shifts in approaches to early detection and treatment of autism.* Keynote presentation at the Annual Meeting of the International Society for Autism Research, Rotterdam, Netherlands.

DeHoff, B. A., Staten, L. K., Rodgers, R. C., & Denne, S. C. (2016). The role of online social support in supporting and educating parents of young children with special health care needs in the United States: A scoping review. *Journal of Medical Internet Research, 18*(12), e333.

Dell, A. G., & Newton, D. A. (2011). Assistive technology. *Journal of Special Education Technology, 26,* 55–59.

Division for Early Childhood. (2018). *RMP: Recommended practices in early childhood.* Chapel Hill, NC: Early Childhood Technical Assistance Center.

Doman, G. (1974). *What to do about your brain-injured child.* New York, NY: Doubleday.

Dunn, L. M. (1968). Special education for the mildly retarded: Is much of it justifiable? *Exceptional Children, 35,* 5–22.

Education for All Handicapped Children Act of 1975, PL 94-142, 20 U.S.C. §§ 1400 *et seq.*

Education of the Handicapped Act Amendments of 1986, PL 99-457, 20 U.S.C. §§ 1400 *et seq.*

Favazza, P., Ostrosky, M. M., & Mouzourou, C. (2016). *The Making Friends Program: Supporting acceptance in your K–2 classroom.* Baltimore, MD: Paul H. Brookes Publishing Co.

Fixsen, D., Blase, K., Metz, A., & Van Dyke, M. (2013). Statewide implementation of evidence-based programs. *Exceptional Children, 79,* 213–230.

Friedman-Krauss, A. H., Barnett, W. S., Weisenfield, G. G., Kasmin, R., Dicrecchio, N., & Horowitz, M. (2018). *The state of preschool, 2017.* New Brunswick, NJ: National Institute on Early Education Research, Rutgers University.

Gallagher, J. J. (Ed.). (1975). *The application of child development research to exceptional children.* Reston, VA: Council for Exceptional Children.

Gallagher, J. J., Danaher, A. C., & Clifford, R. M. (2009). The evolution of the National Early Childhood Technical Assistance Center. *Topics in Early Childhood Special Education, 29,* 7–23.

Garraway, L. A., Verweij, J., & Ballman, K. V. (2013). Precision oncology: An overview. *Journal of Clinical Oncology, 31,* 1803–1805.

Ghate, D. (2015). From programs to systems: Deploying implementation science and practice for sustained real world effectiveness in services for children and families. *Journal of Clinical Child & Adolescent Psychology, 45,* 812–826.

Goldstein, H., Kelly, E., Greenwood, C., McCune, L., Carta, J., Atwater, J., et al. (2016). Embedded instruction improves vocabulary learning during automated storybook reading among high-risk preschoolers. *Journal of Speech, Language, and Hearing Research, 59,* 484–500.

Haartsen, R., Jones, E. J., & Johnson, M. H. (2016). Human brain development over the early years. *Current Opinions in Behavioral Sciences, 10,* 149–154.

Hadden, S. D., & Pianta, R. C. (2006). MyTeachingPartner: An innovative model of professional development. *Young Children, 61,* 42–63.

Hazlett, H. C., Gu, H., Munsell, B. C., Kim, S. H., Styner, M., Wolff, J., et al. (2017). Early brain development at high risk for autism spectrum disorders. *Nature, 542,* 348–351.

Hogan, R. L. (2007). The historical development of program evaluation: Exploring the past and present. *Online Journal of Workforce Education and Development, 2*(4), 1–14.

Institute of Medicine. (2000). *From neurons to neighborhoods: The science of early childhood development.* Washington, DC: National Academies Press.

Jones, W., & Klin, A. (2013). Attention to eyes is present but in decline in 2–6-month-olds later diagnosed with autism. *Nature, 504,* 427–431.

Kavale, K. A., & Forness, S. R. (2000). Auditory and visual perception processes and reading ability: A quantitative reanalysis and historical reinterpretation. *Learning Disability Quarterly, 23,* 253–270.

Kephart, N. (1960). *The slow learner in the classroom.* Columbus, OH: Charles Merrill.

Lorah, E. R. (2018). Evaluating the iPad Mini® as a speech-generating device in the acquisition of a discriminative and repertoire for young children with autism. *Focus on Autism and Other Developmental Disabilities, 33,* 47–54.

Lu, Y. F., Goldstein, D. B., Angrist, M., & Cavalleri, G. (24 July 2014). Personalized medicine and human genetic diversity. *Cold Spring Harbor Perspectives in Medicine, 4*(9), a008581–a008581.

Lyons, A. R., Cook, C. R., Brown, E. C., Locke, J., Davis, C., Ehrhart, M., et al. (2018). Assessing organizational implementation context in the education sector: Confirmatory factor analysis of measures of implementation leadership, climate, and citizenship. *Implementation Science, 13*, 1–13.

McClellan, E. (2013). Computer use with students with disabilities. In C. R. Reynolds, K. J. Vannest, & E. Fletcher-Janzen (Eds.), *Encyclopedia of special education: A reference for the education of children, adolescents, and adults with disabilities and other exceptional individuals* (4th ed.). Hoboken, NJ: Wiley.

Moher, D., Liberati, A., Tetzlaff, J., Altman, D. G., & the PRISMA Group. (2009). Preferred reporting items for systematic reviews and meta-analyses: The PRISMA statement. *PLoS Med, 6*(7), e1000097.

Morgan, P. L., Farkas, G., Cook, M., Strassfeld, N. M., Hillemeier, M. M., Pun, W. H., et al. (2017). Are Black children disproportionately overrepresented in special education? A best-evidence synthesis. *Exceptional Children, 83*, 181–198.

Morgan, P. L., Farkas, G., Cook, M., Strassfeld, N. M., Hillenmeier, M. M., Pun, W. H., et al. (2018). Are Hispanic, Asian, Native American, or language-minority children overrepresented in special education? *Exceptional Children, 84*, 261–279.

Murias, M., Major, S., Davlantis, K., Franz, L., Harris, A., Rardin, B., et al. (2018). Validation of eye-tracking measures of social attention as potential biomarkers for autism clinical trials. *Autism Research, 11*, 166–174.

Murphy, D. G. (2018, May). *Discussant remarks: Autism Biomarker Consortium for Clinical Trials.* Paper presented at the annual meeting of the International Society for Autism Research, Rotterdam, Netherlands.

Murphy, H. J. (1986). Computer technology/special education/rehabilitation: Proceedings of the conference. Northridge, CA. ERIC ED 2090259.

National Academies of Sciences, Engineering, and Medicine (2016). *Parenting matters: Supporting parents of children ages 0–8.* Washington, DC: National Academies Press.

Odom, S. L. (2009). The tie that binds: Evidence-based practice, implementation science, and early intervention. *Topics in Early Childhood Special Education, 29*, 53–61.

Odom, S. L., Brantlinger, E., Gersten, R., Horner, R., Thompson, B., & Harris, K. (2005). Research in special education: Scientific methods and evidence-based practices. *Exceptional Children, 71*, 137–148.

Odom, S. L., Cox, A., & Brock, M. (2013). Implementation science, professional development, and autism spectrum disorders: National Professional Development Center on ASD. *Exceptional Children, 79*, 233–251.

Odom, S. L., & Karnes, M. (Eds.) (1988). *Early intervention for infants and children with handicaps: An empirical base.* Baltimore, MD: Paul H. Brookes Publishing Co.

Odom, S. L., & McLean, M. E. (Eds.) (1996). *Early intervention/early childhood special education: Recommended practices.* Austin, TX: PRO-ED.

Odom, S. L., Thompson, J. L., Hedges, S., Boyd, B. A., Dykstra, J. R., Duda, M. A., et al. (2015). Technology-aided intervention and instruction for adolescents with autism spectrum disorders. *Journal of Autism and Developmental Disorders, 45*, 3805–3819.

Odom, S. L., & Warren, S. F. (1988). Early childhood special education in the year 2000. *Journal of the Division for Early Childhood, 12*, 263–273.

Plavnick, J. (2012). A practical strategy for teaching a child with autism to attend to and imitate a portable video model. *Research and Practices for Persons with Severe Disabilities, 37*, 263–270.

Rosa, E. M., & Tudge, J. (2013). Urie Bronfenbrenner's theory of human development: Its evolution from ecology to bioecology. *Journal of Family Theory & Review, 5*, 243–258.

Sam, A., Cox, A., & Odom, S. L. (2018). *AFIRM: Autism focused intervention resources and materials.* Chapel Hill, NC: Frank Porter Graham Child Development Institute, University of North Carolina at Chapel Hill. Retrieved from http://afirm.fpg.unc.edu/afirm-modules

San Antonio, M., Fenick, A., Shabanova, V., Leventhal, J., & Weitzman, C. (2014). Developmental screening using the Ages and Stages Questionnaire: Standardized versus real-world conditions. *Infants & Young Children, 27*, 111–119.

Sandall, S., McLean, M., & Smith, B. (2001). *DEC recommended practices in early intervention/ early childhood special education.* Reston, VA: Council for Exceptional Children.

Schertz, H. H., Odom, S. L., Baggett, K. M., & Sideris, J. H. (2018). Mediating parent learning to promote social communication for toddlers with autism. *Journal of Autism and Developmental Disorders, 48,* 853–867.

Skiba, R. J., Artiles, A. J., Kozleski, E. B., Losen, D. J., & Harry, E. G. (2016). Risks and consequences of oversimplifying educational inequities: A response to Morgan et al. (2015). *Educational Researcher, 45,* 221–225.

Skiba, R. J., Poloni-Staudinger, L., Gallini, S., Simmons, A. B., & Feggins-Azziz, R. (2006). Disparate access: The disproportionality of African American students with disabilities across educational environments. *Exceptional Children, 72,* 411–424.

Shea, C. M., Jacobs, S. R., Esserman, D. A., Bruce, K., & Weiner, B. J. (2014). Organizational readiness for implementing change: A psychometric assessment of a new measure. *Implementation Science, 9*(7), 1–15.

Shen, M. D., Nordahl, C. W., Young, G. S., Wootton-Gorges, S. L., Lee, A., Liston, S. E., et al. (2013). Early brain enlargement and elevated extra-axial fluid in infants who develop autism spectrum disorder. *Brain, 136,* 2825–2035.

Squires, J., & Bricker, D. (2009). *Ages and Stages questionnaire, third edition.* Baltimore, MD: Paul H. Brookes Publishing Co.

Strain, P. S., & Odom, S. L. (1985). Innovations in the education of severely handicapped preschool children. In R. Horner, L. Voeltz, & H. Fredericks (Eds.), *Education of learners with severe handicaps: Exemplary service strategies* (pp. 61–98). Baltimore: Paul H. Brookes Publishing Co.

Symons, F. J., & Roberts, J. E. (2013). Biomarkers, behavior, and intellectual and developmental disabilities. *American Journal on Intellectual and Developmental Disabilities, 118,* 413–415.

U.S. Department of Education. (2014). *Educational services for immigrant children and those recently arrived to the United States.* Washington DC: Author. Retrieved from https://www2.ed.gov/policy/rights/guid/unaccompanied-children.html

Vernon-Feagans, L., Kainz, K., Hedrick, A., Ginsberg, M., & Amendum, S. (2013). Live webcam coaching to help early elementary classroom teachers provide effective literacy instruction for struggling readers: The Targeted Reading Intervention. *Journal of Educational Psychology, 105,* 1175–1187.

Von Tetzcher, S., Verdel, M., Barstad, B. G., Gravas, E. M., Jahnsen, R., Krabbe, S., et al. (2013). The effect of interventions based on the programs of The Institutes for the Achievement of Human Potential and Family Hope Center. *Journal of Developmental Neurorehabilitation, 16,* 217–229.

Winton, P., Buysse, V., & Rous, B. (2015). *Connect: Modules and courses to build early childhood practitioners' ability to make evidence-based practice decisions.* Chapel Hill, NC: Frank Porter Graham Child Development Institute, University of North Carolina.

Yan, X. S. (2011). Information science: Its past, present and future. *Information, 2,* 510–527.

V

Fifty Years of Progress and Future Directions

In this concluding section, Barbara Wasik and Mary Ruth Coleman identify the 1960s as a time of unprecedented national focus on children and their families—a period that saw the initiation of significant work in research, policy, and practice. They identify the influence that Bronfenbrenner's early ecological theory played in explaining research findings focused on early childhood environments, then suggest that Bronfenbrenner's more advanced model—his Process, Person, Content, and Time (PPCT) model—provides advantages for guiding future research. A critical part of this developmental model are proximal processes, those immediate child–adult interactions that are so critical for children's learning and development. Using examples from the three themes of this volume, the different components of this PPCT model are illustrated and information is provided on how the model can promote critical new research directions.

The authors then identify challenges and potential strategies for the future. Observing that challenges can be described as "wicked problems" (ones that are complex and difficult to solve), Wasik and Coleman identify some of the most compelling problems facing the field of early care and education. Among the wicked problems they identify are ongoing concerns about the achievement gap between minority children and White children and the increasing diversity across language, culture, and income influencing educational experiences for children. Preparation of the workforce continues to be a major issue as classroom learning and achievement cannot be separated from the skills of teachers and other professionals. New ways of thinking about and conducting professional development and in-service training are needed for all who work with children to ensure the implementation of effective practices. The authors also call for adding to the repertoire of research designs, noting the need for alternative paradigms that encompass flexible procedures, enabling interventions to be responsive to changing needs. Relatedly, they call for funding designs that allow for the study of proximal processes between individual children and adults. Underscoring the calls of other authors throughout this volume, they emphasize the need to continue to conduct intensive research on early intervention efforts because the need for quality early intervention remains a highly significant social, educational, and cultural issue in the country.

15

Fifty Years of Progress and Future Directions

Barbara Hanna Wasik and Mary Ruth B. Coleman

> Especially in its early phases, and to a great extent throughout the life course, human development takes place through processes of progressively more complex reciprocal interaction between an active evolving biopsychological human organism and the persons, objects, and symbols in its immediate environment. (Bronfenbrenner, 1995, p. 620)

Historical events in the United States have shaped the contemporary context in which we examine the lives of young children, influencing both the issues we address and the methodology we employ. This situation was clearly seen in the 1960s, which was a time of unprecedented national focus on children and their families (Zigler & Styfco, 2010) as well as the beginning of the modern era of early childhood education (Meisels & Shonkoff, 2000). Driving much of this interest in the 1960s were several merging events: a challenge to long-standing beliefs about the immutability of intelligence, a growing concern with the detrimental effects of poverty on children's development, an interest in addressing the needs of children with disabilities and their families, and an excitement about the potential of changing children's environments in ways that would improve the possibility of school success and adult life-course outcomes. This work was being conducted within a time of increased sensitivity to race relations, civil rights, and the plight of minorities in the United States. Terms such as "cultural deprivation" emerged and the need for "compensatory programs," exemplified by Head Start, gained the support of both researchers and politicians. These events coincided with the political will to begin to fund programs for young children who were most at risk for failure due to poor educational outcomes. Within this social and political framework, 12 research centers were funded in the 1960s, including the Frank Porter Graham Child Development Institute (FPG), to address national priorities for children with intellectual and developmental disabilities. Our early work was founded on the idea that outcomes for children could be improved through targeted research, quality early educational experiences, and policies that fostered family and child well-being (Shaw, 2016). Interest in helping child care workers and parents in their roles began to expand dramatically, with research on early intervention in child care settings expanding simultaneously with research addressing ways parents could enhance their child's development (Lazar et al., 1982).

SEEING THE CHILD WITHIN THE SYSTEM

In the 1960s and early 1970s, research procedures were consistent with viewing the child as part of a larger ecological system, beginning with the family and including the neighborhood, school, and community. Because both the home and preschool were major areas of interests, investigators focused on evaluating overall outcomes for these center and home interventions. Although researchers saw the interactions between adults and children as essential for realizing positive outcomes for children, they generally did not assess the specific interactions in these settings between the adults and the child, but rather focused on major child outcomes for these environmental interventions. This focus on the broader context was consistent with Bronfenbrenner's early work on the ecological theory of development (Bronfenbrenner, 1977, 1979). His model identified a set of increasingly more complex environments within which the child resided and came to influence the methods and analyses employed by researchers. His early theory situated the child in the microsystem, which could be the child's home or a child care setting. His second contextual level, the exosystem, was more removed from the child and included settings such as the parent's place of work and the broader community. Although the child did not usually enter these settings, these settings could have significant indirect influences on the child. The context furthest from the child was the macrosystem, composed of decision makers and policy makers whose actions could and often did have major consequences for children. In addition to these three increasingly more complex systems was a fourth system, the mesosystem. The mesosystem included interactions among the different microsystems, such as between the family and a child care setting or with other parents and children in the neighborhood (Bronfenbrenner & Morris, 1998).

For many researchers and practitioners, Bronfenbrenner's early model emphasizing environmental influences was not only readily accepted as an explanation for understanding contextual influences on child behavior, but environmental influences were viewed as an overarching explanation for children's behavior. During the 1960s and 1970s, the inequities in educational settings for children had become a significant social and cultural issue and, as changes were called for, many individuals began to recognize the importance of context on children's behavior. Changes in the educational system began to take place, especially for children of color and those with disabilities, as schools became desegregated and access to educational opportunities increased for children with disabilities.

In his early theory, Bronfenbrenner visualized his ecological systems theory as illustrated by a set of Russian nesting dolls represented by increased complexity in the environment (Tudge, Rosa, & Payir, 2018). However, he did not intend his model to be simplistic, with development explained almost solely by the influence of context on the individual. Rather, his thinking always included the interactions between the child and adults in the child's life as key to influencing development. As his theory evolved, the emphasis he placed on these interactions began to take center stage.

Illustrating the evolving nature of his model, during the time period from 1980 to 1993, Bronfenbrenner emphasized the impact of multidirectional interactions across the system on the individual's development (Rosa & Tudge, 2013). During this time, he reaffirmed the role the person has in his or her own development (Tudge, Mokrova, Hatfield, & Karnik, 2009). Beginning in the 1990s, he proposed the Process-Person-Context-Time (PPCT) model, his most refined model, which captured a more detailed understanding of children's development. The developing child was seen as both influenced by and influencing the environment (Bronfenbrenner, 1995; Bronfenbrenner & Morris, 2006). By this time, he had replaced the term *ecological model* with that of *bioecological model*, making more explicit his position that influences were not unidirectional (from others in the environment to the child); rather, the child played an essential role in his or her own development by initiating and responding to persons, objects, or symbols in the immediate environment (Bronfenbrenner, 1995). These interactions within the child's microsystem, especially in the home and the child care setting, are identified as *proximal processes*—events providing the strongest influence on the child's development and ones that should receive the most attention for understanding children's development and learning. Thus, it is not the setting or context per se, but the processes that take place with the child in the setting that are the most critical.

The second component of the PPCT model is the *person* component. Three types of person characteristics were identified by Bronfenbrenner, each of which can alter the nature of proximal processes—namely, demand, resource, and force, which are described later in this chapter (Tudge et al., 2018). The third component of this bioecological model is *context*, the aspect that garnered the most early attention. The fourth component is *time*, an inclusion that evolved from the earlier concept of the chronosystem. Time itself focuses attention on the importance of the individual's own developmental life course, which in turn is shaped by conditions and events that take place during the person's life (Bronfenbrenner, 1995; Bronfenbrenner & Morris, 1998).

THE PROCESS-PERSON-CONTEXT-TIME MODEL

Here, we use Bronfenbrenner's PPCT model to highlight some of the significant accomplishments over the past 50 years.

Context

Within an ecological context, both immediate influences (e.g., those in the home and child care setting) and more distal influences (e.g., policies governing educational services for children) have garnered much attention in research focused on young children. Numerous writers over the past decades have emphasized the importance of context, whether it was to recommend that children participate in child care settings that could help promote language, early literacy, and social-emotional development or whether it was to recommend that we provide support to parents to encourage their interactions at home with their children (see Chapters 7, 9, and 10). In the 1960s, Head Start was initiated based on beliefs that modifying the child's immediate environment could bring about positive child outcomes. Many of the most influential research studies, including the Perry Preschool Study and the Abecedarian Project, were based on the assumption that changes in the environmental setting would make a critical difference in children's outcomes.

Setting variables can and do make a difference, whether they are larger in scope (e.g., providing a quality early care and education environment) or smaller (e.g., modifying the classroom arrangement or providing books in the home). Forty years ago, Harms and Clifford (Harms & Clifford, 1980) and their colleague, Debby Cryer, in documenting infant, toddler, and preschool classrooms, began a long line of FPG research and evaluation on the teaching practices and interactions that young children need to thrive. Their focus on both context and process has had an extensive national and international influence on the use of quality rating systems as a way to improve practice (https://ers.fpg.unc.edu/about-environment-rating-scales). Workplace characteristics are also influential because they can determine the times parents can be with their children as well as parental financial resources. Context also includes larger situations, such as residential segregation, which, in turn, often leads to segregated schools. As Barbarin noted in Chapter 3 and Bowman noted in Chapter 5, when these schools are in low-income areas, the educational resources available are usually much less desirable than those in more affluent residential areas, which affects the achievement of students. The emphasis on context is not only noted in the area of early care and education but also for children with disabilities, where the characteristics of the setting can influence children's behavior. Context is also considered a critical component when addressing the needs of children from different cultures or dual-language learners. Although context refers to all the ecological settings in Bronfenbrenner's early model, in his later model the phenomena of most interest are not the broad characteristics of the environment, but rather the interactions or proximal processes the child has with others in the environment.

Proximal Processes

Identified by Bronfenbrenner as the most critical for children's development, *proximal processes* have been recognized by many researchers as having a critical role in early interventions. In larger model programs with children from poverty backgrounds implemented in the 1960s and 1970s, fine-grain analyses of these proximal processes were rarely conducted, even when the intervention called for intensive teacher–child interactions or mother–child interactions. Later in the early intervention literature, an increasing emphasis emerged on documenting teacher–child interactions in which the adult engages with the child to promote learning and development, often using scaffolding procedures (Wasik & Sparling, 2010). In some very specific content areas in education, such as reading, the teacher or parent can be taught to provide detailed guidance to the child through a set of prompts—procedures that are much like scaffolding (Whitehurst & Lonigan, 1998).

An examination of proximal processes has been a mainstay of research with children with disabilities, illustrated by research across the past 50 years (see Chapter 11). Researchers recognized early on that interventions would need to be individualized for each child and that the responsiveness of the caregivers, teachers, or parents to the child was critical for the child's learning. Documentation of these proximal processes focused on the role of the immediate child–adult interactions, with the goal of helping teachers, therapists, or others interact with children in ways that prompted learning. We also see these interactions having an important role in language instruction, whether for children with specific language difficulties or children who are dual-language learners (DLLs), as identified by Espinosa and Zepeda in Chapter 4. These authors noted that these children should not be considered as a homogeneous group; they have distinct early learning environments and their instruction needs to be individualized. Consequently, these authors support culturally responsive teaching for young DLLs and recommend that educators adapt a set of skills and strategies originally proposed for the K–12 educator (Lucas, Villegas, & Freedson-Gonzales, 2008), including the following: 1) knowledge of the language and educational backgrounds of children, 2) understanding the program's expectations for first and second language development, and 3) having the instructional skills needed to scaffold learning to engage DLLs in the learning environment.

More recent research on preschool classrooms and the early elementary grades has provided strong documentation regarding the importance of having teachers ensure that each student is actively engaged and has ample learning opportunities. In writing about ways to improve early childhood education, including children's academic achievement and social skills development, Pianta and Hamre (2009) addressed how teachers instruct and relate with children, identifying this relationship as the most important component for children's learning. These authors are at the forefront of calling for an assessment of teachers' behavioral interactions with students as a way to improve instruction and related social processes (Hamre, Pianta, Mashburn, & Downer, 2007). An examination of their instrumentation, the CLASS, illustrates how closely their work is consistent with the proximal processes identified by Bronfenbrenner, including the importance of emotional and instructional supports. When children are in classrooms with teachers who provide effective teacher–student interactions, children have higher gains in achievement and social skill development (Pianta & Hamre, 2008). Yet, many classrooms in the United States fall considerably below where they need to be. In documenting effective teacher–student interactions defined as emotional support, classroom organization, and instructional support, less than 15% of classrooms in one study were found to display moderately to highly effective teacher–student interactions (LoCasale-Crouch et al., 2007). FPG's Margaret Burchinal (2018) recently raised cogent questions about what measures of teachers, students, and classrooms best predict children's outcomes. Based on a review of outcomes from major early childhood assessment instruments, Burchinal concludes that the assessment of early childhood education quality should include not only the quality and content of instruction but also "the degree to which teachers actively scaffold learning, monitor children's progress, and use that information to individualize instruction and engage parents in their children's education." Furthermore, she concludes that future work must recognize that children "need scaffolded interactions with rich, extended conversations to acquire the language, self-regulations, and executive functioning skills that lay the foundation for school success" (Burchinal, 2018).

The importance of proximal processes is also reflected in professional training and in-service training. The authors in this volume on practice issues—Epinosa and Zepeta on disabilities and culture (Chapter 4), Hyson on early care and education (Chapter 8), and Winton on disabilities (Chapter 12)—all emphasize the necessity of high-quality education and training for professionals who work with young children. These authors note that our current level of preparation of professionals is insufficient to address the needs of young children; furthermore, the number of professionals, especially in areas such as DLLs, is insufficient to ensure that all children needing extra services will receive those services. At the core of what is needed for children's development and learning—well-trained educators in sufficient numbers to provide quality proximal processes—the early childhood field is seriously understaffed to meet the needs of many young children, placing large numbers of children in a vulnerable situation.

Person

The three types of person characteristics identified by Bronfenbrenner—demand, resource, and force—can alter the nature of proximal processes

(Tudge et al., 2018). Demand characteristics are easily observed and facilitate or discourage reactions from others in the environment. These include skin color and other physical characteristics such as attractiveness, age, and gender. Resource characteristics, which are not as immediately recognizable as demand characteristics, include such important variables as mental and emotional resources, intelligence, ability, and knowledge; they contribute to a person's ability to engage in the proximal processes (Bronfenbrenner & Morris, 2006; Rosa & Tudge, 2013). These characteristics can also include those that may limit or disrupt proximal processes, including low birth weight or physical disabilities (Bronfenbrenner & Morris, 2006). The third person characteristic is force or dispositions. These force characteristics can be described as generative—that is, ones where the individual engages in active orientations such as curiosity, or the "tendency to initiate and engage in activity alone or with others" (Bronfenbrenner & Morris, 2006, p. 1009; Rosa & Tudge, 2013). Individuals with disruptive force characteristics such as impulsiveness, distractibility, or an inability to defer gratification would be less likely to be engaged by others due to these characteristics (see Bronfenbrenner & Morris, 2006; Rosa & Tudge, 2013).

In identifying race/skin color, Barbarin provided information in Chapter 3 on one of the key components of the PPCT model. He identified the situation of young African American boys to illuminate how this one specific person characteristic can strongly influence interactions of others with these children. In Chapter 5, Bowman also called out the cost of racial inequality, especially in achievement, and identified the need for effective policies to address these issues. Other critical person characteristics of the child include ethnicity, language, immigrant status, and culture, which are illustrated by the research on DLLs described by Espinosa and Zepeda in Chapter 4. These authors remind us that just one child characteristic can have highly detrimental effects on child outcomes, whether race, gender, or physical appearance.

Low birth weight children and children with physical disabilities also have a higher likelihood of disadvantage and may experience long-term negative educational, medical, and social outcomes. Furthermore, children who demonstrate characteristics such as impulsiveness or disruptiveness can prompt undesirable reactions from others—a situation that requires vigilance on the part of parents and teachers to ensure a positive and healthy environment for the child (see Chapter 13). Many of these person characteristics of young children are known at birth, sometimes resulting in medical and social difficulties across the child's lifetime.

More than 30 years ago, Garcia-Coll et al. (1996) challenged the existing approaches to research with minority children and called for a reconceptualization of the variables that must be considered when addressing the development of minority children. This model emphasizes the importance of five major factors—racism, prejudice, discrimination, oppression, and segregation—on the development of minority children and their families. To provide a heuristic guide to the study of competencies in children of color, the authors placed "these influences (social position, racism and its derivatives, and segregation) at the core rather than at the periphery of a causal framework" and then specified how these influences can impact immediate settings (Garcia-Coll et al., 1996, p. 1908). This theoretical model helps link our understanding of person characteristics in the PPCT model to the realities and complexities of studying minority children and their families.

In summary, many person characteristics have been of concern to numerous educators, researchers, and policy makers over the past 50 years. Considerable accomplishments have been made in addressing the needs associated with person characteristics, especially those of children with disabilities (see Chapters 11, 12, and 14) and children with medical conditions such as low birth weight (see Chapter 7). However, for many other person characteristics, particularly children of color, considerable progress is needed in resources and in the preparation of educational personnel for these children to realize the advantages of nonminority children (Chapters 3 and 5).

Time

When studying children, the concept of time is fundamental to understanding changes that take place across the development of a child. Across all the areas of interest in this volume, the dimension of time in the PPCT model is the one least likely to have been studied, possibly due to the complexity and expenses of following individuals longitudinally to obtain data at different points in a person's life course. However, data over time are essential to draw conclusions about development. To meet the objective of the time dimension, Tudge and colleagues have noted that the same children must be included in studies that address two or more of the other variables (proximal processes, person, or context). To determine how closely contemporary researchers were following Bronfenbrenner's PPCT model, Tudge et al. (2009) examined a large set of research studies that referenced Bronfenbrenner's model. Through their analysis of 25 research papers, they found that only four used Bronfenbrenner's final PPCT model, whereas all others used earlier versions of his model that did not include the full PPCT model—most notably omitting the time dimension.

Of the four studies that did meet the time criteria, one is of particular interest here because the authors conducted a study with participants in the Abecedarian Project to investigate the impact of quality early child care on children from economically disadvantaged families. Using data on the Abecedarian participants in a longitudinal study, FPG's Campbell, Pungello, and Miller-Johnson (2002) specifically noted that they used Bronfenbrenner's ecological model to examine interactions among personal characteristics, proximal processes, contexts, and time to determine how these four factors affected developmental outcomes. The investigators collected measures of proximal processes, person characteristics, and context during the participants' early years and then obtained additional information during adolescence on their feelings of self-worth. Because the study was longitudinal, the authors were able to study the interrelated effects of each process, person, and context over time and used Bronfenbrenner's model to link data from young children to adolescents' feelings of self-worth (Tudge et al., 2009).

A Convergence of Models

A close study of the bioecological theory of development and its placement of proximal processes as central for the child prompts us to identify other theories that also call attention to the importance of proximal processes. It is helpful to draw parallels between Bronfenbrenner's model and other significant models or approaches because these other conceptualizations also address concepts similar to proximal processes. The research arising from applied behavior analysis recognizes the importance of the immediate interactions between a parent and a child or a teacher and a child, identifying conditions under which the adult's interactions can be used to promote appropriate child behavior or mastery of areas such as reading. The transactional theory of Sameroff (2009) has also identified the bidirectional, interdependent interactions between the child and the environment, proposing that the child is a product of the interactions between the child and the child's social setting. The child, parent, and environment all contribute to the child's overall development, while also affecting each other. The writings of Vygotsky propose that a more knowledgeable adult or even a more competent child, acting within the child's zone of proximal development, can provide the prompts and information needed for a child to move from one level of competence to an increasingly more sophisticated one (Tharp & Gallimore, 1988; Wasik & Sparling, 2010). Vygotsky's work emphasizes the role of scaffolding in interactions with children. Researchers have examined the role of both parents (e.g., Hodapp, Goldfield, & Boyatzis, 1984) and teachers (see Wasik & Newman, 2009) scaffolding children's learning. Vygotsky's work is reflected in concepts later proposed by Bronfenbrenner.

We have identified these other major theories and theorists to acknowledge the role of proximal processes in the immediate environment. Although they carry different labels and are associated with different theoretical orientations, they have been recognized as fundamental to children's learning and development. This convergence of models provides further support for the role of proximal processes and future research should continue an intensive analysis of these processes.

DISTAL INFLUENCES: POLICY AND THE IMPACT OF SOCIAL CONDITIONS

We have so far discussed primarily proximal processes, which have the most immediate influence on children. However, distal influences, especially at the macrosystem level, also affect children and have a critical role in the lives of children and parents. When the necessities of food, housing, and medical care are not available at the level needed for healthy development, they interfere with the ability of hundreds of thousands of children to gain the foundation essential for educational and social success. In Chapter 9, Haskins provided a review of the most significant federal policies influencing young children and their families, noting the impact of funding changes. Many of these funding decisions relate to recurring social concerns about the role of mothers regarding their young children and whether mothers should be supported to remain at home with their children or be required to enter the workforce, thus requiring resources for child care.

Other authors have also spoken compellingly about macro-level influences on children's well-being (see Chapter 2). Several national programs do focus directly on children, including the Maternal, Infant, and Early Childhood Home Visiting program; Early Head Start and Child Care Partnerships; Preschool Development Grants; Head Start; and Race to the Top, which includes funding for children with high needs. When these federal programs keep pace with the needs of young children, children benefit in their learning. However, when these federal programs have less available funding and reach fewer families, children and their families are negatively impacted by these macro-level actions.

Other macrosystem influences come through policies and laws for children and their families, as noted in Chapter 12 about children with disabilities. Over the past 50 years, a number of highly significant policies has meant that opportunities previously closed to these children are now available, from education to sports, from housing to transportation. Barriers that may be physical, social, or financial have been reduced. In Chapter 13, Turnbull identified six strands of federal policy that relate to young children and their families who are affected by disabilities. Some are specialized and exceptional, whereas others affect all children. By addressing topics such as health, education, child welfare, and family support, these policies affect the lives of all children—both those with and without disabilities. In each of these situations, where federal and state funding are provided for services for children and families, or policies and laws have increased accessibility for those with disabilities for a wide range of opportunities, macro-level decisions influence what takes place at the microsystem level with children and their families.

In the following section, we turn to a discussion of other challenges that influence our ability to rear children in ways that help to ensure their healthy growth and development, educational achievement, and positive adult outcomes.

FUTURE CHALLENGES

Numerous challenges over the last 50 years concerning children. Considerable progress has been made in understanding the complexity of children's learning, examining effective methods for preparing professionals, and promoting national political actions. However, considerable work must still be done to provide all children with the skills, knowledge, and characteristics needed to be successful in school and life. These challenges can be characterized as "wicked problems"—a term proposed by Rittel and Webber (1973) for problems that are complex, ill-defined, and difficult to solve because they affect multiple stakeholders in different ways. Wicked problems can be defined differently depending on the perspective of the stakeholder group, thus making it difficult to reach consensus on where to start, how to move forward, and how to determine success (Conklin, 2001).

Numerous challenges identified by authors in this volume have characteristics of wicked problems because they are complex and difficult to resolve. One of the most serious challenges is the increasing diversity of our society. This diversity includes language, racial/ethnic identity, country of origin, family composition, ability status, and socioeconomic level, which can have dramatic social, educational, and cultural impacts. We see these impacts, for example, in the achievement gap between racial and ethnic minority children and their White peers. Chapter 6 cited the National Center for Educational Statistics (Aud, Fox, & KewalRamani, 2010) in reporting that Black children, compared to their White peers were, on average, "more likely to be from single female-headed households, live in poverty, have less educated mothers, attend high-poverty schools, have less educated teachers, and be less school ready, as well as less likely to graduate high school and attend college." This problem is manifested in the continued achievement gaps that leave children who are non-White and/or live in poverty behind their White middle-class peers (Coleman, Winn, & Harradine, 2013). Similar challenges exist for children from immigrant families who experience high rates of family poverty and employment and lower educational levels; these problems are compounded when children and their families are viewed through a deficit lens, as noted in Chapter 4.

A second major challenge relates to state and federal policies and funding that directly influence the likelihood that young children will be placed on a pathway to success. For children with disabilities, Chapters 12–14 all noted the advances made possible by federal legislation and funding for children with disabilities. Funding for early childhood education, however, plateaued during the past decade (Kirk, Gallagher, & Coleman, 2015). Furthermore, as Haskins observed in Chapter 9, pressure for other funding priorities, such as an increasingly older population in the United States, will most likely mean future funding levels will not be sufficient to serve all eligible children. Given the intense competition for funding, discussions must be held among all stakeholders to review multiple priorities and make difficult decisions about where and how resources will be distributed. These decisions will be increasingly influenced by beliefs regarding the use of funds for institutions, such as public schools versus private endeavors, and by intense feelings about phenomena that include immigration, support for working mothers, housing, and health insurance.

We also face significant issues regarding research methodologies. Complex issues require multiple views supported by many different sources of data. One current challenge related to research comes from federal funding priorities and preferred research designs that tend to restrict funding for single-case intervention research designs in favor of large randomized trials (Strain, 2018). Yet, many of the significant advances for children with disabilities were based on the findings of single-case intervention research designs (Kratochwill & Levin, 2014), which allow for the examination of proximal processes between adults and children. A limitation on the kinds of designs that are eligible for federal funding may limit the future development of effective strategies for individualizing practices for children with disabilities (Strain, 2018), as well as limit work that requires a detailed analysis of individual child–adult interactions. Other research issues continue to influence today's programs for young children. In Chapter 10, Barnett observed that we should not expect to reproduce the earlier outcomes of small-scale programs when we try to bring these models to scale. He noted that the overall quality of teachers, the duration of the programs, and the level of funding for the model programs such as the Perry Preschool Project, the Chicago Project, and the Abecedarian Project cannot be replicated with our current funding policies because they most likely would not provide the funds for such longitudinal efforts.

Development of the workforce remains a critical component to bring effective evidence-based practices to scale. All writers in this volume who addressed professional education and practice observed major issues with preparing an adequate workforce (see Chapters 4, 8, and 12). In Chapter 10, Barnett also observed that "there is not likely to be one right way to develop a highly effective early childhood workforce, nor is there one right way for all of them to teach young children."

In summary, we face major challenges that must be addressed to provide for children and their families. The challenges of changed and continually changing demographics in our country have intensified the urgency to address the needs of each child. Although we know what children and families require to fulfill the basic needs of housing, food, medical care, and education, we fall short in helping to meet these needs for millions of children and families. In the next section, we offer some suggestions for addressing the complex issues facing the development of young children and their families.

TACKLING WICKED PROBLEMS

The authors in this volume have examined the research, practice, and policies related to diversity, early childhood, and disability, reporting on the knowledge base but also identifying what needs to be done to find solutions to the wicked problems we still face. The oftentimes inability of our educational system to respond consistently and effectively to the changing demographics of our population is an excellent example of the complex and ongoing challenges we have yet to solve. Addressing this problem will require examining and identifying the institutional barriers that undermine the ability of children from culturally and linguistically different families, families facing poverty, and children with disabilities to reach success. Educational variables inside and outside the classroom must be addressed. The pernicious disparities in educational success, for children of color and poverty, however, are not just educational problems. They reflect societal issues of inequity in housing, criminal justice, public health, and access to wealth—all of which have antecedents in the early history of the United States. In addressing wicked problems, we must think systemically, using more flexible, creative, adaptive, and integrative approaches than we have relied on in the past. We must be responsive to the interconnected nature of both the problems we face and the solutions we seek.

The challenges that have been identified exist within socially complex real-world contexts, and solving them often requires engaging stakeholders across all levels of the system—from micro to macro. Collaborative stakeholder engagement, ensuring that all the important voices are heard, is an essential component to successfully addressing complex issues. Simply bringing the critical people together for a short period of time, however, is not sufficient for resolving many of the challenges we face. It takes a long-term commitment to build the trust needed for truly collaborative partnerships that can work systemically with a shared purpose (Weaver, 2017). Some complicated and thorny problems require long ongoing collaboration and may take years to fully resolve. Other issues may never be fully resolved and will require ongoing attention and continual work as we strive for better outcomes.

Because many of the challenges affect society at large, working to address educational problems must include the macrosystem where laws are passed, policies are made, and funding priorities are set (Gallagher, 2006). Policies are part of the macro-level infrastructure needed to support and improve practice. Policy decisions specify the allocation of resources, identifying what the resources are, stipulating who will receive the resources, and determining how the resources will be delivered (Gallagher, 2006). As discussed in Chapter 9, policy decisions at the federal and state levels have a major impact on services and supports for children and families at the microsystem, shaping the context in which children and families live. These policies must be grounded in knowledge from both research and practice.

Researchers play an important role in addressing complex problems by collecting and examining empirical data through both qualitative and quantitative approaches. Although large-scale randomized control and treatment interventions, with a focus on fidelity, have contributed significantly to our understanding of interventions, additional strategies for studying vexing problems may include observational studies, single-subject intervention research, correlational studies, and qualitative studies. FPG researcher Ritchie and her colleagues (Ritchie & Gutmann, 2014) as well as Pianta and his colleagues (Pianta & Hamre, 2009) have successfully utilized the observational study of classroom behavior in their quest to determine factors that promote positive child outcomes. One finding of major concern has been the documentation of a low occurrence of interactions between teachers and students during the school day which, in turn, leads to low academic and social success for many children. These researchers all stress that teachers must engage in intentional teaching and scaffolding children's learning. Furthermore, their work has significant policy implications for the preparation of teachers, as well as implications for the direct assessment of actual teaching as a component of accountability frameworks. Some researchers have successfully utilized the observational study of behavior, illustrated in the work of Pianta and colleagues. By directly observing the proximal processes between teachers and students in preschool and elementary classrooms, they documented the low occurrence of interactions that are known to relate to positive child outcomes. Furthermore, their work has direct policy implications for the preparation of teachers, as well as the direct assessment of actual teaching that can be a component of accountability frameworks (Pianta & Hamre, 2009). Likewise, Coleman and colleagues have shown how a strengths-based school improvement effort, focused on nurturing potential in young learners, can intentionally encompass all levels of the system from micro to macro. This strengths-based school improvement effort includes micro-level changes with teacher observations, improved classroom practices, and family engagement with home-based activities while simultaneously building capacity for change at the macro level through an infrastructure of policy, professional development, and accountability (Coleman, 2016). These observational studies of teachers and students offer strong examples of how to bring together research, practice, and policy efforts in a collaborative and dynamic way. In the next section, we discuss what these collaborative and dynamic approaches might look like.

Collaborative Approaches to Integrating Research, Policy, and Practice

Collaborative approaches must include partnerships across stakeholder groups, including interdisciplinary researchers, practitioners, policy makers, and community members. Complex problems regarding children can rarely be contained within one discipline. Interdisciplinary collaborations bring the benefit of multiple perspectives needed to examine complex problems. The challenge of optimizing each child's development (the focus of the work described in this volume) is a classic example of why we need interdisciplinary approaches to research. Optimizing child outcomes, taking the whole child into account, includes integrating the social, academic, health, and well-being aspects of the child's development. As Odom observed in Chapter 14, this integration requires research teams that bring multiple perspectives, including biomedical, sociological, educational, and psychological, to the work.

Input from all pertinent stakeholders in the design and implementation of research helps to ensure the relevance and applicability of the findings. Practitioners, for example, can conduct field-based research that capitalizes on authentic interactions within natural settings, generating research findings that show how a practice actually works within real-world settings (Strain, 2018). Practitioners, especially early childhood educators, can be actively engaged with researchers in identifying when changes are needed in research procedures, as Barnett noted in Chapter 10. Strong stakeholder partnerships, including parents and other community members, give us a deeper understanding of contextual implications for the successful adaptation of research findings and help us to understand their generalizability with a variety of contexts, thus providing support to bring these practices to scale (see Chapter 8). Implementation science—the study of how we bring good practices to scale—can help us close the research-to-practice gap by identifying core aspects of practice and by examining how these aspects can be used to directly improve services and outcomes for children and their families (Fixsen, 2018). Robust partnerships within the implementation phase of the work also build support for sustainability through early ownership for both the interventions and the outcomes.

Through building collaborative partnerships across stakeholders at all phases of the research process, we can begin to reduce the long-standing difficulty of translating research to meaningful practice and policy (see Chapter 10). Collaborative research findings can provide a powerful force for influencing policy because they can document the evidence of successful approaches to addressing real world, relevant problems (Strain, 2018). Addressing policy is critical for systems change and, because systems are made up of people, the relationships formed across individuals and stakeholder groups are essential. The barriers to change often hinge on the willingness of individuals to engage in, support, and advance the changes authorized by policy (Gallagher, 2006). Thus, successful change at the systems level involves building trust among stakeholders, promoting ownership, and enabling the sharing of time, talent, and resources of the stakeholders (Weaver, 2017; Farka & Duffett, 2014).

Because finding solutions to wicked problems is in part a social challenge, the social nature of solution finding from the initial research design through implementation of practices and policy development is critical for successful systems change (Conklin, 2001). Collaborative work is often challenging, but overcoming these challenges is key to tackling the wicked problems we face. In addition to working more collaboratively, our work must also become more dynamic. We address this need in the next section.

Dynamic Approaches to Integrating Research, Policy, and Practice

Dynamic approaches address interconnectedness within and across systems, intentionally working toward systems change by integrating research, practice, and policy from conception through application. This integration is central to the success of system change. Dynamic approaches are more flexible, responding to a range of contexts, circumstances, and changing needs over time. Because these approaches to research and practice address real-world issues, with all the complexities that these involve, they give us richer results that can more readily be translated into policy. It is not enough, however, to have solid, well-researched information that shapes policies and guides practice; policies and practices must be supported with a strong but flexible infrastructure if they are to be successfully implemented within a variety of contexts (Gallagher, 2006). The infrastructure necessary for success includes support for the process of implementation with technical assistance and personnel preparation; this support must be tailored so that it adapts to the practice, the context, and the stages of implementation (Fixsen, 2018). As an illustration, FPG's Impact Center is scaling up Triple P and other evidenced-based interventions in several states and communities (Aldridge, et al., 2016).

Dynamic research approaches can be incorporated into multiple research designs (e.g., experimental "pre-post," large-scale randomized control/treatment, single-case approaches, qualitative methods). Research designs are dynamic when they intentionally build in the flexibility and responsivity needed to examine child outcomes within real-world circumstances across longer periods of time and/or within a variety of settings. Dynamic designs may also include longitudinal methods to explore outcomes over time, employing an evolutionary examination of treatment impacts that can be adjusted and adapted to circumstances and needs. Such designs are essential for understanding children's development—a phenomenon that must be studied over time. As Barnett pointed out in Chapter 10, the effectiveness of any given treatment or practice designed for children will vary by person, place, and context, and these effects change over time. Because of this variation, there is rarely one right way to implement a treatment or practice. A more dynamic approach to research—one that builds in an expectation of flexibility—is needed to address these variations.

An expectation of flexibility also requires a rethinking of the fidelity of treatment/implementation to include more flexibility and adaptation when supporting the implementation of a treatment or practice across a range of contexts (Coleman, 2016). Fidelity, in this approach, is built around core or defining elements of the practice that act as anchors to support the integrity of implementation, but it also intentionally embraces natural flex-points where adjustments can (and should) be made to adapt to the contexts. Fidelity also includes adherence to the core elements of the practice, as well as thoughtful adaptations made in response to current needs, circumstances, and contexts (Coleman & Shah-Coltrane, 2010; Fixsen, 2018). Fidelity with flexibility also tracks these adaptations and examines their role in the future success of implementations. In Chapter 10, Barnett emphasized that "departures from fidelity are not failures of practice but necessary adaptations for success," focusing our attention on a new way of conducting and evaluating research designs. Despite this proposition by Barnett, current research guidelines often define fidelity as an adherence to design features regardless of the contextual needs within real-world settings (Coleman & Shah-Coltrane, 2010; Strain, 2018).

Sustainability

As we move toward more dynamic approaches to implementation of best practices, we also need to shift our understanding of what sustainability means. Sustainability can no longer be the rigid or static implementation of a model or practice; rather, it must reflect the dynamic nature of real-world contexts, where change is the only constant. If adaptation is a healthy sign of growth and is part of evolution, then sustainability becomes the dynamic and continued commitment of broad-based stakeholder groups to improving outcomes. Sustainability is the ongoing commitment of stakeholders. Redefining sustainability as the continued commitment of multiple stakeholder groups to improve outcomes over time acknowledges the dynamic nature of systems change. This continuous improvement approach to sustainability builds on the initial collaborative partnerships, extends the dynamic research/implementation designs, and advances policy agendas through creating a long-term commitment to improving outcomes (see Chapters 8 and 10; Coleman, 2016). In summary, dynamic designs look at critical research, practice, and policy variables across interactions, individuals, settings, and time and are responsive to Bronfenbrenner's process, person, context, and time model.

CONCLUSIONS

In this volume, the authors presented and reflected on research, practice, and policy with children and families, from 1960 to the present. Through the collective reflections on the three major themes of this volume, we see the innovative and pioneering spirit of the early work of FPG as well as that of many colleagues across the country providing a strong, albeit incomplete, foundation for understanding children's development. As we move into the next 50 years, we can build on this foundation of innovation and explore ways to better integrate research, practice, and policy in order to improve outcomes for children and their families. Addressing all components of the process-person-context-time model may move us forward more rapidly toward understanding the multifaceted variables impacting the child's development. Greater collaboration across all stakeholder groups and a more dynamic approach to integrating research, policy, and practice will be essential to ensuring that every child is placed on a trajectory for success. Although we have focused in this volume on more vulnerable children, we need to remain vigilant to the needs of *all* children as we focus on innovations in research, practice, and policy to make the next 50 years stand out for their own accomplishments in addressing the needs of children and families.

REFERENCES

Aldridge, W. A., II, Boothroyd, R. I., Fleming, W. O., Lofts Jarboe, K., Morrow, J., Ritchie, G. F., & Sebian, J. (2016). Transforming community prevention systems for sustained impact: Embedding activeimplementation and scaling functions. *Translational Behavioral Medicine, 6*, 135–144.

Aud, S., Fox, M. A., & KewalRamani, A. (2010). *Status and trends in the education of racial and ethnic groups* (NCES 2010-015). Washington, DC: U.S. Department of Education National Center for Education Statistics. Retrieved from https://files.eric.ed.gov/fulltext/ED510909.pdf

Bronfenbrenner, U. (1977). Toward an experimental ecology of human development. *American Psychologist, 32*, 515–531.

Bronfenbrenner, U. (1979). *The ecology of human development: Experiments by nature and design.* Cambridge, MA: Harvard University Press.

Bronfenbrenner, U. (1995). Developmental ecology through space and time: A future perspective. In P. Moen, G. H. Elder, Jr., & K. Luscher (Eds.), *Examining lives in context: Perspectives on the ecology of human development* (pp. 619–647). Washington, DC: American Psychological Association.

Bronfenbrenner, U., & Ceci, S. J. (1994). Nature-nurture reconceptualized in developmental perspective: A bioecological model. *Psychological Review, 101*, 568–586.

Bronfenbrenner, U., & Evans, G. W. (2002). Developmental science in the 21st century: Emerging questions, theoretical models, research designs, and empirical findings. *Social Developments, 9*, 115–125.

Bronfenbrenner, U., & Morris, P. A. (1998). The ecology of developmental processes. In W. Damon & R. M. Lerner (Eds.), *Handbook of child psychology, Vol. 1: Theoretical models of human development.* (5th ed., pp. 993–1027). New York: Wiley.

Bronfenbrenner, U., & Morris, P. A. (2006). The bioecological model of human development. In W. Damon (Series Ed.) & R. M. Lerner (Vol. Ed.), *Handbook of child psychology: Vol. 1. Theoretical models of human development* (6th ed., pp. 793–828). New York, NY: Wiley.

Burchinal, M. (2018). Measuring early care and education quality. *Child Development Perspectives, 12*(1). Society for Research in Child Development.

Campbell, F. A., Pungello, E. P., & Miller-Johnson, S. (2002). The development of perceived scholastic competence and global self-worth in African American adolescents from low-income families: The roles of family factors, early educational intervention, and academic experience. *Journal of Adolescent Research, 17*, 277–302.

Campbell, F. A., & Ramey, C. T. (1995). Cognitive and school outcomes for high-risk African-American students at middle adolescence: Positive effects of early intervention. *American Educational Research Journal, 32*(4), 743–772.

Coleman, M. R. (2016). Recognizing young children with high potential: U-STARS~PLUS. In *Annals of the New York Academy of Sciences, Beyond IQ* (pp. 32–43). New York, NY: New York Academy of Sciences.

Coleman, M. R., & Shah-Coltrane, S. (2010). *U-STARS~PLUS: Science and literature connections.* Arlington, VA: Council for Exceptional Children.

Coleman, M. R., Winn, D., & Harradine, C. (2013). *Expanding educational excellence: The power of schools.* Chapel Hill, NC: University of North Carolina, Frank Porter Graham Child Development Institute.

Conklin, J. (2001). Wicked problems and fragmentation. In J. Conklin (Ed.), *Dialog mapping: Making sense of project fragmentation.* Retrieved from http://www.cognexus.org/id29.htm

Farka, S., & Duffett A. (2014). *Maze of mistrust: How district politics and cross talk are stalling efforts to improve public education.* Retrieved from https://www.kettering.org/catalog/product/maze-mistrust-how-district-politics-and-cross-talk-are-stalling-efforts-improve

Fixsen, D. L. (2018). A commentary on personal thoughts on early childhood special education research. *Journal of Early Intervention, 40*(2), 117–120.

Gallagher, J. J. (2006). *Driving change in special education.* Baltimore, MD: Paul H. Brookes Publishing Co.

Garcia-Coll, C., Lamberty, G., Jenkins, R., McAdoo, H. P., Crnic, K., Wasik, B. H., et al. (1996). Toward an integrative theoretical model for the study of developmental competencies in minority children. *Child Development, 67,* 1891–1914.

Harms, T., & Clifford, R. M. (1980). *Early Childhood Environment Rating Scale,* New York: Teachers College Press.

Hamre, B. K., Pianta, R. C. Mashburn, A. J., & Downer, J. T. (2007). *Building a science of classrooms: Application of the CLASS framework in over 4,000 U.S. early childhood and elementary classrooms.* New York, NY: Foundation for Child Development.

Hodapp, R. M., Goldfield, E. C., & Boyatzis, C. J. (1984). The use and effectiveness of maternal scaffolding in mother-infant games. *Child Development, 55,* 772–781

Kirk, S., Gallagher, J., & Coleman, M. R. (2015). *Educating exceptional children* (14th ed.). Belmont, CA: Cengage.

Kratochwill, T. R., & Levin, J. R. (2014). *Single-case intervention research: Methodological and statistical advances.* Washington, DC: American Psychological Association.

Lazar, I., Darlington, R., Murray, H., Royce, J., Snipper, A., & Ramey, C. T. (1982). Lasting effects of early education: A report from the Consortium for Longitudinal Studies. *Monographs of the Society for Research in Child Development, 47*(2/3).

LoCasale-Crouch, J., Konold, T., Pianta, R., Howes, C., Burchinal, M., Bryant, D., et al. (2007). Profiles of observed classroom quality in state-funded pre-kindergarten programs and associations with teacher, program and classroom characteristics. *Early Childhood Research Quarterly, 22*(1), 3–17.

Lucas, T., Villegas, A. M., & Freedson-Gonzales, M. (2008). Linguistically responsive teacher education: Preparing classroom teachers to teach English language learners. *Journal of Teacher Education, 29*(4), 361–373.

Meisels, S. J., & Shonkoff, J. P. (2000). Early childhood intervention: A continuing evolution. In J. P. Shonkoff & S. J. Meisels (Eds.). *Handbook of early intervention* (2nd ed). Cambridge, UK: Cambridge University Press.

Pianta, R. C., & Hamre, B. K. (2008). Using standardized observation to conceptualize, measure, and improve classroom processes. *Teacher Quality, 12,* 59–77.

Pianta, R. C., & Hamre, B. K. (2009). Conceptualization, measurement, and improvement of classroom processes: Standardized observation can leverage capacity. *Educational Researcher, 38*(2), 109–119.

Ritchie, S. (2013). Directions for the future. In S. Ritchie & L. Gutmann (Eds.) *First-School: Transforming PreK-3rd grade for African American, Latino, and low-income children* (pp. 170–186). New York, NY, Teachers College Press.

Rittel, H., & Webber, M. (1973). Dilemma in a general theory of planning. *Policy Science, 4,* 155–159.

Rosa, E. M., & Tudge, J. (2013). Urie Bronfenbrenner's theory of human development: Its evolution from ecology to bioecology. *Journal of Family Theory & Review, 5,* 243–258.

Sameroff, A. (2009). The transactional model. In A. Sameroff (Ed.), *The transactional model of development: How children and contexts shape each other* (pp. 3–21). Washington, DC: American Psychological Association.

Shaw, D. (2016). *The promise of the premise: The first 50 years of the Frank Porter Graham Child Development Institute.* Chapel Hill, NC: The University of North Carolina, FPG Child Development Institute.

Sparling, J. J. (2004). Earliest literacy: From birth to age 3. In B. H. Wasik (Ed.), *Handbook of family literacy* (pp. 45–56). Mahwah, NJ: Erlbaum.

Strain, P. S. (2018). Personal thoughts on early childhood special education research: An historical perspective, threats to relevance, and call to action. *Journal of Early Intervention, 40*(2), 107–116.

Tharp, R. G., & Gallimore, R. (1988). *Rousing minds to life: Teaching, learning, and schooling in social context.* Cambridge, UK: Cambridge University Press.

Tudge, J. R. H., Mokrova, I., Hatfield, B. E., & Karnik, R. B. (2009). Uses and misuses of Bronfenbrenner's bioecological theory of human development. *Journal of Family Theory & Review, 1*, 198–210.

Tudge, J., Rosa, E. M., & Payir, A. (2018). Bioecological model. In Marc H. Bornstein (Ed.), *The SAGE encyclopedia of lifespan human development* (pp. 251–252). Thousand Oaks, CA: Sage.

Wasik, B. H., & Newman, B. A. (2009). Teaching and learning to read. In O. A. Barbarin & B. H. Wasik, *Handbook of child development and early education* (pp. 303–327). New York, NY: Guilford Press.

Wasik, B. H., & Sparling, J. J. (2010). Nested strategies to promote language and literacy skills. In B. H. Wasik (Ed.), *Handbook of family literacy* (pp. 66–86). New York, NY: Routledge.

Weaver, L. (2017). *Turf, trust, co-creation and collective impact.* Retrieved from http://www.tamarackcommunity.ca/library/turf-trust-co-creation-collective-impact

Whitehurst, G., & Lonigan, C. J. (1998). Child development and emergent literacy. *Child Development, 69*(3), 848–872.

Zigler, E., & Styfco, S. J. (2010). *The hidden history of Head Start.* New York, NY: Oxford University Press.

Index

Page numbers followed by *f* and *t* indicate figures and tables, respectively.